STIRRING UP THINKING

Ben E. Johnson

Montana State University—Northern

HOUGHTON MIFFLIN COMPANY   Boston   New York

Senior Sponsoring Editor: Dean Johnson
Editorial Assistant: Mary Healey
Senior Project Editor: Janet Young
Editorial Assistant: Carrie Wagner
Production/Design Coordinator: Jennifer Meyer Dare
Senior Manufacturing Coordinator: Florence Cadran
Senior Marketing Manager: Nancy Lyman

Cover design by Harold Burch/Harold Burch Design, NYC
Additional credits appear on page 480.

Printed in the U.S.A.

Library of Congress Catalog Card Number: 96-76915

ISBN: 0-669-39325-8

123456789-CW-00 99 98 97

CONTENTS

2 Becoming a Critical Thinker   *27*

Part Two   THINKING THAT DEVELOPS THINKING   *49*

3 Gathering Skills   *50*

4 Organizing Skills   *91*

TO THE STUDENT

LEARN THE MOST FREQUENTLY EMPLOYED CRITICAL THINKING SKILLS NOW, OTHERS LATER

There is an important fact to understand as you begin your study of critical thinking. This fact is the foundation for this book and the basis on which you will begin developing your critical thinking skills. It is this: *Because critical thinking skills are so interrelated that one skill depends to some degree on another, becoming adept at thinking critically involves learning to use a variety of reasoning abilities effectively in many different contexts and in many different combinations.*

Learning to be a critical thinker means acquiring several critical thinking abilities. But which abilities? There are probably close to two hundred abilities that have been identified by someone or other as critical thinking skills, but many of them are so specialized you might not need to call upon them in a lifetime. So why learn them now? You don't have to. In this introductory book in critical thinking you will learn the general ideas, concepts, and methods of focused thinking that lead to being a critical thinker. Specifically, you will be introduced to nineteen of the most important, applicable, and widely useful critical thinking skills, and you will be encouraged to develop and strengthen them.

Observing	Deducing
Comparing and contrasting	Questioning
Identifying cause and effect	Classifying and sequencing
Summarizing	Inferring
Generating ideas	Synthesizing
Recognizing fact and opinion	Recognizing purpose
Recognizing bias	Recognizing tone
Recognizing underlying assumptions	Recognizing organization
	Analyzing
Evaluating	Inducing

Only nineteen? What about the other one hundred eighty or so critical thinking skills? Don't worry about them. There isn't much to be gained at this point by studying them. Later, when the need arises, you will be able to acquire those additional specialized thinking skills. This book will give you a solid critical thinking foundation on which to build.

What you do need to know how to use now is the small group of basic critical thinking skills that you will use frequently in college and afterward to stir up your thinking. These basic critical thinking skills (some prefer to call them *dispositions*) are grouped in the following chapters into classifications (gathering skills, organizing skills, generating skills, recognizing skills, and analyzing skills) and subskills (observing, questioning, inferring, summarizing, and so forth). These are the important thinking activities that you will find yourself using all the time. Some of these skills you are already familiar with and are using now, but not all of them. Once you become familiar with all of them through the readings, exercises, and applications in the chapters, you will find yourself using them without consciously thinking about them. They will become a way of thinking.

THERE'S NOTHING SPECIAL ABOUT THE ARRANGEMENT OF SKILLS IN THIS BOOK

The organization of this book is the author's choice. There is nothing special about learning the skills in the order they are presented here. What is important is that you begin with an understanding of the usefulness of these nineteen thinking abilities as a basis for the development of your other critical thinking skills. It is also important that you know that this is just one of the ways that critical thinking skills can be classified. Various other critical thinking professors and writers choose to arrange the same critical thinking skills and others into a different order and classification. The order and grouping of the skills isn't important. Acquiring proficiency in using these skills is important.

Although the classifications and order of the critical thinking skills in *Stirring Up Thinking* follow a general progression from the less-complicated thinking skills to the more-complicated, at times an arbitrary choice had to be made in determining which skill would be presented next. It was not the author's intention to create a skill hierarchy in which one skill must be learned before the next skill could be considered. In nearly every context, the execution of some skills or subskills presupposes the use of others. It is worthwhile to emphasize that these critical thinking skills (in fact, all critical thinking skills) are so

ESSENTIAL THINKING SKILLS

CHAPTER	WHAT THEY'RE CALLED	WHAT THEY MEAN
Chapter 3	**The Gathering Skills**	**Gathering all the information.**
	Observing	Actively seeking information through one or more senses.
	Questioning	Seeking information by asking questions.
Chapter 4	**The Organizing Skills**	**Organizing for the purpose of making sense.**
	Comparing and Contrasting	Noting similarities and differences between two or more things, events, or ideas.
	Classifying and Sequencing	Arranging things or concepts into categories and into sequential order.
	Identifying Cause and Effect	Recognizing the relationship between an effect and its cause.
Chapter 5	**The Generating Skills**	**Generating additional information.**
	Inferring	Making an assumption, stating a hypothesis, or coming to a conclusion based on limited information.
	Summarizing	Condensing the essence of the information accurately and efficiently.
	Synthesizing	Creating new information by combining two or more pieces of information.
	Generating Ideas	Creating new information, alternatives, or applications.
Chapter 6	**The Recognizing Skills**	**Recognizing what has been left unsaid.**
	Recognizing Purpose	Identifying a writer's or speaker's intention.
	Recognizing Fact and Opinion	Distinguishing between a statement of fact and a statement of opinion.
	Recognizing Tone	Identifying a sentiment or mood by assessing the writer's or speaker's choice of words.
	Recognizing Bias	Noting the presence and nature of a writer's or speaker's prejudice.
	Recognizing Organization	Identifying the organizational pattern of a thought, statement, passage, or plan.
	Recognizing Underlying Assumptions	Recognizing the suppositions that are taken for granted and are the foundation of a proposition, notion, or idea.
Chapter 7	**The Analyzing Skills**	**Analyzing for the purpose of coming to a conclusion.**
	Analyzing	Identifying and separating ideas, attributes, situations, and/or components in order to form a conclusion as to their relationship.
	Evaluating	Appraising something according to certain criteria and forming a judgment as to its worth or quality.
	Inducing	Analyzing individual facts or premises in order to derive a general conclusion.
	Deducing	Applying general principles or a broad framework to a situation in order to come to a conclusion about it.

interrelated that any one skill depends to some degree on other think-ing skills. It is likely that several skills are actively involved *at the same time* whenever you are thinking critically.

TAKE THE EXERCISES IN THIS BOOK SERIOUSLY

Each chapter in this book has an assortment of exercises, writing and thinking assignments, and three kinds of puzzles, called "Thinkers," "Any Questions?" and "Think About This!" All are designed to accom-modate various ability levels and to stir up your thinking in different ways and for different reasons. Most of these exercises and assignments will be interesting to you, some will be entertaining, and all of them will challenge your thinking. Sometimes the exercises and questions are easily read, understood, answered, and completed, but at other times they appear to be more difficult and you may not be able to answer them completely without help. That's the way it is supposed to be. Take them seriously and do each of them as you are directed. You will find that the ones that are a bit more difficult are just as effective as the easy ones in making you think in ways that you are not used to. In perform-ing these activities, you will find that your habitual, inefficient habits of thinking get shaken up and you begin to establish new patterns of thinking, leading to prowess in critical thinking. All the questions, assignments, puzzles, "Thinkers," and exercises are phrased so that you can answer them from your own experience, but expect that collabora-tion with other students and class discussion will allow you to explore these questions and exercises to their fullest depth. Here's a sample puzzle.

THINK ABOUT THIS!

Mental Muscle

In your head, count the number of capital letters that contain curved lines.

Start now.

THE READINGS ARE FOR APPLICATION

The wide assortment of readings included in this book have one purpose: to give you information on a variety of subjects and at a range of difficulty levels that allow you to demonstrate your grasp of one or more critical thinking skills. The readings are selected from periodicals and newspapers, as well as college textbooks in women's studies, minority studies, American history, physical science, urban history, Holocaust studies, marketing, Native American studies, communications, multicultural issues, environmental studies, advertising, chemistry, economics, biology, writing, education, history of the Vietnam War, and other subjects. Some of the passages (actually most of them) are of high interest and are entertaining—but some aren't. Some read like textbooks—and that is not an accident. Much of what you read in college will be interesting and entertaining, but much will be dense and slow going. You will have to read it anyway. In short, in this book you will be asked to read and respond to the kind and level of materials you will typically experience during your college studies. Not only will you find your thinking challenged with each reading selection as you are asked to process the information in new ways, but you will find that by the end of the book you will have acquired a great deal of information about these subject areas. By the time you have completed this book, you will find that you never look at simple textbook reading or straight lecture as "simple" or "straight" again. Instead, you will be questioning, challenging, relating—in short, *processing* what you read and hear. You will begin to *really* learn. And, at the risk of being obvious: to *begin* to *really* learn is why you are in college.

IT'S TIME TO BEGIN

And now it is time to begin. This book has been carefully designed to lead you into developing valuable critical thinking skills. All you need to do is faithfully work your way through the chapters and apply what you are learning to daily experience, and the results will speak for themselves. You will have the thinking edge, and that will make the difference for you in college and in life.

THINKERS

A Sure Thing?

If I say to you, "I will bet you $1 that if you give me $2, I will give you $3 in return," would this be a good bet for you to take?

Need a Hint?
How many dollars are you actually risking? What happens if I give you less than $3 in return? Solution is on the next page.

ACKNOWLEDGMENTS

My thanks to the many colleagues who offered helpful observations and suggestions on the content and structure of this book in its manuscript form: Michael Berberich, Galveston College; Betty Cassidy, Adirondack Community College; Gary Christensen, Macomb Community College; Robert Dees, Orange Coast College; Carolyn Gramling, Suffolk Community College; and Nora Hernandez Hendrix, Miami-Dade Community College.

My appreciation also goes to the staff of Houghton Mifflin, especially Dean Johnson, Mary Healey, and Janet Young—and to Jacqueline Rebisz and Lisa De George.

B.E.J.

SOLUTION to Thinkers (page xxii)

No. This would be a bad bet for you, a good bet for me. I would accept your $2, then say, "I lose the bet," and give you the $1 I lost in the wager. I would now be $1 richer, and you $1 poorer.

Dedication

*With great admiration and affection,
this book is dedicated to my friend
Shirley A. Ritchey
for thirty years the single best friend
Sarasota County, Florida, students and teachers have had.*

THINKING ABOUT THINKING

"There are one-story intellects, two-story intellects, and three-story intellects with sky-lights. All fact collectors who have no aim beyond their facts are one-story men. Two-story men compare, reason, generalize, using the labor of fact collectors as their own. Three-story men idealize, imagine, predict—their best illumination comes from above the skylight."
—Oliver Wendell Holmes

"I am putting myself to the fullest possible use, which is all, I think, that any conscious entity can ever hope to do."
—Hal 9000 computer, from the novel *2001: A Space Odyssey*, Arthur C. Clarke

Chapter 1

THINKING vs. THINKING CRITICALLY

What happens when critical thinking becomes a usable tool?

> " . . . as a nation, we have gone from being resource-rich in the old economy to resource-poor in the new economy almost overnight! Our public education has not successfully made the shift from teaching the memorization of facts to achieving the learning of critical thinking skills. We are still trapped in a K–12 public education system which is preparing our youth for jobs that no longer exist. "
> —John Sculley

STIR UP YOUR THINKING BEFORE YOU START READING

One of the most valuable and basic forms of research is the interview. In this book, you will be asked several times to interview other people and find out what they know, think, and believe. This information will provide you with important insights and ideas for what you learn in these chapters. Begin now.

Before you start reading this chapter, take an informal survey and then compare the answers you receive with what you learn in this chapter. Ask three people to answer the questions below. Briefly record their answers.

Do you think there is any difference between thinkers and critical thinkers? If there is a difference, how is that difference shown in what they learn in college?

Responses:

1. _____

_____

2. _____

_____

_____

3. _____

_____

_____

> **"**We must return to basics, but the basics of the 21st century are not only reading, writing, and arithmetic. They include communication and higher order problem-solving skills, and scientific and technological literacy—the thinking *tools that allow us to understand the technological world around us. . . . Development of students' capacities for problem-solving and critical thinking in all areas of learning is presented as a fundamental goal.***"**
> —Educating Americans for the 21st Century

What questions am I going to have answered in this chapter?

1. What is the difference between thinking and critical thinking?
2. Is critical thinking a process or a combination of thinking behaviors—or both?
3. How are specific critical thinking skills related to the development of critical thinking prowess?
4. Is there any relationship between critical thinking and negative thinking?
5. What is the relationship between learning and thinking in my college education?

WHY TEACH THINKING?

- How are a CD-ROM, a laser disc, and a battery-operated flashlight similar?
- What would you have to do in order to make ice burst into flames?
- What are five different uses for the spare watch parts found in an abandoned watch factory?
- In what ways are the possible causes of the resurgence of Nazism related to fluctuations in world stock market daily averages?
- What does that advertisement really say about the buying habits of Canadians?

These are examples of questions that are not easily answered, and probably not answerable at all for people who haven't developed their critical thinking skills. You'll understand why as you read further.

WHY SHOULD I (OR ANYONE) ENGAGE IN CRITICAL THINKING?

"Why should I engage in or value critical thinking?" is a question that has to be addressed, especially at the beginning of a book that proposes to guide students to understand, develop, and use a broad array of critical thinking skills.

THINK ABOUT THIS!

Where Does Thinking Take Place?

Hey! Don't I mean *how* does thinking take place?

No, I mean *where*.

Brain surgeons can tell us about the physical aspects of thinking, but that's not what I am referring to.

Try the following mental exercise: Pretend that you are required for some strange reason (perhaps because you are a very highly paid business consultant) to determine the number of hamburgers your local McDonald's serves in one year. To find the answer you will be placed in an absolutely empty room. You will have no furniture, books, telephone, computer, radio, paper, or pencil. Nothing. You will be kept there for fifteen minutes, and then you will be asked for your answer. Certainly you can think while you are in the room, but that's about all you can do. What do you think the chances are of coming up with the answer? Not very good.

On the other hand, what if that room were a well-equipped office with telephone, computer with modem, fax machine, books, paper, pencils, and even a small group of reference librarians? Do you think that you could figure out how to determine the number of hamburgers sold in a year? It's very likely you could, because *your thinking is enhanced, enriched, clarified, tested, and made possible by everything and everyone around you*. Just writing ideas on paper produces more thinking than is possible without writing thoughts down. Collaboration with others produces expanded thinking. Computers, writing materials, and books make productive thinking possible. Without these aids to thinking, very little thinking, other than superficial or personal reflection, is possible.

So where do you think thinking takes place?

_____

_____

_____

_____

One rather simplistic answer to that question comes immediately to mind: You should engage in critical thinking because if you don't, you are left with thinking that is characterized by a thoughtless intellectual acceptance and passivity. Most of our learning has been heavily *memorizing dependent*. This means that we have focused most of our learning time on acquiring content from primary sources, periodicals, and textbooks, and we have depended, to some degree, on lectures for information. Because of the largely one-way nature of these information sources, which don't routinely challenge us to question, verify, relate, think, and reason about what we are learning, most of us don't have frequent opportunities to develop skill in reasoning, that is, in critical thinking. The focus of our education has been on getting us to remember details rather than on getting us to understand the relationships and interactions between those details and what ever else we know. Meanwhile, national standardized tests and assessments are changing. Their creators are adding reasoning to the "skills" being measured and expecting you to have acquired critical thinking expertise that you can demonstrate on the tests.

What all this means is that it is up to you to learn to be a critical thinker. But we are not yet finished answering the question, Why should I engage in critical thinking? The next several pages should provide you with a more complete answer.

THERE IS A BIG DIFFERENCE BETWEEN THINKING AND CRITICAL THINKING

You will not be able to understand just what critical thinking is until you understand that it is related to what we refer to as *thinking*, but goes considerably beyond simple thinking.

THINKERS

A Cool Byrd

Why was it necessary for Admiral Byrd to take along a refrigerator on his Antarctic expedition? Hmmm.

Need a Hint?
What is the single biggest problem in the Antarctic? What else does a refrigerator do besides keep things cold?

Thinking About Thinking

Without asking anyone for help with this, and without resorting to a dictionary, take a stab at defining for yourself the word *thinking* before it is defined for you. Don't read any further in this chapter until you have done this. Write your definition here:

_____

_____

_____

Now look up *thinking* in your dictionary and compare that definition with the one you just wrote.

How close were you to the dictionary's "official" definition? You may not have used the same words, but you probably came pretty close. Just about any dictionary's basic definition of *thinking* will read something like this: "the action of using one's mind to produce thoughts." Sometimes the definition will then go on to describe a range of thinking operations that could be employed consciously or unconsciously. Actually, these definitions really don't tell us much. We already sort of know what thinking is, even if we can't put it into words.

Thinking and Critical Thinking
Are Easier to Illustrate Than to Define

Perhaps the following definition of *thinking* will help, especially in the next few pages where we discuss *critical* thinking.

THINKING:
The process of producing thoughts based on recall of remembered and memorized information

---

As you can see from this definition, thinking depends on recall of remembered information (acquired passively, without trying) or memorized information (acquired actively, by planning). Try the following "thinking" exercise.

STIR UP YOUR THINKING

Without checking with your fellow students, answer this question with the first answer that comes to mind, no matter what it is. *A student went to the campus bookstore and bought two pencils for a total of 10 cents. How much did each pencil cost?*

If you answered 5 cents (a total of 10 cents divided by two pencils equals 5 cents), your thinking fits the definition of *thinking* given above and was based on simple recall of memorized information. You fell back on all those math formulas you memorized in school in order to answer the question. On the other hand, if you had any other answer, you weren't simply thinking, you were thinking *critically,* because you were doing more than relying on recall of information.

Here's probably what happened: You first thought about your thinking on an almost unconscious level. Your thinking/reasoning warning light went off. Perhaps you said to yourself, "I can't tell. Maybe one pencil is bigger than the other, so maybe one pencil cost 6 cents and the other cost 4 cents," or perhaps you thought, "Wait a minute, I need more information." Perhaps you questioned the whole idea of two pencils being so cheap, or perhaps you were thinking that this had to be some type of trick question because it was so simple. *If you did more than passively employ memorized math formulas to answer—or challenge—the question, you were going beyond thinking to thinking critically.*

WHAT IS CRITICAL THINKING?

In order to study critical thinking and understand its important contribution to success in college and in life, it is necessary that we be clear about what critical thinking is. We can't do that by simply turning to a dictionary, because there are over a dozen related but different definitions of the term *critical thinking.* On top of this, critical thinking is sometimes called *higher-order thinking, reflective thinking, productive thinking, inquiry thinking,* or *logical reasoning!* These multiple terms reveal that critical thinking is viewed by some as a process of thinking, whereas others see critical thinking as a composite of thinking skills.

A Process or a Composite of Many Skills?

When described as a process, critical thinking is seen as the *way* in which a particular result is pursued. As early as 1949, the *Dictionary of Education* had defined critical thinking as a process, as "thinking that proceeds on the basis of careful evaluation of premises and evidence and comes to conclusions cautiously through the consideration of all pertinent factors." In 1985, Robert Ennis, a college professor, defined critical thinking more simply as "reflective and reasonable thinking that is focused on deciding what to believe or do." Since then, most people have agreed that this is a reasonably good description of critical thinking as a process, as a *way* of thinking. The problem, however, with defining critical thinking as a process is that the steps or stages in the process are frequently either unclear or so lengthy that they frustrate anyone who tries to implement the process.

The majority of approaches to critical thinking appear to agree that critical thinking involves *a broad collection of separate thinking skills or thinking operations*—a composite of elements of reasoning, attitudes, knowledge, intellectual standards, and specific thinking skills—*which, when necessary, are called upon so that analysis and evaluation can take place.* These separate thinking skills are developed by individuals and then used singly or in combination. We use them to get below the surface of information when the need arises to analyze, make decisions, solve problems, create solutions, reflect, think creatively, and face challenges to our thinking.

This is very close to how *critical thinking* is defined in this book.

> **CRITICAL THINKING:**
> The use of any and all appropriate thinking skills when intellectual tasks call for anything more than information recall

> **CRITICAL THINKING SKILL(S):**
> Just about every thinking ability or behavior that can be taught, including such mental operations as questioning, classifying, synthesizing, comparing, recognizing bias, inducing, deducing, and inferring

An Important Observation: Critical Doesn't Mean Negative

Critical thinking may be a lot of things, but what it isn't is negative or fault-finding thinking. The word *critical*, when used in combination with words like *viewing, listening,* or *thinking,* means "examined" or "analyzed." For example, film critics, drama critics, book critics, and music critics, although they sometimes display negative attitudes toward whatever they are evaluating, are really committed to analyzing and examining their subjects. They are not committed to being negative.

STIRRING UP THINKING

Much of our thinking is habitually biased, partial, uninformed, or even prejudiced because we seldom think about our thinking and so do not apply any standards to it. We merely respond. Any time that your thinking is stirred up so that you force yourself to think about your thinking and apply standards to it, you are using thinking skills that go beyond recall of information—you are exercising some degree of critical thinking. There are many ways that this is done, and nearly all of them are interesting and sometimes entertaining. Systematically cultivating the process of critical thinking leads to an increased ability to conceptualize, analyze, synthesize, and evaluate information fairly and accurately. You'll experience stirred-up-thinking opportunities frequently in this book.

THE SHIFT FROM LEARNING TO THINKING

What then is the relevance of critical thinking to the enhancement of your college education? Why are this book's author and so many of your professors convinced that critical thinking skills are so important to your learning? The answer lies in the steady shift that has occurred over the last several years in education, a steady shift from focusing on *learning* to focusing on *thinking*. In 1987, the American Philosophical Association published a consensus statement addressing the importance of critical thinking. This brief statement captured the feeling of educators concerning the importance of critical thinking:

> We understand critical thinking to be purposeful, self-regulatory judgment which results in interpretation, analysis, evaluation, and inference, as well as explanation of the evidential, conceptual, methodological, criteriological, or contextual considerations upon which that judgment is based. Critical thinking is essential as a tool of inquiry. As such, critical thinking is a liberating force in education and a powerful resource in one's personal and civic life.[1]

---

[1] This statement was recorded by Peter A. Facione, in "Critical Thinking: A Statement of Expert Consensus for Purposes of Educational Assessment and Instruction" (*Institute for Critical Thinking Resource Publication*, Series 4, No. 6, 1991, p. 3).

Teachers at all levels, elementary, secondary, and college, have concluded that it is better for students to think for themselves than merely to learn what other people have thought. They declare that effective and meaningful education requires that teaching and learning at all levels be coordinated so as to foster in students the mental skills and the habits of unemotional questioning associated with critical thinking. They have long made the case that educating students to be critical thinkers is vital for the students themselves and for society in general. Recently, however, with the explosive growth of new information, information retrieval systems, and individualized access to information through computers, it has become even more important that every person be trained to be an independent thinker.

Over a decade ago, in a 1984 poll of professional educators, nine out of ten respondents said that better instruction in thinking skills should be a major priority.[2] It appears that most educators believe that instruction in critical thinking is not merely an educational option, but that students have the *right* to be taught how to think critically. Even government officials, business leaders, and a sizable segment of the American public support the teaching of critical thinking.[3] The U.S. Department of Labor's Secretary's Commission on Achieving Necessary Skills in 1992 even went so far as to identify the acquisition of critical thinking skills as one of three essentials for successful entry into the workplace of the future.

THE VERDICT IS IN: CRITICAL THINKING IS ESSENTIAL

Your professors want you to be able to exercise good judgment in interpreting, evaluating, and applying what you read and hear in their classes, and this good judgment cannot be brought to bear unless it rests upon proficient thinking skills. If developing your critical thinking skills can produce an improvement in your education, it will be because it brings you academic empowerment. We live in what frequently has

---

[2]For more information about this poll, see B. Z. Presseisen, *Thinking Skills: Meanings, Models, and Materials* (Research for Better Schools, Inc., Philadelphia, Pa., National Institute of Education, Washington, D.C., 1984 [ERIC ED 257 858]).

[3]See, for example, *Academic preparation for college: What students need to know and be able to do* (New York: College Board, 1983).

been referred to as an information age because of all the information that is brought to us daily by way of newspapers, magazines, books, radio, television, and computer networks. Sorting it all out and determining what information to act upon and what information to question requires developed thinking skills. Acquiring critical thinking skills enables you to think more and more independently, skillfully, and efficiently apart from what you are told on the information highway and even in classes and assigned textbooks. If by the time you finish this book your thinking is characterized by the use of critical thinking skills, you will have developed thinking habits that will serve you well through life.

THE GOAL OF CRITICAL THINKING IS INDEPENDENT THINKING

Students who develop and practice critical thinking are able to think independently. They recognize the limits to their knowledge, they analyze important issues before acting, and they are not easily manipulated. Now that kind of independence is a worthy goal for every person.

STIR IT UP 1.1   Whether we are currently computer literate or not, and whether we have ever "surfed the Net" or not, the use of computers and the Internet promises to play a very big part in our future careers and lives. Why? Let's find out. With a group of four or five classmates, make a list of possible reasons for college students to become active users of Internet services such as Prodigy, America Online, or CompuServe. Do some brainstorming and write down all the ideas that you can think up, without evaluating them. When you have a list of reasons, go through them and prioritize them, starting with the best ones and ending with the least useful ones. Notice how brainstorming stirs up your thinking and allows you to feed off other people's ideas and thinking. Many of you will recognize brainstorming as a useful *prewriting* activity.

STIR IT UP 1.2   Surprise! It's time to write. Writing is the single best activity for stirring up your thinking and for developing your many different thinking abilities. It causes you to reflect on information and ideas, synthesize information from all sources, question relevance and value, and so on. So, it is not surprising that you will frequently be asked to write in this book.

Write a letter to your parents (or your grandparents, a rich uncle, a philanthropic foundation, or other source of funds) asking for support in the amount of twenty dollars a month to enable you to connect to the Internet and spend a "reasonable" amount of time (up to twenty dollars' worth) using the Internet services. Using the lists of reasons developed in Stir It Up 1.1, select the most persuasive reasons to make your case for this monthly allowance. How will you be a better student, be better off intellectually, get better grades, or learn more and faster if you are connected? Consider well who you are writing to when you give your reasons. Who knows—you may be able to send this letter if you craft it well and persuasively enough.

On the other hand, if you are *not* convinced of the value of the Internet for college students, write a letter convincing your audience that its use should not be encouraged.

STIR IT UP 1.3 First, examine the letter you wrote for Stir It Up 1.2 and try to find weaknesses or flaws in your reasoning. Make a list of what your letter reader might find weak or wrong in your argument. Next, exchange letters with a classmate and evaluate the reasoning and arguments in his or her letter. Just how persuasive is the letter? On a separate piece of paper, shoot down (nicely, please) the reasoning if you can. Then, suggest ways to strengthen the arguments. Discuss with each other why you were not persuaded and what your suggestions are for making a stronger case. Compare the list of probable weak spots you prepared for your own letter with the weaknesses that your classmate found. Were they the same? What does that tell you?

STIR IT UP 1.4 Do some research in the library or on the Internet. See if you can find ten different definitions of critical thinking. Record the definitions and the sources where they were found. Speculate on why there is such a difference in definitions and a seeming lack of agreement on a definition. Is there any relationship between each definition and the source where it was found? In other words, is a definition of critical thinking found in a psychology textbook uniquely *psychological* in its application, or can it be applied to nonpsychology situations also?

JOURNAL WRITING

In each chapter in this book you will find lined pages labeled "Journal Observations," where you will be asked to keep a journal of your thinking (and perhaps of your actions) related to what you are reading and experiencing in this book. Beginning in Chapter 3, there will be journal pages for each critical thinking skill discussed. Ideally, you will step back from reading about and discussing critical thinking, reflect on what you have learned, and record your reactions to it, perhaps writing down the concepts that seem especially clear and useful, and the things that are still a bit confusing. You might even describe the times you experience examples of muddy, faulty, lazy, noncritical thinking outside of this class (on your part and on the part of others: roommates, friends, professors, employers).

The journal pages are a good place to make "real-life" connections to what you are learning and discussing in class. They are also an especially good place to jot down questions that arise when you are away from class. Later, these questions can be raised in class with your instructor or further researched by you. The journal pages can become a personal chronology of your growth in critical thinking, a record of your discussions with others as you work through some of the "Thinkers" and other thinking exercises in this book, a planning guide for what you need to do to accomplish your goal of becoming an active critical thinker, a place to record reactions to the readings, and a repository for your active reflection on each chapter.

For each chapter or for each thinking skill section, set aside at least three different times when you will think about the material covered in the section, and write your thoughts on the journal pages that follow. Writing on three different occasions, rather than filling all the lines at one sitting, will allow you to "reflect on your reflections" and even to change your mind or disagree with yourself. Becoming a better thinker, a critical thinker, is an ongoing process. By the way, you will find it interesting when you finish this book to go back and reread your journal observations. You will be able to see the changes in your thinking patterns.

Journal Observations (see page 13)

THINKING vs. THINKING CRITICALLY

1st Writing _____

_____

_____

_____

_____

_____

_____

_____

_____

_____

_____

_____

2nd Writing _____

_____

_____

_____

_____

_____

_____

_____

_____

_____

_____

_____

_____

3rd Writing _____

_____

_____

_____

_____

_____

_____

_____

_____

_____

Owl Activists Don't Give a Hoot About the Economy

Susan Mercier
The Orange County Register, June 21, 1990

Dear fellow members of SHAFT:
   Without the Spotted Owl's very photogenic and undeniably appealing presence, the fight against all logging in the Pacific Northwest would be nearly impossible to win.

We have toiled long and arduous hours against the evil logging industry, and now we see forest-product companies quivering with deserved fear.

Their paramount goal of eliminating our majestic forests, and reaping obscene profits by cheerfully slicing and hacking their way through old-fir forests with happy impunity and gleeful destruction will soon come to a halt.

Insuring many years of profitable lumber production, the timber industry replants two trees for every one they harvest, but that's an insignificant fact we'll keep to ourselves.

The Spotted Owl prefers to roost in old-growth trees, furnishing us with a fortuitous excuse to accomplish our objective of stopping all logging in the "old-growth" evergreen national forests.

New-growth trees have been found to attract nesting owl pairs as well, but that bit of information could detract from our plan and shouldn't be too widely publicized.

Never mind the 60,000 logging jobs and thousands of other timber-dependent occupations threatened under the guise of saving the Spotted Owl.

To rescue our feathered mascot, government wildlife biologists spent six months studying the Spotted Owl, and concluded the owls are threatened.

The 300 acres of forest per pair of owls already set aside was found to be too constricting, as the smaller Spotted Owls unwisely drifted out of their allotted 300 acres and were consumed by horned owls.

What tremendous news! This indicates to us that even more acreage is required to save the Spotted Owl. At least 21 miles for each owl pair just might do the trick. That would mean virtually ending all logging in the entire Pacific Northwest's national forest.

Joining our battle, Congressman Jim Jontz of Indiana backs us 100 percent. His empathy with the Spotted Owl, and environmental solicitude for the Pacific Northwest's forest surprised us, since he hails from Indiana. He stridently disagrees with Representative Bob Smith of Oregon, who predicts the demise of the Pacific Northwest if all federally owned lands are barred from logging.

We say, "Let the people find other means of sheltering their families, and putting food on their tables." Saving our forests and owls from human threat, and silencing the timber industry once and for all, justifies our campaign.

Five million acres of national forest inhabited by the owls, and an additional 900,000 acres of protected wilderness, which can't be logged, insure pristine forests for owls, hikers, and campers to enjoy.

We expect a great influx of backpackers in the coming years. Perhaps the out-of-work mill employees and other timber-related workers will be able to grub sustenance from the land, munching wild blackberries and roots. We intend to guarantee the forest will be there, providing foraging grounds for all those Americans forced from their homes and jobs.

Declining housing availability, skyrocketing lumber prices, and the livelihood of all those concerned are but a small price to pay for the lives of 3,000 Spotted Owls.

By the way, ever hear of the yellow-striped weaving spider? Its habitat and existence depend on the corn fields in Indiana. The problem arises when the harvesting of corn destroys the spiders' cornstalk-dependent webs.

The greedy farmers, thinking only of profits, continue to harvest their corn, with total disregard for this tiny spider. Also, the landscape is blighted with the gathering of corn. Once-verdant fields become unsightly brown tracts of barren land. It is our hope Rep. Jontz will support our efforts to stop the willful massacre of the innocent yellow-striped weaving spider and preserve the lush fields of corn.

God bless America! Home of the free and land of a political system our forefathers never even dreamed of.

Very truly yours,

SHAFT
(Stop Harvest of All Forest Timber)

Examine Your Thinking About What You Just Read

Pay attention to your thinking processes as you answer the following questions.

1. What is this article *really* about? Is it about owls, activists, the economy, logging, or what? And what is the impression being created of Congressman Jim Jontz of Indiana?

2. What is the SHAFT organization? What are we supposed to believe about SHAFT and its purposes? How does the tone of this article influence what we believe?

3. What are some of the facts presented in this article, and how would you go about validating them? What are some of the opinions woven into this article? How do you know that they are opinions?

4. How did the organization of this article contribute to making it a particularly effective piece of writing?

Write about this In a short essay, use this article as a model and write a similar piece advocating some environmentally related cause. Perhaps you could write about saving the whales, saving water, not littering, or refraining from eating any of the endangered species.

Critical Inquiry and Political Reality: A Window of Opportunity

Walter C. Veit

To those of us who believe that the long period of hysteria that has gripped the American consciousness since the Bolshevik revolution may be drawing to a close, there is some cause for a new optimism in the area of a critical questioning of political values. The red scares of the 20's, the red baiting of the 50's and the more recent flirtation with a particularly banal Americanism of the 80's, culminating in the pillaging of both corporate and banking resources by an irresponsible deregulation of public agencies, could provide the background for the emergence of critical social and political forces that have been hitherto fragmented and unfocused. The discovery that the Soviet Bogeyman was as much a creation of mindless market capitalism as it was a reaction by the Soviet bureaucracy itself to such western fears, might open the doors to a kind of criticism whose very absence has seriously weakened the democratic process at a time when some new institutions need desperately to be examined. One of these latter institutions, although strictly speaking not new, has been so transmogrified by the exponential growth of technology that its form could almost be thought of as new. I am referring to a worldwide corporate media that has only just begun to flex its muscles.

Such a new climate of openness will not sustain itself, however, unless new political factions emerge which can serve to institutionalize the kind of political, social and economic critique that is a fixture in other political democracies. Debate is seriously hobbled by the absence of a genuine critical political consciousness here in America. In virtually all of the West except the United States, there are political parties which, if I were to pick out their most significant function, serve to keep issues in front of citizens and do so in a constant and relentless fashion. Such single-mindedness is essential if we are ever going to be able to break out of a media dependency which has become a surrogate for political participation. Such a condition as now exists makes it possible to focus on personalities to the exclusion of issues; on pragmatic possibilities rather than long range theoretical solutions.

At the heart of the present vacuum is the ability of elites to define and create the permissible language of public discourse. Instead of wearing a label, so effortlessly applied by such elites, with pride and honor, we shrink from such badges out of a fear of being stigmatized. We lack the organization which would rally to our side and provide the solidarity that gives courage to principle. The paucity of political organization on the bottom—or indeed even in the middle—multiplies the power of the top. It is organized. It is ideologically and philosophically cohesive. Given its huge advantage of prestige that private wealth can buy, we look to it rather than ourselves for definition and clarification of values. That such values become shallow, consumerist and disorganizing simply reifies the system. The long and difficult road out of such a miasma has to be built by a political consciousness that eschews present establishment politics. The present winter of discontent may provide such an opening, but the window isn't open very wide and if it isn't wedged open, it may close when new substitutes for the old Communist bully-boy are discovered.

Read and Respond

1. Did you understand the majority of what this writer was saying in this short article? Perhaps the writer's choice of words was a problem for you. But wait, one mark of good writing is the use of a rich and diversified vocabulary. This helps the writer express his or her thoughts more accurately. However, if the reader doesn't know what the words mean, then the writing can be confusing and ineffective and the point of the writing gets lost. This article has a lot of interesting and descriptive words. Do you know what they mean? Be certain that you do. What do the following words and phrases mean as used in this article: *red baiting, banal Americanism, pillaging, deregulation, Soviet Bogeyman, mindless market capitalism, transmogrified, exponential growth, critique, hobbled, critical political consciousness, media dependency, pragmatic possibilities, theoretical solutions, the present vacuum, elites, stigmatized, solidarity, paucity, consumerist, reifies, miasma, eschews, establishment?* After you have noted the meanings of these words, read the article again. What is the difference now in your understanding of the article? How important is a good and growing vocabulary to your education, to your future success, and to your awareness in general?

2. Just what is a "window of opportunity," and what is the specific opportunity referred to in this article?

3. What do the following sentences mean? Express them in your own words, making certain to maintain the accuracy of the writer's words and intentions in your interpretation?

   a. "At the heart of the present vacuum is the ability of elites to define and create the permissible language of public discourse."

   b. "The paucity of political organization on the bottom—or indeed even in the middle—multiplies the power of the top."

   c. "It is ideologically and philosophically cohesive."

   d. "That such values become shallow, consumerist and disorganizing simply reifies the system."

4. Are there any questionable assertions in the article? Identify them and indicate why you believe them to be questionable.

ASKING CRITICAL QUESTIONS

After you read the articles that follow, what critical questions come to mind? Everything you read will stir up your thinking if you read and question critically. What questions would you like to have answered in order for you to put the articles in proper context and to completely understand what is being said or reported? *On the lines following each article, write three questions that, if answered, will help you understand what is really being said.*

Children of a Marriage

Richard Rodriguez

What is culture?

The immigrant shrugs. Latin American immigrants come to the United States with only the things they need in mind—not abstractions like culture. Money. They need dollars. They need food. Maybe they need to get out of the way of bullets.

Most of us who concern ourselves with Hispanic-American culture, as painters, musicians, writers—or as sons and daughters—are the children of immigrants. We have grown up on this side of the border, in the land of Elvis Presley and Thomas Edison; our lives are prescribed by the mall, by the DMV and the Chinese restaurant. Our imaginations yet vascillate between an Edenic Latin America (the blue door)—which nevertheless betrayed our parents—and the repellent plate glass of a real American city—which has been good to us.

Hispanic-American culture is where the past meets the future. Hispanic-American culture is not an Hispanic milestone only, not simply a celebration at the crossroads. America transforms into pleasure what America cannot avoid. Is it any coincidence that at a time when Americans are troubled by the encroachment of the Mexican desert, Americans discover a chic in cactus, in the decorator colors of the Southwest? In sand?

Hispanic-American culture of the sort that is now showing (the teen movie, the rock song) may exist in an hourglass; may in fact be irrelevant to the epic. The U.S. Border Patrol works through the night to arrest the flow of illegal immigrants over the border, even as Americans wait in line to get into "La Bamba." Even as Americans vote to declare, once and for all, that English shall be the official language of the United States, Madonna starts recording in Spanish.

But then so is Bill Cosby's show irrelevant to the 10 o'clock news, where families huddle together in fear on porches, pointing at the body of the slain boy bagged in tarpoline. Which is not to say that Bill Cosby or Michael Jackson is irrelevant to the future or without neo-Platonic influence. Like players within the play, they prefigure, they resolve. They make black and white audiences aware of a bond that may not yet exist.

Before a national TV audience, Rita Moreno tells Geraldo Rivera that her dream as an actress is to play a character rather like herself: "I speak English perfectly well . . . I'm not dying from poverty . . . I want to play *that* kind of Hispanic woman, which is to say, an American citizen." This is an actress talking, these are show-biz pieties. But Moreno expresses as well the general Hispanic-American predicament. Hispanics want to belong to America without betraying the past.

Hispanics fear losing ground in any negotiation with the American city. We come from an expansive, an intimate culture that has been judged second-rate by the United States of America. For reasons of pride, therefore, as much as of affection, we are reluctant to give up our past. Hispanics often express a fear of "losing" culture. Our fame in the United States has been our resistance to assimilation.

The symbol of Hispanic culture has been the tongue of flame— Spanish. But the remarkable legacy Hispanics carry from Latin America is not language—an inflatable skin—but breath itself, capacity of soul, an inclination to live. The genius of Latin America is the habit of synthesis.

We assimilate. Just over the border there is the example of Mexico, the country from which the majority of U.S. Hispanics come. Mexico is *mestizo*—Indian and Spanish. Within a single family, Mexicans are light-skinned and dark. It is impossible for the Mexican to say, in the scheme of things, where the Indian begins and the Spaniard surrenders.

In culture as in blood, Latin America was formed by a rape that became a marriage. Due to the absorbing generosity of the Indian, European culture took on new soil. What Latin America knows is that people create one another as they marry. In the music of Latin America you will hear the litany of bloodlines—the African drum, the German accordion, the cry from the minaret.

The United States stands as the opposing New World experiment. In North America the Indian and the European stood apace. Whereas Latin America was formed by a medieval Catholic dream of one world—of meltdown conversion—the United States was built up from Protestant individualism. The American melting pot washes away only embarrassment; it is the necessary initiation into public life. The American faith is that our national strength derives from separateness, from "diversity." The glamour of the United States is a carnival promise: You can lose weight, get rich as Rockefeller, touch up your roots, get a divorce.

Immigrants still come for the promise. But the United States wavers in its faith. As long as there was space enough, sky enough, as long as economic success validated individualism, loneliness was not too high a price to pay. (The cabin on the prairie or the Sony Walkman.)

As we near the end of the American century, two alternative cultures beckon the American imagination—both highly communal cultures— the Asian and the Latin American. The United States is a literal culture. Americans devour what we might otherwise fear to become. Sushi will make us corporate warriors. Combination Plate #3, smothered in mestizo gravy, will burn a hole in our hearts.

Latin America offers passion. Latin America has a life—I mean *life*— big clouds, unambiguous themes, death, birth, faith, that the United States, for all its quality of life, seems without now. Latin America offers communal riches: an undistressed leisure, a kitchen table, even a full sorrow. Such is the solitude of America, such is the urgency of American need, Americans reach right past a fledgling, homegrown Hispanic-American culture for the real thing—the darker bottle of Mexican beer; the denser novel of a Latin American master.

For a long time, Hispanics in the United States withheld from the United States our Latin American gift. We denied the value of assimilation. But as our presence is judged less foreign in America, we will produce a more generous art, less timid, less parochial. Carlos Santana, Luis Valdez, Linda Ronstadt—Hispanic-Americans do not have a "pure" Latin American art to offer. Expect bastard themes, expect ironies, comic conclusions. For we live on this side of the border, where Kraft manufactures bricks of "Mexican style" Velveeta, and where Jack in the Box serves "Fajita Pita."

The flame-red Chevy floats a song down the Pan American Highway: From a rolled-down window, the grizzled voice of Willie Nelson rises in disembodied harmony with the voice of Julio Iglesias. Gabby Hayes and Cisco are thus resolved.

Expect marriage. We will change America even as we will be changed. We will disappear with you into a new miscegenation.

Along the border, real conflicts remain. But the ancient tear separating Europe from itself—the Catholic Mediterranean from the Protestant north—may yet heal itself in the New World. For generations, Latin America has been the place—the bed—of a confluence of so many races and cultures that Protestant North America shuddered to imagine it.

Imagine it.

My Critical Questions

1. _____
   _____ **?**

2. _____
   _____ **?**

3. _____
   _____ **?**

Teaching Thinking

Wilbert J. McKeachie

Everyone agrees that students learn in college, but whether they learn to think is more controversial.

Thinking is defined in so many ways that the boundary between "learning" and "thinking" is fuzzy and perhaps nonexistent. The two processes are inextricably entwined—even a simple learning task, such as reading a textbook assignment, requires thinking.

Thus the preceding chapter, "Teaching Students How to Learn," is actually about teaching students to think. Setting goals, thinking about what strategy to use in tackling an assignment, accessing relevant previous knowledge, and monitoring one's progress—these are all important components of critical thinking and problem solving.

When faculty members talk about teaching critical thinking, problem solving, or reasoning, they typically mean teaching students to use what they already know.

Can We Teach Thinking?

Can we teach thinking? Some would argue that we can only give students the knowledge necessary for thinking—that the intellectual ability required for thinking is not teachable. There is increasing evidence, however, that measures of thinking, such as tests of general, verbal, and spatial/technical intelligence, improve with education (McKeachie, Pintrich, Lin, Smith, and Sharma, 1990).*

How?

So we do teach thinking skills, but how?

Almost every chapter of this book has dealt with methods of teaching thinking. Effective methods of learning discussions, lecturing, and testing are critical elements in a program for teaching students to think more effectively. Writing, laboratory work, field work, peer learning, project methods, case method, instructional games, journals, role playing, and computers can all contribute to teaching thinking. This chapter would be excessively long if we reviewed, or even summarized, all of the foregoing material on thinking. Therefore I shall simply highlight a few general points.

Knowledge is not enough. Our ever present pressure to "cover" the content may, in fact, militate against effectiveness in teaching thinking because we fail to allow time for thinking. Thinking, like other skills, requires practice, particularly practice that brings our thinking into the open where it can be challenged, corrected, or encouraged. Thus we teachers need to give students opportunities to talk, write, do laboratory or field projects, or carry out other activities that stimulate and reveal their thinking. One doesn't become a skillful musician or basketball player by listening to an expert three hours a week.

The bottleneck is time. I can only read one paper, or listen to one student, at a time. Fortunately the teacher does not have to be the only source of feedback. Other studies can help. . . .

Even though knowledge is not sufficient, thinking requires knowledge. Our own research has shown that measures of thinking relate to how well students have achieved an organized structure of concepts.

Surprisingly, standard courses in logic do not seem to improve practical reasoning skills unless the abstract concepts are coupled with concrete examples. Training in statistics, however, can be generalized—

---

*The full titles of books mentioned in parentheses appear at the end of the book this excerpt is drawn from, but we don't provide them with this excerpt.

even brief training (either by giving rules or examples) in the law of large numbers results in generalization, probably because students have intuitive ideas approximating statistical abstraction (Nisbett, Fong, Lehman, and Cheng, 1987). Typical laboratory courses in science have a poor track record in teaching thinking. Yet they, too, can have a positive effect when taught with specific emphasis upon thinking (Bainter, 1955).

If knowledge of subject matter, knowledge of logic, and knowledge of laboratory procedures fail to produce more effective thinkers, what can we do?

Learning to think usually begins by 1) bringing order out of chaos, 2) discovering uncovered ideas, and 3) developing strategies while avoiding jumping to conclusions. Teaching students to describe the elements of a problem or to create a schematic or graphic representation may help them bring order out of chaos. Verbalizing the reason for taking a step before the step is actually taken also can lead to improved thinking.

Bloom and Broder (1950) asked good students to think aloud while answering mock exam questions requiring problem solving. Other students were asked to compare their own thought processes with those used by the good students and to practice thinking procedures that were successful. Although this procedure was not effective for all students, thinking aloud has often been used since, both in research and training in thinking, and is an additional strategy for you to use in teaching thinking.

Alverno College has made measurable progress in teaching critical thinking by stressing explicitness, multiple opportunities to practice in differing contexts, and emphasis on developing student self-awareness and self-assessment (Loacker, Cromwell, Fey, and Rutherford, 1984).

Research on teaching problem solving in particular courses suggests explicitly focusing on the specific methods and strategies to be used in solving particular types of problems. Noting different approaches also helps.

Student participation, teacher encouragement, and student-to-student interaction positively relate to improved critical thinking. These three activities confirm other research and theory stressing the importance of active practice, motivation, and feedback in learning thinking skills as well as other skills. As we saw earlier, discussions are superior to lectures in improving thinking and problem solving.

Many studies point to the importance of developing understanding rather than simply teaching routine steps for problem solving.

Increasing understanding and skill lead in turn to increased intrinsic motivation for thinking.

In conclusion, at least three elements of teaching seem to make a difference in student gains in thinking skills: 1) student writing and discussion, 2) explicit emphasis on problem-solving procedures and methods using varied examples, and 3) verbalization of methods and strategies to encourage development of metacognition.

My Critical Questions

1. _____

   _____ **?**

2. _____

   _____ **?**

3. _____

   _____ **?**

SOLUTION to Thinkers (p. 5)

To keep things from freezing. Some things needed to be kept cool but could not be frozen.

Chapter 2

BECOMING A CRITICAL THINKER

It's the attitude that counts.

> *"Compared to what we ought to be, we are only half awake, we are making use of only a small part of our physical and mental resources. Stating the thing broadly, the human individual thus lives far within his limits. He possesses power of various sorts which he habitually fails to use."*
> —William James

> *"Put some magic in your thinking by asking 'what if?' questions. What if animals became more intelligent than people? What if we had mouths in the palms of our hands? What if men also had babies? What if we had edible clothing? What if we elected our officials by lottery? What if people exuded a foul smell from every pore whenever they did something bad? Such questions will stretch your thinking and lead to new ideas."*
> —Roger von Oech

> *"Thinking is the hardest work in the world; and most of us will go to great lengths to avoid it."*
> —Louise Dudley

What questions am I going to have answered in this chapter?

1. Isn't the development of critical thinking skills a natural result of aging?
2. What qualities of mind or personality become the *foundation* for developing critical thinking skills?
3. What intellectual habits do I need in order to employ critical thinking skills?

DOESN'T SKILLFUL THINKING DEVELOP ON ITS OWN?

If you were able to survey the population of your community, you would probably find that the majority of people believe erroneously that skillful thinking develops on its own. After all, don't people just become better thinkers as they get older? Unfortunately, or perhaps fortunately, if people are left to develop their thinking skills on their own, they frequently fail to progress beyond basic, unthinking acceptance of much of what they see, hear, and read, and never really progress to the think-

THINK ABOUT THIS!

Rate Your Level of Mental Fitness

"Strength of mind comes from exercising it, not resting it." Alexander Pope said it well, but then, he was just an eighteenth-century poet—a world-class poet, but a poet—so what could he possibly know about the thinking process?

How would you rate your mental fitness, your objectivity, your reasoning and questioning ability, your ability to be fairminded—to judge persons, events, issues, and information in an impartial and accurate way?

☐ **Really Sharp**   My thinking is exceptional: objective, creative, precise, deeply grounded in reality, fairmindedness, and accuracy. I'm even thinking of writing a critical thinking book. Just call me Marie Curie.

OK, let's see if you really belong in this category. Pick a number, any number, but don't tell me what it is. Double it. Add 17. Divide your total by 2. Now subtract from your total the number you started with. The number you have left is 8 1/2, or 8.5 if you prefer decimals. How did I know that would be your answer, especially since I had no idea what number you were starting with? If you can figure out how I accomplished this example of long-distance ESP, you can stay in the Really Sharp category.

☐ **Not Bad/Not Good**   I sometimes reach amazing heights of reasoning and awareness, but much of the time I don't really think at all. I mostly tend to jump to conclusions, to simply fall back on memorized information to answer questions or solve problems. I frequently am fooled, come to the wrong conclusion, or make the wrong decision. But I survive OK. So far. Just call me Gilligan.

Do you really belong in this category? Here is a little scenario: You are confronted with a decision that has two possible alternatives—a yes-or-no decision or a this-or-that decision. You take out a coin and assign one alternative to heads and the other alternative to tails. You flip the coin. When it lands you look at it and ask yourself how you feel about that alternative. If you feel good, you go with it. If you feel uncomfortable, then you go with the other alternative. Under what circumstances is this a wise policy to follow, and why? If you can figure this out, you belong in the Not Bad/Not Good category.

☐ **Oops!**   I can't believe how easily and regularly I am fooled, make hasty decisions, jump to the wrong conclusions, and fail to think things through. My thinking most often resembles a bowl of mush—with occasional hard lumps, but still mush. Just call me True Grits.

If you are now thinking, "I'd really rather go play pool or watch TV than read this stuff about improving thinking," then you belong in the Oops! category.

ing levels of which they may be capable. Students do not tend "naturally" to develop an urge to consider thoughtfully the subjects and issues they are confronted with. There is little evidence, unfortunately, that students acquire critical thinking skills as a byproduct of studying any subject in school. Prowess in critical thinking must be actively sought and learned and then practiced.

This may be easier to understand if we compare thinking to climbing, another "natural" skill. We learn to climb as children, frequently beginning with stairs, then progressing to chairs and couches and perhaps later to ladders and trees. However, if given the opportunity, we would not dream of attempting to climb the sheer face of a cliff without specialized training. We may know how to climb, but rock-climbing is an advanced type of climbing, requiring greater expertise. As with climbing, people develop thinking skills naturally to some degree, *but not sufficiently* to take on the specialized thinking tasks necessary to consciously control their own thinking at all times. If you are to acquire good thinking skills, you must work with that objective in mind. Thinking skills are not likely to be realized spontaneously or as a consequence of merely getting older. Schools, classes, and books like this one provide the appropriate setting within which specialized critical thinking instruction can take place. But is that all there is to becoming a critical thinker, just having an appropriate setting in which to learn? Becoming a critical thinker has certain additional requirements.

BECOMING A CRITICAL THINKER ASSUMES CERTAIN MENTAL DISPOSITIONS

It is not only possible, but it is likely that you already have the qualities that will enable you to acquire, develop, and employ at an efficient and skillful level the critical thinking skills that this book addresses. Some of these qualities are fairly obvious, such as politeness and willingness to listen, but in addition, there are fundamental thinking dispositions that are necessarily present if critical thinking is going to become a way of life. In 1987, the American Philosophical Association, through its Committee on Pre-College Philosophy, published a summary statement regarding the ideal critical thinker:

> The ideal critical thinker is habitually inquisitive,
> well-informed, trustful of reason, open-minded, flexible,
> fair-minded in evaluation, honest in facing personal biases,
> prudent in making judgments, willing to reconsider, clear

about issues, orderly in complex matters, diligent in seeking relevant information, reasonable in the selection of criteria, focused in inquiry, and persistent in seeking results which are as precise as the subject and the circumstances of inquiry permit. Thus, educating good critical thinkers means working toward this ideal. It combines developing CT skills with nurturing those dispositions which consistently yield useful insights and which are the basis of a rational and democratic society.[1]

In addition to possessing the critical thinking skills just identified, the good critical thinker can be characterized as being especially strong when it comes to the following habits of mind:

Curiosity and Courage

Along with an overall inquisitiveness and intellectual perseverance with regard to issues and questions, there is an abiding concern to become and remain generally well-informed. The desire to know, to know more, to ask questions, raise objections, and seek causes, is at the heart of independent learning. Essential to critical thinking is the courage to consider "dangerous" ideas and to question opinions even when they are held by powerful groups or individuals.

A Drive for Competence and Accuracy

An accurate thinker recognizes the need to be consistent in the use of intellectual standards and to give close attention to such qualities as orderliness in dealing with complicated, complex, or multiple details. A competent thinker is flexible in dealing with ambiguity and change but maintains willingness to hold to rigorous standards and to exercise great care in focusing attention on the concern at hand. Watchfulness, a lack of "mind wandering," and precision to the degree permitted by subject and circumstances, are maintained. Understanding the question or concern and demanding clarity in stating it are always a top priority.

---

[1]For the complete text, see Peter A. Facione, "Critical Thinking: A Statement of Expert Consensus for Purposes of Educational Assessment and Instruction," *Institute for Critical Thinking Resource Publication*, Series 4, No. 6 (Upper Montclair, NJ: Montclair State University, 1991), pp. 1–51.

A Desire for Truth and Self-Honesty

Because we are products of our families, our backgrounds, and our communities, honesty in facing our biases, prejudices, stereotypes, and egocentric or sociocentric tendencies is important to becoming critical thinkers. The best thinkers today, as well as throughout history, acknowledge the need to consider all viewpoints dispassionately, without giving special weight to their own feelings or the feelings of friends, family, and community, or to what they can gain by unfairly taking advantage of facts or situations.

A Willingness to Reason and Reflect

The most efficient thinkers are the ones who build in "wait time," who constantly guard against a "rush to judgment," and who are willing to reflect and consider before they make decisions and take action. Drawing reasonable conclusions is the stated goal. Skillful thinkers know from past experience that in order to complete any task successfully, they will need thoughtful effort rather than routine application of prior knowledge.

Open-Mindedness and Empathy

Two related fundamental attitudes required for developing critical thinking skills are open-mindedness and empathy. An open-minded thinker is willing to be nonjudgmental, to search out solutions or alternatives, and to take alternative points of view seriously. Empathy is demonstrated by respect for others, that is, by sensitivity to their feelings, fairmindedness, readiness to listen, and willingness to consider their points of view. Also involved in these qualities is a willingness to admit error, wrong thinking, or shoddy reasoning.

THINKERS

Three Errors

There are three errers in these two sentences. You must detect all three of them to recieve credit as a Thinker.

Need a Hint?
Not all errors in sentences are spelling errors.

WHAT STANDARDS DO YOU SET FOR YOUR THINKING?

Critical thinking is shaped by standards. The degree to which we set and hold to standards for our thinking determines to a large degree the quality of our thinking. Everyone reasons, but not everyone reasons according to high standards. Thinkers who demand of themselves that their thinking be characterized by the following qualities are certain to be honored thinkers:

Clarity	Precision
Relevance	Accuracy
Logic	Consistency
Significance	Depth
Fairness	Thoroughness

Without these standards, thinking will be characterized by errors in reasoning leading to faulty solutions. This in turn will lead inevitably to frustration and disappointment.

STIR IT UP 2.1   Look again at the qualities of a critical thinker identified in this chapter. There seem to be a lot of them. Are they all really necessary? Can you have some of them—but not all—and still be a critical thinker? Probably, but which ones? Begin with your own understanding of the *minimum* intellectual standards necessary for being a critical thinker. What are the minimum standards, the minimum qualities you must have if you are to call yourself a critical thinker? Are some of these qualities more important than others? Why or why not? What determines which of these qualities you choose as essential? What thinking is going on in your head when you make this determination? Describe it. Compare your minimum qualities with those of other students. What accounts for the differences in your lists?

STIR IT UP 2.2   Writing for a particular audience for a particular purpose is an effective way to produce clear, concise thinking. Choose one of the following objects: a paper clip, a tape dispenser, a calculator, a key, a stapler, a necktie, a computer diskette, or any other common object. Now choose one of the assignments from the list below, and without stating which assignment you chose or naming the object you are referring to, write a paragraph according to the directions for the assignment. Be ready to read your paragraph to the class and see how easily class members can identify your object.

1. Examine the object and describe it so that your reader can walk into a store and pick it out from all others similar to it.

2. Write a memo to your favorite professor convincing him or her that this object should be purchased for all the students in your class.

3. Explain to someone who has never seen this object how to use it efficiently.

4. You are an archaeologist two hundred years from now. Write in your journal about this object you have just unearthed.

5. Suppose you came to school and discovered *you were the object*. How would you spend your day?

6. Tell a story about the object to a kindergarten class.

STIR IT UP 2.3   Are you already a critical thinker? Rate yourself below. The checklist doesn't show what you want to be, but what kind of thinker you are now, so be honest. It can give you an idea of the areas you need to strengthen.

I'm a Critical Thinker!

How do I know? Because my thinking and behavior are characterized by the following qualities. How many of these descriptions may honestly be applied to you? Check them off.

☐ I'm willing to consider another's point of view.
☐ I put myself in the place of others.
☐ I recognize the limits of my knowledge.
☐ I don't claim to know more than others know.
☐ I suspend judgment when information is inadequate.
☐ I rethink conclusions in light of new evidence.
☐ I'm willing to deal with unpopular ideas, beliefs, and viewpoints.
☐ I challenge sacred cows.
☐ I'm true to my own thoughts.
☐ I hold myself to the same intellectual standard to which I hold others.
☐ I pursue intellectual truths and insights in spite of difficulties and frustrations.
☐ I think logically (at least I attempt to).
☐ I have a strong desire to understand deeply, to figure things out.
☐ I raise reasonable questions to probe for more information.
☐ I offer evidence that is relevant, valid, complete, and reliable.

THINKERS

Which Ending Is More Frequent?

Are there more words that end in *-ing,* or are there more words in which the letter *n* is the next-to-the-last letter in the word? What is your proof?

Need a Hint?
What is the next-to-the-last letter in *-ing?*

Journal Observations (see page 13)

BECOMING A CRITICAL THINKER

1st Writing _____

_____

_____

_____

_____

_____

_____

_____

_____

_____

2nd Writing _____

_____

_____

3rd Writing

Student Markets Primer on the Art of Cheating

Anthony Flint
Boston Globe, February 3, 1992

One of the hottest books on college campuses isn't the latest collection of Calvin and Hobbes—it's a book about cheating.

"Cheating 101" is a how-to guide on shortcuts to a degree—effective places to hide crib sheets, systems of foot signals for sharing multiple-choice answers, places to buy term papers and dozens of other tips.

Michael Moore, 24, a Rutgers University senior and author of the book, has sold 5,000 copies, mostly at Rutgers, Ohio State and the University of Maryland. He recently returned from a marketing road trip to Penn State. And he plans to go to Boston, home to 11 colleges and universities, to hawk the $7 book around spring break.

"We're going to hit Boston right after we hit Daytona Beach in March."

Moore, a journalism major, contracts with a printer to produce the 86-page book and sells it mostly out of his home in Hopewell, N.J. But because of the book's popularity, he takes sales operations on the road from time to time. Sometimes aided by a pre-visit article in a student newspaper, he sets up a table in a fraternity house or a room on campus and watches the money roll in.

"Students love it," said Moore, who described his weekend selling session at Penn State University and St. Francis College as "a mob scene." The trip was good for 1,150 copies.

Moore said that in addition to students snapping up the guide, several college administrators, lawyers and clinical psychologists have ordered it too—presumably as a form of counterintelligence.

Moore makes no excuses about the profits he reaps from the book, and acknowledges that he set out to make money. But he also considers "Cheating 101" to be a commentary on the shortcomings of higher education: ill-prepared professors more concerned with research, dreary required courses and the lack of training for real-world applications.

"I thought it would be a good opportunity to point out what I believe are the permanent problems in education," said Moore, who said his experience in college has been sour. "It's an indictment of the system. Maybe somebody will make some changes, to curb cheating and make college a better place."

Cheating, Moore said, is a response to the shortcomings that students see. It flourishes because often professors are not interested or look the other way, he said.

"Students just don't cheat because they're lazy or hung over," he said. "They see a professor who's not interested in what they're doing, so students aren't going to be interested in learning. That's a natural defense mechanism."

Rutgers officials, while praising Moore's entrepreneurial skills, have sharply criticized "Cheating 101" as a blatant violation of academic ethics. Some have drawn parallels to Michael Milken and Ivan Boesky, describing the book as the scholar's quick-and-dishonest route to success.

The penalties for cheating vary from school to school, but frequently include suspension or expulsion. Most colleges spell out the rules against cheating or plagiarizing in student codes provided to all freshmen.

Some educators are using the book as an opportunity to teach about ethics. Carol Oppenheim, a communications professor at Boston's Emerson College, recently led a discussion with students on whether a student newspaper should run an advertisement for the book.

"It's an interesting teaching opportunity about a real ethical dilemma," Oppenheim said.

Moore said the wrath of college administrators is to be expected. "It's a manual about their mistakes, their shortcomings and failures. It's like a bad audit."

But he denies that he is engaging in anything dishonest or unethical.

"I don't think people that are buying the book have never cheated before. They already know a lot of the methods. I'm not making a cheater out of anybody," he said.

"There's 'Final Exit,' a book on how to get out of drunk driving, a book on how to get out of speeding tickets," Moore said. "I'm making an honest living. I'm not dealing drugs. I'm just exercising my First Amendment rights."

Examine Your Thinking About What You Just Read

Pay close attention to your thinking processes as you answer the following questions.

1. In your observations of friends, acquaintances, and fellow students, what conditions are you aware of that make it possible for students to cheat? How are these conditions created? Are these conditions inevitable, that is, are there no ways to eliminate or alter them?

2. What specific cheating techniques have you personally seen being employed by students? Did any of the cheaters get caught?

3. Is it your observation that these students *want* to cheat, or are they *forced* to cheat because of conditions? If conditions force students to cheat, is there any obvious way to change the conditions? If so, what is it?

4. What other ethically questionable "shortcuts" have you personally heard other students say they used or planned to use in an attempt to get a higher score or a better grade? Was there any hesitation on the part of these students to talk about their use of the shortcuts? What do you conclude from this hesitation or lack of hesitation?

5. In your experience, how closely do teachers and professors monitor situations in which students may try to cheat? Does it appear to you that instructors "look the other way" in potential cheating situations? Why would that be even a possibility?

6. What "shortcuts" have you seen advertised on your campus? Where is this advertising done? Is there an ethical dilemma involved in advertising these shortcuts on campus?

The Costs of Going 55

Charles Lave
Newsweek, October 23, 1978

There is evidence that people who commute value their travel time at about 42 percent of their hourly wage. If commuters are allowed to travel at 65 mph rather than 55 mph, the value of the commuting time saved is about $6 billion. Traveling 55 mph rather than 65 mph, however, saves about 4,500 lives each year. Therefore, the 55 mph limit saves a single life at the cost of about $1.3 million. Calculated in a different way, saving a life by lowering the speed limit from 65 mph to 55 mph costs 102 person-years of extra travel time.

Vehicles use fuel slightly more efficiently when they travel 55 mph rather than 65 mph. For example, evidence suggests that for automobiles traveling 55 mph rather than 65 mph uses between 1 and 2 percent less gasoline. This saving is trivial—an identical saving in fuel could be achieved through proper tire maintenance alone.

Thus, the primary benefit of the 55 mph limit is the savings in lives, but at an opportunity cost of $1.3 million per life. Life is important. There are a large number of substantially less expensive ways of saving an equivalent number of lives, however. Putting a smoke detector in every home would cost about $5,000 per life saved. Additional kidney dialysis machines would cost about $30,000 per life saved. Mobile cardiac care units would cost about $2,000 per life saved. Changing the design of roads would cost between $20,000 and $100,000 per life saved, depending upon the type of change made. Clearly, a 55 mph law is a very costly way of saving lives.

If this approach strikes you as too insensitive to the value of human life, driving at 45 mph or less would save even more lives. Indeed, a 5 mph limit would result in virtually no deaths from automobile accidents. The costs of imposing such a limit would be enormous.

Read and Respond

1. In five or six words, what is this article about?

2. Is there any proof for the assertions made in this article concerning the saving of lives? For example, who says putting in smoke detectors would cost about $5,000 per life saved? How do you know that is true? Are you willing to believe that assertion—and the others? Why or why not? What personal knowledge can you bring to bear on this article that would lead you to believe or disbelieve what the author says?

3. What are some possible implications and consequences of believing the information presented in this article?

For Some U.S. Immigrants, Paradise Becomes a Trap

Fakhrudd Ahmed
Herald Tribune (International), January 9, 1987

Even in an age of unprecedented immigration, leaving one's homeland behind is a painful process. The place where a person first tastes the beauty and evil of this world is very special. The values absorbed there endure throughout life. The morality that nourishes him becomes the yardstick against which he makes moral judgments. There is no other place where the person is truly "at home."

Yet people do leave their homes for the politics or the economics of it, mostly the latter. The United States is the country where most people want to make their new home. It is the most prosperous and powerful nation. Unlike many West European countries, where an immigrant feels cornered by the homogeneous indigenous population, America, with its diverse ethnic mix, is still considered an immigrant's paradise.

Things are not the same for every arrival. While the experience of European immigrants who share a Judeo-Christian culture with Americans is less traumatic, someone coming from a Third World country such as Bangladesh can be overwhelmed. He is dazzled by the affluence, yet shocked by the permissiveness. He speaks differently, thinks differently and, of course, eats different food. The first person he wants to look up is someone from his homeland with whom he can talk in his native tongue and have a native meal.

If he came for a college degree, he may promise to himself and his family to return home the day after graduation. However, as he settles down and becomes comfortable in his studies and the American way, the seduction begins. He will stay "just a few years" after graduation to earn some money. He will start dating American girls, though more often he goes home to get a spouse.

He will struggle to get a job and the immigration "green card," which would give his stay some measure of permanence. His U.S.–born children will be U.S. citizens—a status for which he will have to wait for five years after the green card. With the proliferation of Indian grocery stores and cultural centers in the United States, his life as an expatriate will be nicely spiced in these ways.

The dream of returning home will begin to fade. He will not get the "appropriate" job and will be incensed to find that people back home do not much value his American experience.

Eventually the children will decide the issue. They will not like to hear about returning to an impoverished country. To the consternation of the parents, the children, who will not have experienced a second country, will start growing up like American kids. At school they may be subjected to blatant and subtle forms of racism. This they will try to counter by aiming to be superachievers.

Parents will tell the kids they should not forget their heritage, stressing, for example, that they should speak Bengali at home and that if they are born to a Moslem family they should pray five times a day and refrain from eating pork or sipping alcoholic drinks. To that the children, who will probably understand Bengali but not speak it, may respond: "Spanish would be more relevant to us!"

The coup de grace will usually be delivered by the adolescent daughter wanting to go out on a date. Parents will explain in great detail why it is not allowed in their culture and will insist that she meet, under strict supervision, only with Bangladeshi boys. Sometimes the girl will relent, on condition that it is a Bangladeshi boy born and brought up in the United States. More often, after her eighteenth birthday, the daughter will politely but firmly inform her parents that according to U.S. law they cannot interfere in her personal life—and that, to avoid further conflict over the boyfriend, she is going to move in with him.

The parents will be devastated. Doubts and questions flood in. The decision to stay begins to haunt them. While the second generation begins to adjust completely in its single homeland, the aging parents become more despondent and think desperately of returning home. Passing old age among grandchildren in the native land is a much better proposition than being among strangers in an American old people's home, they will tell each other.

For the first time, they will begin to doubt the friendship of neighbors. "Do they really like us, or do they simply tolerate us because we are the so-called model minority?" they will ask. Taking a renewed sentimental pride in the glorious Indian civilization of the past, they will assure each other that in terms of science, culture and human stock, their heritage is as refined as anyone's.

Nevertheless, the stubborn questions return in an avalanche and gnaw at the heart: Do we amount to much in this society? One can be comfortable in two cultures, but can he belong to both? Are we anything more than some superior minds from an "inferior" country? Have we been trapped by paradise?

Read and Respond

1. Just what is the "trap" described in this article? Who is trapped, parents or children or both? From your perspective, is it a trap or is it an opportunity? What makes the difference?

2. In this article, values play a big role in turning paradise into a trap. Explain this.

3. Are the issues described in this article important to you personally? Why or why not?

ASKING CRITICAL QUESTIONS

After you read the articles that follow, what critical questions come to mind? Everything you read will stir up your thinking if you read and question critically. What questions would you like to have answered in order for you to put the articles in proper context and to completely understand what is being said or reported? *On the lines following each article, write three questions that, if answered, will help you understand what is really being said.*

Effects of Technology on Teaching and Learning

Wilbert J. McKeachie

Under the influence of computer technologies, teaching and learning will change in dramatic ways. These effects have been anticipated by Collins (1991) in terms of eight "shifts" that he believes computers will bring to pre-college education. In essence, these shifts put greater emphasis "on the activity of the student than on that of the teacher" (p. 29). I believe that we should begin to anticipate how the shifts he describes are likely to challenge colleges and universities.

1. A shift from lecture and recitation to coaching. When subject matter is available via interactive technologies, there is less burden on the teacher to present information and more opportunity to diagnose learning problems and help learners find solutions. Research shows that when students work with computers, teachers reduce the time they spend directing students; they spend more of their time facilitating student learning.

2. A shift from whole-class instruction to small group instruction. When students work with computers, they progress at different rates. Therefore, it makes less sense to teach the class as a whole, expecting students to move in lockstep. Teachers interact more with individual students and small groups, becoming better informed about individual students' understandings and misunderstandings.

3. A shift from working with better students to working with weaker students. The need to choose a single level of difficulty for class instruction disappears when the teacher can work with individuals and small groups. The teacher is then able to aim instruction at one specific target group and to devote time to those who most need help.

4. A shift from all students learning the same things to different students learning different things. It has always been naive to expect that all students will learn the same things, that is, that they will learn what the teacher intends to teach them. Students learn what they need and want to learn, and, while there are some common attainments, there is also much individuality. When resources for learning are available through electronic technologies, it becomes possible to recognize, accept, and even reward the attainments of individuals.

5. A shift toward more engaged students. In most college classrooms the great majority of students are passive most of the time. Classes

proceed whether or not everyone is engaged and whether or not everyone understands. With interactive technology, attention is ensured. Instruction comes to a halt when there are no responses from learners. Well-designed computer-mediated instruction is more likely to engage individuals than are the words of a professor in front of a room filled with students.

6. A shift from assessment based on test performance to assessment based on products and progress. Rather than repeating or paraphrasing information from lectures and textbooks, students devote their energies to more creative projects. The best projects include realistic tasks that generalize what is being learned and show how it applies to new areas.

7. A shift from a competitive to a cooperative goal structure. Collaboration is encouraged when students have access to extensive data bases and share their own developing work through networked communications. Under these circumstances, products are truly collaborative, and teachers must learn how to assess work in light of the collaborative nature of student projects.

8. A shift from the primacy of verbal thinking to the integration of visual and verbal thinking. Students have more extensive experience with video than with print, yet instruction is based primarily on print. Visual literacy is poorly understood and poorly utilized in the service of instruction. We need to consider what capacities for visual knowledge and skills educated citizens should possess, and determine how we can ensure progress toward developing those capacities.

These shifts suggested by Collins also imply a shift in the teacher's role—liberation from the role of content provider to a more flexible, helping role.

My Critical Questions

1. _____

   _____ **?**

2. _____

   _____ **?**

3. _____

   _____ **?**

Why Americans Fight in Viet-Nam

Lyndon B. Johnson

Why must this nation hazard its ease, its interest, and its power for the sake of a people so far away?

We fight because we must fight if we are to live in a world where every country can shape its own destiny, and only in such a world will our own freedom be finally secure.

This kind of world will never be built by bombs or bullets. Yet the infirmities of man are such that force must often precede reason and the waste of war, the works of peace.

We wish that this were not so. But we must deal with the world as it is, if it is ever to be as we wish.

The world as it is in Asia is not a serene or peaceful place.

The first reality is that North Viet-Nam has attacked the independent nation of South Viet-Nam. Its object is total conquest.

Of course, some of the people of South Viet-Nam are participating in the attack on their own government. But trained men and supplies, orders and arms, flow in a constant stream from North to South.

This support is the heartbeat of the war.

And it is a war of unparalleled brutality. Simple farmers are the targets of assassination and kidnaping. Women and children are strangled in the night because their men are loyal to their government. And helpless villages are ravaged by sneak attacks. Large-scale raids are conducted on towns, and terror strikes in the heart of cities.

The confused nature of this conflict cannot mask the fact that it is the new face of an old enemy.

Over this war—and all Asia—is another reality: the deepening shadow of Communist China. The rulers in Hanoi are urged on by Peking. This is a regime which has destroyed freedom in Tibet, which has attacked India and has been condemned by the United Nations for aggression in Korea. It is a nation which is helping the forces of violence in almost every continent. The contest in Viet-Nam is part of a wider pattern of aggressive purposes.

Why are these realities our concern? Why are we in South Viet-Nam?

We are there because we have a promise to keep. Since 1954 every American President has offered support to the people of South Viet-Nam. We have helped to build, and we have helped to defend. Thus, over many years, we have made a national pledge to help South Viet-Nam defend its independence.

And I intend to keep that promise.

To dishonor that pledge, to abandon this small and brave nation to its enemies, and to the terror that must follow, would be an unforgivable wrong.

We are also there to strengthen world order. Around the globe from Berlin to Thailand are people whose well-being rests in part on the belief that they can count on us if they are attacked. To leave Viet-Nam to its fate would shake the confidence of all these people in the value of an American commitment and in the value of America's word. The result would be increased unrest and instability, and even wider war.

We are also there because there are great stakes in the balance. Let no one think for a moment that retreat from Viet-Nam would bring an end to conflict. The battle would be renewed in one country and then another. The central lesson of our time is that the appetite of aggression is never satisfied. To withdraw from one battlefield means only to prepare for the next. We must say in Southeast Asia—as we did in Europe—in the words of the Bible: "Hitherto shalt thou come, but no further."

There are those who say that all our effort there will be futile—that China's power is such that it is bound to dominate all Southeast Asia. But there is no end to that argument until all of the nations of Asia are swallowed up.

There are those who wonder why we have a responsibility there. Well, we have it there for the same reason that we have a responsibility for the defense of Europe. World War II was fought in both Europe and Asia and when it ended we found ourselves with continued responsibility for the defense of freedom.

Our objective is the independence of South Viet-Nam and its freedom from attack. We want nothing for ourselves—only that the people of South Viet-Nam be allowed to guide their own country in their own way.

We will do everything necessary to reach that objective and we will do only what is absolutely necessary.

In recent months attacks on South Viet-Nam were stepped up. Thus, it became necessary for us to increase our response and to make attacks by air. This is not a change of purpose. It is a change in what we believe that purpose requires.

We do this in order to slow down aggression.

We do this to increase the confidence of the brave people of South Viet-Nam who have bravely borne this brutal battle for so many years with so many casualties.

And we do this to convince the leaders of North Viet-Nam—and all who seek to share their conquest—of a simple fact:

We will not be defeated.

We will not grow tired.

We will not withdraw, either openly or under the cloak of a meaningless agreement.

We know that air attacks alone will not accomplish all of these purposes. But it is our best and prayerful judgment that they are a necessary part of the surest road to peace.

We hope that peace will come swiftly. But that is in the hands of others besides ourselves. And we must be prepared for a long continued conflict. It will require patience as well as bravery—the will to endure as well as the will to resist.

I wish it were possible to convince others with words of what we now find it necessary to say with guns and planes: armed hostility is futile— our resources are equal to any challenge—because we fight for values and we fight for principle, rather than territory or colonies, our patience and our determination are unending.

Once this is clear, then it should also be clear that the only path for reasonable men is the path of peaceful settlement. . . .

These countries of Southeast Asia are homes for millions of impoverished people. Each day these people rise at dawn and struggle through until the night to wrestle existence from the soil. They are often wracked by diseases, plagued by hunger, and death comes at the early age of forty.

Stability and peace do not come easily in such a land. Neither independence nor human dignity will ever be won by arms alone. It also requires the works of peace. The American people have helped generously in times past in these works, and now there must be a much more massive effort to improve the life of man in that conflict-torn corner of our world.

The first step is for the countries of Southeast Asia to associate themselves in a greatly expanded co-operative effort for development. We would hope that North Viet-Nam would take its place in the common effort just as soon as peaceful co-operation is possible.

The United Nations is already actively engaged in development in this area, and as far back as 1961 I conferred with our authorities in Viet-Nam in connection with their work there. And I would hope tonight that the Secretary General of the United Nations could use the prestige of his great office and his deep knowledge of Asia to initiate, as soon as possible, with the countries of that area, a plan for co-operation in increased development.

For our part I will ask the Congress to join in a billion-dollar American investment in this effort as soon as it is underway.

And I would hope that all other industrialized countries, including the Soviet Union, will join in this effort to replace despair with hope and terror with progress.

The task is nothing less than to enrich the hopes and existence of more than a hundred million people. And there is much to be done.

The vast Mekong River can provide food and water and power on a scale to dwarf even our own T.V.A.

The wonders of modern medicine can be spread through villages where thousands die every year from lack of care.

Schools can be established to train people in the skills needed to manage the process of development.

And these objectives, and more, are within the reach of a cooperative and determined effort.

I also intend to expand and speed up a program to make available our farm surpluses to assist in feeding and clothing the needy in Asia. We should not allow people to go hungry and wear rags while our own warehouses overflow with an abundance of wheat and corn and rice and cotton.

So I will very shortly name a special team of outstanding, patriotic, and distinguished Americans to inaugurate our participation in these programs. This team will be headed by Mr. Eugene Black, the very able former president of the World Bank.

This will be a disorderly planet for a long time. In Asia, and elsewhere, the forces of the modern world are shaking old ways and uprooting ancient civilizations. There will be turbulence and struggle and even violence. Great social change—as we see in our own country—does not always come without conflict.

We must also expect that nations will on occasion be in dispute with us. It may be because we are rich, or powerful, or because we have made some mistakes, or because they honestly fear our intentions. However, no nation need ever fear that we desire their land, or to impose our will, or to dictate their institutions.

But we will always oppose the effort of one nation to conquer another nation.

We will do this because our own security is at stake.

But there is more to it than that. For our generation has a dream. It is a very old dream. But we have the power, and now we have the opportunity to make that dream come true.

For centuries nations have struggled among each other. But we dream of a world where disputes are settled by law and reason. And we will try to make it so.

For most of history men have hated and killed one another in battle. But we dream of an end to war. And we will try to make it so.

For all existence most men have lived in poverty, threatened by hunger. But we dream of a world where all are fed and charged with hope. And we will help to make it so.

My Critical Questions

1. _____

_____ **?**

2. _____

_____ **?**

3. _____

_____ **?**

SOLUTIONS to Items in This Chapter

Thinkers (p. 31)

1. errers
2. recieve
3. The third error is the assertion that there is a third error. There isn't.

Thinkers (p. 34)

Words in which the letter *n* is the next-to-the-last letter. Proof? All -*ing* words include *n* as the next-to-the-last letter. In addition, there are other, non -*ing* words in which *n* is the next-to-the-last letter.

Part Two

THINKING THAT DEVELOPS THINKING

"He who has imagination without learning has wings and no feet. Education does not consist merely in adorning the memory and enlightening the understanding. Its main business should be to direct the will."
—Joseph Joubert

Chapter 3

GATHERING SKILLS

- **Observing**
- **Questioning**

Gathering all the information

> *"The mind can store an estimated 100 trillion bits of information—compared with which a computer's mere billions are virtually amnesiac."*
> —Sharon Begley et al., *Newsweek*

STIR UP YOUR THINKING BEFORE YOU START READING

Before you start reading this chapter, take an informal survey of what you believe concerning observation and questioning. As you go through the chapter, compare these beliefs with what you learn. Jot down your responses to this question:

Can you improve your skills of observation and questioning? If so, how would you go about it, and how will you know when they are improved?

Responses:

1. _____

_____

_____

2. _____

_____

_____

3. _____

_____

_____

Observing

ESSENTIAL THINKING SKILLS		
CHAPTER	**WHAT THEY'RE CALLED**	**WHAT THEY MEAN**
Chapter 3	**The Gathering Skills**	**Gathering all the information.**
	Observing	Actively seeking information through one or more senses.
	Questioning	Seeking information by asking questions.
Chapter 4	**The Organizing Skills**	**Organizing for the purpose of making sense.**
	Comparing and Contrasting	Noting similarities and differences between two or more things, events, or ideas.
	Classifying and Sequencing	Arranging things or concepts into categories and into sequential order.
	Identifying Cause and Effect	Recognizing the relationship between an effect and its cause.
Chapter 5	**The Generating Skills**	**Generating additional information.**
	Inferring	Making an assumption, stating a hypothesis, or coming to a conclusion based on limited information.
	Summarizing	Condensing the essence of the information accurately and efficiently.
	Synthesizing	Creating new information by combining two or more pieces of information.
	Generating Ideas	Creating new information, alternatives, or applications.
Chapter 6	**The Recognizing Skills**	**Recognizing what has been left unsaid.**
	Recognizing Purpose	Identifying a writer's or speaker's intention.
	Recognizing Fact and Opinion	Distinguishing between a statement of fact and a statement of opinion.
	Recognizing Tone	Identifying a sentiment or mood by assessing the writer's or speaker's choice of words.
	Recognizing Bias	Noting the presence and nature of a writer's or speaker's prejudice.
	Recognizing Organization	Identifying the organizational pattern of a thought, statement, passage, or plan.
	Recognizing Underlying Assumptions	Recognizing the suppositions that are taken for granted and are the foundation of a proposition, notion, or idea.
Chapter 7	**The Analyzing Skills**	**Analyzing for the purpose of coming to a conclusion.**
	Analyzing	Identifying and separating ideas, attributes, situations, and/or components in order to form a conclusion as to their relationship.
	Evaluating	Appraising something according to certain criteria and forming a judgment as to its worth or quality.
	Inducing	Analyzing individual facts or premises in order to derive a general conclusion.
	Deducing	Applying general principles or a broad framework to a situation in order to come to a conclusion about it.

> **"**We cannot create observers by saying 'observe,' but by giving them the power and the means for this observation, and these means are procured through education of the senses.**"**
> —Maria Montessori

> **"**One of life's most fulfilling moments occurs in that split second when the familiar is suddenly transformed into the dazzling aura of the profoundly new. . . . [W]hat seems mundane and trivial is the very stuff discovery is made of. The only difference is our perspective, our readiness to put the pieces together in an entirely new way and to see patterns where only shadows appeared just a moment before.**"**
> —Edward Lindaman

What questions am I going to have answered in this discussion of observing?

1. Why is skillful observing the foundation for good thinking?

2. Are most of us skillful observers?

3. How much do passive observers see and hear? How much do active observers see and hear?

4. How do we improve our observation skills?

THINK ABOUT THIS!

What If Time Ran Backwards?

If time ran backwards, would our usual sense of good and bad be inverted? For example, firefighters would probably be bad guys because they would approach a building, pull water from it into their hoses, watch it burst into flames, and then drive away as fast as they could. An arsonist, on the other hand, would be a good guy because when the firefighters have left, he would approach the fire, watch it get smaller until it soaked into pools of gasoline, which he would put into containers. The arsonist would contain the fire in the head of a match and take the gasoline to a gas station, which would send it back to the refinery.

What would an automobile accident be like, or college, or even dinner preparations, if time ran backwards? Pick something to describe in a world where time runs backwards. Jot down your ideas below.

_____

_____

_____

> **OBSERVING:**
> **Actively seeking information through one or more senses**

Good thinkers are good observers—they have to be. Becoming conscious, purposeful, productive thinkers doesn't just happen to us when we begin college or at some later point in life. We all wish it did, but it doesn't. We have to work at it, and we must begin by developing the thinking skill of observing.

HOW WELL DO WE OBSERVE?

We see things every day, but we can't say that we really notice them. To demonstrate this to yourself, take the Ultimate Observing Skills Test that follows and see just how observant you have been up to now.

STIR IT UP 3.1 **The Ultimate Observing Skills Test**

If you have well-developed observing skills, or if you are a connoisseur of trivia games, you will do well on this test. If you are like most people, you'll be surprised by the results and by just how little you pay attention to common things.

1. The names of what twenty-six things are "hidden" on the back of a five-dollar bill?

   _____

2. On a standard traffic light, is the green at the top or the bottom?

   _____

3. How many sides are there on a standard pencil?

   _____

4. Name the five colors on a Campbell's soup label, excluding the colors in the photo.

   _____

5. On a standard typewriter/computer keyboard, over which number is the symbol %?

   _____

6. Which two letters of the alphabet do not appear on a telephone dial?

_____

7. In which direction does the lettering run on a standard pencil (eraser to tip or tip to eraser)?

_____

8. What is the lowest number on an FM radio dial?

_____

9. What's in the center on the back of a one-dollar bill?

_____

10. Which two numbers on a telephone dial are not accompanied by letters?

_____

11. Sleepy, Sneezy, Doc, Happy, Grumpy, and Dopey. Name the seventh dwarf.

_____

12. How many hot dogs are there in a standard package?

_____

Compare your answers with the correct answers at the end of this chapter. How did you do? Only one wrong? Either your observing skills are quite good or you've been playing a lot of trivia games. Two or more wrong? You'll benefit from this chapter.

And now, off to Paris.

It is a

a well-known fact

that people love

Paris in the

the springtime.

Did you notice anything wrong with this sentence about Paris? What? There is an extra *a* and an extra *the* in the sentence. Did you spot both errors the first time? Just one?

Becoming a powerful thinker requires that we go through a process of learning first how to observe, how to stay aware even when things seem familiar (as in the Paris-in-springtime statement), and then how to gather and organize new information in light of what we already know. If the new information is gathered improperly, if it is faulty, unclear, inaccurate, or sketchy because our observation was casual, incomplete, or undisciplined, then any thinking we do based on the information will have the same sloppy characteristics.

And just one more thing. Simply reading here that you need to be more observant won't make you observant. You have to work at it. Here's an example of what I mean. The Paris-in-springtime sentence above made you see that you weren't really using your observing skills efficiently. But now you are aware of the problem, so it is unlikely that you could be so unobservant a second time, right? Let's see. Read the following sentence aloud:

> **FINISHED FILES ARE THE RE-**
> **SULT OF YEARS OF SCIENTIF-**
> **IC STUDY COMBINED WITH**
> **THE EXPERIENCE OF YEARS.**

Now count aloud the letter F's in the sentence. But count them *only once*. Do *not* go back and count them again. How many F's are there in the sentence? Record your answer here: _____

Most people say there are three F's. Is that how many you counted?

Surprisingly, there are six F's. Even when told that there are six F's, many people have a difficult time finding all six. Where are the other three F's? The F in the little word *of* is usually missed the three times the word appears in the sentence. We take the preposition *of* for granted and don't really see it. After all, it is merely a common connector between words and phrases and doesn't convey much of an image all by itself. Consequently, we don't pay any attention to it. It is only through working at being observant that we will develop our observing skills.

OBSERVING IS AN *ACTIVE* PROCESS

We need to understand that observing, the very important active thinking ability that we use to gather information, is different from mere passive seeing and hearing. It involves employing all of our senses in an ***active effort to note, discern, be aware of, acquire, and retain critical information.*** When we observe well, we lay a foundation for seeing and interpreting details that frequently contain the key to solving problems or generating ideas. Observing is a means of coming to know *clearly,* of learning by carefully studying and actively remembering. When we work at developing our observation skills, we benefit by becoming more aware of what we see and hear and better able to infer, to recognize emerging insights, and to differentiate between what is true and false and between what is fact and what is speculation.

? ANY QUESTIONS

What's really pretty dumb about the statement "No two snowflakes are exactly alike"?

_____

_____

_____

_____

_____

THINKERS

How can you physically stand behind another person while he/she is standing behind you?

Need a Hint?
I think you should turn your back on this one.

THE HINDRANCE WITHIN US

So what's so hard about observing efficiently, and why make such a big deal out of something when we all agree we ought to improve our observation skills? The problem is one of knowing but not doing. The hindrance to well-developed observation skills is rooted in our laziness. All our lives we have taken a relatively casual attitude toward observing, largely because careful observing was not required of us. We have a habit of observing in a sloppy, casual way. We see what we see. But that is no longer good enough. Real-world thinking, learning in college, and reasoning to solve problems demand increasingly developed observation skills. There is so much that we have missed because we haven't wanted to take the time or make the effort to *really* observe. Now, however, we must break that habit and establish a new habit of careful, focused observing.

HOW DO WE DO IT?

Because developing observation skills is a matter of establishing patterns of observing, the exercises in this chapter require that you observe. In doing the exercises, you will find your observation skills improving not just in your ability to do the exercises but in all areas of your daily routine. The need for well-developed observation skills becomes especially apparent when we are asked to give thorough and accurate answers to typical classroom questions such as these:

- What words or phrases make this story sad? Exciting? What words influence the way we feel about the characters?

- What nonverbal behavior or mannerisms did the speaker exhibit, and what did they communicate about what was being said?

- What evidence can you give in support of that observation?

STIR IT UP 3.2   Observing with all your senses is more difficult than you may think. Answer the following questions:

1. What was the name of the last person you talked to? _____

2. What was the person wearing (style, colors, type of shoes, etc.)?

   _____

   _____

3. What color were the person's eyes? _____

4. Was the person wearing glasses? _____ Describe them.

   _____

5. What was the last book you used (not read, used), not counting this one? Describe the cover. Did it have an index? What subject matter was covered in the index? _____

_____

6. What was the subject of the last magazine article you read, and who was the author? _____

_____

7. What were the main points? _____

_____

8. What was the subject of the last lecture you heard? _____

9. What were the main points? _____

_____

10. What kind of a skill is observing? (Hint: What's the title of this chapter?) _____

_____

How did you do? Were you able to recall the information that these questions called for? Perhaps you are already a skillful observer—but perhaps not.

STIR IT UP 3.3 In a short essay, answer the following questions:

1. What possible difference will it make *to your critical thinking patterns* if you become more skillful in your observing?

2. What difference will it make *to you in your college career* if you are more skillful and active in your observing?

3. What possible side effects will there be *for your life* if you become a highly skilled observer?

STIR IT UP 3.4 Frequently, we are least observant about the things that are most familiar to us. Check this out. Compose a paragraph that is loaded with concrete details about something you own. Don't look at the thing, but try to visualize it and remember how it feels to handle it. Include the answers to the following questions in your finished paragraph.

1. What color is the thing?

2. What size is it?

3. How is it shaped?

4. How does it work?

5. What is its use (function)?

6. What does it smell (taste) like?

7. How does it feel to the touch?

8. Does it make any sound? What kind?

9. How did you get it?

10. How long have you had it?

11. Anything else?

THINKERS

If you were to take two apples from three apples, how many would you have?

Need a Hint?
Note that the question doesn't ask, "How many would be left?"

Journal Observations (see page 13)

OBSERVING

1st Writing _____

_____

_____

_____

_____

_____

2nd Writing _____

3rd Writing _____

Federal Judge Orders Lawyer Not to Use Her Maiden Name

Tara Bradley-Steck
Contra Costa Times, July 14, 1988

PITTSBURGH—A federal judge told an attorney he doesn't allow anyone to "use that Ms." in his courtroom, ordered her to use her husband's name or go to jail and found her colleague in contempt for protesting.

"Do what I tell you or you're going to sleep in the county jail tonight. You can't tell me how to run my courtroom," Senior U.S. District Judge Hubert I. Teitelbaum told attorney Barbara Wolvowitz.

The judge told Wolvowitz, whose husband is University of Pittsburgh law professor Jules Lobel, that she must go by the name Mrs. Lobel in his courtroom.

When her co-counsel, Jon Pushinsky, protested, Teitelbaum found him in contempt of court for "officious intermeddling" and gave him a suspended sentence of 30 days in jail.

During a disjointed dialogue Friday that covered about 20 pages of court transcript, Teitelbaum told Wolvowitz that Mrs. Lobel is her legal name "under the laws of the state of Pennsylvania.

"And that's what I want you to be, to call yourself from here on in this courtroom," he said. "That's an intolerable kind of thing."

The judge claimed a married woman must petition Common Pleas Court for permission to use her maiden name. The Pennsylvania Family Law Practice and Procedure Handbook said no legal proceedings are required if a woman chooses to use her maiden name.

Teitelbaum, presiding over a race discrimination suit against PPG Industries Inc., also asked each of the six female jurors on Friday if she used her husband's name or maiden name. All used their husbands' names.

Wolvowitz, 36, said she was "in shock for two days."

"I've practiced for 10 years. I've gotten into arguments with judges but never over something like this. I can't quite understand what happened," said Wolvowitz, who had never previously argued a case before Teitelbaum. "After it was over and the jury left, I had tears in my eyes."

When the trial resumed Monday, Teitelbaum denied Wolvowitz's request for a mistrial, and the attorney again refused to be called Mrs. Lobel.

"What if I call you sweetie?" said Teitelbaum, 73, a former U.S. attorney appointed to the federal bench by President Nixon in 1970.

The judge declared he would refer to Wolvowitz only as "counselor."

Examine Your Thinking About What You Just Read

Pay attention to your thinking processes as you answer the following questions:

1. What was the real issue in this bizarre courtroom incident? Was it really a question of law?

2. Think about bias for just a minute or two. Which of the individuals in this incident showed considerable bias? Toward or against what? Was there more than one bias at work throughout the incident?

3. What was the judge really trying to find out from the six female jurors when he asked if they used their husbands' names or their maiden names?

4. Was there right or wrong in this incident? How could that be determined?

5. What have you concluded about the people involved in this incident: Judge Teitelbaum, Ms. Wolvowitz, and attorney Pushinsky? Think about your answer to this. What are your answers based on? After all, there are only 384 words in this article. Why are those few words sufficient for you to form opinions about the people involved, and probably strong opinions at that? How is that possible?

Write about this   In a short essay, relate what happened in this article to what happens outside of a courtroom. Could using the title *Ms.* cause a similar confrontational situation today in a business or school? Under what conditions? Give some examples that support your opinion.

Would Your Textbook Authors Be Better Off If the Used Book Market Were Banned?

James R. Kearl

There are almost always "used" markets for *durable* goods. It is sometimes argued that these markets hurt the original producers because, obviously, the original producer doesn't receive any of the money that changes hands in the used markets. If, for example, you purchase a new car or a new textbook, the automobile manufacturer or the textbook publisher gets a share of the purchase price. However, if you purchase a used car or a used textbook, the person selling the automobile or textbook to you keeps the full price the two of you agree upon. It appears, then, that automobile producers and textbook publishers (and, therefore, textbook authors) would be better off if resale were prohibited because they would then sell more cars or books. How can you evaluate this argument?

Begin by noting that because automobiles and textbooks are durable goods, they last for more than one year. Then to evaluate the argument, assume that a textbook lasts two years and resale is allowed. If you and the person that you sell it to each get, say, twenty dollars' worth of service from the textbook, the publisher could charge you more than $20 for it because you have the opportunity to sell it to someone else. How much more could the publisher charge? If the interest rate is 10 percent and you expect to be able to sell the textbook for $20 a year from now, the present value to you would be

$$PV = \$20 + \frac{\$20}{1 + 0.10} = \$38.18$$

Suppose that the author gets 10 percent of the retail price. If 2 one-year books were sold, the author would receive at most $2.00 each year. (You would be willing to pay no more than $20 for a book that only you could use.) Because $2.00 wouldn't be paid to the author until next year, however, the present value of this arrangement is

$$PV = \$2 + \frac{\$2}{1 + 0.10} = \$3.82$$

The author would receive $3.82 immediately from the sale of the two-year book, however. Thus, authors don't stand to gain from the increased sales that might come if resale markets were prohibited.

Read and Respond

1. What did you think of this short article? In your own words, summarize what was said, including the conclusion. What is the crucial point on which the whole argument rests?

2. The author's argument seems to be based on the idea that used books are similar to used cars. Do you see any differences between books and cars that might make this analogy faulty? What are they?

3. Is there a better analogy for used textbooks than used cars?

Reputation and Contracts in Russia and the U.S. Diamond Market

Louis Uchitelle
The *New York Times,* January 17, 1992

We take for granted that our legal system will provide broad guidelines for transactions and enforce deals made within those guidelines. As a consequence, we enter into short- and long-term contracts without much thought about enforcement. Contracts are not so simple in Russia, however, because there is little law to provide a backdrop for negotiation. As one U.S. businessman noted, "In New York, you don't have to say that much in a contract because the obligations are clear in laws and in precedent, but here you have to spell everything out." In the turmoil in Russia following the breakup of the Soviet Union, however, contracting is more risky because expectations are difficult to tie down and enforcement is an open issue. As a consequence, there are few incentives to make long-term agreements. The only secure deals are those in which all parties benefit from proceeding at any given moment. This arrangement, however, provides little incentive to enter into the longer-term exchanges that are important for the allocation of resources within the Russian economy. At one time or another in virtually every long-term contract, one party has an incentive to behave opportunistically and take advantage of efforts or commitments of the other party.

In some cases, exchanges that extend over time cannot be avoided, however. Instead of relying on formal contracts and enforcement through the legal system, many Russians must rely on informal contracts and reputation when making exchanges. As a Russian entrepreneur noted, "There is already a blacklist of people with whom we don't deal anymore." The blacklisted individuals have taken advantage of commitments made by others in informal contracts.

Using reputation to enforce contracts is not unique to Russia, of course. For a very long time, for example, using reputation and its incentives to adhere to agreed-upon deals has been the norm in the wholesale diamond market in the United States. Thus, much of the wholesale diamond trade in the United States occurs without any formal contracts. Agreements worth millions of dollars are made on the basis of a handshake. Although these trades obviously have much lower transaction costs than they would if they were based on carefully negotiated contracts, they also provide incentives for one or both parties to behave opportunistically and take advantage of the other party. How can this form of exchange persist in the face of these incentives?

The market for diamonds is dominated by a close-knit community of individuals, who frequently live near each other and are of the same religious and ethnic background. The traders know each other and know each other's reputations. In general, they will not trade with outsiders in the same way that they trade with those within the community and continued membership in the community depends on abiding by one's agreements. Hence, although a person may be tempted to take advantage of someone else on a particular transaction, if he did, he would be ostracized from the community, and thus would no longer be able to transact in this market at all. In other words, a person's future trading opportunities and income depend on being reliable in each current transaction. Thus, reputation alone policies the agreements and overcomes the natural inclination some might have to behave opportunistically.

Read and Respond

1. Business transactions are the same all over the world, right? Apparently not. According to this article, what problems arise for Americans and Russians doing business with one another? How are these problems related to differences in the two countries' legal systems, economies, and traditions? What might have led to the differences between the countries?

2. Explain this statement: "[T]here are few incentives to make long-term agreements." Why would Russian entrepreneurs and business executives be reluctant to make long-term agreements? What assumptions do Russian businesspeople make?

3. The U.S. wholesale diamond trade is described as being conducted similarly to the Russian way of doing business, without any formal contracts. Speculate as to how this practice developed in the United States. How easily could an outsider enter the U.S. diamond business? Explain your answer: what is your reasoning?

ASKING CRITICAL QUESTIONS

After you read the article that follows, what critical questions come to mind? Everything you read will stir up your thinking if you read and question critically. What questions would you like to have answered in order for you to put the articles in proper context and to completely understand what is being said or reported? *On the lines following each article, write three questions that, if answered, will help you understand what is really being said.*

The Woman Worker

U.S. Department of Labor, Women's Bureau

H alf a million women were estimated early this year [1942] to be serving their country in war industries. The number of these increases day by day. In some 30 plants making small-arms and artillery ammunition, where 40,000 women were employed in the last quarter of 1941, over 70,000 are expected to be at work by late summer. In some of these the women labor force will be doubled, in others trebled, and some will employ 10 times as many women as before. These are chiefly new jobs, not those vacated by men. Before 1941 almost no women were in aircraft.

Women in Jobs Vacated by Men

Many reports from all parts of the country show that men called to war service actually have been replaced by women in types of work formerly not done, or done only very rarely, by women, though of course there is no way to discover the full number of these. They include clerks, cashiers, and pharmacists in drug stores, theater ushers, hotel elevator operators, taxi drivers, bank tellers, electricians, acetylene welders, milling-machine operators, riveters, tool-keepers, gauge checkers, gear cutters, turret and engine lathe operators. Women are operating service stations. They are replacing men as finger-print classifiers. A southern city reports a woman manager of a parking lot.

One of the country's major airfields has women on maintenance work, engaging them chiefly in cleaning spark plugs and painting luminous dials. One woman hired as a secretary now directs landings and take-offs by radio. In another city a woman has entered for the first time an airfield office as a meteorologist. Both an eastern and a southern airport have definite plans to place women in their reservations departments, and in flight watch or in the traffic operations departments, and the Civil Aeronautics Administration is considering training women as radio operators.

Women telegraph messengers now number 325 in New York City alone, and in the country as a whole 3,000 women are expected to do such work this year. In New York, they must be at least 21 years of age. Girls also are performing other messenger services, formerly done by boys, in many plants and offices. A major chemical company is now training a few women as its chemists.

Labor Shortages Open Jobs to Women

There are many types of work long done by women but in which women now are being taken on in large numbers, because of plant expansion as well as declining supply of male labor. For example, as armature winders, inspectors, power-press and drill-press operators, assemblers. Shortages of workers are reported in many places in fields usual for women; for example, in hotel and restaurant work, as retail clerks, stenographers, and as sewing-machine operators in certain great clothing centers. Shortages of school teachers are growing, because of better-paid jobs in industry as well as the drafting of men, and the National Education Association reports that the enrollment in teachers' colleges and normal schools has declined by 11 per cent. Certain of the army camps already have employed considerable numbers of women in their offices and laundries, jobs formerly done by men but of a type frequently performed by women. A woman's job at present done by men in camps is canteen work, but serious consideration is being given to employing women in this.

My Critical Questions

1. _____

_____ **?**

2. _____

_____ **?**

3. _____

_____ **?**

Questioning

ESSENTIAL THINKING SKILLS		
CHAPTER	**WHAT THEY'RE CALLED**	**WHAT THEY MEAN**
Chapter 3	**The Gathering Skills**	**Gathering all the information.**
	Observing	Actively seeking information through one or more senses.
	Questioning	Seeking information by asking questions.
Chapter 4	**The Organizing Skills**	**Organizing for the purpose of making sense.**
	Comparing and Contrasting	Noting similarities and differences between two or more things, events or ideas.
	Classifying and Sequencing	Arranging things or concepts into categories and into sequential order.
	Identifying Cause and Effect	Identifying the relation between and effect and its cause.
Chapter 5	**The Generating Skills**	**Generating additional informaton.**
	Inferring	Making an assumption, stating an hypothesis, filling in gaps, or coming to a conclusion based on limited or partial information.
	Summarizing	Condensing the essence of the information accurately and efficiently
	Synthesizing	Creating new information by combining two or more pieces of information
	Generating Ideas	Creating additional information, alternatives, applications.
Chapter 6	**The Recognizing Skills**	**Recognizing what has been left unsaid.**
	Recognizing Purpose	Identifying a writer's or speaker's purpose.
	Recognizing Fact & Opinion	Distinguishing between a statement of fact and a statement of opinion.
	Recognizing Tone	Identifying a sentiment or mood by assessing the writer's or speaker's choice of words.
	Recognizing Bias	Evaluating an observation or passage and noting the presence and nature of the writer's or speakers' prejudgment.
	Recognizing Organization	Examining a thought, statement, passage, or plan for the purpose of identifying theorganizational pattern.
	Recognizing Underlying Assumptions	Recognizing the suppositions that are taken for granted and are foundation for a proposition, notion or idea.
Chapter 7	**The Analyzing Skills**	**Analyzing for the purpose of coming to a conclusion.**
	Analyzing	Identifying separate components in order to form a conclusion as to the relationship between those components.
	Evaluating	Appraising something according to certain criteria and forming a judgment as to its worth or quality.
	Inducing	Analyzing individual facts or premises in order to derive a general conclusion about something.
	Deducing	Applying general principles or board frameworks to a particular situation in order to come to a reasoned conclusion about the particular situation.

"Instead of parents asking their children, 'What did you learn in school today?' they should ask them, 'What good questions did you ask today?'"
—Anonymous

"There is a quiet revolution happening in education. Subtly, questions are becoming instruments to open engaged minds to unsuspected possibilities. Softly, teachers are encouraging student interactions which encourage students to depend on themselves as thinkers and learners."
—E. P. Torrance and K. Goff

What questions am I going to have answered in this section on questioning?

1. How important can asking good questions be to my college education?
2. What four different kinds of questions are important to my learning and thinking?
3. In what way can questioning interfere with my learning and thinking?

THINK ABOUT THIS!

Outlaw Humor?

What if humor were outlawed? Would telling a bad joke be a greater offense than telling a good joke? Would people lose their sense of humor over time? Would there be underground schools to teach what it means to be funny, and underground comedy clubs to demonstrate humor? Would laughter be considered a pathological condition? Would it be possible to eliminate humor from the world? What would that take? What would life be like if there were no humor possible? Jot down your thoughts below.

_____

_____

_____

_____

_____

_____

_____

**QUESTIONING:
Seeking information by asking questions**

For most of us, a good deal of what we learned in high school was factual knowledge, requiring little, if any, mental effort on our part. The high school curriculum tended to emphasize studying and remembering facts, and learning tended to be dependent upon a textbook. Consequently, teachers tended to ask fact-recall questions of their students nearly all the time, resulting in very little thinking or reasoning and a heavy dependence on memorization and factual recall. By everyone's admission, not much critical thinking went on in high school. Fortunately for your learning and success, that style of educating is over. In college, students are expected to take the initiative in their learning, to dig below the surface, to challenge, to question. Why the change in emphasis?

LIVING AND LEARNING
REQUIRE QUESTIONING

Educators have known for thousands of years that living and learning with a questioning mind results in powerful learning and thinking. Ever since Socrates first exemplified their use, questions have played a key role in teaching and learning. For years, educators have been seeking an expanded place in the classroom for student-raised questions. Why? Because questions raised by students show an active attempt at learning. These questions are formed in ignorance and curiosity and are based on the students' desire to know, to clarify, to satisfy a curiosity.

This questioning attitude is important because it shifts learning from a relatively passive role to an active role, stimulates thinking, and heightens retention of information. Unfortunately, not all the teachers you will have in college are skillful at encouraging students to ask questions. Sometimes you will have the impression that your questions are nothing more than an unwelcome interruption. Don't accept that situation or be intimidated. Continue to raise questions. It is your learning that is at stake.

A major goal of all teaching should be to make students independent learners and thinkers. As you read and study, you ought to keep a list of questions that you want to raise about what you are studying. After reading, seek answers for those questions so that you may acquire complete information and study the most effectively. Your thinking and learning is facilitated when you seek answers to questions that have been raised in your mind by what you have heard or read.

THOSE BASIC QUESTIONS

Just what do you have to do to become a skillful questioner and therefore an independent learner? What is required is very little more than knowing when to ask questions and what kind of questions to ask.

When should you raise questions? Whenever you are unsure of what you are reading, hearing, experiencing, and learning.

What kind of questions should you ask? There are four basic kinds of questions that college students should keep in mind and seek answers for as they attend classes and study. You'll notice that there is a pattern, a hierarchy, to these questions: if the questions are asked in the proper order, they will lead you to practice increasingly complex thinking operations (for example, classifying, contrasting, evaluating, synthesizing) in acquiring answers to them. Seeking answers to these questions will lead naturally to more questions and ultimately to important answers as well as to the development of your higher-order thinking skills.

1. *Questions requiring information clarification.* What is it (fact, event, idea, argument) that I need to know? (What occurred? What was said? Who is involved? When? Where? Is it verifiable? What is meant by these statements? Why is that so?)

2. *Questions requiring processing of that information.* What else do I need to know about this? (What values, unstated assumptions, viewpoint, perspective, bias, or vested interests are behind this? Is this an argument or a report? Is this relevant? How credible is this? What has been left unsaid? What evidence is there?)

3. *Questions requiring application of that information.* What does this mean in light of what I already know? (Are there examples, patterns, applications of this? How does this fit with what else I know? How does this relate to . . . ?)

4. *Questions requiring assessment of the questions and responses.* What did I learn from raising these questions? (Were these the right questions to ask? Was the additional information thorough, sufficient, and clear? Do I now understand what I didn't before? What additional questions do I need to ask?)

ANY QUESTIONS

Are there any questions that have no answer? Really? If you believe there are questions that have no answers, what are some of them?

_____

_____

_____

_____

_____

_____

_____

_____

THINKERS

Can you see it?

Find a perfect star in the pattern below.

Need a Hint?
Finding the star while looking at the whole pattern is tough. Try quartering the pattern and covering all but one quarter at a time.

THE IMPORTANCE OF QUESTIONING OURSELVES

Sometimes the answers to important questions will come from other people or sources, faculty members, fellow students, the library, and so forth. At other times the answers to the questions we raise when we are learning can come only from ourselves. These are questions that prompt us to examine our own long-held beliefs and values in light of what we are exposed to in our classes and elsewhere. Perhaps we begin to question the logic of our thinking on some issues and our feelings about something. Learning encourages us to examine ourselves. Instead of simply accepting the beliefs and views of others (including parents and teachers), as we did when we were younger, we gradually develop the ability and insight to question our own thinking and to decide whether long-held beliefs should be kept or rejected. Through this continual process of questioning, our thinking matures and we are less likely to accept unthinkingly the things we hear and read. We will no longer be easily fooled. Living and learning with a questioning mind is an important step in becoming a mature person and a productive thinker.

A WARNING ABOUT QUESTIONING

Is it possible to have too much questioning going on and not enough learning? Yes. How can that be? Establishing a pattern of raising questions and seeking clarification and information as you attend classes and study is a good thing, but only as long as the questioning remains focused on what you need to learn. It is possible for students to slip into the "challenge everything" mode and thereby hinder their learning. Questioning of what you are learning must be interspersed with time to reflect on and assimilate the responses to your questions, and then time to relate that information to what it is that you are learning. Students waste learning time when they routinely (and unnecessarily) challenge everything, thereby having little time left to absorb what needs to be learned. There is little to be gained by questioning well and learning little.

STIR IT UP 3.5   In a sentence, answer these questions about learning. Be ready to discuss your answers in class.

1. What makes something, or someone, "logical"?

   _____

2. What can you do to make the information you receive in class more understandable to your thinking?

   _____

3. What makes a fact accurate? Inaccurate?

   _____

4. How do the emotions and attitudes of others in class influence our opinions?

   _____

5. Are you aware of your thoughts and emotions when you try to verify your conclusions? Always?

   _____

6. What is the connection between your most difficult subjects and your emotional dislike of them?

   _____

7. How independent do you think you are in making decisions for yourself?

   _____

8. How might you revise your thinking and decide to learn more effectively?

   _____

9. What does the phrase "reflective thinking" suggest to you?

   _____

10. In which class(es) could you most benefit from developing your questioning skills?

    _____

STIR IT UP 3.6 For each of the statements below, indicate a possible question you might raise to foster your learning.

1. A star radiates energy because of nuclear fusion reactions inside its core.

   _____

2. The difference between eutrophic and oligotrophic lakes is that the oligotrophic lake contains many nutrients.

   _____

3. Witchcraft was itself a crime, and witches were criminals of a special sort.

   _____

4. The most famous example of the impact of women's colleges may be Jane Addams's experience at Rockford Seminary.

   _____

5. A target market must be defined so that the most appropriate segment of consumers can be reached.

   _____

6. Writing for radio has some parallels to writing for television in that the goal is a script that includes sound effects.

   _____

7. There is little question that Eastern Europe and the former Soviet Union need assistance as they try to reconstruct their economies.

   _____

8. When market demand is stable, collusion is more likely to occur.

   _____

9. Kennedy's decision-making system failed to correct the president's false image of Vietnam's prospects.

   _____

10. Students for a Democratic Society wishes to reiterate emphatically its intention to pursue its opposition to the war in Vietnam, undeterred by the diversionary tactics of the administration.

   _____

STIR IT UP 3.7   Well-thought-out questions, asked in the proper sequence, can gain you much information. For each of the statements below, create no more than three questions that, when answered, will give you a complete picture of the events that led up to each statement being made. List the questions in the order that you would ask them. Compare your questions with those of your classmates.

1. Suddenly, everything became black.

    a. _____

    b. _____

    c. _____

2. Wow! I did it!

    a. _____

    b. _____

    c. _____

3. She paused to look back at the now quiet, empty classroom, and then shut and locked the door.

    a. _____

    b. _____

    c. _____

4. Finally, I knew I had succeeded; I started to cry.

    a. _____

    b. _____

    c. _____

5. The last twenty-four hours I will never forget.

    a. _____

    b. _____

    c. _____

6. [Name] is really my best friend, not you.

    a. _____

    b. _____

    c. _____

7. The sweet, sugary taste lingered in my mouth.

    a. _____

    b. _____

    c. _____

8. Thank goodness that's over; it was worse than I had been told to expect!

   a. _____

   b. _____

   c. _____

9. We just smiled at each other, suddenly feeling uncomfortable and embarrassed.

   a. _____

   b. _____

   c. _____

10. He slammed the door as he stomped out.

   a. _____

   b. _____

   c. _____

   _____

THINKERS

Pick-up Straws

In what order should these straws be removed so as not to disturb the rest of the pile?

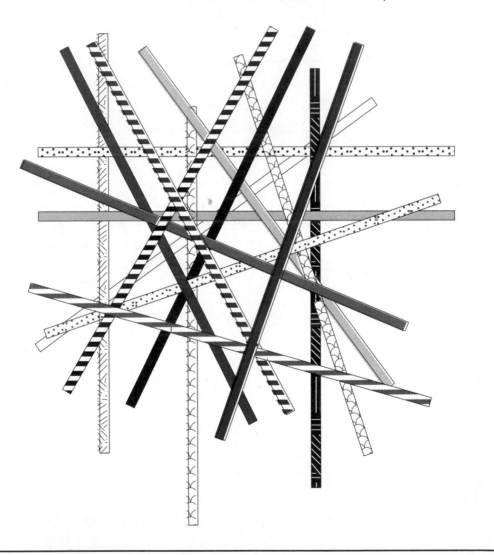

Need a Hint?
Try numbering the straws as you "remove" them one at a time.

Journal Observations (see page 13)

QUESTIONING

1st Writing _____

_____

_____

_____

_____

_____

_____

_____

_____

_____

_____

_____

2nd Writing _____

_____

_____

_____

_____

_____

_____

_____

_____

_____

_____

_____

_____

3rd Writing _____

_____

_____

_____

_____

_____

_____

_____

_____

_____

READINGS

The Okies in California

Carey McWilliams

The most characteristic of all housing in California in which migrants reside at the moment is the shacktown or cheap subdivision. Most of these settlements have come into existence since 1933 and the pattern which obtains is somewhat similar throughout the State. Finding it impossible to rent housing in incorporated communities on their meager incomes, migrants have created a market for a very cheap type of subdivision of which the following may be taken as being representative:

In Monterey County, according to a report of Dr. D. M. Bissell, county health officer, under date of November 28, 1939, there are approximately three well-established migrant settlements. One of these, the development around the environs of Salinas, is perhaps the oldest migrant settlement of its type in California. In connection with this development I quote a paragraph of the report of Dr. Bissell:

"This area is composed of all manners and forms of housing without a public sewer system. Roughly, 10,000 persons are renting or have established homes there. A chief element in this area is that of refugees from the Dust Bowl who inhabit a part of Alisal called Little Oklahoma. Work in lettuce harvesting and packing and sugar beet processing have attracted these people who, seeking homes in Salinas without success because they aren't available, have resorted to makeshift adobes outside the city limits. Complicating the picture is the impermeable substrata which makes septic tanks with leaching fields impractical. Sewer wells have resulted with the corresponding danger to adjacent water wells and to the water wells serving the Salinas public. Certain districts, for example, the Airport Tract and parts of Alisal, have grown into communities with quite satisfactory housing, but others as exemplified by the Graves district are characterized by shacks and lean-tos which are unfit for human habitation." . . .

Typical of the shacktown problem are two such areas near the city limits of Sacramento, one on the east side of B Street, extending from Twelfth Street to the Sacramento city dump and incinerator; and the other so-called Hoovertown, adjacent to the Sacramento River and the city filtration plant. In these two areas there were on September 17, 1939, approximately 650 inhabitants living in structures that, with scarcely a single exception, were rated by the inspectors of this division as "unfit for human occupancy." The majority of the inhabitants were white Americans, with the exception of 50 or 60 Mexican families, a few single Mexican men, and a sprinkling of Negroes. For the most part they are seasonally employed in the canneries, the fruit ranches, and the hop fields of Sacramento County. Most of the occupants are at one time or another upon relief, and there are a large number of occupants in these shacktowns from the Dust Bowl area. Describing the housing, an inspector of this division reports:

"The dwellings are built of brush, rags, sacks, boxboard, odd bits of tin and galvanized iron, pieces of canvas and whatever other material was at hand at the time of construction."

Wood floors, where they exist, are placed directly upon the ground, which because of the location of the camps with respect to the Sacramento River, is damp most of the time. To quote again from the report:

"Entire families, men, women, and children, are crowded into hovels, cooking and eating in the same room. The majority of the shacks have no sinks or cesspools for the disposal of kitchen drainage, and this, together with garbage and other refuse, is thrown on the surface of the ground."

Because of the high-water table, cesspools, where they exist, do not function properly; there is a large overflow of drainage and sewage to the surface of the ground. Many filthy shack latrines are located within a few feet of living quarters. Rents for the houses in these shacktowns range from $3 to $20 a month. In one instance a landlord rents ground space for $1.50 to $5 a month, on which tenants are permitted to erect their own dugouts. The Hooverville section is composed primarily of tents and trailers, there being approximately 125 tent structures in this area on September 17, 1939. Both areas are located in unincorporated territory. They are not subject at the present time to any State or county building regulation. In Hooverville, at the date of the inspection, many families were found that did not have even a semblance of tents or shelters. They were cooking and sleeping on the ground in the open and one water tap at an adjoining industrial plant was found to be the source of the domestic water supply for the camp. . . .

Read and Respond

1. This article describes some pretty awful housing. What are the implications of having thousands of individuals living in such substandard housing?

2. Suppose that next year our country (and probably the world as a result) suffered a sudden and serious depression, with bank and business failures and millions of people suddenly out of work and forced to leave their homes. Could you live in housing similar to the housing described in this article? What would be your action plan to avoid a similar fate? How would you survive?

Race Riot in Chicago

Chicago Commission on Race Relations

Sunday afternoon, July 27, 1919, hundreds of white and Negro bathers crowded the lake-front beaches at Twenty-sixth and Twenty-ninth streets. This is the eastern boundary of the thickest Negro residence area. At Twenty-sixth Street Negroes were in great majority; at Twenty-ninth Street there were more whites. An imaginary line in the water separating the two beaches had been generally observed by the two races. Under the prevailing relations, aided by wild rumors and reports, this line served virtually as a challenge to either side to cross it. Four Negroes who attempted to enter the water from the "white" side were driven away by the whites. They returned with more Negroes, and there followed a series of attacks with stones, first one side gaining the advantage, then the other.

Eugene Williams, a Negro boy of seventeen, entered the water from the side used by Negroes and drifted across the line supported by a railroad tie. He was observed by the crowd on the beach and promptly became a target for stones. He suddenly released the tie, went down and was drowned. Guilt was immediately placed on Stauber, a young white man, by Negro witnesses who declared that he threw the fatal stone.[1]

White and Negro men dived for the boy without result. Negroes demanded that the policeman present arrest Stauber. He refused; and at this crucial moment arrested a Negro on a white man's complaint. Negroes then attacked the officer. These two facts, the drowning and the refusal of the policeman to arrest Stauber, together marked the beginning of the riot.

Two hours after the drowning, a Negro, James Crawford, fired into a group of officers summoned by the policeman at the beach and was killed by a Negro policeman. Reports and rumors circulated rapidly, and new crowds began to gather. Five white men were injured in clashes near the beach. As darkness came Negroes in white districts to the west suffered severely. Between 9:00 P.M. and 3:00 A.M. twenty-seven Negroes were beaten, seven stabbed, and four shot. Monday morning was quiet, and Negroes went to work as usual.

Returning from work in the afternoon many Negroes were attacked by white ruffians. Street-car routes, especially at transfer points, were the centers of lawlessness. Trolleys were pulled from the wires, and Negro passengers were dragged into the street, beaten, stabbed, and shot. The police were powerless to cope with these numerous assaults. During Monday, four Negro men and one white assailant were killed, and thirty Negroes were severely beaten in street-car clashes. Four white men were killed, six stabbed, five shot, and nine severely beaten. It was rumored that the white occupants of the Angelus Building at Thirty-fifth Street and Wabash Avenue had shot a Negro. Negroes gathered about the building. The white tenants sought police protection, and one hundred policemen, mounted and on foot, responded. In a clash with the mob the police killed four Negroes and injured many.

Raids into the Negro residence area then began. Automobiles sped through the streets, the occupants shooting at random. Negroes retaliated by "sniping" from ambush. At midnight surface and elevated car service was discontinued because of a strike for wage increases, and thousands of employees were cut off from work.

---

[1]The coroner's jury found that Williams had drowned from fear of stone-throwing which kept him from the shore.

On Tuesday, July 29, Negro men en route on foot to their jobs through hostile territory were killed. White soldiers and sailors in uniform, aided by civilians, raided the "Loop" business section, killing two Negroes and beating and robbing several others. Negroes living among white neighbors in Englewood, far to the south, were driven from their homes, their household goods were stolen, and their houses were burned or wrecked. On the West Side an Italian mob, excited by a false rumor that an Italian girl had been shot by a Negro, killed Joseph Lovings, a Negro.

Wednesday night at 10:30 Mayor Thompson yielded to pressure and asked the help of the three regiments of militia which had been stationed in nearby armories during the most severe rioting, awaiting the call. They immediately took up positions throughout the South Side. A rainfall Wednesday night and Thursday kept many people in their homes, and by Friday the rioting had abated. On Saturday incendiary fires burned forty-nine houses in the immigrant neighborhood west of the Stock Yards. Nine hundred and forty-eight people, mostly Lithuanians, were made homeless, and the property loss was about $250,000. Responsibility for the fires was never fixed.

The total casualties of this reign of terror were thirty-eight deaths—fifteen white, twenty-three Negro—and 537 people injured. Forty-one per cent of the reported clashes occurred in the white neighborhood near the Stock Yards between the south branch of the Chicago River and Fifty-fifth Street, Wentworth Avenue and the city limits, and 34 per cent in the "Black Belt" between Twenty-second and Thirty-ninth streets, Wentworth Avenue and Lake Michigan. Others were scattered.

Responsibility for many attacks was definitely placed by many witnesses upon the [white] "athletic clubs," including "Ragen's Colts," the "Hamburgers," "Aylwards," "Our Flag," the "Standard," the "Sparklers," and several others. The mobs were made up for the most part of boys between fifteen and twenty-two. Older persons participated, but the youth of the rioters was conspicuous in every clash. Little children witnessed the brutalities and frequently pointed out the injured when the police arrived.

Read and Respond

1. If you were asked to identify an incident that sparked the rioting, what would that incident be? Was there more than one incident? Was there one riot or more than one?

2. Was the *cause* of the riot the same as the incident that you identified in question 1? How would you describe the difference between cause and incident?

3. Speculate about the purpose and makeup of the white "athletic clubs" that played such a prominent part in the riot. What do you think they were? In the article, the phrase "athletic clubs" is in quotation marks. Why?

4. It has been stated that whenever friction arises between the races, the suffering is usually endured by the innocent. Is this true of the riot described in this article? What evidence of this statement do you see in the article?

Chemistry: A Science for Today and Tomorrow

William R. Shine

The time is 7:30 A.M. Your clock radio has just started to talk, waking you out of a sound sleep. The announcers have just finished the news, and summarize the weather by saying that it is going to be a great day.

But what do they know? They don't have a chemistry class to go to at 9 A.M. So you push the snooze alarm for another 5 minutes of sleep. You put your head down on your pillow stuffed with polyurethane foam and snuggle under the polyester sheets. After three more bouts with the alarm, you find yourself staring into a mirror, brushing your teeth with a fluoride toothpaste. Since you stayed up late the night before studying chemistry, you have a slight headache and you decide to take some aspirin or acetaminophen (the active ingredient of Tylenol). You jump into the shower and scrub with your favorite coconut oil soap, and head off for breakfast.

Your breakfast consists of fruit juice (fructose, citric acid, orange flavoring), eggs (protein, fat, cholesterol), toast (starch, protein), cereal (carbohydrate, protein), bacon (fat, protein), and coffee (flavoring, caffeine) with milk (lactose, casein, butterfat) and sugar (sucrose). You sweeten your cereal with sugar, Sweet N' Low (saccharin), or Equal (NutraSweet). You put butter or hydrogenated margarine on your toast. The butter comes from milk that came from a cow that was fed with agricultural products grown with fertilizers. The margarine is derived from soybean oil hardened with hydrogen gas.

The eggs are cooked in a metal pan coated with nonstick Teflon. The toaster uses electricity from the local utility company that burns coal or uses nuclear fission as a source of energy to generate electricity. You sit on a plastic, wood, or metal chair while you eat off melamine-formaldehyde dishes at a table with a Formica surface. After you sit down, you realize that you need eating utensils, and get a silverplated knife and fork (nickel coated with silver).

After breakfast, you dress in clothing made of cotton, acrylics, and polyesters. You put on your glasses consisting of plastic frames and plastic lenses, and slip on your 10-karat-gold high school class ring (42% gold, 38% copper, 13% silver, and 7% zinc.) As you prepare to leave for class, you recall a matter that will require your attention later in the day, and you make yourself a note on chemically processed paper using a pencil made of wood and graphite (carbon) or a pen containing ink. You dispose of some old notes in a polyethylene waste basket and head out to the car.

You look with pride at your shiny car, washed the previous day with a detergent and protected by wax. It is an older car that has been protected from corrosion with rustproofing materials. You turn the key and electrons flow from the electrochemical cell (the battery) to the starter and sparks begin to ignite the hydrocarbons that are flowing to the engine from the gas tank. Octane boosters added to the gasoline make the car run smoothly. Since your car sat outside in the cold overnight, you use the windshield washer containing soap, water, and methanol to remove a coating of frost on the windows. Lubricating oils allow you to start the car easily regardless of temperature. Antifreeze in the coolant system has protected the engine from the cold and now protects it from the heat that is generated by burning the fuel.

Since you got off to a late start, you are rather impatient as you find yourself delayed at a traffic light, even though you are sitting on a comfortable seat cushioned with polyurethane foam and covered with a polyester fabric. You notice the envelope you placed on the dashboard the day before. You admire the colorful stamp held in place on the letter by an adhesive made of carbohydrate and you grumble at the sticky adhesive that makes the envelope hard to open. Just then you notice that the traffic light is now shining through the green Plexiglas covering; it is your turn to go. The car in front of you is making a turn, so you go around it by turning your plastic steering wheel and pointing your vulcanized rubber tires in the proper direction.

You find a place to park, and gather up your book bag made of polyvinyl chloride with plasticizer added. You then walk across the asphalt parking lot, enter the door, and go to the classroom where you are about to listen to a chemistry lecture. And you think to yourself, "Why do I have to learn chemistry? What does it have to do with me anyway?"

Read and Respond

1. How effective is this article in answering the question it raises? What method is used to influence your thinking? How would you describe the reasoning that led the author to write this article in this manner? Was the approach just a lucky guess, or was it planned, thought out, carefully considered? How do you know?

2. What evidence, information, or data is presented here? Does the presentation have any weaknesses? If so, what are they? What other evidence or data would you add if you were writing this article?

3. Using this article as a model, what would you say if asked, "Why do we have to study economics (or American history, British literature, calculus, etc.)?" Are some college subjects easier than others to defend by means of this approach? Why?

ASKING CRITICAL QUESTIONS

After you read the article that follows, what critical questions come to mind? Everything you read will stir up your thinking if you read and question critically. What questions would you like to have answered in order for you to put the article in proper context and to completely understand what is being said or reported? *On the lines following the article, write three questions that, if answered, will help you understand what is really being said.*

The Creative Leap

Michael L. Rothschild

According to one popular theory, the left brain thinks orderly, logical, linear thoughts, while the right brain thinks melodies, pictures, diagrams, and signs. Even though this dichotomy is an oversimplification of the way the brain actually works, it is a useful image because it summarizes a phenomenon we all know to be true: People are sometimes logical and sometimes intuitive. And some of us are generally more logical and less intuitive than others.

Most textbooks make it appear that complex marketing and advertising problems are almost always solved by "left-brain" procedures. The problem solver gets a situation analysis, an orderly, logical presentation of the facts, a thorough knowledge of consumer preferences and brand perceptions, and then the one-and-only correct solution pops out, like wheat bread from a toaster. The process is portrayed as more complicated but essentially the same as $2 + 2 = 4$.

That is not the way the real world works.

In the real world, one rarely has time to collect and analyze all the "left-brain" data. A great many important decisions are made under strict deadlines set by schedules and events beyond any researcher's control. And even on those occasions when enough time is available, the data that emerge are always questionable, messy, and subject to a variety of more or less reasonable interpretations.

This means that the "left-brain" work is only the first, and sometimes the least important, step in solving a complex marketing or advertising problem. When all the "left-brain" work has been done, someone must make a creative leap from information to policy. This leap may be a timid, tentative hop, in which case the policy will be thoroughly and literally pedestrian. Or it may be a new creative synthesis of half-formed old facts, new data, semi-knowledge, and dimly perceived ideas. That's where the "right brain" comes in. And that's what's exciting, challenging, demanding, frustrating, and fun.

So don't think that the process of solving real marketing problems is as orderly or logical as the textbooks make it seem to be. This game isn't only for "left-brain" people.

The most interesting part of the work begins when the computer has been disconnected; and it ends (to quote James Joyce) in "the most delicate and evanescent of moments when the whatness of a thing leaps to us from the vestment of its appearance."

The intuitive skill with which that part of the work gets done is what makes the difference between a brilliant solution and a dud.

My Critical Questions

1. _____

_____ **?**

2. _____

_____ **?**

3. _____

_____ **?**

SOLUTIONS to Items in This Chapter

The Ultimate Observing Skills Test (p. 53)

As you note the correct answer to each question, speculate on why that answer is correct. For example, as you read the answer to question 1, try to figure out why only twenty-six states are printed on the back of the bill. Where can you go to confirm whether or not your "why" answer is correct?

1. Twenty-six states. Grab a magnifying glass and see if you can find all twenty-six.
2. Bottom.
3. Six.
4. Black, white, red, gold, and yellow.
5. The number 5.
6. Q and Z.
7. From tip to eraser.
8. 88 (megahertz).
9. The word *ONE*.
10. 1 and 0.
11. Bashful.
12. Hot dogs mostly come in packages of ten. How many hot-dog buns are in a standard package? Hot dog buns mostly come in packages of eight. Why the difference?

Any Questions? (p. 56)

No two examples of anything are exactly alike, so why keep marveling over snowflakes? No two dogs, flowers, people, bicycles, trees, or banana splits are exactly alike either, but we don't walk around marveling over that fact.

THINKERS (p. 56)

Stand back-to-back.

THINKERS (p. 59)

You would have two apples. How many you take is how many you have.

Any Questions? (p. 72)

Here are a couple that don't seem to have an answer that isn't pure speculation:
  Why did everything begin? How is everything going to end?
What questions can you come up with?

THINKERS (p. 72)

THINKERS (p. 78)

Straws should be removed in the following order:

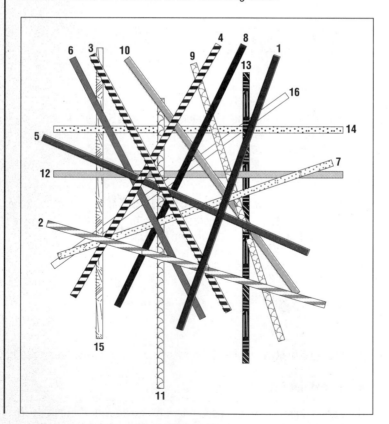

Chapter 4

ORGANIZING SKILLS

- ■ **Comparing and Contrasting**
- ■ **Classifying and Sequencing**
- ■ **Identifying Cause and Effect**

Now *it makes sense—when you look at it that way.*

"Readers are plentiful; thinkers are rare."
—Harriet Martineau

"All men see the same objects, but do not equally understand them. Intelligence is the tongue that discerns and tastes them."
—Thomas Traherne

*"To show our simple skill,
That is the true beginning of our end."*
—William Shakespeare

STIR UP YOUR THINKING BEFORE YOU START READING

Before you start reading this chapter, take an informal survey. Compare the results you get with what you learn in this chapter. Ask three people to answer this question:

If we never developed the thinking skills that allow us to organize our thinking (for example, comparing and contrasting, classifying and sequencing, what effect would this have on our ability to learn? On our ability to survive? And what happens if some of those skills are inadequately developed?

Responses:

1. _____

_____

_____

Comparing and Contrasting

ESSENTIAL THINKING SKILLS		
CHAPTER	**WHAT THEY'RE CALLED**	**WHAT THEY MEAN**
Chapter 3	**The Gathering Skills**	**Gathering all the information.**
	Observing	Actively seeking information through one or more senses.
	Questioning	Seeking information by asking questions.
Chapter 4	**The Organizing Skills**	**Organizing for the purpose of making sense.**
	Comparing and Contrasting	Noting similarities and differences between two or more things, events, or ideas.
	Classifying and Sequencing	Arranging things or concepts into categories and into sequential order.
	Identifying Cause and Effect	Recognizing the relationship between an effect and its cause.
Chapter 5	**The Generating Skills**	**Generating additional information.**
	Inferring	Making an assumption, stating a hypothesis, or coming to a conclusion based on limited information.
	Summarizing	Condensing the essence of the information accurately and efficiently.
	Synthesizing	Creating new information by combining two or more pieces of information.
	Generating Ideas	Creating new information, alternatives, or applications.
Chapter 6	**The Recognizing Skills**	**Recognizing what has been left unsaid.**
	Recognizing Purpose	Identifying a writer's or speaker's intention.
	Recognizing Fact and Opinion	Distinguishing between a statement of fact and a statement of opinion.
	Recognizing Tone	Identifying a sentiment or mood by assessing the writer's or speaker's choice of words.
	Recognizing Bias	Noting the presence and nature of a writer's or speaker's prejudice.
	Recognizing Organization	Identifying the organizational pattern of a thought, statement, passage, or plan.
	Recognizing Underlying Assumptions	Recognizing the suppositions that are taken for granted and are the foundation of a proposition, notion, or idea.
Chapter 7	**The Analyzing Skills**	**Analyzing for the purpose of coming to a conclusion.**
	Analyzing	Identifying and separating ideas, attributes, situations, and/or components in order to form a conclusion as to their relationship.
	Evaluating	Appraising something according to certain criteria and forming a judgment as to its worth or quality.
	Inducing	Analyzing individual facts or premises in order to derive a general conclusion.
	Deducing	Applying general principles or a broad framework to a situation in order to come to a conclusion about it.

2. _____

_____

_____

3. _____

_____

_____

"*Question: What do John the Baptist and Winnie the Pooh have in common?
Answer: They both have the same middle name.***"**
—Unknown Riddler

"*Shall I compare thee to a summer's day?***"**
—William Shakespeare

What questions am I going to have answered in this section on comparing and contrasting?

1. What do we do when we compare and contrast?
2. Why is it so important to study and develop the thinking skills of comparing and contrasting?
3. What things cannot be easily compared or contrasted?

> **COMPARING:**
> Noting similarities between two or more things, events, or ideas

> **CONTRASTING:**
> Noting differences between two or more things, events, or ideas

If there are any fundamental thinking skills that are the foundation for all other thinking skills, they are the skills of comparing and contrasting. A person who cannot compare and contrast cannot think. These two thinking skills are essential to our continued mental and intellectual growth from the time of our birth. Comparing and contrasting are apparent in small children when they indicate their

THINK ABOUT THIS!

Two Definitions

"The happiest person is the person who thinks the most interesting thoughts."
—Timothy Dwight, nineteenth-century educator

"The happiest person is the person who thinks the most interesting thoughts that result in accomplishing something."
—The Author of This Book, twentieth-century educator

Which of these definitions makes the most sense to you? Why? What does this tell you about your thinking and yourself?

_____

_____

_____

_____

_____

preferences for shapes, colors, food, toys, experiences, and even people. As children grow, so does their dependence on the skills of comparing and contrasting. In school, as in the rest of life, we frequently think in terms of comparisons and contrasts. Our teachers not only engage us in comparing and contrasting activities, but they use comparing and contrasting to determine what we know and to elicit information from us.

- How was the Civil War similar to the Spanish-American War?

- List three differences between these two leaves.

- Which of the following sentences best describes how Shakespeare and Mozart were alike?

- You have just read a discussion concerning the members of the European Economic Community. Which of these sentences describes a difference in their economies?

- Do the words in each poem sound the same or different to you? Are they harsh, soft, angry, gentle, or what?

- Write a comparison and contrast essay.

WHY THE SKILLS OF COMPARING AND CONTRASTING ARE IMPORTANT

In college, not just our learning but also the quality of our learning frequently depend on these organizing skills. Comparing and contrasting are powerful tools for helping us understand. They are a part of nearly everything we do in college, from choosing an item in the school cafeteria to writing a paper or to selecting a college major. Comparing and contrasting are so basic to college thinking that the term *comparative* is used in the names of several fields of study: comparative literature, comparative anatomy, comparative religion. College classes use comparing and contrasting as the method for presenting material: in literature classes we frequently compare and contrast characters, plots, structures; in history we compare and contrast periods, rulers, wars, and discoveries; in political science we compare and contrast government; in education we match learning styles to students and environment; in psychology and sociology we look for similarities and differences in behavior patterns. When we compare and contrast we look at something in a different way, adding a new dimension to it.

We routinely compare and contrast objects, events, organisms, institutions, and ideas. We analyze features that match and features that don't. We use comparing and contrasting in several of the more complex organizing processes, such as classifying, sequencing, identifying cause and effect, and identifying underlying assumptions.

So, if we already have a lot of experience with these two skills, why do we need to spend time on them in this book? Good (thinking) question.

Because we get better at it! A major problem with the way we compare and contrast is that we do so with varying degrees of thoroughness. Sometimes we attend only to surface characteristics, like how things look, when other things are more relevant or important. But if we can learn to be thorough, precise, and aware of the implications of similarities and differences, we will become significantly better at reasoning, decision making, and problem solving. Being better at comparing and contrasting, we become better at the other thinking skills that depend upon comparing and contrasting.

WHAT IT MEANS TO COMPARE AND CONTRAST

When we compare, we note similarities; when we contrast, we note differences. Simple. But is that all we do? Sometimes, but to get the greatest benefit from comparing and contrasting we should be doing some additional thinking and questioning. Not just:

- How are they similar?

- How are they different?

But also:

- What similarities and/or differences *seem significant?*

- What *categories or patterns do we see* in the significant similarities and differences?

- What *interpretation or conclusion is suggested* by the significant similarities and differences?

STIR IT UP 4.1   Although points of comparison can be found in most things, some things just cannot be reasonably compared with one another because they have no common characteristics. For example, it is difficult to compare an ibis with a rainbow or nuclear fission with an oak tree. What pairings can you make of things that cannot be easily compared? Write them below. Be ready to explain why they are not easily compared. After you have written the noncomparisons below, suggest a third thing that *has* obvious comparing possibilities with one of the two original items. An example is given.

noncomparisons		new item compared with old item	
pizza	*porcupines*	*pin cushion*	*porcupines*

THINKERS

Without being separated, these four shapes can be folded to form a triangle or a square. Can you tell which?

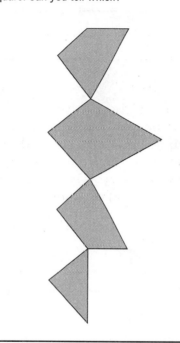

Need a Hint?
Try cutting out the shape—or a copy of it—and folding it. You'll have the answer fast! But don't assume your first answer is the only answer.

ANY QUESTIONS?

If you had to pick four books—and only four—to take with you to a new planet, which books would you take? Why those four?

_____

_____

_____

_____

My choices are the following. Can you guess why I selected them?
1. *Roget's Thesaurus*
2. *Webster's Unabridged Dictionary*
3. *Bartlett's Familiar Quotations*
4. My hometown *Yellow Pages*

STIR IT UP 4.2   There is an old saying, "You can't compare apples and oranges." But is it true? Explain, with illustrations, why you *can* compare apples and oranges.

_____

_____

_____

_____

STIR IT UP 4.3   This exercise asks you to do some writing, one of the best ways to develop thinking skills. In a substantial paragraph or series of paragraphs, answer the comparison and contrast questions below. The completed paragraphs may be read aloud for the class, and your classmates may indicate at what point they knew what your "most valued possession" was and what specific details they liked the best.

1. If your most valued possession were an animal, what would it be? Why?

   _____

2. If it were a fruit or vegetable, what would it be? Why?

   _____

3. What season does it remind you of? Why?

   _____

4. Would it be a Republican, a Democrat, or an independent voter? Why?

   _____

5. How do you feel when you don't have it around?

   _____

6. Would it be enjoyed most by a young person, a middle-aged person, or an old person? Why?

   _____

7. What object in nature does it most remind you of? Why?

   _____

8. What object in your house does it most remind you of? Why?

   _____

9. Does it make you think of any person you know? Why?

_____

10. What emotion best suits it? Why?

_____

STIR IT UP 4.4   An excellent way to stir up your comparing and contrasting thinking is to use it to say something in another way. But that is not always as easy as it sounds. Below are some quotations that will limber up your mental muscles. Say what these famous thinkers have said in another way. Be careful to say the same thing—just differently. Compare your versions with those of your classmates. Are some versions more accurate than others? Why?

1. "A word to the wise is sufficient." (Titus Plautus)

_____

2. "To those who are awake, there is one ordered universe common to all, whereas in sleep each man turns away from this world to one of his own." (Heraclitus)

_____

_____

3. "One great use of words is to hide our thoughts." (Voltaire)

_____

4. "It takes a very long time to become young." (Pablo Picasso)

_____

5. "Nothing comes of doing nothing." (William Shakespeare)

_____

6. " A man may dwell so long upon a thought that it may take him prisoner." (Sir George Savile)

_____

7. "Freedom of will is the ability to do gladly that which I must do." (Carl Jung)

_____

8. "The only way to get rid of temptation is to yield to it." (Oscar Wilde)

_____

9. "Every decision you make is a mistake." (Edward Dahlberg)

_____

10. "When they tell you to grow up, they mean stop growing."
    (Tom Robbins)

_____

_____

THINKERS

Why are 1998 dollar bills worth more than 1997 dollar bills, and why will 1999 dollar bills be worth more than 1997 or 1998 dollar bills?

Need a Hint?
What makes you think these numbers are years?

Journal Observations (see page 13)

COMPARING AND CONTRASTING

1st Writing _____

_____

_____

_____

_____

_____

2nd Writing

3rd Writing

READINGS

The Costs of a Volunteer Army

James R. Kearl

Maintaining an army will impose costs on the government or society as a whole because its resources such as labor are not used to produce goods and services that it might consume or use in other ways. But does a volunteer army cost more than a conscript or draft army? In considering this question, you might first ask: "costs to whom?"

First consider the costs to the government. With a volunteer army, the government must pay a wage rate sufficient to attract the number and quality of personnel it requires to maintain its desired military force. Suppose that this wage is $10 per hour. (It is often helpful in thinking through problems to put numbers with the ideas.) With a draft army, where individuals are forced into service on threat of jail, the government could set this wage much lower, say $4 per hour. Note that if the government could get all the volunteers it needed at $4 per hour, then even if it had a draft, it would not need to actually draft anyone. Thus, it appears that if the government actually uses the draft, the cost to the government of a volunteer army is likely to be higher than the cost of a draft army.

What about the costs to society as a whole? With a volunteer army, the wage rate would have to be at least as great as the opportunity cost of those entering the military. That is, in terms of our example, all those volunteering would have alternatives with wages at or below $10 per hour. This opportunity cost is the value of output lost elsewhere in the economy. (Resources are being used for military purposes instead of being used to produce goods and services.) Therefore, even though a draft army costs *the government* less than a volunteer army of the same size, the draft army costs *society at least as much* as the volunteer army. In both cases an equal number of resources are moved from elsewhere in the economy to the military.

Who pays the difference between the cost to the government and the cost to society? The difference is paid by the draftees, who are paid less than their opportunity costs (otherwise they would have volunteered). Thus, a draft army is paid for by a large, hidden tax on those who are drafted, whereas a volunteer army is paid for by a large, visible tax on the citizens who are being defended.

Are there other possible costs? With a draft, individuals with opportunity costs above and below the volunteer army wage would be forced to serve because the draft takes individuals without regard to opportunity cost. For example, it might be that someone with an opportunity cost of $20 per hour was drafted as well as someone with an opportunity cost of $5 per hour. With a volunteer army, however, only individuals with opportunity costs below $10 per hour will join the army because joining a volunteer army where the pay was $10 per hour would not be attractive to someone with options that would pay $20 per hour. *If* the opportunity costs for individuals represent their contributions to the economy (that is, if a person being paid $20 per hour produces goods and services worth $20 and a person being paid $5 per hour produces goods and services worth $5), the draft army will probably be more costly than a volunteer army, since it will take more valuable resources from the economy than will a volunteer army. That is, the draft will occasionally take a person with opportunity costs of, say, $20 per hour, whereas only those with opportunity costs below $10 per hour will volunteer.

Examine Your Thinking About What You Just Read

Pay attention to your thinking processes as you answer the following questions.

1. Examine carefully how this article is written. Analyze it. This article is organized around the classic question-and-answer format: ask questions and then answer them. What five key questions does the writer raise, and were these questions sufficient to give a complete picture of the issue? Should there have been another question or two added? If so, what might those questions be? In order to determine believability about what is said when an article uses this organizational technique, what things must the reader decide before reading, during reading, and after reading?

2. Besides the question-and-answer organizational structure of this article, it also employs a second organizational device: comparison and contrast. What is being compared and contrasted in this article? Was there a conclusion attached to this comparison and contrast? If so, what was it? How was this compare and contrast technique integrated with the question-and-answer organization of the article? Could one of these organizational techniques have been eliminated and still leave an effective article? If so, which device could have been left out? What would be the result?

3. What is being assumed or taken for granted in this article? Identify as many underlying assumptions as possible for what is stated. For example, this article suggests that $10 an hour is a wage sufficient to

attract volunteers into the army. What assumptions does this suggestion rest upon? Are the assumptions correct, or must these assumptions be qualified in some way? Is there an assumption that this is a peacetime army? Is $10 an hour sufficient to attract enlistees if the nation is at war? What other assumptions are hidden in this article?

4. How would you explain to someone what "opportunity costs" are and what the importance is of these costs in evaluating what is stated in this article?

5. This article discusses the economic costs of an army. What other "costs" are associated with an army besides the economic costs?

Three Mile Island

William R. Shine

The accident at Three Mile Island (TMI) was minor compared with the one at Chernobyl. Nevertheless, it was the most serious nuclear accident that has yet happened in the United States.

The events began on March 28, 1979. The unit 2 reactor was the PWR type. The PWR has a steam generator that is separated from the reactor core. Thus water flows through the core, picking up heat generated by fission. This component of the system is known as the *primary loop.* Water also flows through the steam generator or *secondary loop;* it comes in contact with the primary loop, allowing heat to pass from the primary to the secondary loop to be carried to the turbine generator.

A series of problems occurred at TMI beginning with a failure of water pumps in the secondary loop. Since the power plant was designed to provide backups in the event of malfunctions, additional pumps were activated in the secondary loop. Unknown to the operators, valves had been closed in the secondary loop, preventing the backup pumps from delivering water to the secondary loop. Since heat was still being transferred from the primary loop, the secondary loop went dry—all of the water was converted to steam. This automatically caused the turbine generator to trip (shut down) and led to the insertion of some control rods into the reactor. Since the secondary loop was no longer able to draw heat away from the primary loop, the pressure in the primary loop began to rise above normal. At an elevated pressure, a pilot-operated relief valve (PORV) opened to allow steam to escape and to prevent the pressure from rising too high. Shortly after, the reactor tripped—control rods were inserted and the fission was stopped.

At that point, the reactor was under control, but although fission had ceased, generation of heat in the core had not. Up to 7% of the heat released in a nuclear reactor is from the decay of radioactive fission products, particularly γ emitters. The amount of heat from this source depends on the length of time the fuel has been in the reactor. When the fuel is fresh, few fission products are present, and radioactive decay contributes little heat. But when the fuel has been in the reactor for many months, fission products make their greatest contribution to the heat liberated within the core. It so happened that the fuel in the TMI reactor was near the end of its lifetime, and thus the level of fission products was near a maximum. This made the reactor particularly vulnerable at the time of the accident.

Recall that the transfer of heat from the primary loop was still not taking place since no water was in the secondary loop. Therefore, the temperature in the primary loop continued to rise. This caused the ECCS in the primary loop to activate and dump more water into the core. However, unknown to the operators, another problem had developed. As the core cooled, the pressure relief valve was supposed to close, and indications inside the control room were that it had. But the PORV had actually become stuck in an open position and remained that way for more than 2 hours. Consequently, a large amount of water flowed out of the reactor onto the floor of the containment building, and the pressure became lower than normal in the primary loop. When the operators discovered the low pressure, they deactivated the ECCS. About 10 minutes after the start of the accident, the operators recognized that the valves in the secondary loop were closed and they restored the flow of water to the secondary loop. Although several minutes passed between the time the pumps were activated and water actually began to flow, this malfunction did not lead to any significant damage to the plant. It did add to the confusion, however, and provided a distraction from the serious problem of the stuck-open PORV.

With the PORV still open and indications of low pressure in the primary loop, the operators had a condition that was considered impossible: high temperature and low pressure. Therefore, they decreased the flow of cooling water to the core to allow some pressure to develop; this caused a portion of the core, which is normally completely covered with water, to be uncovered because of formation of steam bubbles. This allowed the core to heat up to temperatures in excess of 2200 °C and caused approximately half of the core to melt. This type of "core meltdown" is commonly known as the "China principle" in which it is imagined that the nuclear core would melt its way through the center of the earth and come out in China.

Approximately 4 hours into the accident the stuck PORV was discovered and cooling was restored to the core. With the whole world watching events unfold, the accident was a continuing concern for another 48 hours until it was decided that no further danger existed.

Comparing TMI and Chernobyl

We have seen that operator errors contributed heavily to each accident. At Chernobyl, the fission process went totally out of control, causing a massive power surge resulting in an explosion and virtually total destruction of the plant. At TMI, heat from the fission products, rather than the fission process itself, led to overheating and melting of a substantial portion of the core.

At TMI, 17 Ci of radioiodine was released because the containment building effectively trapped the liquid and solid radioactive materials that escaped from the reactor. Greater amounts, thought to be a few million curies of noble gases, ^{133}Xe and ^{85}Kr, escaped and were dispersed into the atmosphere. Whereas radiation detectors some distance away detected the noble gases, no people were exposed to any significant dose of radiation.

In contrast, massive amounts of radioactive elements of several kinds were released at Chernobyl and spread over a wide area, partly due to the fires that followed the explosion and burned for many hours. Many individuals received large doses of radiation. Some died within a short time after the accident; for others the effects will be observed in future decades and even in future generations. A study supported by the U.S. Department of Energy estimates that 21,000 Europeans may die of cancer in the next 50 years because of exposure to radiation from the accident. Potassium iodide tablets were distributed to inhabitants of the area around Chernobyl to try to protect them from the effects of ^{131}I, which was released in large amounts from the reactor. Since iodine is efficiently captured by the thyroid gland for incorporation into thyroid hormones, it was hoped that nonradioactive potassium iodide would be able to saturate each person's thyroid and prevent uptake of the radioactive iodine.

Many lessons were learned from these two accidents. Designs that are under consideration for future construction rely heavily on passive components, such as systems that do not require operator intervention, to bring reactors under control in the event of malfunctions. Smaller, modularized units are also being contemplated to permit less costly construction and greater ease of operation. Above all, designs like the RBMK, with a positive void coefficient, are no longer being considered.

Through proper design of reactor core and moderators, it is possible to ensure that a reactor will always have a negative void coefficient so that the fission process cannot run out of control. More efficient passive cooling systems seem to be the way to prevent meltdowns. Meanwhile, for existing plants, more safety measures have been included, such as more extensive training of operators.

Other than the $1 billion required to clean up the TMI plant and the financial devastation of the utility that owns it, no great harm has resulted from that accident. The consequences of Chernobyl will be studied and discussed for many decades, just as are the effects of nuclear bombs on the Japanese citizens in World War II.

Read and Respond

1. Is it important for you to know what happened at Three Mile Island and at Chernobyl even though you may have little interest in science or engineering? Why or why not?

2. Were there differences in what happened at Three Mile Island and at Chernobyl? Were there similarities? What were they?

3. Do you believe that "it is possible to ensure that a reactor . . . cannot run out of control"? Are there any fallacies in the underlying assumptions for that statement?

A Forced Marriage in Texas

Rose Williams

What I say am the facts. If I's one day old, I's way over ninety, and I's born in Bell County, right here in Texas, and am owned by Massa William Black. He owns Mammy and Pappy, too. Massa Black has a big plantation, but he has more niggers than he need for work on that place, 'cause he am a nigger trader. He trade and buy and sell all the time.

Massa Black am awful cruel, and he whip the colored folks and works 'em hard and feed 'em poorly. We-uns have for rations the corn meal and milk and 'lasses and some beans and peas and meat once a week. We-uns have to work in the field every day from daylight 'til dark, and on Sunday we-uns do us washing. Church? Shucks, we-uns don't know what that mean.

I has the correct memorandum of when the war start. Massa Black sold we-uns right then. Mammy and Pappy powerful glad to git sold, and they and I is put on the block with 'bout ten other niggers. When we-uns gits to the trading block, there lots of white folks there what come to look us over. One man shows the interest in Pappy. Him named Hawkins. He talk to Pappy, and Pappy talk to him and say, "Them my woman and childs. Please buy all of us and have mercy on we-uns." Massa Hawkins say, "That gal am a likely-looking nigger; she am portly and strong. But three am more than I wants, I guesses."

The sale start, and 'fore long Pappy am put on the block. Massa Hawkins wins the bid for Pappy, and when Mammy am put on the block, he wins the bid for her. Then there am three or four other niggers sold before my time comes. Then Massa Black calls me to the block, and the auction man say, "What am I offer for this portly, strong young wench. She's never been 'bused and will make the good breeder."

I wants to hear Massa Hawkins bid, but him say nothing. Two other men am bidding 'gainst each other, and I sure has the worriment. There am tears coming down my cheeks 'cause I's being sold to some man that would make separation from my mammy. One man bids $500, and the auction man ask, "Do I hear more? She am gwine at $500." Then someone say, "$525," and the auction man say, "She am sold for $525 to Massa Hawkins." Am I glad and 'cited! Why, I's quivering all over.

Massa Hawkins takes we-uns to his place, and it am a nice plantation. Lots better than Massa Black's. There is 'bout fifty niggers what is growed and lots of children. The first thing Massa do when we-uns gits home am give we-uns rations and a cabin. You must believe this nigger when I says them rations a feast for us. There plenty meat and tea and coffee and white flour. I's never tasted white flour and coffee, and Mammy fix some biscuits and coffee. Well, the biscuits was yum, yum, yum to me, but the coffee I doesn't like.

The quarters am pretty good. There am twelve cabins all made from logs and a table and some benches and bunks for sleeping and a fireplace for cooking and the heat. There am no floor, just the ground.

Massa Hawkins am good to he niggers and not force 'em work too hard. There am as much difference 'tween him and Old Massa Black in the way of treatment as 'twixt the Lord and the devil. Massa Hawkins 'lows he niggers have reasonable parties and go fishing, but we-uns am never tooken to church and has no books for larning. There am no education for the niggers.

There am one thing Massa Hawkins does to me what I can't shunt from my mind. I knows he don't do it for meanness, but I always holds it 'gainst him. What he done am force me to live with that nigger, Rufus, 'gainst my wants.

After I been at he place 'bout a year, the massa come to me and say, "You gwine live with Rufus in that cabin over yonder. Go fix it for living." I's 'bout sixteen year old and has no larning, and I's just ignomus child. I's thought that him mean for me to tend the cabin for Rufus and some other niggers. Well, that am start the pestigation for me.

I's took charge of the cabin after work am done and fixes supper. Now, I don't like that Rufus, 'cause he a bully. He am big and 'cause he so, he think everybody do what him say. We-uns has supper, then I goes here and there talking, till I's ready for sleep, and then I gits in the bunk. After I's in, that nigger come and crawl in the bunk with me 'fore I knows it. I says, "What you means, you fool nigger?" He say for me to hush the mouth. "This am my bunk, too," he say.

"You's teched in the head. Git out," I's told him, and I puts the feet 'gainst him and give him a shove, and out he go on the floor 'fore he know what I's doing. That nigger jump up and he mad. He look like the wild bear. He starts for the bunk, and I jumps quick for the poker. It am 'bout three feet long, and when he comes at me I lets him have it over the head. Did that nigger stop in he tracks? I's say he did. He looks at me steady for a minute, and you could tell he thinking hard. Then he go and set on the bench and say, "Just wait. You thinks it am smart, but you am foolish in the head. They's gwine larn you something."

"Hush your big mouth and stay 'way from this nigger, that all I wants," I say, and just sets and hold that poker in the hand. He just sets, looking like the bull. There we-uns sets and sets for 'bout an hour, and then he go out, and I bars the door.

The next day I goes to the missy and tells her what Rufus wants, and Missy say that am the massa's wishes. She say, "You am the portly gal, and Rufus am the portly man. The massa wants you-uns for to bring forth portly children."

I's thinking 'bout what the missy say, but say to myself, "I's not gwine live with that Rufus." That night when him come in the cabin, I grabs the poker and sits on the bench and says, "Git 'way from me, nigger, 'fore I bust your brains out and stomp on them." He say nothing and git out.

The next day the massa call me and tell me, "Woman, I's pay big money for you, and I's done that for the cause I wants you to raise me childrens. I's put you to live with Rufus for that purpose. Now, if you doesn't want whipping at the stake, you do what I wants."

I thinks 'bout Massa buying me offen the block and saving me from being separated from my folks and 'bout being whipped at the stake. There it am. What am I's to do? So I 'cides to do as the massa wish, and so I yields. . . .

I never marries, 'cause one 'sperience am 'nough for this nigger. After what I does for the massa, I's never wants no truck with any man. The Lord forgive this colored woman, but he have to 'scuse me and look for some others for to 'plenish the earth.

Read and Respond

1. What, if anything, did you learn from this article about the personal side of slavery? We all know that slaves didn't have any rights. Can you imagine yourself in Rose Williams's place? Can you imagine living with no rights at all? Would you act any differently?

2. What are the key ideas related to loss of freedom that are embedded in this account? To be a slave meant to have no freedom in several areas. Which of those areas are identified in this article?

3. Compare and contrast Hawkins and Black as slave owners. How much of your comparison is based on inference and how much on statements (assumed to be fact) from this article?

ASKING CRITICAL QUESTIONS

After you read the articles that follow, what critical questions come to mind? Everything you read will stir up your thinking if you read and question critically. What questions would you like to have answered in order for you to put the articles in proper context and to completely understand what is being said or reported? *On the lines following each article, write three questions that, if answered, will help you understand what is really being said.*

Aria

Richard Rodriguez

Supporters of bilingual education today imply that students like me miss a great deal by not being taught in their family's language. What they seem not to recognize is that, as a socially disadvantaged child, I considered Spanish to be a private language. What I needed to learn in school was that I had the right—and the obligation—to speak the public language of *los gringos*. The odd truth is that my first-grade classmates could have become bilingual, in the conventional sense of that word, more easily than I. Had they been taught (as upper-middle-class children are often taught early) a second language like Spanish or French, they could have regarded it simply as that: another public language. In my case such bilingualism could not have been so quickly achieved. What I did not believe was that I could speak a single public language.

Without question, it would have pleased me to hear my teachers address me in Spanish when I entered the classroom. I would have felt much less afraid. I would have trusted them and responded with ease. But I would have delayed—for how long postponed?—having to learn the language of public society, I would have evaded—and for how long could I have afforded to delay?—learning the great lesson of school, that I had a public identity.

Fortunately, my teachers were unsentimental about their responsibility. What they understood was that I needed to speak a public language. So their voices would search me out, asking me questions. Each time I'd hear them, I'd look up in surprise to see a nun's face frowning at me. I'd mumble, not really meaning to answer. The nun would persist, "Richard, stand up. Don't look at the floor. Speak up. Speak to the entire class, not just to me!" But I couldn't believe that the English language was mine to use. (In part, I did not want to believe it.) I continued to mumble. I resisted the teacher's demands. (Did I somehow suspect that once I learned public language my pleasing family life would be changed?) Silent, waiting for the bell to sound, I remained dazed, diffident, afraid.

Because I wrongly imagined that English was intrinsically a public language and Spanish an intrinsically private one, I easily noted the difference between classroom language and the language of home. At school, words were directed to a general audience of listeners. ("Boys and girls.") Words were meaningfully ordered. And the point was not self-expression alone but to make oneself understood by many others. The teacher quizzed: "Boys and girls, why do we use that word in this sentence? Could we think of a better word to use there? Would the sentence change its meaning if the words were differently arranged? And wasn't there a better way of saying much the same thing?" (I couldn't say. I wouldn't try to say.)

Three months. Five. Half a year passed. Unsmiling, ever watchful, my teachers noted my silence. They began to connect my behavior with the difficult progress my older sister and brother were making. Until one Saturday morning three nuns arrived at the house to talk to our parents. Stiffly, they sat on the blue living room sofa. From the doorway of another room, spying the visitors, I noted the incongruity—the clash of two worlds, the faces and voices of school intruding upon the familiar setting of home. I overheard one voice gently wondering, "Do your children speak only Spanish at home, Mrs. Rodriguez?" While another voice added, "That Richard especially seems so timid and shy."

That Rich-heard!

With great tact the visitors continued, "Is it possible for you and your husband to encourage your children to practice their English when they are home?" Of course, my parents complied. What would they not do for their children's well-being? And how could they have questioned the Church's authority which those women represented? In an instant, they agreed to give up the language (the sounds) that had revealed and accentuated our family's closeness. The moment after the visitors left, the change was observed, "*Ahora,* speak to us *en inglés,* my father and mother united to tell us.

At first, it seemed a kind of game. After dinner each night, the family gathered to practice "our" English. (It was still then *inglés,* a language foreign to us, so we felt drawn as strangers to it.) Laughing, we would try to define words we could not pronounce. We played with strange English sounds, often overanglicizing our pronunciations. And we filled the smiling gaps of our sentences with familiar Spanish sounds. But that was cheating, somebody shouted. Everyone laughed. In school, meanwhile, like my brother and sister, I was required to attend a daily tutoring session. I needed a full year of special attention. I also needed my teachers to keep my attention from straying in class by calling out, *Rich-heard*—their English voices slowly prying loose my ties to my other name, its three notes, *Ri-car-do.* Most of all I needed to hear my mother and father speak to me in a moment of seriousness in broken—suddenly heartbreaking—English. The scene was inevitable: One Saturday morning I entered the kitchen where my parents were talking in Spanish. I did not realize that they were talking in Spanish however until, at the moment they saw me, I heard their voices change to speak English. Those *gringo* sounds they uttered startled me. Pushed me away. In that moment of trivial misunderstanding and profound insight, I felt my throat twisted by unsounded grief. I turned quickly and left the room. But I had no place to escape to with Spanish. (The spell was broken.) My brother and sisters were speaking English in another part of the house.

Again and again in the days following, increasingly angry, I was obliged to hear my mother and father: "Speak to us *en inglés*" (*Speak.*) Only then did I determine to learn classroom English. Weeks after, it happened: One day in school I raised my hand to volunteer an answer. I spoke out in a loud voice. And I did not think it remarkable when the entire class understood. That day, I moved very far from the disadvantaged child I had been only days earlier. The belief, that calming assurance that I belonged in public, had at last taken hold.

Shortly after, I stopped hearing the high and loud sounds of *los gringos*. A more and more confident speaker of English, I didn't trouble to listen to *how* strangers sounded, speaking to me. And there simply were too many English-speaking people in my day for me to hear American accents anymore. Conversations quickened. Listening to persons who sounded eccentrically pitched voices, I usually noted their sounds for an initial few seconds before I concentrated on *what* they were saying. Conversations became content-full. Transparent. Hearing someone's *tone* of voice—angry or questioning or sarcastic or happy or sad—I didn't distinguish it from the words it expressed. Sound and word were thus tightly wedded. At the end of a day, I was often bemused, always relieved, to realize how "silent," though crowded with words, my day in public had been. (This public silence measured and quickened the change in my life.)

At last, seven years old, I came to believe what had been technically true since my birth: I was an American citizen.

But the special feeling of closeness at home was diminished by then. Gone was the desperate, urgent, intense feeling of being at home, rare was the experience of feeling myself individualized by family intimates. We remained a loving family, but one greatly changed. No longer so close; no longer bound tight by the pleasing and troubling knowledge of our public separateness. Neither my older brother nor sister rushed home after school anymore. Nor did I. When I arrived home there would often be neighborhood kids in the house. Or the house would be empty of sounds.

Following the dramatic Americanization of their children, even my parents grew more publicly confident. Especially my mother. She learned the names of all the people on our block. And she decided we needed to have a telephone installed in the house. My father continued to use the word *gringo*. But it was no longer charged with the old bitterness or distrust. (Stripped of any emotional content, the word simply became a name for those Americans not of Hispanic descent.) Hearing him, sometimes, I wasn't sure if he was pronouncing the Spanish word *gringo* or saying gringo in English.

Matching the silence I started hearing in public was a new quiet at home. The family's quiet was partly due to the fact that, as we children learned more and more English, we shared fewer and fewer words with our parents. Sentences needed to be spoken slowly when a child addressed his mother or father. (Often the parent wouldn't understand.) The child would need to repeat himself. (Still the parent misunderstood.) The young voice, frustrated, would end up saying, "Never mind"—the subject was closed. Dinners would be noisy with the clinking of knives and forks against dishes. My mother would smile softly between her remarks; my father at the other end of the table would chew and chew at his food, while he stared over the heads of his children.

My *mother!* My *father!* After English became my primary language, I no longer knew what words to use in addressing my parents. The old Spanish words (those tender accents of sound) I had used earlier—*mamá* and *papá*—I couldn't use anymore. They would have been too painful reminders of how much had changed in my life. On the other hand, the words I heard neighborhood kids call their parents seemed equally unsatisfactory. *Mother* and *Father; Ma, Papa, Pa, Dad, Pop* (how I hated the all American sound of that last word especially)—all these terms I felt were unsuitable, not really terms of address for my parents. As a result, I never used them at home. Whenever I'd speak to my parents, I would try to get their attention with eye contact alone. In public conversations, I'd refer to "my parents" or "my mother and father."

My mother and father, for their part, responded differently, as their children spoke to them less. She grew restless, seemed troubled and anxious at the scarcity of words exchanged in the house. It was she who would question me about my day when I came home from school. She smiled at small talk. She pried at the edges of my sentences to get me to say something more. (What?) She'd join conversations she overheard, but her intrusions often stopped her children's talking. By contrast, my father seemed reconciled to the new quiet. Though his English improved somewhat, he retired into silence. At dinner he spoke very little. One night his children and even his wife helplessly giggled at his garbled English pronunciation of the Catholic Grace before Meals. Thereafter he made his wife recite the prayer at the start of each meal, even on formal occasions, when there were guests in the house. Hers became the public voice of the family. On official business, it was she, not my father, one would usually hear on the phone or in stores, talking to strangers. His children grew so accustomed to his silence that, years later, they would speak routinely of his shyness. (My mother would often try to explain: Both his parents died when he was eight. He was raised by an uncle who treated him like little more than a menial servant. He was never encouraged to speak. He grew up alone. A man of few words.) But my father was not shy, I realized, when I'd watch him speaking Spanish with relatives. Using Spanish, he was quickly effusive. Especially when talking with other men, his voice would spark, flicker, flare alive with sounds. In Spanish, he expressed ideas and feelings he rarely revealed in English. With firm Spanish sounds, he conveyed confidence and authority English would never allow him.

The silence at home, however, was finally more than a literal silence. Fewer words passed between parent and child, but more profound was the silence that resulted from my inattention to sounds. At about the time I no longer bothered to listen with care to the sounds of English in public, I grew careless about listening to the sounds family members made when they spoke. Most of the time I heard someone speaking at home and didn't distinguish his sounds from the words people uttered in public. I didn't even pay much attention to my parents' accented and ungrammatical speech. At least not at home. Only when I was with them in public would I grow alert to their accents. Though, even then, their sounds caused me less and less concern. For I was increasingly confident of my own public identity.

I would have been happier about my public success had I not sometimes recalled what it had been like earlier, when my family had conveyed its intimacy through a set of conveniently private sounds. Sometimes in public, hearing a stranger, I'd hark back to my past. A Mexican farmworker approached me downtown to ask directions to somewhere, "¿*Hijito* . . . ?" he said. And his voice summoned deep longing. Another time, standing beside my mother in the visiting room of a Carmelite convent, before the dense screen which rendered the nuns shadowy figures, I heard several Spanish-speaking nuns—their busy, singsong overlapping voices—assure us that yes, yes, we were remembered, all our family was remembered in their prayers. (Their voices echoed faraway family sounds.) Another day, a dark-faced old woman—her hand light on my shoulder—steadied herself against me as she boarded a bus. She murmured something I couldn't quite comprehend. Her Spanish voice came near, like the face of a never-before-seen relative in the instant before I was kissed. Her voice, like so many of the Spanish voices I'd hear in public, recalled the golden age of my youth. Hearing Spanish then, I continued to be a careful, if sad, listener to sounds. Hearing a Spanish-speaking family walking behind me, I turned to look. I smiled for an instant, before my glance found the Hispanic-looking faces of strangers in the crowd going by.

Today I hear bilingual educators say that children lose a degree of "individuality" by becoming assimilated into public society. (Bilingual schooling was popularized in the seventies, that decade when middle-class ethnics began to resist the process of assimilation—the American melting pot). But the bilingualists simplistically scorn the value and necessity of assimilation. They do not seem to realize that there are *two* ways a person is individualized. So they do not realize that while one suffers a diminished sense of *private* individuality by becoming assimilated into public society, such assimilation makes possible the achievement of *public* individuality.

The bilingualists insist that a student should be reminded of his difference from others in mass society, his heritage. But they equate mere separateness with individuality. The fact is that only in private—with intimates—is separateness from the crowd a prerequisite for individuality. (An intimate draws me apart, tells me that I am unique, unlike all others.) In public, by contrast, full individuality is achieved, paradoxically, by those who are able to consider themselves members of the crowd. Thus it happened for me: Only when I was able to think of myself as an American, no longer an alien in *gringo* society, could I seek the rights and opportunities necessary for full public individuality. The social and political advantages I enjoy as a man result from the day that I came to believe that my name, indeed, is *Rich-heard Road-ree-guess.* It is true that my public society today is often impersonal. (My public society is usually mass society.) Yet despite the anonymity of the crowd and despite the fact that the individuality I achieve in public is often tenuous—because it depends on my being one in a crowd—I celebrate the day I acquired my new name. Those middle-class ethnics who scorn assimilation seem to me filled with decadent self-pity, obsessed by the burden of public life. Dangerously, they romanticize public separateness and they trivialize the dilemma of the socially disadvantaged.

My awkward childhood does not prove the necessity of bilingual education. My story discloses instead an essential myth of childhood—inevitable pain. If I rehearse here the changes in my private life after my Americanization, it is finally to emphasize the public gain. The loss implies the gain: The house I returned to each afternoon was quiet. Intimate sounds no longer rushed to the door to greet me. There were other noises inside. The telephone rang. Neighborhood kids ran past the door of the bedroom where I was reading my school-books—covered with shopping-bag paper. Once I learned public language, it would never again be easy for me to hear intimate family voices. More and more of my day was spent hearing words. But that may only be a way of saying that the day I raised my hand in class and spoke loudly to an entire roomful of faces, my childhood started to end.

My Critical Questions

1. _____

_____ **?**

2. _____

   _____ **?**

3. _____

   _____ **?**

Isaac Newton

James Shipman, Jerry Wilson, and Aaron Todd

I saac Newton and Albert Einstein are usually considered to be the two greatest scientists in history. Newton's laws of motion were some of many contributions he made to a variety of subjects in physics. Newton was born on Christmas day in 1642 in the village of Woolsthorpe in Lincolnshire, England. He showed no particular genius in his early schooling, but fortunately a teacher encouraged him to pursue his education, and in 1661 he entered Trinity College at Cambridge.

Four years later he received his degree. He planned to continue studying for a master's degree, but an epidemic of the bubonic plague broke out and the university was closed. Newton returned to Woolsthorpe, and in the next two years he laid the groundwork for many of his contributions in physics, mathematics, and astronomy. In Newton's own words, "I was in the prime of my age for invention, and minded mathematics and philosophy [science] more than any time since."

Over the next 20 years Newton was very productive, and at the age of 45 he published his famous treatise, *Philosophiae Naturalis Principia Mathematica* [*Mathematical Principles of Natural Philosophy*],[1] or *Principia* for short. In this book he set forth his laws of motion, together with the theory of gravitation. The publication of the *Principia* was financed by a friend, Edmund Halley, who used Newton's theories to predict the return of the comet that bears his name.

Newton was reportedly a shy man, but he often got into disputes about his theories and achievements. His dispute with Gottfried Leibniz about who first developed calculus is famous. Newton was elected to Parliament and later appointed Master of the Mint, where he supervised the task of recoining the English currency. He was knighted by Queen Anne in 1705.

----

[1]Physics was once called natural philosophy.

Sir Isaac Newton died in 1727 at the age of 85 and was buried with honor in Westminster Abbey. Some insight about this austere bachelor and giant of science may be gleaned from the following excerpts from his writings.

I seem to have been only like a boy playing on the seashore and diverting myself in now and then finding a smoother pebble or a prettier shell than ordinary, whilst the great ocean of truth lay all undiscovered before me.

If I have been able to see farther than some, it is because I have stood on the shoulders of giants.

About Newton, the poet Alexander Pope wrote:

Nature and Nature's laws lay hid in night:
God said, Let Newton be! and all was light.

My Critical Questions

1. _____

_____ **?**

2. _____

_____ **?**

3. _____

_____ **?**

The "Wasty Ways" of Pioneers

by James Fenimore Cooper

Elizabeth was awakened by the exhilarating sounds of the martins, who were quarreling and chattering around the little boxes that were suspended above her windows, and the cries of Richard, who was calling, in tones as animating as the signs of the season itself—

"Awake! awake! my lady fair! the gulls are hovering over the lake already, and the heavens are alive with the pigeons. You may look an hour before you can find a hole, through which to get a peep at the sun. Awake! awake! lazy ones! Benjamin is overhauling the ammunition, and we only wait for our breakfasts, and away for the mountains and pigeon shooting." . . .

If the heavens were alive with pigeons, the whole village seemed equally in motion, with men, women, and children. Every species of fire-arms, from the French ducking-gun, with its barrel of near six-feet in length, to the common horseman's pistol, was to be seen in the hands of the men and boys; while bows and arrows, some made of the simple stick of a walnut sapling, and others in a rude imitation of the ancient crossbows, were carried by many of the latter. . . .

Among the sportsmen was to be seen the tall, gaunt form of Leather-stocking [Natty Bumppo], who was walking over the field, with his rifle hanging on his arm, his dogs following at his heels, now scenting the dead or wounded birds, that were beginning to tumble from the flocks, and then crouching under the legs of their master, as if they participated in his feelings at this wasteful and unsportsmanlike execution.

The reports of the fire-arms became rapid, whole volleys rising from the plain, as flocks of more than ordinary numbers darted over the opening, covering the field with darkness, like an interposing cloud; and then the light smoke of a single piece would issue from among the leafless bushes on the mountain, as death was hurled on the retreat of the affrighted birds, who were rising from a volley, for many feet into the air, in a vain effort to escape the attacks of man. Arrows, and missiles of every kind, were seen in the midst of the flocks; and so numerous were the birds, and so low did they take their flight, that even long poles, in the hands of those on the sides of the mountain, were used to strike them to earth. . . .

So prodigious was the number of the birds, that the scattering fire of the guns, with the hurling of missiles, and the cries of the boys, had no other effect than to break off small flocks from the immense masses that continued to dart along the valley, as if the whole creation of the feathered tribe were pouring through that one pass. None pretended to collect the game, which lay scattered over the fields in such profusion as to cover the very ground with the fluttering victims.

Leather-stocking was a silent, but uneasy spectator of all these proceedings, but was able to keep his sentiments to himself until he saw the introduction of the swivel into the sports.

"This comes of settling a country!" he said—"here have I known the pigeons to fly for forty long years, and, till you made your clearings, there was nobody to skear or to hurt them. I loved to see them come into the woods, for they were company to a body; hurting nothing; being, as it was, as harmless as a garter-snake. But now it gives me sore thoughts when I hear the frighty things whizzing through the air, for I know its only a motion to bring out all the brats in the village at them. . . .

Among the sportsmen was Billy Kirby, who, armed with an old musket, was leading, and without even looking into the air, was firing and shouting as his victims fell even on his own person. He heard the speech of Natty, and took upon himself to reply—

"What's that, old Leather-stocking!" he cried, "grumbling at the loss of a few pigeons! If you had to sow your wheat twice, and three times, as I have done, you wouldn't be so massyfully feeling'd to'ards the divils.—Hurrah, boys! Scatter the feathers. This is better than shooting at a turkey's head and neck, old fellow."

"It's better for you, maybe, Billy Kirby," replied the indignant old hunter, "and all them as don't know how to put a ball down a rifle barrel, or how to bring it up ag'n with a true aim; but it's wicked to be shooting into flocks in this wasty manner; and none do it, who know how to knock over a single bird. If a body has a craving for pigeon's flesh, why! it's made the same as all other creater's, for man's eating, but not to kill twenty and eat one. When I want such a thing I go into the woods till I find one to my liking, and then I shoot him off the branches without touching a feather of another, though there might be a hundred on the same tree. But you couldn't do such a thing, Billy Kirby—you couldn't do it if you tried."

"What's that you say, you old dried cornstalk! you sapless stub!" cried the wood-chopper. "You've grown mighty boasting, sin' you killed the turkey; but if you're for a single shot, here goes at that bird which comes on by himself."

. . . A single pigeon . . . was approaching the spot where the disputants stood, darting first from one side, and then to the other, cutting the air with the swiftness of lightning, and making a noise with its wings, not unlike the rushing of a bullet. Unfortunately for the woodchopper, notwithstanding his vaunt, he did not see his bird until it was too late for him to fire as it approached, and he pulled his trigger at the unlucky moment when it was darting immediately over his head. The bird continued its course with incredible velocity.

Natty lowered the rifle from his arm, when the challenge was made, and, waiting a moment, until the terrified victim had got in a line with his eyes, and had dropped near the bank of the lake, he raised it again with uncommon rapidity, and fired. It might have been chance, or it might have been skill, that produced the result; it was probably a union of both; but the pigeon whirled over in the air, and fell into the lake with a broken wing. At the sound of his rifle, both his dogs started from his feet, and in a few minutes the "slut" brought out the bird, still alive.

The wonderful exploit of Leather-stocking was noised through the field with great rapidity, and the sportsmen gathered in to learn the truth of the report.

"What," said young Edwards, "have you really killed a pigeon on the wing, Natty, with a single ball?"

"Haven't I killed loons before now, lad, that dive at the flash?" returned the hunter. "It's much better to kill only such as you want, without wasting your powder and lead, than to be firing into God's creaters in such a wicked manner. But I come out for a bird, and you know the reason why I like small game, Mr. Oliver, and now I have got one I will go home, for I don't relish to see these wasty ways that you are all practysing, as if the least thing wasn't made for use, and not to destroy."

"Thou sayest well, Leather-stocking," cried Marmaduke, "and I begin to think it time to put an end to this work of destruction."

"Put an ind, Judge, to your clearings. An't the woods His work as well as the pigeons? Use, but don't waste. Wasn't the woods made for the beasts and birds to harbour in? And when man wanted their flesh, their skins, or their feathers, there's the place to seek them. But I'll go to the hut with my own game, for I wouldn't touch one of the harmless things that kiver the ground here, looking up with their eyes on me, as if they only wanted tongues to say their thoughts."

With this sentiment in his mouth, Leather-stocking threw his rifle over his arm, and followed by his dogs, stepping across the clearing with great caution, taking care not to tread on one of the wounded birds that lay in his path, he soon entered the bushes on the margin and was hid from view.

My Critical Questions

1. _____

   _____ **?**

2. _____

   _____ **?**

3. _____

   _____ **?**

Classifying and Sequencing

ESSENTIAL THINKING SKILLS		
CHAPTER	**WHAT THEY'RE CALLED**	**WHAT THEY MEAN**
Chapter 3	**The Gathering Skills**	**Gathering all the information.**
	Observing	Actively seeking information through one or more senses.
	Questioning	Seeking information by asking questions.
Chapter 4	**The Organizing Skills**	**Organizing for the purpose of making sense.**
	Comparing and Contrasting	Noting similarities and differences between two or more things, events, or ideas.
	Classifying and Sequencing	Arranging things or concepts into categories and into sequential order.
	Identifying Cause and Effect	Recognizing the relationship between an effect and its cause.
Chapter 5	**The Generating Skills**	**Generating additional information.**
	Inferring	Making an assumption, stating a hypothesis, or coming to a conclusion based on limited information.
	Summarizing	Condensing the essence of the information accurately and efficiently.
	Synthesizing	Creating new information by combining two or more pieces of information.
	Generating Ideas	Creating new information, alternatives, or applications.
Chapter 6	**The Recognizing Skills**	**Recognizing what has been left unsaid.**
	Recognizing Purpose	Identifying a writer's or speaker's intention.
	Recognizing Fact and Opinion	Distinguishing between a statement of fact and a statement of opinion.
	Recognizing Tone	Identifying a sentiment or mood by assessing the writer's or speaker's choice of words.
	Recognizing Bias	Noting the presence and nature of a writer's or speaker's prejudice.
	Recognizing Organization	Identifying the organizational pattern of a thought, statement, passage, or plan.
	Recognizing Underlying Assumptions	Recognizing the suppositions that are taken for granted and are the foundation of a proposition, notion, or idea.
Chapter 7	**The Analyzing Skills**	**Analyzing for the purpose of coming to a conclusion.**
	Analyzing	Identifying and separating ideas, attributes, situations, and/or components in order to form a conclusion as to their relationship.
	Evaluating	Appraising something according to certain criteria and forming a judgment as to its worth or quality.
	Inducing	Analyzing individual facts or premises in order to derive a general conclusion.
	Deducing	Applying general principles or a broad framework to a situation in order to come to a conclusion about it.

"One can live in the shadow of an idea without grasping it."
—Elizabeth Bowen

"Sometimes I sits and thinks, and then again I just sits."
—Punch

What questions am I going to have answered in this section on classifying and sequencing?

1. What are classifying and sequencing, how are they different, and how do they work together?
2. What thinking process do we go through when we classify?
3. What thinking process do we go through when we sequence?

> **CLASSIFYING:**
> **Arranging things or concepts into groups or categories according to a shared characteristic**

> **SEQUENCING:**
> **Putting things or concepts in sequential order according to some criterion**

The two thinking skills of classifying and sequencing—really just extensions of comparing and contrasting—are usually learned together because of the natural relationship between them.

TO CLASSIFY IS TO SORT

When we classify things or ideas, we sort and group them according to one or more attributes that they have in common—and we do this kind of thing all the time. We classify when we call one person a friend, another person an enemy, and a third person a stranger, or when we describe ourselves as college freshmen, or when we call *Gone With the Wind* a great American movie (as opposed to a British or Australian movie). Our houses are great examples of classifying in action. The house itself is divided into rooms according to the activities that occur

THINK ABOUT THIS!

Step One, Step Two, Step Three . . .

Every plan of action needs to be broken down into simpler actions, or steps. Select a project from the list below and write down the steps you need to take to carry out the project successfully. Some of the suggested projects are easier than others. Don't be a wimp and choose an easy one. Go for a tough project. List alternatives where appropriate, if things don't go according to plan at any point in your steps.

Projects

Buying a home computer sufficient for your needs for the next three years
Opening a Mexican restaurant
Writing a thirty-page research paper for a world history class
Making a fortune in real estate
Keeping and training a pot-bellied pig
Organizing and conducting a fund-raising campaign for a campus organization
Convincing an acquaintance who detests you to fall in love with you
Clearing your neighborhood streets of drug dealers
Making a violin
Creating a new variety of rose
Losing thirty pounds and keeping it off for five years

_____

_____

_____

_____

_____

_____

_____

_____

_____

in them: "living" in the living room, sleeping in the bedrooms, bathing in the bathroom. In organizing our kitchens, we classify when we group things (put things in cupboards and drawers) according to certain shared attributes or functions: silverware in the silverware drawer, pots and pans in one cupboard, dishware in another cupboard, and canned goods, spices, soap, and so on in other locations. Classifying the contents of our kitchen this way makes it easier for us to locate items when we want to, and it makes cooking in the kitchen more efficient. In like manner, understanding how to classify enables us to answer questions like these:

- Which basic food groups are represented in this meal?

- Based on the lecture you have just heard about the solar system, what do Earth, Mars, Venus, and Neptune have in common?

- On what basis are the life forms listed below determined to be part of the phylum Chordata?

THINKERS

Which number among the choices below is next in this series, and why?

4, 10, 11, 3, 14 . . .

Choices: 44, 1, 41, 12

Need a Hint?
Numbers can have relationships that aren't mathematical. How about shape relationships?

TO SEQUENCE THINGS IS
TO ARRANGE THEM IN ORDER

When we sequence things or ideas, we may also sort them, but we sort them according to *an order or priority within the group*. We put them in some order according to an identified criterion: small to large, first to last, light to dark, oldest to newest, and so forth. Like classifying, sequencing allows for more efficient use of the sequenced things or ideas. In many activities, sequencing is vital to success. A recipe is a sequence that assures (usually) a cook a certain uniformity of food product when the sequence is followed. Librarians are *classifying* when they arrange periodicals on shelves according to the periodical name, but they are *sequencing* those periodicals when they arrange them according to date of publication, from the oldest to the current edition. Sequencing is used in answering the following questions:

- In what order should we arrange these dinosaur teeth if we want the most ancient to come first and the most recent to come last?

- Which countries have the lowest infant mortality rate?

- List Columbus, Marco Polo, Magellan, and Cortez in order according to distance traveled.

HOW DO WE CLASSIFY?

The procedure we go through when we classify things or ideas is relatively simple.

1. *We first identify our purpose or goal.* (We want to place the animals we have been studying in zoology into as few categories as possible.)

2. *We then glance at the information or list of items to note interesting features that may give us an idea for our classifications.* What similarities do the items have (the items being bears, cattle, chickens, coyotes, deer, foxes, frogs, grasshoppers, humans, lions, mice, rabbits, seals, squirrels, wolves)?

3. *Try out a set of criteria to see if it works.* (These animals all eat something. Group them according to what they eat: herbivores eat only plant material, carnivores eat meat, omnivores eat both.)

4. *Take the first "label" and describe its classifying feature.* (Herbivores are animals that eat only plant material.)

5. *Identify the items or ideas that share that label, that classifying feature.* (Cattle, chickens, deer, grasshoppers, rabbits, and squirrels eat plant material.)

6. *Repeat, starting another group.* (Coyotes, foxes, lions, seals, and wolves eat meat, so they are carnivores. Bears and humans eat both meat and plant material, so they are omnivores.)

7. *Check to see that all items or ideas are classified.* (Oops. What about mice and frogs? They eat bugs and other critters, but don't they also eat some plant material?)

8. *Decide what to do with the "leftovers."* (Put mice and frogs with the omnivores until you check their diets.)

9. *Decide if combining groups or subclassifications are possible or desirable.* (Herbivores could be divided into mammals, birds, and insects, but it isn't necessary for your present purposes.)

ANY QUESTIONS?

Many questions have humorous answers, but can you come up with some questions that are funny no matter what the answer is? Here are some examples to stimulate your thinking:

Should men who wear skirts shave their legs?

Who invented circumcision, and how did he or she convince someone to try it?

When people are born they are very small and gradually they grow tall to a certain height. How come when they stop growing, they don't start to gradually diminish in size?

How can a family of three make twenty-seven bags of garbage out of six bags of groceries?

Do fish have necks?

Where did barn swallows nest before there were barns?

I've heard that rabbits have a very high body temperature and that the heat dissipates through their long ears. How many rabbits would it take to heat a three-room apartment when the temperature outside is forty-five degrees?

When you cut a few matted tangles of fur on your pet, how does that hair know to grow back to the same length as the surrounding, uncut hair?

Many people have seen UFOs with lights on them. Why would a UFO need lights on it?

Why did Mother Nature use wood when she decided to make a tree?

Why is C the third letter of the alphabet? Q would have been a better choice.

HOW DO WE SEQUENCE?

For most of us, putting items and ideas in some sort of order is a relatively simple task.

1. *First we look at the items or ideas and determine the possible ways to order them.* Some options are: general to specific, least understandable to most understandable, largest to smallest, least interesting to most interesting, oldest to newest, loudest to quietest, brightest to darkest, least expensive to most expensive, first to last, softest to hardest, and so forth.

2. *We select the most appropriate sequence type for our purpose.* Nearly all items and ideas can be sequenced in many different ways. Choose the most appropriate for your purpose. For example, a company in financial difficulty can implement a variety of cost-cutting ideas. Its managers will most likely choose to implement those ideas in an order (a sequence) that produces the greatest savings the quickest. The managers aren't likely to implement the cost-cutting ideas in the order of most enjoyable to least enjoyable, although that too is an option. On the other hand, the enjoyability factor might be very appropriate for determining in what order you do things while on a three-day vacation.

STIR IT UP 4.5   Test your sequencing abilities by determining what you need in order to survive on another planet. Try this exercise by determining your own priorities first, and then team up with one or more students in the class to work together. Be ready to share your rankings and the group's rankings with the class, along with the reasons for your rankings.

The Lambda Orionis IV Survival Test

Your spaceship has just landed on the daylight side of the planet Lambda Orionis IV. You were scheduled to rendezvous with your mother ship 200 miles away on the surface of the planet, but the rough landing has ruined your ship and destroyed all the equipment on board, except for the 15 items listed below. You and your crew's survival depends on reaching the mother ship, so you must choose the most critical items available for the 200-mile trip. Your task is to rank the 15 items in terms of their importance for survival. Place the number 1 by the most important item, number 2 by the second most important, and so on through 15, the least important. On the line next to each item briefly indicate why you think it is important or for what purpose you plan to use the item.

_____ Box of matches _____

_____ Food concentrate _____

_____ Fifty feet of nylon rope _____

_____ Parachute silk _____

_____ Solar-powered portable heating unit _____

_____ Two 45-caliber pistols _____

_____ One case of dehydrated milk _____

_____ Two 100-pound tanks of oxygen _____

_____ Local stellar map _____

_____ Self-inflating life raft _____

_____ Magnetic compass _____

_____ Five gallons of water _____

_____ Signal flares _____

_____ First-aid kit including hypodermic needles _____

_____ Solar-powered FM receiver-transmitter _____

THINKERS

What letter comes next in this series?

W L C N I T

Need a Hint?
The answer is built into the question.

STIR IT UP 4.6   The Desert Dilemma

One of the best methods of problem solving is listing options and then ranking them, something most of us fail to do very often. Assume the following: You are stranded in the desert dressed in summer clothing. In your desperation you have driven fifty miles off the road, and now your car is out of gas. There is nothing around you but cactus and sand, and it is 110 degrees in the shade—but there is no shade. You must try to reach the highway. You can carry only a limited number of things with you. Look at the list below. Your task is to rank the fifteen items in order of their importance and utility in ensuring your survival. Place 1 by the most important item, 2 by the second most important, and so on through 16, the least important survival item. Consider what you know about the desert in making your decisions. When you are finished, be ready to discuss your reasons for ranking each item as you did.

_____ Any part of the car   _____ First-aid kit

_____ Sunglasses   _____ AM-FM radio

_____	50 feet of nylon rope	_____	Lipstick
_____	Four chocolate bars	_____	Blanket
_____	Map of the state	_____	Slingshot
_____	Box of matches	_____	Pair of boots
_____	Silk scarf	_____	Propane lamp
_____	Packet of powdered soft-drink mix	_____	Wallet or purse

STIR IT UP 4.7   Another successful element of problem solving involves breaking up a large complex plan of action into a series of actions and then sequencing them in the most effective order. Select any five of the following projects and write out the steps you need to take to accomplish them. Sequence the steps in the most effective order. List two possible alternative steps for each project you select if things don't go according to plan.

Traveling to Timbuktu

Becoming fluent in Japanese

Becoming a lighting designer for a rock band

Building an addition to your home

Making a zip gun

Buying a coin collection

Organizing an immunization campaign in a third-world country

Starting a local newspaper

Starting a Chinese restaurant

Journal Observations (see page 13)

CLASSIFYING AND SEQUENCING

1st Writing _____

_____

_____

_____

_____

_____

_____

_____

_____

_____

_____

2nd Writing _____

_____

_____

_____

_____

_____

_____

_____

_____

_____

_____

_____

3rd Writing _____

_____

_____

_____

_____

_____

_____

_____

_____

_____

READINGS   **Is Sex Doomed?**

Joseph Levine and Kenneth Miller

One of the most widely known flowering plants is *Taraxacum offici-nale.* This organism thrives in areas of high light intensity, including frequently mowed lawns. It is exceptionally hardy, blooms early in the spring, and produces hundreds of seeds just a few days after blooming. The dandelion, as *Taraxacum officinale* is more commonly known, is one of a handful of plants that have adapted well to twentieth-century suburban life. It has survived even the most vigorous attempts to exterminate it. Could the dandelion be an example of how sexual recombination shuffles genes to achieve the greatest degree of fitness in a population? Not really. Beneath the fields of glistening yellow flowers, the humble, successful dandelion conceals a dark secret: it is one of a handful of plants that have abandoned sex.

For years, evolutionary biologists have been puzzled about why sexual reproduction is so widespread. Although sexual recombination does produce new combinations of genes, the constant and random mixing also makes it more difficult for a beneficial gene to be passed on to the next generation. Asexually reproducing organisms face no such problems; offspring are identical to parents, so beneficial genes take hold in a population quickly. The dandelion seems to have taken a first step along the road to producing identical offspring by abandoning the sexual process.

Although dandelions seem to be typical composite flowers, the pollen they produce is sterile. Furthermore, the female megagametophyte mother cell does not undergo meiosis to produce a haploid gametophyte. Instead, the diploid egg cell begins to develop into an embryo and quickly produces seeds that are genetically identical to the mother plant. The technical name for this process in plants is *apomixis*. Interestingly, although fertilization of the egg does not occur, pollination is still important to development in dandelions: the application of pollen to the carpel seems to serve as a signal that development should proceed. Thus the dandelion has discarded the gametophyte stage of the plant life cycle along with sex. The significance of a "higher" plant going asexual has not been lost on biologists. One might also say that dandelions have discarded our concept of *species* as well. Our definition of this term depends in part on the ability of organisms to interbreed. Because dandelions do not interbreed under any circumstances, they have led biologists to wonder whether the species concept can still be applied to them.

It is possible that dandelions are onto a good thing. They may have discovered that sex is too much trouble, too chancy, too random, and too conservative in the evolutionary sense. They retain the appearance of normal flowers and the need for a pollination signal as evolutionary remnants of processes that they have not yet completely discarded, suggesting that their not-too-distant ancestors at one time reproduced by means of a typical sexual cycle.

Only time will tell whether the dandelions are just an interesting experiment or the harbinger of things to come. Certainly we need not yet conclude that the sexual processes of flowering plants, which have filled the world with such beauty and provided so much inspiration, are about to be pushed off the scene. Just further motivation, perhaps, for those homeowners who resolutely set the lawn mower blades a little lower and cut off every little yellow flower they can reach.

Read and Respond

1. What do we know for a fact about dandelions? Not what do we *think* is true, what do we *know*? Make a list of dandelion facts presented in this article. How do these facts compare with what we assumed to be true about dandelions? Do you know to be true more than you

assumed before this article or are you assuming more than you really know?

2. What are the implications for us of this information on dandelion reproduction? Where does it lead researchers? What might it suggest?

Moving Pictures Evoke Concern

Henry Myers

Moving pictures, their educational influence for good or for bad, their growing importance as a factor in our civilization, the announced determination of those controlling the industry boldly to enter politics, and the desirability of regulation by law through censorship constitute a subject of acknowledged importance to the American people. . . .

The motion picture is a great invention, and it has become a powerful factor for good or bad in our civilization. It has great educational power for good or bad. It may educate young people in the ways of good citizenship or in ways of dissoluteness, extravagance, wickedness, and crime. It furnishes recreation, diversion, and amusement at a cheap price to many millions of our people—largely the young. It is the only form of amusement within the means of millions. It possesses great potential possibilities for good. It may furnish not only amusement but education of a high order.

Through motion pictures the young and the old may see depicted every good motive, laudable ambition, commendable characteristic, ennobling trait of humanity. They may be taught that honesty is the best policy; that virtue and worth are rewarded; that industry leads to success. Those who live in the country or in small interior towns, and who never visit large cities, may see pictured the skyscrapers, the crowded streets, the rush and jam of metropolitan cities. Those who live in the interior, and never see the seacoast, may see on the screen the great docks and wharves of seaports and see the loading and unloading of giant ocean steamers. Those who live in crowded cities, and never see the country or get a glimpse of country life, may have depicted to them all the beauties of rural life and scenery. All may see scenes of the luxuriant Tropics, the grandeur of Alpine Mountains, polar conditions, life in the Orient. The cities, palaces, cathedrals, ports, rural life, daily routine, scenic attractions, mode of living of every country on the globe, may be brought to our doors and eyes for a small price. The industry may be made an education to the young.

However, from all accounts, the business has been conducted, generally speaking, upon a low plane and in a decidedly sordid manner. Those who own and control the industry seem to have been of the opinion that the sensual, the sordid, the prurient, the phases of fast life, the ways of extravagance, the risqué, the paths of shady life, drew the greatest attendance and coined for them the most money, and apparently they have been out to get the coin, no matter what the effect upon the public, young or old; and when thoughtful people have suggested or advocated official censorship, in the interest of good citizenship and wholesome morals, the owners of the industry have resented it and, in effect, declared that it was nobody's business other than theirs and concerned nobody other than them what kind of shows they produced; that if people did not like their shows they could stay away from them; that it was their business, and they would conduct it as they might please. At least they have vigorously fought all attempts at censorship and resented them. . . .

I have no doubt young criminals got their ideas of the romance of crime from moving pictures. I believe moving pictures are doing as much harm to-day as saloons did in the days of the open saloon—especially to the young. They are running day and night, Sunday and every other day, the year round, and in most jurisdictions without any regulation by censorship. I would not abolish them. They can be made a great force for good. I would close them on Sunday and regulate them week days by judicious censorship. Already some dozen or more States have censorship laws, with the right of appeal to the courts, and the movement is on in many other States.

When we look to the source of the moving pictures, the material for them, the personnel of those who pose for them, we need not wonder that many of the pictures are pernicious.

The pictures are largely furnished by such characters as Fatty Arbuckle, of unsavory fame, notorious for his scandalous debauchery and drunken orgies, one of which, attended by many "stars," resulted in the death of Virginia Rappe, a star artist; William Desmond Taylor, deceased, murdered for some mysterious cause; one Valentino, now figuring as the star character in rape and divorce sensations. Many others of like character might be mentioned.

At Hollywood, Calif., is a colony of these people, where debauchery, riotous living, drunkenness, ribaldry, dissipation, free love, seem to be conspicuous. Many of these "stars," it is reported, were formerly bartenders, butcher boys, supers, swampers, variety actors and actresses, who may have earned $10 or $20 a week, and some of whom are now paid, it is said, salaries of something like $5,000 a month or more, and they do not know what to do with their wealth, extracted from poor people, in large part, in 25 or 50 cent admission fees, except to spend it in riotous living, dissipation, and "high rolling."

These are some of the characters from whom the young people of today are deriving a large part of their education, views of life, and character-forming habits. From these sources our young people gain much of their views of life, inspiration, and education. Rather a poor source is it not? Looks like there is some need for censorship, does it not? There could be some improvement, could there not? . . .

Read and Respond

1. What are the issues raised in this article, and what would you say is the primary point that the writer is attempting to make? Is the main point of this article the same as the conclusion as expressed in the last two sentences?

2. Even though this article was written over seventy-five years ago about the fledgling movie industry, it seems that the arguments both in support of and opposed to the industry are similar to those being raised today. Just what are these arguments for and against regulating the movie industry? Are there any fallacies in the reasoning?

3. How much of what is said here is persuasive to you? Why are some things more persuasive than others? What, if anything, does that tell you about your "leanings"?

ASKING CRITICAL QUESTIONS

After you read the article that follows, what critical questions come to mind? Everything you read will stir up your thinking if you read and question critically. What questions would you like to have answered in order for you to put the articles in proper context and to completely understand what is being said or reported? *On the lines following each article, write three questions that, if answered, will help you understand what is really being said.*

The Metric System

James Shipman, Jerry Wilson, and Aaron Todd

Historians generally agree that the metric system originated with Gabriel Moulton, a French mathematician, when in 1670 he proposed a comprehensive decimal system based on a physical quantity of nature and not on human anatomy. Moulton proposed that the fundamental base unit of length be equal to one minute of arc of a great circle of Earth. This would be divided into submultiples of 10, and an appropriate length would be selected as a standard unit. A pendulum constructed with this length was to be used to define the unit of time.

Over 120 years later, in the 1790s during the French Revolution (1789–1799), the French Academy of Science recommended the adoption of a decimal system with a unit of length equal to one ten-millionth the distance on the surface of Earth from the equator to the North Pole. The unit of length was named the metre from the Greek *metron,* meaning "to measure."

A cubing of this length was proposed to be a unit of volume, and a unit of mass was proposed to be equal to the amount of pure water needed to fill a portion of the cube. Thus an easily usable system was established based on multiples or submultiples of 10 and defined on a single base unit related to a physical quantity of nature.

The metric system as originally conceived had problems, especially with standard units. To solve these problems, the French government in 1870 legalized a conference to work out standards for a unified measurement system. Five years later on May 20, 1875, the Treaty of the Meter was signed in Paris by 17 nations, including the United States.

The treaty established a General Conference on Weights and Measures as the supreme authority for all actions. It also established an International Committee of Weights and Measures with responsibility for supervising the International Bureau of Weights and Measures—a permanent laboratory and world center of scientific metrology (science of measurement).

The United States officially adopted the metric system in 1893. Congress enacted the Metric Conversion Act of 1975 that stated that "the policy of the United States shall be to coordinate and plan the increasing use of the metric system in the United States and to establish a United States Metric Board to coordinate the voluntary conversion to the metric system." However, no mandatory requirements were made, and the United States continues to use the British units of measurement.

In 1960 a modified metric system consisting of six basic standard units (meter, kilogram, second, ampere, kelvin, candela) was established by the 11th General Conference of Weights and Measures. Today this system is known as the International System of Units, or SI for short (SI is an abbreviation for the French Le Système International d'Unités).

The metric mass unit (kilogram) adopted in 1960 did not meet the needs of chemistry, so the 14th General Conference meeting in

1971 established the seventh base unit, the mole, for the amount of substance.

My Critical Questions

1. _____

   _____ **?**

2. _____

   _____ **?**

3. _____

   _____ **?**

Identifying Cause and Effect

ESSENTIAL THINKING SKILLS		
CHAPTER	**WHAT THEY'RE CALLED**	**WHAT THEY MEAN**
Chapter 3	**The Gathering Skills**	**Gathering all the information.**
	Observing	Actively seeking information through one or more senses.
	Questioning	Seeking information by asking questions.
Chapter 4	**The Organizing Skills**	**Organizing for the purpose of making sense.**
	Comparing and Contrasting	Noting similarities and differences between two or more things, events, or ideas.
	Classifying and Sequencing	Arranging things or concepts into categories and into sequential order.
	Identifying Cause and Effect	Recognizing the relationship between an effect and its cause.
Chapter 5	**The Generating Skills**	**Generating additional information.**
	Inferring	Making an assumption, stating a hypothesis, or coming to a conclusion based on limited information.
	Summarizing	Condensing the essence of the information accurately and efficiently.
	Synthesizing	Creating new information by combining two or more pieces of information.
	Generating Ideas	Creating new information, alternatives, or applications.
Chapter 6	**The Recognizing Skills**	**Recognizing what has been left unsaid.**
	Recognizing Purpose	Identifying a writer's or speaker's intention.
	Recognizing Fact and Opinion	Distinguishing between a statement of fact and a statement of opinion.
	Recognizing Tone	Identifying a sentiment or mood by assessing the writer's or speaker's choice of words.
	Recognizing Bias	Noting the presence and nature of a writer's or speaker's prejudice.
	Recognizing Organization	Identifying the organizational pattern of a thought, statement, passage, or plan.
	Recognizing Underlying Assumptions	Recognizing the suppositions that are taken for granted and are the foundation of a proposition, notion, or idea.
Chapter 7	**The Analyzing Skills**	**Analyzing for the purpose of coming to a conclusion.**
	Analyzing	Identifying and separating ideas, attributes, situations, and/or components in order to form a conclusion as to their relationship.
	Evaluating	Appraising something according to certain criteria and forming a judgment as to its worth or quality.
	Inducing	Analyzing individual facts or premises in order to derive a general conclusion.
	Deducing	Applying general principles or a broad framework to a situation in order to come to a conclusion about it.

"There are no evil thoughts except one: the refusal to think."
—Ayn Rand

"Lucky is he who has been able to understand the causes of things."
—Paul Verlaine

What questions am I going to have answered in this section on identifying cause and effect?

1. Why is it important to be able to identify cause and effect?
2. What is the role of establishing a sequence of events when identifying cause and effect?
3. What problems am I likely to face in attempting to identify cause and effect?

> **IDENTIFYING CAUSE AND EFFECT:**
> **Recognizing the relationship between an effect and its cause**

As soon as children are old enough to begin talking they begin asking questions, and the questions they ask are mostly attempts to identify cause and effect in everything they see, hear, touch, or taste. "Why?" is the most frequently asked question. Children want to know what causes things and what will happen as a result of something occurring. "Why is this happening?" "Why does it taste (or look, smell, sound, feel) that way?" "What will happen if . . . ?" Children ask these questions because they are struggling to understand and give meaning to the world around them.

Later, as children grow older, go to school, and mature to adulthood, these attempts to identify cause and effect in life don't stop. Instead, cause-and-effect questions become a bit more sophisticated, complicated, and frequently harder to answer, but they are still asked. "Why is this happening?" "Why don't the authorities do something about it?" "Why did she have to die so young?" "Why is he behaving like that?" "What will be the result of that congressional action?"

THINK ABOUT THIS!

Another Possibility

A good way to keep your mental muscles toned is to come up with a number of possible causes, not just one, for any given effect. For example, say the telephone hasn't rung in over a week and you usually receive several calls a day from your friends and family. What are some possible causes of this unusual situation? You may hypothesize that your phone is out of order, that you have alienated your family and friends, that since you haven't bothered to call anyone, no one has thought to call you, that your friends are all sick, or perhaps that all your family and friends have been kidnapped.

What are some possible causes for the following effects?

Another student in one of your classes takes a sudden interest in you.

_____

One of your professors seems to be calling on you frequently in class.

_____

Your right arm is stiff and aching.

_____

You have lost your appetite for the last few days.

_____

You have been eating constantly for the last few days.

_____

You don't seem to be able to sleep past 6 A.M. any day of the week.

_____

Your favorite professor doesn't seem to have time to speak with you after class anymore.

_____

Your father has been sending you fifty dollars a week for the past month without saying why.

_____

Several of your favorite items of clothing seem to have disappeared.

_____

Your car frequently makes strange noises.

_____

Your cat hasn't been around in nearly two weeks.

_____

The bank says that you have more money in your checking account than your checkbook says you have.

_____

THE IMPORTANCE OF EXPLORING RELATIONSHIPS AND SEQUENCE OF EVENTS

In order to answer the cause-and-effect questions we raise, we must explore the relationships between different events and examine how these events interact with each other over time. When we seek to understand why something has occurred, we attempt to identify the events that led up to it and the factors that were involved. For example, if you are driving home from class and your car gets hit by another car at a busy intersection (fortunately, no one is hurt), both you and the police will attempt to examine the sequence of events that led up to (that caused) the accident (the effect) by tracing events back in time.

The same process, but in reverse, is used to predict what is likely to happen when a sequence or combination of events is examined and projected into the future. For example, you might ask yourself (rather naively), "What will be the most likely result (effect) of my not going to composition class regularly, not turning in daily assignments, just skimming the assigned chapters in the textbook, and skipping the midterm exam?" The effect (a poor or failing grade) can be easily predicted.

IT'S NOT ALWAYS THAT EASY

Analyzing cause and effect can be very difficult when we face complicated questions and problems. It may be that we are unable to easily identify sufficient causes or that there is no seemingly sequential or

? ANY QUESTIONS?

Is it better to be skillful or lucky? Illustrate or explain your answer.

_____

_____

_____

_____

_____

relational connection between the causes. At other times there can be a question as to whether or not causes are *necessary* to an effect or merely *possible contributors* to an effect or outcome. For example, no easy answers, no sufficient causes can be found when we attempt to explain why one individual became a mass murderer and another became a dedicated humanitarian. In cases like this, where there is no simple answer to the Why? or What will happen? questions, the best you can do is speculate about possible causes and effects while qualifying your conclusions with words such as *usually, probably, may, most,* and *likely.*

THINKERS

In baseball, which pitch can be hit farther—a slow ball or a fast ball?

Your opinion isn't good enough. What is your corroborating evidence?

Need a Hint?
Don't speculate. Try it. Get a ball and. . . .

STIR IT UP 4.8   The following rather outlandish "what if" statements will focus your thinking on the consequences of actions. What might be a few "effects" of the following "causes"? Pay special attention to your thinking process and the sequence of events you foresee.

1. What if all the junk food in vending machines were replaced by health food?

    _____

    _____

    _____

2. What if everyone were required to come to class on a skateboard?

    _____

    _____

    _____

3. What if you were asked (and you agreed) to be the instructor of this class for a week?

    _____

_____

_____

4. What if your college or university required that you listen to rap music for a minimum of three hours a day?

_____

_____

_____

5. What if students were not permitted to speak at all when inside school buildings?

_____

_____

_____

6. What if students were permitted to take only one course each semester?

_____

_____

_____

STIR IT UP 4.9   For each of the "effects" below, suggest at least three possible causes.

1. All campus parking lots are closed.

_____

_____

_____

2. Amazingly, all students on campus appear to be more physically fit today than they were a year ago.

_____

_____

_____

3. Campus police patrols have ceased entirely.

_____

_____

_____

4. Neither you nor your parents will have to pay any federal income tax for the foreseeable future.

_____

_____

_____

5. You walk into a bank with no money, and you walk out with $100,000.

_____

_____

_____

6. You are monumentally depressed.

_____

_____

_____

7. You are happier than you have ever been.

_____

_____

_____

8. You have just failed an exam in your favorite class.

_____

_____

_____

STIR IT UP 4.10   **Standards for Thinking and Reasoning**

Identify the three most important critical thinking standards to be applied to the skill of identifying cause and effect. Put a check (✓) next to your three choices. Be ready to explain your thinking. Why these three?

☐ Clear   ☐ Precise   ☐ Specific
☐ Accurate   ☐ Relevant   ☐ Consistent
☐ Logical   ☐ Deep   ☐ Significant
☐ Complete   ☐ Fair   ☐ Adequate

Journal Observations (see page 13)

IDENTIFYING CAUSE AND EFFECT

1st Writing _____

_____

_____

_____

_____

_____

_____

_____

_____

_____

_____

_____

2nd Writing _____

_____

_____

_____

_____

_____

_____

_____

_____

_____

_____

_____

3rd Writing _____

_____

_____

_____

_____

_____

_____

_____

_____

_____

_____

A Warning to Mothers (1839)

READINGS

The Female Moral Reform Society

Beloved Sisters,
   Will you permit an associated band, most of whom share responsibilities similar to your own, and know with yourselves the deep yearnings of maternal love, to call your attention, for a few moments, to a forbidding, but most important subject. Be assured that nothing but the fixed conviction that it is a subject affecting the temporal and eternal well-being of the young immortals committed to your care, would induce us to commend it to your consideration through the Press. We refer to a species of licentiousness from which neither age nor sex is exempt; a vice that has done its work of ruin, physical, mental, and moral, when no eye but that of Omniscience could behold it, a vice that has been practised in ten thousand instances, without a correct knowledge of its consequences, or its guilt, until it has paved the way for the most revolting excesses in crime. . . .

   Recently it has pleased, our Heavenly Father to bring before our minds a flood of light, by which we have been solemnly convinced, that in nine cases out of ten, "solitary vice" is the first cause of social licentiousness, and the foundation and hidden source of the present corrupt state of society. . . .

The dangers to which all classes of the rising generation are exposed, are great beyond expression, they are dangers, too, that may stain the soul with guilt, and yet elude the vigilance of the most watchful parent, unless obviated *from the cradle,* by proper training and correct instruction. . . .

"A pupil in a select school, a child but ten years of age, confessed to her teacher, that she had been guilty of the sin alluded to for years, although she had never been taught it, and knew not that any one living practised it but herself. Her mind was fast sinking, she was wholly unable to reckon even small sums. This child had been religiously educated, but she was reared where the table was made a snare. Rich and high seasoned food, and abundance of dainties were given her, bathing was neglected, and a precocious development of the passions, and their consequent indulgence, was, in this case, the result."

"A child, under 12 years of age, whose morals in every respect had been carefully guarded, and who had never, except in one instance, been exposed, to the influence of an evil associate; on being questioned by her mother, confessed with tears that the sin had been taught her by the suspected individual."

Read and Respond

1. So, just what is this vice that mothers are being warned against? How do you know? Could it be anything else, perhaps drinking alcoholic beverages or even chewing fingernails?

2. The writer gives examples of what happens to people who are victims of this vice. Are the examples factual, believable, reasonable? Why or why not?

3. Why has the Female Moral Reform Society selected this vice for particular attention? What is the stated reason, and do you believe it? Why or why not? Is this issue important to society today? Was it important to society in 1839?

DNA: The Ultimate Fingerprint?

Joseph Levine and Kenneth Miller

Fingerprints are ideal for identifying individuals because they differ so widely from one person to the next. But fingerprints are useful only in those rare cases where a criminal leaves clean, complete prints that can be matched with police records. Today, however, molecular biology has developed a new tool that may become the ultimate weapon of criminology: the *DNA fingerprint*.

DNA fingerprinting makes use of the fact that certain DNA regions between genes are extremely variable from one individual to the next. When probes to these "hypervariable" regions are constructed, Southern blotting can be used to produce a pattern of RFLPs that differs markedly from one individual to the next.

If the probe recognizes a large number of fragments from around the genome, a single gel can produce a "fingerprint" that is unique for one individual. Scientists hoped that by using several probes, they could produce a gel pattern so specific that it could be distinguished from the pattern of any other individual in the world. DNA fingerprints can be prepared from cells found in a drop of blood or semen and even from fragments of skin caught under the fingernails of a crime victim.

In 1988 this technique came to the aid of a 27-year-old computer operator at Disney World in Florida who had been attacked, beaten, and raped in her home in Orlando in 1986. Although she caught a brief glimpse of her assailant's face during the rape, she faced the terrifying prospect of having to convince a jury that her brief eyewitness identification of the suspect, 24-year-old Tommie Lee Andrews, was absolutely certain.

Andrews claimed that he was at home during the evening the rape occurred, and he even produced a witness to substantiate that claim. It was a classic case of the victim's word against that of the accused. The prosecuting attorneys sought the aid of a molecular biologist to perform the "DNA fingerprinting" test on a semen sample taken by police the night of the rape. When the DNA fingerprint of this sample was compared with a blood sample taken from Andrews, the results were conclusive: It was a perfect match. The jury returned a verdict of guilty, resulting in a jail sentence of 22 years for Andrews.

As the legal issues of this technique were explored, the Andrews trial turned out to be no more than the opening legal chapter on DNA fingerprinting. In several trials, defense attorneys correctly pointed out that there was not enough data to be absolutely certain that identical patterns could not appear in two different individuals. This could lead to a false DNA identification.

After 3 years of study, in 1992 the National Academy of Sciences attempted to settle the matter by issuing a report that recognized the scientific standing of DNA fingerprinting. The report proposed a new, conservative way to estimate the possibility that a DNA identification could be mistaken and proposed DNA testing standards for laboratories to meet. At this writing it remains to be seen whether or not courts throughout the country will agree that evidence meeting the new standards will be routinely admitted in court.

Only when uniform, court-approved standards are developed will DNA fingerprinting have the chance to fulfill its early promise as the ultimate weapon of criminal identification.

Read and Respond

DNA fingerprinting requires some intense scientific validating and an agreement to maintain certain testing standards. Why? Why must "uniform, court-approved standards" be developed for DNA fingerprints? What might occur if there are never any court-approved standards?

Prohibition Nonobserved

U.S. National Commission on Law Enforcement, 1931

There is a mass of information before us as to a general prevalence of drinking in homes, in clubs, and in hotels; of drinking parties given and attended by persons of high standing and respectability; of drinking by tourists at winter and summer resorts; and of drinking in connection with public dinners and at conventions. In the nature of the case it is not easy to get at the exact facts in such a connection, and conditions differ somewhat in different parts of the country and even to some extent from year to year. This is true likewise with respect to drinking by women and drinking by youth, as to which also there is a great mass of evidence. In weighing this evidence much allowance must be made for the effect of new standards of independence and individual self-assertion, changed ideas as to conduct generally, and the greater emphasis on freedom and the quest for excitement since the war. As to drinking among youth, the evidence is conflicting. Votes in colleges show an attitude of hostility to or contempt for the law on the part of those who are not unlikely to be leaders in the next generation. It is safe to say that a significant change has taken place in the social attitude toward drinking. This may be seen in the views and conduct of social leaders, business and professional men in the average community. It may be seen in the tolerance of conduct at social gatherings which would not have been possible a generation ago. It is reflected in a different way of regarding drunken youth, in a change in the class of excessive drinkers, and in the increased use of distilled liquor in places and connections where formerly it was banned. It is evident that, taking the country as a whole, people of wealth, business men and professional men, and their families, and, perhaps, the higher paid workingmen and their families, are drinking in large numbers in quite frank disregard of the declared policy of the National Prohibition Act. . . .

Read and Respond

1. What is the conclusion arrived at in this 1931 report?

2. What is the evidence on which this conclusion is based? Is there, in fact, any evidence other than assertions of fact? What is the quality of the personal observations recorded here? What significant information is omitted from this article that would prove the author's point (that prohibition is not working)?

3. How much of what is said here could also be said about the prevalence of drinking today?

ASKING CRITICAL QUESTIONS

After you read the article that follows, what critical questions come to mind? Everything you read will stir up your thinking if you read and question critically. What questions would you like to have answered in order for you to put the articles in proper context and to completely understand what is being said or reported? *On the lines following each article, write three questions that, if answered, will help you understand what is really being said.*

The Concept of Time

James Shipman, Jerry Wilson, and Aaron Todd

In Chapter 1 time was defined as the continuous forward flowing of events. This definition implies that time relates to motion, has a forward direction, and cannot be quantized.

Things change from one position to another, and an interval of time is noted for the change to occur. This is something we observe in our physical world, and we call this changing of position *motion*. Everything appears to be in motion. The things we say are at rest are at rest only in reference to something else. A book on a table is at rest, but the table and book are on a moving Earth. Our thoughts concerning the concept of time are meaningless unless we include the concept of motion.

Do the events that take place in our physical world have a forward direction? That is, does time flow in a forward direction? If the answer is yes, how can we differentiate between forward and backward events? The answer can be found in the concept of entropy.

One of the most important laws of nature is the second law of thermodynamics, which can be and has been stated in many ways. One way, which gives the direction of time, is with the entropy concept. Entropy is a measure of disorder, and the second law of thermodynamics states that the total entropy of the universe increases in every natural process. Thus, as events occur (the flow of time), disorder becomes greater.

We do not observe and cannot measure extremely short (less than 10^{-13} s) intervals of time. Does this mean that things we cannot measure are meaningless? Not necessarily. For example, calculations concerning the Big Bang theory for the origin of the universe specify that during the extremely brief interval 1.35×10^{-43} s (known as Planck time) following the Big Bang all forces were unified. Although we cannot measure this time interval, scientists use it in theories concerning the origin and expansion of the universe.

Is time absolute? The answer is a definite no. One of the outcomes from Albert Einstein's special theory of relativity was time dilation. This concept refers to the measurement of time by observers in different reference frames. For example, clocks run slower or time is stretched out in a moving reference frame as observed by a stationary observer. Also, biological processes proceed at a slower rate on a moving reference frame than on a stationary one. See Appendix VII for an equation showing how to calculate relativistic time dilation.

Scientists performed an experiment that measured the time difference between clocks, four moving and one stationary. Four cesium-beam atomic clocks were flown on jet flights around the world twice, once eastward and once westward. The times recorded by the clocks on the jet flights were compared with the corresponding clock at the U.S. Naval Observatory, and time differences were recorded that were in good agreement with relativity theory.

Einstein's special theory of relativity also binds three-dimensional space with time, ranking time as a basic reference coordinate and labeling it as a fourth dimension. Thus, to give the complete location of an event, we must state where it is in three spatial dimensions plus the time it is there. Space and time are relative concepts. They are dependent on the relative velocity of the reference frame in which they are measured. Space and time are related in a fundamental way in what we call the four-dimensional continuum, or space-time.

Although the concept of time is difficult to comprehend, the existence of time, as we experience it, is related to change. We, as individuals, experience the universe in our own time-frame, which is different from everybody else's.

My Critical Questions

1. _____

_____ **?**

2. _____

_____ **?**

3. _____

_____ **?**

SOLUTIONS to Items in This Chapter

THINKERS (p. 97)

Both answers are correct. The shapes are pivoted on their adjoining points: to the right to form a square and to the left to form a triangle.

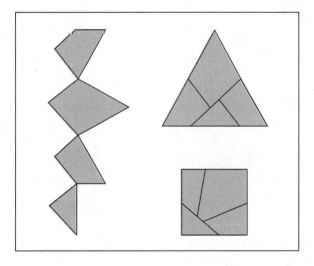

THINKERS (p. 100)

The numbers are amounts, not years.

THINKERS (p. 125)

The number 12 comes next. The numbers in the series alternate, with a number composed of straight lines followed by a number with curves. The number 12 has curves.

THINKERS (p. 129)

The letter S comes next. Each letter in the series is the first letter of a word in the question. The word *series* is next.

ANY QUESTIONS (p. 142)

I think skillful is better than lucky. Would you rather be operated on by a surgeon who is lucky or a surgeon who is skillful?

THINKERS (p. 143)

A fast ball. Want proof? Try this. Throw a ball gently against a wall. Then throw it hard against the wall. It will bounce back farther when you throw it hard.

GENERATING SKILLS

- **Inferring**
- **Summarizing**
- **Synthesizing**
- **Generating Ideas**

There's more that can be said about this.

> "When thou hast done, thou hast not done,
> For, I have more."
> —John Donne

> "To expect a man to retain everything . . . is like expecting him to carry about in his body everything he has ever eaten."
> —Arthur Schopenhauer

> "Some people become so expert at reading between the lines they don't read the lines."
> —Margaret Millar

STIR UP YOUR THINKING BEFORE YOU START READING

Before you start reading this chapter, take an informal survey. Compare the answers you receive with what you learn in this chapter. Ask three students to answer this question:

How important to your learning and your success in college is being able to accurately infer, summarize, and synthesize information?

Responses:

1. _____

_____

_____

2. _____

_____

_____

Inferring

	ESSENTIAL THINKING SKILLS	
CHAPTER	**WHAT THEY'RE CALLED**	**WHAT THEY MEAN**
Chapter 3	**The Gathering Skills**	**Gathering all the information.**
	Observing	Actively seeking information through one or more senses.
	Questioning	Seeking information by asking questions.
Chapter 4	**The Organizing Skills**	**Organizing for the purpose of making sense.**
	Comparing and Contrasting	Noting similarities and differences between two or more things, events, or ideas.
	Classifying and Sequencing	Arranging things or concepts into categories and into sequential order.
	Identifying Cause and Effect	Recognizing the relationship between an effect and its cause.
Chapter 5	**The Generating Skills**	**Generating additional information.**
	Inferring	Making an assumption, stating a hypothesis, or coming to a conclusion based on limited information.
	Summarizing	Condensing the essence of the information accurately and efficiently.
	Synthesizing	Creating new information by combining two or more pieces of information.
	Generating Ideas	Creating new information, alternatives, or applications.
Chapter 6	**The Recognizing Skills**	**Recognizing what has been left unsaid.**
	Recognizing Purpose	Identifying a writer's or speaker's intention.
	Recognizing Fact and Opinion	Distinguishing between a statement of fact and a statement of opinion.
	Recognizing Tone	Identifying a sentiment or mood by assessing the writer's or speaker's choice of words.
	Recognizing Bias	Noting the presence and nature of a writer's or speaker's prejudice.
	Recognizing Organization	Identifying the organizational pattern of a thought, statement, passage, or plan.
	Recognizing Underlying Assumptions	Recognizing the suppositions that are taken for granted and are the foundation of a proposition, notion, or idea.
Chapter 7	**The Analyzing Skills**	**Analyzing for the purpose of coming to a conclusion.**
	Analyzing	Identifying and separating ideas, attributes, situations, and/or components in order to form a conclusion as to their relationship.
	Evaluating	Appraising something according to certain criteria and forming a judgment as to its worth or quality.
	Inducing	Analyzing individual facts or premises in order to derive a general conclusion.
	Deducing	Applying general principles or a broad framework to a situation in order to come to a conclusion about it.

3. _____

_____

_____

> **"**_Life is the art of drawing sufficient conclusions from insufficient premises._**"**
> —Samuel Butler

> **"**_Of making many books there is no end; and much study is a weariness of the flesh._**"**
> —Ecclesiastes

> . . . _And I sure wish I'd started studying for this exam two weeks ago._
> —Nearly every student in the world

What questions am I going to have answered in this section on inferring?

1. What is inferring, and how difficult is it to do?
2. Are conclusions that are inferred as reliable as conclusions that are based on factual data?
3. Why is inferring necessary when reading, studying, or listening to lectures in class?
4. Are some inferences stronger than others?

INFERRING:
Making an assumption, stating a hypothesis, or coming to a conclusion based on limited information

---

Nearly all reasoning, both good and poor, includes the act of observation followed by inference. An inference is a statement about the _unknown_ based on the _known_. When you reason, you start with what you know to be fact, or what you observe, and proceed to a reasonable conclusion about what you don't know to be fact, or can't observe.

Frequently you do not have enough information to make a fact-based decision, so you interpret what facts you have as best you can. In these cases, you use inferring to arrive at a conclusion. When you have limited or partial information and the conclusions you come to are based

THINK ABOUT THIS!

Famous Last Words

Throughout history, the last words of people have been regarded as important. I suppose that's because we like to believe that in the moments before we die, we will have some insight, totally unselfish, that we can share with family and friends that will enrich their lives after we are gone. But that doesn't happen very often, does it? Here are the not-so-famous last words of some famous figures and one anonymous judge:

• *Billy the Kid: "Who is there?"*

• *Benedict Arnold: "Let me die in my old uniform. God forgive me for ever putting on another."*

• *Alexander Graham Bell: "So little done, so much to do."*

• *An anonymous judge: "Case dismissed."*

• *Alexander the Great (when asked who should get his crown): "The strongest."*

What makes last words so interesting to us is that they frequently reflect the life, accomplishments, or failures of the speaker. What do you think your own last words will be? Think about it. In fact, suggest some famous last words for the people listed below. Be certain to make the last words reflective in some way of the person supposedly saying them.

Richard Nixon ——————————————————

Michael Jordan ——————————————————

The instructor for this class ————————————————

Your best friend ——————————————————

Santa Claus ——————————————————

Your boss ——————————————————

Your mother ——————————————————

Your father ——————————————————

on assumptions that go beyond that partial information, you are inferring. Of course, sometimes your inferences are logical because the information you have is clear. Your inferences are closely and directly tied to the information available. At other times, your inferences may be weak because they have little foundation in fact. You still infer, but you are aware that you may be making an error.

THINKERS

What's the Rule?

Ben has a weird rule for deciding which words he likes and which words he dislikes. He says, "I like *scowl,* but not *frown.* I like *grapes,* but not *fruit.* I love *kayak,* but not *canoe.* I love *pottery,* but I don't like *clay.*" What is Ben's rule?

Need a Hint?
"What's in a word?" he said with a chuckle.

INFERRING SKILLS BEGIN DEVELOPING EARLY

Skillfully drawing inferences in the course of your studies is less difficult than you may think. In fact, it is really quite simple, because you are already highly skilled at it. Every day you draw conclusions about people you meet, things that are said to you, and things that you see and hear in the media. You developed your inferring skills when you were very young. You learned to gauge the moods of family members by considering their facial expressions, body language, and tone of voice. You learned to interpret what was said and what wasn't said. However, it is not as easy to infer things other than moods, because often you are expected to come to conclusions and make decisions on limited information. You have to rely also on your stockpiled information, that is, information you have accumulated over the years. For example, if you visit your grandmother in Florida and see an orange tree in her backyard with most of the oranges on the ground under it, you mentally run through the various things that could have occurred:

- Orange pickers didn't have enough baskets to put the oranges in.
- Neighborhood kids were playing in the tree and knocked off the fruit.
- A strong wind blew the fruit off.
- A winter frost hit the area, knocking off the fruit.
- Grandma let the fruit fall off, and no one has gathered it.

After doing some thinking, you conclude that the fruit ripened and Grandma just let it fall off. Your reasoning goes something like this: The orange trees in the neighbors' yards still have all their fruit, so you rule out wind and frost. Grandma lives in a community where everyone is at least fifty-five years old, so chances are that children didn't knock the oranges off. You happen to know that Grandma has never hired orange pickers in the past, so she probably didn't hire them this year. Consequently, you conclude that Grandma just let the fruit fall off and hasn't picked it up. Your conclusion is an inference because it is based on incomplete information and general knowledge that you have.

INFERRING SKILLS SHARPEN THROUGH USE

By constantly making inferences, we sharpen our ability to make sound, rational decisions. When we are faced with a situation about which we don't have all the facts, we call to mind principles, examples, generalizations, our own observations, or statements of authorities that we know to be true and that were made about similar situations. For example, we may infer that a particular exercise machine is not reliable without testing it. We can do this because we can cite evidence concerning other, similar machines, and we know as well that other products manufactured by the same company have proved to be faulty. We may not know for a fact that this particular product is faulty or unreliable, but by citing other evidence, we infer unreliability. The more evidence that can be cited, the stronger the inference that can be made.

INFERRED CONCLUSIONS COULD BE WRONG

It is important to remember that even though inferring is an essential part of good thinking, the conclusions and predictions arrived at by inferring may be wrong. Inferences are based partially on our past experiences and partially on the information we possess at the moment. Even though our reasoning is sound, it may be faulty because it is based on insufficient information. That is why the English language gives us a rich supply of words we can use to qualify our inferences: *seems, appears, might be, could be,* and so on. "She *seems* to be deep in thought most of the time." "David and Karen *appear* happy now that Ken is out of the picture." "Sulfuric acid *might be* the missing element." "Item B *could be* the correct answer to this question."

WHY THE INFERRING SKILL IS NECESSARY IN COLLEGE

Inferring is an essential thinking skill for learning in college. For a variety of reasons authors and professors "don't come right out and say it," and so you must be able to identify correctly the message the writer/speaker is presenting. You need to infer what is going on when you don't have all the facts. Often there are several possible inferences that you can make about any situation. To try your hand at this, do Stir It Up 5.1.

STIR IT UP 5.1   What is going on? Make two *possible*, but *contradictory*, inferences for each scene described.

1. Two young men dressed in T-shirts and jeans are pushing a high-priced sports car down the street. _____

   _____

2. You arrive at American literature class after being absent for the last two class sessions and find the classroom empty. _____

   _____

3. The last two Thursdays, the dormitory cafeteria has served mackerel patties and creamed peas. It is Thursday again. _____

   _____

4. The new student is gorgeous, makes a point of saying hello to you every day, smiles frequently at you, and always seems to be leaving the classroom at exactly the same moment that you do.

   _____

   _____

5. Your professor has spent the last four class sessions on the Battle of Gettysburg. The midterm exam is next week. _____

   _____

WHY WE HAVE TO INFER

Among the reasons authors and teachers don't always say what they want to say, clearly and plainly, are the following:

- Writers and speakers usually cannot include (often because of limited space or time) all the information that might be relevant to their subject. Thus, they must rely on their audience's ability to infer.

- Writers and speakers sometimes leave out information because including it would divert attention from the point being made or from the train of reasoning.

- Writers and speakers sometimes leave out information because they assume their readers or listeners are already familiar with it.

- Writers and speakers often rely on inference to create or sustain emotional power and artistic value. This technique is often applied in creative writing such as poetry or fiction. Leaving something unstated often contributes to humor, fear, irony, or a climax when the reader has to infer a point or draw a conclusion.

- Writers and speakers sometimes leave out information they don't want their audience to know when they want to present a one-sided argument. They hope that their audience will not be aware of the facts left out. This is questionable writing at worst, and editorial writing at best. Be aware of calculated evasions.

- Writers or speakers sometimes must trust their audience's inferential skills because including specific information may be illegal or dangerous (in some countries), or it may leave the writer/speaker open to a lawsuit.

For these reasons and many others, students must hone their inferring skills and use them continuously, in the classroom, while reading, and while getting information from the media.

INFERRING ON TESTS

Frequently, inferring is useful, even necessary, on quizzes and exams when you don't have complete information and you need to answer questions like the following:

- The number 4 is the answer to which question?

- If the ozone layer is destroyed, what will happen to plant life over the next few years?

- In the paragraph you just read, what does the writer's description imply about the athletes?

? ANY QUESTIONS?

Why do stores that never close have locks on their doors? If they are open 24 hours a day, 365 days a year, what's the point of locks? Suggest as many reasonable possibilities as you can.

_____

_____

_____

_____

_____

Using the information you have at hand, and adding to it related facts and information that you have stored in your memory, it is possible for you to infer an acceptable answer.

STIR IT UP 5.2   Each of the following descriptions is for the same person. After each description, jot down your inference concerning the character or situation of the person being described. As the descriptions for this person begin to pile up, do your inferences become more difficult to make? Why or why not?

What can you infer about a person who:

1. watches the clock when working? _____

2. never mentions a personal life? _____

3. has no friends at work? _____

4. eats lunch alone? _____

5. never takes breaks? _____

6. is the last person to leave work? _____

What's your overall conclusion about this person? Who is he or she? Is there something wrong with the person? Or, could it be that these are the actions of a person who is in charge, for example, a manager or a shift supervisor?

STIR IT UP 5.3   The following questions were taken from a test. What is the test designed to measure? What led you to make that inference?

1. Have you changed your living conditions or moved?
2. Have you had trouble with in-laws?
3. Have you taken out a large loan?
4. Have you frequently had trouble falling asleep?
5. Have you found that you eat, drink, or sleep more now than before?
6. Have you changed jobs recently?
7. Has a close friend or relative died recently?
8. Have you been dissatisfied with your sex life?
9. Have you or your wife recently gotten pregnant?
10. Have you and your significant other discussed separating lately?

_____

_____

_____

———————————————

THINKERS

What number should go in the shaded area?

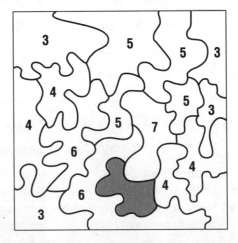

Need a Hint? The number has nothing to do with size or shape. What's left?

Journal Observations (see page 13)

INFERRING

1st Writing _____

_____

_____

_____

_____

_____

_____

_____

_____

_____

_____

2nd Writing _____

_____

_____

_____

_____

_____

_____

_____

_____

_____

_____

3rd Writing _____

_____

_____

_____

_____

_____

_____

_____

_____

_____

_____

READINGS

Sound Too Good to Be True?
Behind the Boom in Subliminal Tapes

Kevin Krajick
Newsweek, *July 30, 1990*

Rob Gregory wanted to do better at his job selling used factory-ventilation systems in Kansas City. So three years ago he bought a "subliminal" audiotape called "Unconditional Love." All Gregory heard was "some synthesized music and weird gongs." But buried beneath the sounds, supposedly, were inaudible messages subconsciously persuading him to feel better about other people. It worked, he says. His sales went up because "people sense if you really care." Encouraged, he bought another tape, this one called "Stop Hair Loss." He says he soon stopped losing his hair. Now Gregory, 30, owns 15 different improvement tapes—none of whose "hidden" messages he can hear. "Subliminals are both practical and spiritual," he says. "They're a smorgasbord for human potential."

Sound too good to be true? Not to the millions of people snapping up subliminal tapes that promise to help them shed weight or regain faith in God. Sales have doubled since 1985, and this year cassettes are expected to bring in $50 million, mostly from middle-class buyers under 45. Once sold only through the mail by small New Age firms, subliminals are now found in chain bookstores. At least 20 publishers, including Bantam, Simon and Schuster and Random House, have jumped into the business. "The whole idea that a $9.95 tape can change your life and you don't have to do anything seems so absurd," says Harriet Pironti, a spokesperson for Random House. "But it's the American way."

The tapes are said to work because their "messages" bypass conscious defense mechanisms. One hears only music or relaxing sounds; underneath, encouraging words are "embedded" at decibel levels perceived only subconsciously. Some manufacturers even speed up messages to a blur or run them through electronic filters to disguise them further. An audible voice at the start of "How To Be Popular," one of more than 170 titles from Potentials Unlimited of Grand Rapids, Mich., says, "The messages will enter your subconscious . . . so that changes will take place in your life as they should; without effort, without thought, without strain." Ocean waves and aimless harp music well up, the voice vanishes; results are guaranteed in 30 days.

The top sellers are cassettes to lose weight or quit smoking; from there, the world is at your earlobes. Single and lonely? Get "How To Attract Love." Or maybe it's time for "Divorce—Yes." For other vital concerns, there is "Agoraphobia," "Freedom From Acne," "Winning at the Track" and "I Am a Genius." Credence Cassettes of Kansas City, Mo., offers tapes designed to "correct and heal . . . concepts of God that are negative, distorted or even hostile." Inmates at Utah's South Point Prison use one called "Pedophilia" to quell criminal impulses; Texas Rangers pitchers use custom-made cassettes to increase confidence. Kids' tapes, such as "I Am a Great Reader," are popular, says Patricia Mounteer, owner of Mind Mint, a Salt Lake City self-help store. "Prenatal mothers play it to the fetus and the kids come out more intelligent and walk sooner," she claims. "Positive Thoughts for Children" offers the sounds of a seashore and, somewhere in there, the assurance: "I am loved."

One needs no scientific credentials to make tapes. Potentials Unlimited president and chief "hypnotherapist" Barrie Konicov, 51, whose soothing voice is heard on his firm's cassettes, sold aluminum hair curlers, fire alarms and life insurance (his license was yanked in

1973 for forgery) before discovering self-help tapes in 1977. A federal judge once summed up Konicov's qualifications as a degree in marketing and "approximately three weekend seminars on hypnosis." Potentials Unlimited sells a million tapes a year, mostly through chains like Barnes and Noble.

Subliminal cassettes generate ridicule as well as riches. They're "worthless trash," says Brooklyn College psychology professor Arthur Reber. "People want to make their lives better by some kind of magical pseudoscience." Most psychologists, while acknowledging that experiments show people can sometimes process sounds or sights so slight they can't be consciously perceived, say there's no evidence such stimuli change lives. Even the advertising industry, which flirted with the tantalizing idea of subliminal manipulation in the 1950's, has long since abandoned the concept as ineffective.

Examine Your Thinking About What You Just Read

Pay attention to your thinking processes as you answer the following questions.

1. So, what do you think? Are you encouraged to run right out and buy some subliminal tapes to improve your life, to make you rich or smart? Why or why not? What do you already know or believe that leads you to either accept or reject the idea of subliminal learning? How does what you know shape your attitude toward what you hear or read?

2. What is the tone of this article? Is it supportive of subliminal tapes, or is it ridiculing and skeptical? Which words can you identify as tone words that influence the way the information is received by the reader?

3. Examine this article for fact and opinion. How much of what is written here can be verified, and how much must be called opinion? How much is a mix of fact and opinion?

Write about this In a short essay, suggest a marketing plan for a new subliminal tape to help people stop biting their nails. How will you find those nail biters? How will you get them to buy the tape? What will you call the tape, and how will you describe it? Before you begin, choose the tone that you want to convey, and then consciously select your words so that the tone comes across consistently in your essay.

The Attitudes and Work Habits of Successful Academic Writers

Edited by Joseph M. Moxley

What is your fantasy of how writers work? Do you believe that writers are unusually talented people who write in lonely garrets and occasionally—like those lucky $35 million lottery winners—write a novel, or a nonfiction book, or even a screenplay that hits the jackpot? Do you imagine writers doing research by cruising the Bahamas in a private yacht and hanging out with movie stars and power brokers at the Full Moon Golf and Racket Club?

As someone who is determined to become a competent, confident writer, it is important for you to start by analyzing your attitudes about writing. After all, your attitude about writing and your assumptions about how writers work can limit your imagination and the quality of your finished product. You can debunk a truckload of myths about writing by analyzing how you write, how your peers write, and how professional writers write.

Writing Myths

Below are eleven of the common myths that many of us hold about writers. To help you identify blind spots—that is, opinions and attitudes you hold that you are not even conscious of—you should discuss these misconceptions with friends outside of class and with your peers in class. You should also explore in writing (or in your writer's journal, if you have one) any attitudes and myths you tend to subscribe to that might interfere with your writing success.

Writers Are Born Rather Than Nurtured

Or, writers are unusual, especially intelligent people. *Reality:* Perhaps a few people are born with a special ability to express themselves through language. Yet ability without desire or experience nets an empty page. Despite countless attempts, researchers have been unable to prove that writers are uniquely intelligent or original. What is unique, however, is that writers discipline themselves to write and revise. When their thoughts are muddy, successful writers persist until they achieve clarity.

Writers Always Enjoy Writing

Reality: Even professionals agonize about their writing from time to time. For example, Sue Lorch, an accomplished writing teacher and author, writes,

> I do not like to write. Most people to whom I reveal this small, personal truth find it exceedingly odd, suggesting by their expressions that I ought either to repair my attitude or develop the discretion necessary not to go around telling people about it. Apparently these people hear my confession as an admission of fraud. Because my professional life centers on the written word—on producing it, interpreting it, teaching it, and teaching others to teach it—people assume that I should enjoy writing. Not at all. I inevitably view the prospect of writing with a mental set more commonly reserved for root canals and amputations: If it must be done, it must be done, but for God's sake, let us put it off as long as possible.

Although experienced writers may dislike the act of writing, they know, nonetheless, that if they are to develop ideas, they need to put their pen to the page or their fingers to the keyboard. Like the forty-niners prospecting for gold in the Sierras, many of us write with the hope of eventually experiencing the "Eureka Phenomenon"—the inspirational moment when our passion finds form and we discover what we want to say by writing.

Gifted Writers Are Overflowing with Ideas

Reality: Experienced writers do not have a monopoly on good ideas. Like most other people, they suffer through long, weary days when good ideas seem as rare as a lunar eclipse. Even on the worst days, however, they have faith in the creative process; their experience tells them that the chaos and frustration of early drafting will subside once a few drafts are written. Also, they look outside of themselves for ideas by reading extensively, observing their world, and building relationships with people.

Writing Is a Lonely Craft Conducted Best by Introverts

Or, only a weak writer seeks help from others. *Reality:* Contrary to the myth of the lonely writer in the garret, you do not need to chain yourself to a desk in order to create. Writing need not be a solitary, lonely act. In fact, writers who do not enjoy working in isolation either coauthor essays or they make arrangements with friends to meet together and write on their separate subjects. Others find it useful to write in noisy college cafeterias. And even if you do your best writing in a quiet room away from other people, you can probably do your best revising by observing how your words influence actual readers. When you can no longer find fault with your manuscript, there's nothing more invigorating than sharing it with trusted peers.

In business settings, authors often coauthor corporate reports and interoffice memoranda. Even the stereotypical author in the garret is responding line by line to how his or her words are likely to be received by the intended reader. Most writers routinely seek advice from colleagues and editors.

Writers Work Best at Their Desks

Reality: Thoughts about what you are going to write about do not only occur when you are sitting at your desk. If you are receptive to sudden insights, you will find that some of your best ideas originate when you are puttering about in the world, playing golf, or driving in busy traffic. Sutdies of the creative processes of scientists and artists suggest that our most innovative breakthroughs occur in the slack moments between work and play, so you would be wise to keep a notepad or tape recorder handy to record promising thoughts.

Writers Are Most Critical When They Are Planning and Drafting

Reality: When they are just beginning a writing project, experienced writers ignore doubts about the quality of their ideas. They often set aside questions about how best to organize their ideas or whether their rough drafts contain grammatical and mechanical errrors. Experienced writers understand that it is impossible to evaluate the originality of an idea based on a first or second draft.

Truly Skilled Writers Rarely Revise

Or, quality writing always develops spontaneously; revision is a form of punishment inflicted by nit-picking teachers. *Reality:* Professional writers do not perceive revision as merely a process of correcting errors; instead, they value revision as a method for developing and discovering their ideas.

Once Written, the Word Is Final

Reality: Sure, when you submit your finished essays to your teachers, you should believe in what you have said. Ideally, your essays represent your best thinking on your subject. However, you should feel free to change your mind when reviewing your work at a later date. In fact, your teachers want to help you recognize that thinking is an ongoing process. Rigid thinkers, like rigid writers, are characterized by bitterness and sarcasm rather than invigorated by the challenges of an ever-changing world.

It Is Inappropriate to Use "I" in Writing

Reality: You *should* use the first person when you are discussing personal experiences and when you want your readers to understand that the ideas in the text are your ideas or your opinions. Because the "I" voice is so integrated with the insightful, energetic inner voice that helps us create, you might find it useful to write all your first drafts in the first person. Later on, if required by your communication situation, you can remove or rework the first-person references.

The First Paragraph of Every Essay Should Define Your Thesis

Reality: Rigid rules about structuring ideas need to be shattered when serious thinking is going on. No single structure or format can satisfy diverse audiences and purposes. When you are revising your work, you will want to respond to the conventions for structuring ideas that exist for your specific communication situation.

Teachers Care Primarily about Grammar, Punctuation, and Spelling

Reality: More than anything else, your teachers care that you have thought deeply about a subject and written about it in such a way that they can understand your thinking. Your teachers are much more concerned with the quality and depth of your ideas than with spelling, grammatical, or punctuation errors. However, because stylistic errors can intrude on your reader's understanding of your subject, teachers understandably are concerned with these sorts of errors as well.

Read and Respond

1. Were there any writing myths that you know of that were not listed here? Before reading this article, did you subscribe to any of the myths listed? How does knowing that these writing "truths" are really myths affect your attitude about writing? Is it possible to believe these myths about writing and still get a substantital amount of writing done? How?

2. Truth is the opposite of myth. What are some helpful truths about writing? For example: A good writer establishes a comfortable place to write, a place that is free of distractions. What are some other truths?

3. If you had to select three pieces of good advice about writing to give to a high school student, what would that advice be? Would your advice be myth or truth?

Hot-Blooded Dinosaurs?

Joseph Levine and Kenneth Miller

M any body tissues, including muscles, operate well when body temperature is within a narrow range. The ability to move rapidly, either to capture prey or to avoid becoming prey, thus depends on a constant, optimal body temperature. Living reptiles are all ectotherms that make use of environmental conditions to regulate body temperature. To get warm, they bask in the sun. To avoid overheating, they shelter in the shade. This strategy works well in warm climates, but in very cold weather many ectotherms must become dormant.

Endothermic mammals and birds use insulation such as feathers, fat, and fur to retain metabolic heat. When it gets cold, endotherms metabolize food to keep warm. When it gets too hot, they sweat or pant to get rid of extra heat. Endotherms can perform muscular work for longer periods and under more widely varying environmental conditions than ectotherms. They can also grow faster. This vitality is expensive; an endotherm needs between *10* and *50 times* more food than a reptile of the same size.

Some paleontologists, led by Robert Bakker of the University of Colorado Museum, argue that dinosaurs were endotherms that regulated body temperatures as modern mammals do. This theory would account for dinosaurs' adaptive superiority and high growth rates, and it would explain how birds became endothermic.

Other paleontologists point out that dinosaurs were diverse and that not all were necessarily endothermic. It is not unlikely, says Yale's John Ostrom, that small, carnivorous dinosaurs were endothermic. Indeed, endothermy among the small dinosaurs that gave rise to birds would explain the role of the first feathers. But Ostrom and others point out that mammalian-style endothermy in large herbivorous dinosaurs is unlikely for practical reasons; they could never have eaten enough to survive. Elephants spend up to 15 out of every 24 hours stuffing 300-odd pounds of leaves and branches into their huge mouths. Could tiny-headed apatosaurs have gathered the daily *2000* pounds of conifers and lower plants needed to maintain endothermic metabolism in their enormous bodies?

Bakker's supporters point out that elephants use their large mouths for chewing and grinding. Dinosaurs, however, used their jaws only for *taking in* food; grinding was done by a gizzardlike arrangement in which stones that were swallowed were rubbed together by muscles inside the digestive tract.

Many researchers agree that dinosaurs had body temperatures higher than those of modern lizards. The debate over how they maintained those temperatures will continue for some time. Extinction, Ostrom says, ensures a certain amount of ambiguity. "When the dinosaurs died," he writes, "they took many of their secrets with them."

Read and Respond

1. From this brief discussion of the body temperature of dinosaurs, select the one statement that best summarizes what you believe to be the crucial argument for or against endothermic dinosaurs.

2. What is the quality of the personal observations and analogies in this argument? Are they decisive and persuasive? What else, if anything, is necessary before a definitive conclusion about dinosaur body temperatures can be reached?

ASKING CRITICAL QUESTIONS

After you read the article that follows, what critical questions come to mind? Everything you read will stir up your thinking if you read and question critically. What questions would you like to have answered in order for you to put the articles in proper context and to completely understand what is being said or reported? *On the lines following each article, write three questions that, if answered, will help you understand what is really being said.*

Excerpts from *Silent Spring*

Rachel Carson

There was once a town in the heart of America where all life seemed to live in harmony with its surroundings. The town lay in the midst of a checkerboard of prosperous farms, with fields of grain and hillsides of orchards where, in spring, white clouds of bloom drifted above the green fields. In autumn, oak and maple and birch set up a blaze of color that flamed and flickered across a backdrop of pines. Then foxes barked in the hills and deer silently crossed the fields, half hidden in the mists of the fall mornings.

Along the roads, laurel, viburnum and alder, great ferns and wildflowers delighted the traveler's eye through much of the year. Even in winter the roadsides were places of beauty, where countless birds came to feed on the berries and on the seed heads of the dried weeds rising above the snow. The countryside was, in fact, famous for the abundance and variety of its bird life, and when the flood of migrants was pouring through in spring and fall people traveled from great distances to observe them. Others came to fish the streams, which flowed clear and cold out of the hills and contained shady pools where trout lay. So it had been from the days many years ago when the first settlers raised their houses, sank their wells, and built their barns.

Then a strange blight crept over the area and everything began to change. Some evil spell had settled on the community: mysterious maladies swept the flocks of chickens; the cattle and sheep sickened and died. Everywhere was a shadow of death. The farmers spoke of much illness among their families. In the town the doctors had become more and more puzzled by new kinds of sickness appearing among their patients. There had been several sudden and unexplained deaths, not only among adults but even among children, who would be stricken suddenly while at play and die within a few hours.

There was a strange stillness. The birds, for example—where had they gone? Many people spoke of them, puzzled and disturbed. The feeding stations in the backyards were deserted. The few birds seen anywhere were moribund; they trembled violently and could not fly. It was a spring without voices. On the mornings that had once throbbed with the dawn chorus of robins, catbirds, doves, jays, wrens, and scores of other bird voices there was now no sound; only silence lay over the fields and woods and marsh.

On the farms the hens brooded, but no chicks hatched. The farmers complained that they were unable to raise any pigs—the litters were small and the young survived only a few days. The apple trees were coming into bloom but no bees droned among the blossoms, so there was no pollination and there would be no fruit.

The roadsides, once so attractive, were now lined with browned and withered vegetation as though swept by fire. These, too, were silent, deserted by all living things. Even the streams were now lifeless. Anglers no longer visited then, for all the fish had died.

In the gutters under the eaves and between the shingles of the roofs, a white granular powder still showed a few patches; some weeks before it had fallen like snow upon the roofs and the lawns, the fields and streams.

No witchcraft, no enemy action had silenced the rebirth of new life in this stricken world. The people had done it themselves.

This town does not actually exist, but it might easily have a thousand counterparts in America or elsewhere in the world. I know of no community that has experienced all the misfortunes I describe. Yet every one of these disasters has actually happened somewhere, and many real communities have already suffered a substantial number of them. A grim specter has crept upon us almost unnoticed, and this imagined tragedy may easily become a stark reality we all shall know . . . .

The history of life on earth has been a history of interaction between living things and their surroundings. To a large extent, the physical form and the habits of the earth's vegetation and its animal life have been molded by the environment. Considering the whole span of earthly time, the opposite effect, in which life modifies its surroundings, has been relatively slight. Only within the moment of time represented by the present century has one species—man—acquired significant power to alter the nature of his world.

During the past quarter century this power has not only increased to one of disturbing magnitude but it has changed in character. The most alarming of all man's assaults upon the environment is the contamination of air, earth, rivers, and sea with dangerous and even lethal materials. This pollution is for the most part irrecoverable; the chain of evil it initiates not only in the world that must support life but in living tissues is for the most part irreversible. In this now universal contamination of the environment, chemicals are the sinister and little-recognized partners of radiation in changing the very nature of the world—the very nature of its life. Strontium 90, released through nuclear explosions into the air, comes to earth in rain or drifts down as fallout, lodges in soil, enters into the grass or corn or wheat grown there, and in time takes up its abode in the bones of a human being, there to remain until his death. Similarly, chemicals sprayed on croplands or forests or gardens lie long in soil, entering into living organisms, passing from one to another in a chain of poisoning and death. Or they pass mysteriously by underground streams until they emerge and, through the alchemy of air and sunlight, combine into new forms that kill vegetation, sicken cattle, and work unknown harm on those who drink from once pure wells. As Albert Schweitzer has said, "Man can hardly even recognize the devils of his own creation."

It took hundreds of millions of years to produce the life that now inhabits the earth—eons of time in which that developing and evolving and diversifying life reached a state of adjustment and balance with its surroundings. The environment, rigorously shaping and directing the life it supported, contained elements that were hostile as well as supporting. Certain rocks gave out dangerous radiation; even within the light of the sun, from which all life draws its energy, there were short-wave radiations with power to injure. Given time—time not in years but in millennia—life adjusts, and a balance has been reached. For time is the essential ingredient; but in the modern world there is no time.

The rapidity of change and the speed with which new situations are created follow the impetuous and heedless pace of man rather than the deliberate pace of nature Radiation is no longer merely the background radiation of rocks, the bombardment of cosmic rays, the ultra-violet of the sun that have existed before there was any life on earth; radiation is now the unnatural creation of man's tampering with the atom. The chemicals to which life is asked to make its adjustment are no longer merely the calcium and silica and copper and all the rest of the minerals washed out of the rocks and carried in rivers to the sea; they are the synthetic creations of man's inventive mind, brewed in his laboratories, and having no counterparts in nature.

To adjust to these chemicals would require time on the scale that is nature's; it would require not merely the years of a man's life but the life of generations. And even this, were it by some miracle possible, would be futile, for the new chemicals come from our laboratories in an endless stream; almost five hundred annually find their way into actual use in the United States alone. The figure is staggering and its implications are not easily grasped—500 new chemicals to which the bodies of men and animals are required somehow to adapt each year, chemicals totally outside the limits of biologic experience.

Among them are many that are used in man's war against nature. Since the mid-1940's over 200 basic chemicals have been created for use in killing insects, weeds, rodents, and other organisms described in the modern vernacular as "pests"; and they are sold under several thousand different brand names.

These sprays, dusts, and aerosols are now applied almost universally to farms, gardens, forests, and homes—nonselective chemicals that have the power to kill every insect, the "good" and the "bad," to still the song of birds and the leaping of fish in the streams, to coat the leaves with a deadly film, and to linger on in soil—all this though the intended target may be only a few weeds or insects. Can anyone believe it is possible to lay down such a barrage of poisons on the surface of the earth without making it unfit for all life? They should not be called "insecticides," but "biocides."

The whole process of spraying seems caught up in an endless spiral. Since DDT was released for civilian use, a process of escalation has been going on in which ever more toxic materials must be found. This has happened because insects, in a triumphant vindication of Darwin's principle of the survival of the fittest, have evolved super races immune to the particular insecticide used, hence a deadlier one has always to be developed—and then a deadlier one than that. It has happened also because . . . destructive insects often undergo a "flareback," or resurgence, after spraying, in numbers greater than before. Thus the chemical war is never won, and all life is caught in its violent crossfire.

Along with the possibility of the extinction of mankind by nuclear war, the central problem of our age has therefore become the contamination of man's total environment with such substances of incredible potential for harm—substances that accumulate in the tissues of plants and animals and even penetrate the germ cells to shatter or alter the very material of heredity upon which the shape of the future depends.

Some would-be architects of our future look toward a time when it will be possible to alter the human germ plasm by design. But we may easily be doing so now by inadvertence, for many chemicals, like radiation, bring about gene mutations. It is ironic to think that man might determine his own future by something so seemingly trivial as the choice of an insect spray.

All this has been risked—for what? Future historians may well be amazed by our distorted sense of proportion. How could intelligent beings seek to control a few unwanted species by a method that contaminated the entire environment and brought the threat of disease and death even to their own kind? Yet this is precisely what we have done. We have done it, moreover, for reasons that collapse the moment we examine them. We are told that the enormous and expanding use of pesticides is necessary to maintain farm production. Yet is our real problem not one of *overproduction*? Our farms, despite measures to remove acreages from production and to pay farmers *not* to produce, have yielded such a staggering excess of crops that the American taxpayer in 1962 is paying out more than one billion dollars a year as the total carrying cost of the surplus-food storage program. And is the situation helped when one branch of the Agriculture Department tries to reduce production while another states, as it did in 1958, "It is believed generally that reduction of crop acreages under provisions of the Soil Bank will stimulate interest in use of chemicals to obtain maximum production on the land retained in crops."

All this is not to say there is no insect problem and no need of control. I am saying, rather, that control must be geared to realities, not to mythical situations, and that the methods employed must be such that they do not destroy us along with the insects.

My Critical Questions

1. _____
   _____ **?**

2. _____
   _____ **?**

3. _____
   _____ **?**

Summarizing

ESSENTIAL THINKING SKILLS

CHAPTER	WHAT THEY'RE CALLED	WHAT THEY MEAN
Chapter 3	**The Gathering Skills**	**Gathering all the information.**
	Observing	Actively seeking information through one or more senses.
	Questioning	Seeking information by asking questions.
Chapter 4	**The Organizing Skills**	**Organizing for the purpose of making sense.**
	Comparing and Contrasting	Noting similarities and differences between two or more things, events, or ideas.
	Classifying and Sequencing	Arranging things or concepts into categories and into sequential order.
	Identifying Cause and Effect	Recognizing the relationship between an effect and its cause.
Chapter 5	**The Generating Skills**	**Generating additional information.**
	Inferring	Making an assumption, stating a hypothesis, or coming to a conclusion based on limited information.
	Summarizing	Condensing the essence of the information accurately and efficiently.
	Synthesizing	Creating new information by combining two or more pieces of information.
	Generating Ideas	Creating new information, alternatives, or applications.
Chapter 6	**The Recognizing Skills**	**Recognizing what has been left unsaid.**
	Recognizing Purpose	Identifying a writer's or speaker's intention.
	Recognizing Fact and Opinion	Distinguishing between a statement of fact and a statement of opinion.
	Recognizing Tone	Identifying a sentiment or mood by assessing the writer's or speaker's choice of words.
	Recognizing Bias	Noting the presence and nature of a writer's or speaker's prejudice.
	Recognizing Organization	Identifying the organizational pattern of a thought, statement, passage, or plan.
	Recognizing Underlying Assumptions	Recognizing the suppositions that are taken for granted and are the foundation of a proposition, notion, or idea.
Chapter 7	**The Analyzing Skills**	**Analyzing for the purpose of coming to a conclusion.**
	Analyzing	Identifying and separating ideas, attributes, situations, and/or components in order to form a conclusion as to their relationship.
	Evaluating	Appraising something according to certain criteria and forming a judgment as to its worth or quality.
	Inducing	Analyzing individual facts or premises in order to derive a general conclusion.
	Deducing	Applying general principles or a broad framework to a situation in order to come to a conclusion about it.

"*He replied that I must needs be mistaken, or that I said the thing which was not.***"**
—Jonathan Swift

"*How often misused words generate misleading thoughts.***"**
—Herbert Spencer

What questions am I going to have answered in this section on summarizing?

1. What is summarizing, and how does it differ from reporting?
2. What do we do when we summarize?
3. What are the steps to take in summarizing, and how do the steps for summarizing brief passages differ from the steps for summarizing lengthy passages?
4. In what ways does a well-developed summarizing ability help create efficient learning, good grades, and superior students?

SUMMARIZING:
Condensing the essence of the information accurately and efficiently

When you summarize material, you actively engage your thinking abilities in order to condense it, to determine its essence. You are deciding "what counts." As you might assume, summarizing is a thinking ability that you are expected to use frequently in college. One study habit that most good students in college have in common is their reliance on summarizing. They declare that the way they get the most from an article or textbook is to summarize it in writing. Doing so helps them better understand and remember what they read. They also establish early the practice of mentally summarizing lectures as they hear them and then writing accurate summaries of the lectures after class. These students then review the summaries at a later time and when studying for tests.

STIR IT UP 5.4   Can you summarize what you just read? Condense the preceding paragraph into one sentence.

THINK ABOUT THIS!

Why Do We Say That?

Many common expressions have their origins in some past event or practice. Below are three such expressions. Stimulate your thinking and reasoning by attempting to figure out where the expressions came from. Summarize your explanation under each expression. The real explanation is given at the end of the chapter.

Chew the fat

_____

_____

_____

A ham actor

_____

_____

_____

Lick into shape

_____

_____

_____

SUMMARIZING IN COLLEGE

In essay exams you are frequently called upon to summarize content from lectures and textbooks as a demonstration of what you have learned. Even when an essay question doesn't contain the word *summarize,* it may still ask you to summarize. For example, What were the major causes of World War I? asks for a summary of the causes of the war, but in essay form. Chapters in college textbooks frequently begin and end with summary paragraphs or statements. In your English classes you are often expected to include summaries in your essays (for example, thesis statements and topic sentences). You are called upon to read books and write summaries of them (book reviews), and during class discussions you are called upon to summarize orally what you know on a particular subject. In research papers you are expected to summarize the statements of authorities and the research you've done. You read summaries (abstracts) at the beginning of journal articles in order to determine if you want to read the entire article. Whenever you answer questions like the ones below, you are relying on the thinking skill of summarizing.

- What was that essay about?

- What important idea was this philosopher attempting to get us to understand?

- Which of the sentences listed below best summarizes what the paragraph was about?

STIR IT UP 5.5   Summarize the preceding paragraph in one sentence.

_____

_____

HOW LONG IS A SUMMARY?

A summary can be as short as one word (for example, "What was that book about?" "Dinosaurs.") or as long as an entire book (for example, *A Short History of Dinosaurs from the First Ones to Extinction* by Richard Arthur). The longer the summary, the more details that are included; the shorter the summary, the fewer details. When the summary must be brief, the summarizer must choose which points are most important to include and which words best convey the points. When you summarize, you are attempting to identify only a few things: the main point, the purpose of the discussion, reasons or facts that support the main point, and any conclusion that is drawn.

THE STEPS IN SUMMARIZING

Summarizing is a tool for understanding because it helps you focus on the necessary and eliminate the unnecessary. In order to summarize, you have to shorten the information and identify the most important ideas, argument, or facts.

THINKERS

How many squares are on a chessboard?

Need a Hint? Don't forget the definition of a square.

Summarizing the Shorter Passage

Ask yourself these three key questions about the passage to be summarized:

1. What is this passage about? (What is the topic?) For example, you might conclude that the topic in a particular section of a marketing textbook is *car* manufacturing.

2. What is the purpose of discussing this subject (manufacturing cars)? You may determine that the purpose is to describe an innovative marketing plan for a specific model and year, say the 1965 Mustang.

3. What is the main thing that the writer wants you to know about this specific subject (marketing 1965 Mustangs)? It may be this: The marketing plan for the 1965 Mustang revolutionized the selling of new cars and set the industry pattern for the next ten years.

Raising these three questions about the reading passage or lecture material may seem cumbersome and a bit time-consuming, and maybe it is at first—but only at first. Soon you will find it easier to raise these questions as you read and study. Practice will make you an efficient summarizer.

Summarizing the Longer Passage

For longer passages such as chapters in textbooks and even entire books, the steps in summarizing are a bit different. You will need to call on additional thinking skills such as analyzing, evaluating, comparing, contrasting, and synthesizing in order to' avoid misinterpretations of what is important.

1. As you read, eliminate what appears to be unnecessary material. Anything that is trivial should be deleted.

2. Eliminate redundant material. Even if it's important, don't put it in your summary more than once.

3. Use a summary word wherever possible instead of listing items, ideas, or arguments. If a writer or speaker discusses a series of related things such as cars, trucks, and buses, substitute a single word, such as *vehicles*.

4. Use an encompassing word or phrase for a series of actions or events. For example, the sentence *General Electric changed their marketing plan* summarizes "General Electric fired their in-house marketing staff, recruited industry outsiders and Panasonic marketing staff, refocused marketing priorities, and developed a new marketing and advertising program for its microwave and refrigerator lines."

5. When summarizing lengthy or complicated passages, begin by selecting a key sentence or a topic sentence for each paragraph. You can often find the author's own topic sentences. However, less than a third of all expository paragraphs have topic sentences. Fiction seldom has topic sentences because fiction writers feel that topic sentences slow down the narrative.

6. If the passage or paragraph has no topic sentence, create your own.

7. Combine your summary statements into a "summary of summaries." If necessary, reduce the length of this final summary still further.

Apply these seven steps to your summary until it is the length you want it to be.

Summarizing may not be easy to do at first because it requires you to analyze what is said and determine what is important. However, it is one of those thinking skills that become easier and easier as you use it. Soon you will find accurate summarizing to be second nature and you'll do it without thinking about it.

STIR IT UP 5.6   Summarize what you have just learned in twenty-five words or less.

_____

_____

_____

_____

THINKERS

Useless Letters?

In the line of letters below, cross out six letters so that the remaining letters spell a familiar English word. Do not change the order of the letters.

BSAINXLEATNTEARS

Need a Hint? The solution is simple if you do *exactly, literally* what you are directed to do.

ANY QUESTIONS?

What is common sense, and how important is it to success? Why?

_____

_____

_____

_____

_____

_____

_____

_____

_____

Journal Observations (see page 13)

SUMMARIZING

1st Writing _____

_____
_____
_____
_____
_____
_____
_____
_____
_____
_____
_____

2nd Writing _____

_____
_____
_____
_____
_____
_____
_____
_____
_____
_____
_____
_____

3rd Writing _____

_____

_____

_____

_____

_____

_____

_____

_____

_____

READINGS

Tribal Colleges: Shaping the Future of Native Americans

The Carnegie Foundation for the Advancement of Teaching

Twenty years ago in Arizona, Native Americans created a new institution—the first tribally controlled college. Today twenty-four higher learning institutions, founded and controlled by Indians, are serving Native communities from Michigan to Washington State. While most of these colleges are no more than a decade old—a blink in time for higher education—they have undergone dramatic growth, expanding and gaining recognition in spite of conditions others would regard as impossible. . . .

Tribal colleges are truly *community* institutions. After years of brutal physical hardship and disorienting cultural loss, Native Americans—through the tribal college movement—are building new communities based on shared traditions. They are challenging the conditions that plague their societies and continue to threaten their survival. . . .

At the heart of the tribal college movement is a commitment by Native Americans to reclaim their cultural heritage. The commitment to reaffirm traditions is a driving force fed by a spirit based on shared history passed down through generations, and on common goals. Some tribes have lost much of their tradition, and feel, with a sense of urgency, that they must reclaim all they can from the past even as they confront problems of the present. The obstacles in this endeavor are enormous but, again, Indians are determined to reaffirm their heritage, and tribal colleges, through their curriculum and campus climate, are places of great promise. . . .

Today, there are twenty-four tribally controlled colleges scattered in eleven Western and Midwestern states—from California to Michigan, and from Arizona to North Dakota. Together these institutions have a full-time equivalent enrollment of more than 4,400 students and serve over 10,000 Native American individuals.

The Carnegie Foundation spent two years studying these colleges and the ideas they represent. During our visits, we were greatly impressed by the educational opportunities tribal colleges provide and by the pride these institutions inspire in both students and tribal members. In their cultural rootedness and powerfully considered purposes, tribal colleges are unparalleled.

At the same time, the challenges these institutions confront cannot be overstated. A typical tribal college necessarily charges low tuition but lacks a tax base to support the full education costs. Meanwhile, the limited federal support these colleges receive—the backbone of their funding—fails to keep pace with their enrollment growth.

Classes at tribal colleges frequently are held in shabby buildings, even trailers, and students often use books and laboratory equipment that are embarrassingly obsolete. At the same time, the colleges are educating many first-generation students who usually have important but competing obligations to their families and local communities.

Tribal colleges also offer vital community services—family counseling, alcohol abuse programs and job training—with little financial or administrative support. Successful programs frequently end abruptly because of budget cuts.

Considering the enormously difficult conditions tribal colleges endure, with resources most collegiate institutions would find unacceptably restrictive, their impact is remarkable. It became unmistakably clear during our visits that, even as they struggle to fulfill their urgent mandates, tribal colleges are crucial to the future of Native Americans, and of our nation.

. . . The greatest challenge to tribal colleges is the persistent search for funding. Indeed the ability to secure adequate financial support will determine if several of the colleges continue to exist.

Most of the nation's community colleges are supported through local tax dollars; tribal colleges are not. Because their students live in poverty-ridden communities, tuition must be kept low. Few tribal colleges have local benefactors, and regionally based foundations are scarce in the areas where most of the colleges are found. As a result, all must look for support beyond reservation boundaries if they are to survive. They exist on a collection of grants, gifts, and federal appropriations that are unpredictable and frequently threatened. It's a frustrating pursuit, administrators said.

Most tribal colleges are located in isolated regions, away from the agencies and institutions that can offer support. Still, the colleges have been successful in finding some important financial assistance. Grants from foundations and corporations, and occasionally from state governments, play a crucial role in building college facilities and maintaining academic and vocational programs. Without such help, some colleges probably could not have survived. . . .

College presidents are increasingly alarmed, however, that federal funding is not keeping up with the growth in tribal college enrollment. The total amount appropriated has climbed, but there has been a far greater growth in enrollment. This means that the amount available for each college student has substantially declined.

Read and Respond

1. Summarize this article in a sentence or two, identifying the "new crisis" in Native American education. Just what is "Native American education"?

2. Compare your college experience with the experience a student at a Native American college is likely to have. What are the causes for this difference in college experience? What might be done to eliminate the difference? Should the difference be eliminated?

Balancing Benefits, Costs, and Unintended Consequences

James R. Kearl

A bill was introduced for Congressional action in 1991 to increase the average fuel economy standards for new automobiles from 27.7 miles per gallon to 34 miles per gallon by 1996 and 40 miles per gallon by 2001. Since automobile producers would be penalized if they could not meet the standards, they would have a substantial incentive to produce more fuel-efficient automobiles. One of the consequences of meeting these standards, however, is that driving will become more dangerous. Why?

There are two methods of increasing fuel efficiency. First, producers can find technological improvements that increase the efficiency of using fuel. Second, they can produce lighter cars. Because it is difficult to invent technological improvements on demand and these improvements are difficult to mandate by law, making cars lighter is a much easier and more controllable way for manufacturers to plan on meeting the guidelines. Thus, in 1991, the average new car sold in the United States weighed 23 percent less than the average car sold in 1974 did. In 1978, about a quarter of all cars made weighed more than 4,000 pounds and 70 percent weighed more than 3,500 pounds. By 1984, only 1 percent of the cars made weighed more than 4,000 pounds and by 1988, only 37 percent of the automobiles made weighed more than 3,500 pounds. This 500-pound weight reduction appears to be directly related to earlier fuel economy standards.

Lighter cars are not as safe, however. This reduction in weight was estimated to increase fatalities over the life of a new car model between 14 and 27 percent—an additional 2,200 to 3,900 deaths. Injuries were estimated to increase by between 11,000 and 19,500 over each lighter car model's life. The additional weight reductions required to raise fuel efficiency to 40 mpg using existing technologies would increase fatalities by an estimated 4,800 to 8,600 for each car model.

Read and Respond

1. The writer of this article claims that weight reductions in new cars cause additional traffic fatalities, but an awful lot is being assumed here on the part of the writer. He assumes that the reader is making the inferences necessary to understand what is *not* being said. What inferences must the reader make in order to follow the author's argument and concur with his conclusion? For example, just how are these cars losing weight, and what does that have to do with fatalities?

2. Can you infer from this article that automobile manufacturers have *not* found technological improvements that increase fuel efficiency? If so, is this true?

3. If automobile manufacturers *have* found technological improvements that increase fuel efficiency and have implemented these improvements in new cars, what does that fact imply about the conclusion reached by the author of this article?

Girl Pilots: Air Force Trains Them at Avenger Field, Texas

Life, *July 19, 1943*

The time-honored belief that Army flying is for men only has gone into the ash can. At Avenger Field, near Sweetwater, Texas, girls are flying military planes in a way that Army officers a year or so ago would never have thought possible. These girls, who so joyously scramble into the silver airplanes of the Women's Flying Training Detachment each day, fly with skill, precision and zest, their hearts set on piloting with an unfeminine purpose that might well be a threat to Hitler. Each month scores of them complete their training in Texas and go to the Ferry Command to relieve fighting men for combat duty.

Behind the Army decision to train girl pilots was the personality of a smart and pretty woman, Miss Jacqueline Cochran, a famous pilot herself. Miss Cochran's proof of practicability of using America's 3,000 licensed women pilots came after her ferry flight to England in 1941 and close study of what women fliers were doing there. Shortly after, she demonstrated [the] ability of U.S. girl pilots by taking 25 with ample flying experience to England for the R.A.F. ferry setup. About the time that Nancy Love and a score of others with lots of flight hours formed the Women's Auxiliary Ferrying Squadron, Miss Cochran offered the U.S. Air Force a training plan for developing U.S. girl pilots with limited flying time to meet Army needs. That the plan is working is attested by the W.F.T.D. program now flourishing under Major General Barton K. Yount, commanding general of the Flying Training Command, and by the new job General "Hap" Arnold gave Miss Cochran last week—director of all women in the Army Air Forces and special assistant to Major General Barney Giles of the air force staff in Washington.

Under present requirements, any girl pilot with 35 hours flying time in light planes, who is between ages 21 and 34 and has a high-school education, is eligible for the Women's Flying Training Detachment after passing the regular Army Air Force physical examination and a personal interview test. After assignment to Avenger Field, [the] new trainee is under Army supervision but remains a civilian. Upon graduation she is competent to fly any size Army trainer and has the ground work for flying fast combat planes. One curious fact has come out of mass training of girl pilots: the instructors say that girls are faster on instruments than boys, more smooth and gentle in flying characteristics. But on the male side of the ledger goes credit for less mechanical flying and better memory for details. . . .

Girls are very serious about the chance to fly for the Army at Avenger Field, even when it means giving up nail polish, beauty parlors, and dates for a regimented 22 ½ weeks. On the go from 6:15 in the morning till 10 at night, they follow a stepped-up version of the nine-month course developed for male aviation cadets, learning every thing that regular Army pilots master except gunnery and formation flying. Every morning after straightening barracks and marching to breakfast, half of them have calisthenics or drill and attend three classes of ground school, while the other half reports to the flight line to take off in primary Fairchilds, basic Vultees or advanced planes of single and twin-engine types. Every afternoon the schedule is reversed. Every evening girls study in the barracks or are on night-flying assignment. For the whole course under Army command the trainee's life revolves around living and talking one thing—flying.

Though the program is physically strenuous, Avenger Field girls thrive on it, eating more heartily than ever before and sleeping like babes, even in short snatches between flights. On rainy days when they can't fly, they are skittish with excess energy that is turned to editing a newspaper called *The Avenger,* organizing plays or concerts, and writing gay parodies on modern songs. After dinner each evening trainees linger in the recreation hall, playing ping-pong, singing or dancing. On weekends, they sunbathe or swim and see movies in Sweetwater—that is, if flight schedules are up to date. If not, they stay home and fly. Fly first, then relax is the unwritten rule for trainees, most of whom have immediate relatives on active duty with the Army and Navy. That flying agrees with them anyone can see as Uncle Sam's suntanned girl pilots march along at Avenger Field, lustily singing the Air Corps' [anthem,]

Off we go into the wild blue yonder,
Climbing high into the sun!

Read and Respond

1. This article was written in 1943. Note the word choice in the title and throughout the article. What does the word choice tell us about attitudes toward women when this article was written? What things would be said differently if a similar article on women flyers in the armed services were to be written today?

2. What does this article sound like to you? What is being assumed or taken for granted in this article? Imagine this article surrounded by photos in *Life* magazine in 1943. Do you sense any purpose behind what is being said? What gives you that impression?

3. What criteria will you use to evaluate the importance (worth, accuracy, appropriateness, need) of this article for readers when it was written and for readers today? Will the criteria be different for readers today? If the criteria are different (or the same), what does that tell us about the criteria? Why?

ASKING CRITICAL QUESTIONS

After you read the articles below, what critical questions come to mind? Everything you read will stir up your thinking if you read and question critically. What questions would you like to have answered in order for you to put the articles in proper context and to completely understand what is being said or reported? *On the lines following each article, write three questions that, if answered, will help you understand what is really being said.*

School Segregation Is Unconstitutional

Chief Justice Earl Warren

Today, education is perhaps the most important function of state and local governments. Compulsory school attendance laws and the great expenditures for education both demonstrate our recognition of the importance of education to our democratic society. It is required in the performance of our most basic public responsibilities, even service in the armed forces. It is the very foundation of good citizenship. Today it is a principal instrument in awakening the child to cultural values, in preparing him for later professional training, and in helping him to adjust normally to his environment. In these days, it is doubtful that any child may reasonably be expected to succeed in life if he is denied the opportunity of an education. Such an opportunity, where the state has undertaken to provide it, is a right which must be made available to all on equal terms.

We come then to the question presented: Does segregation of children in public schools solely on the basis of race, even though the physical facilities and other "tangible" factors may be equal, deprive the children of the minority group of equal education opportunities? We believe that it does.

In *Sweatt* v. *Painter*, . . . in finding that segregated law school for Negroes could not provide them equal educational opportunities, this Court relied in large part on "those qualities which are incapable of objective measurement but which make for greatness in a law school." In *McLaurin* v. *Oklahoma State Regents,* . . . the Court, in requiring that a Negro admitted to a white graduate school be treated like all other students, again resorted to intangible considerations: ". . . his ability to study, to engage in discussions and exchange views with other students, and, in general, to learn his profession." Such considerations apply with added force to children in grade and high schools. To separate them from others of similar age and qualifications solely because of their race generates a feeling of inferiority as to their status in the community that may affect their hearts and minds in a way unlikely ever to be undone. The effect of this separation on their educational opportunities was well stated by a finding in the Kansas case by a court which nevertheless felt compelled to rule against the Negro plaintiffs:

> Segregation of white and colored children in public schools has a detrimental effect upon the colored children. The impact is greater when it has the sanction of the law; for the policy of separating the races is usually interpreted as denoting the inferiority of the Negro group. A sense of inferiority affects the motivation of the child to learn. Segregation with the sanction of law, therefore, has a tendency to [retard] the educational and mental development of Negro children and to deprive them of some of the benefits they would receive in a racial[ly] integrated school system.

. . . We conclude that in the field of public education the doctrine of "separate but equal" has no place. Separate educational facilities are inherently unequal. Therefore, we hold that the plaintiffs and others similarly situated for whom the actions have been brought are, by reason of the segregation complained of, deprived of the equal protection of the laws guaranteed by the Fourteenth Amendment. . . .

My Critical Questions

1. _____

_____ **?**

2. _____

_____ **?**

3. _____

_____ **?**

Statement of Purpose

National Organization for Women

We, men and women who hereby constitute ourselves as the National Organization for Women, believe that the time has come for a new movement toward true equality for all women in America, and toward a fully equal partnership of the sexes, as part of the world-wide revolution of human rights now taking place within and beyond our national borders.

The purpose of NOW is to take action to bring women into full participation in the mainstream of American society now, exercising all the privileges and responsibilities thereof in truly equal partnership with men.

We believe the time has come to move beyond the abstract argument, discussion and symposia over the status and special nature of women which has raged in America in recent years; the time has come to confront, with concrete action, the conditions that now prevent women from enjoying the equality of opportunity and freedom of choice which is their right as individual Americans, and as human beings.

NOW is dedicated to the proposition that women first and foremost are human beings, who, like all other people in our society, must have the chance to develop their fullest human potential. We believe that women can achieve such equality only by accepting to the full the challenges and responsibilities they share with all other people in our society, as part of the decision-making mainstream of American political, economic and social life.

We organize to initiate or support action, nationally or in any part of this nation, by individuals or organizations, to break through the silken curtain of prejudice and discrimination against women in government, industry, the professions, the churches, the political parties, the judiciary, the labor unions, in education, science, medicine, law, religion and every other field of importance in American society. . . .

There is no civil rights movement to speak for women, as there has been for Negroes and other victims of discrimination. The National Organization for Women must therefore begin to speak.

WE BELIEVE that the power of American law, and the protection guaranteed by the U.S. Constitution to the civil rights of all individuals, must be effectively applied and enforced to isolate and remove patterns of sex discrimination, to ensure equality of opportunity in employment and education, and equality of civil and political rights and responsibilities on behalf of women, as well as for Negroes and other deprived groups.

We realize that women's problems are linked to many broader questions of social justice; their solution will require concerted action by many groups. Therefore, convinced that human rights for all are indivisible, we expect to give active support to the common cause of equal rights for all those who suffer discrimination and deprivation, and we call upon other organizations committed to such goals to support our efforts toward equality for women.

WE DO NOT ACCEPT the token appointment of a few women to high-level positions in government and industry as a substitute for a serious continuing effort to recruit and advance women according to their individual abilities. To this end, we urge American government and industry to mobilize the same resources of ingenuity and command with which they have solved problems of far greater difficulty than those now impeding the progress of women.

WE BELIEVE that this nation has a capacity at least as great as other nations, to innovate new social institutions which will enable women to enjoy true equality of opportunity and responsibility in society, without conflict with their responsibilities as mothers and homemakers. In such innovations, America does not lead the Western world, but lags by decades behind many European countries. We do not accept the traditional assumption that a woman has to choose between marriage and motherhood, on the one hand, and serious participation in industry or the professions on the other. We question the present expectation that all normal women will retire from job or profession for ten or fifteen years, to devote their full time to raising children, only to reenter the job market at a relatively minor level. This in itself is a deterrent to the aspirations of women, to their acceptance into management or professional training courses, and to the very possibility of equality of opportunity or real choice, for all but a few women. Above all, we reject the assumption that these problems are the unique responsibility of each individual woman, rather than a basic social dilemma which society must solve. True equality of opportunity and freedom of choice for women requires such practical and possible innovations as a nationwide network of child-care centers, which will make it unnecessary for women to retire completely from society until their children are grown, and national programs to provide retraining for women who have chosen to care for their own children full time.

WE BELIEVE that it is as essential for every girl to be educated to her full potential of human ability as it is for every boy—with the knowledge that such education is the key to effective participation in today's economy and that, for a girl as for a boy, education can only be serious where there is expectation that it will be used in society. We believe that American educators are capable of devising means of imparting such expectations to girl students. Moreover, we consider the decline in the proportion of women receiving higher and professional education to be evidence of discrimination. This discrimination may take the form of quotas against the admission of women to colleges and professional schools; lack of encouragement by parents, counselors and educators; denial of loans or fellowships; or the traditional or arbitrary procedures in graduate and professional training geared in terms of men, which inadvertently discriminate against women. We believe that the same serious attention must be given to high school dropouts who are girls as to boys.

WE REJECT the current assumptions that a man must carry the sole burden of supporting himself, his wife, and family, and that a woman is automatically entitled to lifelong support by a man upon her marriage, or that marriage, home and family are primarily woman's world and responsibility—hers, to dominate, his to support. We believe that a true partnership between the sexes demands a different concept of marriage, an equitable sharing of the responsibilities of home and children and of the economic burdens of their support. We believe that proper recognition should be given to the economic and social value of homemaking and child care. To these ends, we will seek to open a reexamination of laws and mores governing marriage and divorce, for we believe that the current state of "half-equality" between the sexes discriminates against both men and women, and is the cause of much unnecessary hostility between the sexes.

WE BELIEVE that women must now exercise their political rights and responsibilities as American citizens. They must refuse to be segregated on the basis of sex into separate-and-not-equal ladies' auxiliaries in the political parties, and they must demand representation according to their numbers in the regularly constituted party committees—at local, state, and national levels—and in the informal power structure, participating fully in the selection of candidates and political decision-making, and running for office themselves.

IN THE INTERESTS OF THE HUMAN DIGNITY OF WOMEN, we will protest and endeavor to change the false image of women now prevalent in the mass media, and in the texts, ceremonies, laws, and practices of our major social institutions. Such images perpetuate contempt for women by society and by women for themselves. We are similarly opposed to all policies and practices—in church, state, college, factory, or office—which, in the guise of protectiveness, not only deny opportunities but also foster in women self-denigration, dependence, and evasion of responsibility, undermine their confidence in their own abilities and foster contempt for women.

NOW WILL HOLD ITSELF INDEPENDENT OF ANY POLITICAL PARTY in order to mobilize the political power of all women and men intent on our goals. We will strive to ensure that no party, candidate, President, senator, governor, congressman, or any public official who betrays or ignores the principle of full equality between the sexes is elected or appointed to office. If it is necessary to mobilize the votes of men and women who believe in our cause, in order to win for women the final right to be fully free and equal human beings, we so commit ourselves.

WE BELIEVE THAT women will do most to create a new image of women by *acting* now, and by speaking out in behalf of their own equality, freedom, and human dignity—not in pleas for special privilege, nor in enmity toward men, who are also victims of the current half-equality between the sexes—but in an active, self-respecting partnership with men. By so doing, women will develop confidence in their own ability to determine actively, in partnership with men, the conditions of their life, their choices, their future and their society.

My Critical Questions

1. _____

_____ **?**

2. _____

_____ **?**

3. _____

_____ **?**

Synthesizing

ESSENTIAL THINKING SKILLS		
CHAPTER	**WHAT THEY'RE CALLED**	**WHAT THEY MEAN**
Chapter 3	**The Gathering Skills**	**Gathering all the information.**
	Observing	Actively seeking information through one or more senses.
	Questioning	Seeking information by asking questions.
Chapter 4	**The Organizing Skills**	**Organizing for the purpose of making sense.**
	Comparing and Contrasting	Noting similarities and differences between two or more things, events, or ideas.
	Classifying and Sequencing	Arranging things or concepts into categories and into sequential order.
	Identifying Cause and Effect	Recognizing the relationship between an effect and its cause.
Chapter 5	**The Generating Skills**	**Generating additional information.**
	Inferring	Making an assumption, stating a hypothesis, or coming to a conclusion based on limited information.
	Summarizing	Condensing the essence of the information accurately and efficiently.
	Synthesizing	Creating new information by combining two or more pieces of information.
	Generating Ideas	Creating new information, alternatives, or applications.
Chapter 6	**The Recognizing Skills**	**Recognizing what has been left unsaid.**
	Recognizing Purpose	Identifying a writer's or speaker's intention.
	Recognizing Fact and Opinion	Distinguishing between a statement of fact and a statement of opinion.
	Recognizing Tone	Identifying a sentiment or mood by assessing the writer's or speaker's choice of words.
	Recognizing Bias	Noting the presence and nature of a writer's or speaker's prejudice.
	Recognizing Organization	Identifying the organizational pattern of a thought, statement, passage, or plan.
	Recognizing Underlying Assumptions	Recognizing the suppositions that are taken for granted and are the foundation of a proposition, notion, or idea.
Chapter 7	**The Analyzing Skills**	**Analyzing for the purpose of coming to a conclusion.**
	Analyzing	Identifying and separating ideas, attributes, situations, and/or components in order to form a conclusion as to their relationship.
	Evaluating	Appraising something according to certain criteria and forming a judgment as to its worth or quality.
	Inducing	Analyzing individual facts or premises in order to derive a general conclusion.
	Deducing	Applying general principles or a broad framework to a situation in order to come to a conclusion about it.

> **"***In training a child to the activity of thought, above all things we must beware of what I will call 'inert ideas'—that is to say, ideas that are merely received into the mind without being utilized, or tested, or thrown into fresh combinations.***"**
> —Alfred North Whitehead

> **"***Man is only a reed, the weakest thing in nature; but he is a thinking reed.***"**
> —Blaise Pascal

What questions am I going to have answered in this section on synthesizing?

1. What is synthesizing, and how is synthesizing like a disk operating system for a computer?
2. What is the difference between synthesizing as a process and synthesizing as a product?
3. How important is the thinking skill of synthesizing to success in college? What are some examples of the synthesizing I do as part of my daily learning experience?

> **SYNTHESIZING:**
> Creating new information by combining two or more
> pieces of information

You use your synthesizing ability whenever you reach into your memory to combine two or more things that you know in order to come to a conclusion or create new information.

SYNTHESIZING IS LIKE DOS FOR YOUR MIND

Your purpose in thinking varies. At any one time it may be to make an inference about what you are reading in a textbook, to identify an underlying assumption in an argument, or even to classify a series of behaviors. In order to accomplish any of these thinking activities you need something similar to a computer operating system integrated into your thinking. That is what synthesizing is.

The Process

As a process synthesizing functions like thinking software, allowing the rest of your thinking skills to operate both independently of one

THINK ABOUT THIS!

Putting It All Together

Synthesis involves putting together pieces of information in order to create new information. A good way to enhance the skill of synthesizing is to practice holding as much information in your head as possible when trying to solve problems. Without writing down any of the information, try to answer the following questions. Later, after you have synthesized the information and reached conclusions in your head, check your conclusions by drawing up simple charts in the space below.

1. *Joan and Robert are the same age. Joan is older than Mary, who in turn is older than Tom. Dick is older than Tom, but he is younger than Joan and Mary. Robert is younger than Harry. What is the order of age of these six people?*

2. *Bob is twice as old as Dick will be when Mary is as old as Bob is now. Who is the oldest? Who is the youngest? Who is in between?*

another and together. It allows you—in fact, it forces you—to combine what you already know with what you learn, sometimes in unusual and unique ways, in order to come to conclusions.

In order to answer the questions below, you are required to synthesize information.

- Which of these birds, plants, and animals will be able to live both in cold weather and in hot weather? (You combine what you know about birds, plants, and animals with what you know about weather in order to determine which birds, plants, and animals will be able to live where.)

- Is wood, fur, cotton, or silk the best heat insulator for a chicken egg incubator? (You combine what you know about the properties of wood, fur, cotton, and silk with what you know about the requirements for heating and insulating an incubator. The result will be new information: a determination of the best heat insulator.)

- Given that a room measures 8 feet by 10 feet and that carpet costs $15 a square yard, how much would it cost to carpet the room? (You combine the price and the measurements—new information—with a math formula—prior knowledge—to get the new information: the cost of the carpet.)

- What decisions should Mrs. Smith make about her medical care, considering the costs of treatment and the state of her health? (Combining the costs and the need for health care with the possible results of treatment will allow Mrs. Smith to come to a decision about her care. This conclusion is new information that comes as a result of synthesizing.)

A COMMON FORM OF SYNTHESIZING

Sometimes students have difficulty getting the main idea of an assigned reading. When that occurs, "study-wise" students break the reading up into smaller parts—paragraphs or sections—and identify a main point in each part. They then combine the main points and attempt to pull together a general statement by combining the main points. This pulling together of parts, this synthesizing, frequently allows students to generalize the main idea of the reading quite easily. The same technique can be applied to getting the main ideas from lectures and lecture notes.

THINKERS

By adding a single line, you can turn the Roman numeral 7 (VII) into an 8 (VIII).

But, by adding only a single line to the Roman numeral 9 below, can you turn it into a 6 (VI)?

IX

Need a Hint?
There are at least three ways to do this. Be creative.

STIR IT UP 5.7 On a separate sheet of paper, identify the main point of each paragraph of the following reading. Then combine the main points and come up with a main idea for the entire reading.

Hoyt v. *Florida*

Mr. Justice Harlan delivered the opinion of the Court.

Appellant, a woman, has been convicted in Hillsborough County, Florida, of second degree murder of her husband. On this appeal from the Florida Supreme Court's affirmance of the judgment of conviction, we noted probable jurisdiction to consider appellant's claim that her trial before an all-male jury violated rights assured by the Fourteenth Amendment. The claim is that such jury was the product of a state jury statute which works an unconstitutional exclusion of women from jury service.

The jury law primarily in question is Fla Stat, 1959, § 40.01 (1). This Act, which requires that grand and petit jurors be taken from "male and female" citizens of the State possessed of certain qualifications, contains the following proviso: "provided, however, that the name of no female person shall be taken for jury service unless said person has registered with the clerk of the circuit court her desire to be placed on the jury list."

Showing that since the enactment of the statute only a minimal number of women have so registered, appellant challenges the constitutionality of the statute both on its face and as applied in this case. For reasons now to follow we decide that both contentions must be rejected.

At the core of appellant's argument is the claim that the nature of the crime of which she was convicted peculiarly demanded the inclusion of persons of her own sex on the jury. She was charged with killing her husband by assaulting him with a baseball bat. . . . As described by the Florida Supreme Court, the affair occurred in the context of a marital upheaval involving, among other things, the suspected infidelity of appellant's husband, and culminating in the husband's final rejection of his wife's efforts at reconciliation. It is claimed, in substance, that women jurors would have been more understanding or compassionate than men in assessing the quality of appellant's act and her defense of "temporary insanity." No claim is made that the jury as constituted was otherwise afflicted by any elements of supposed unfairness.

Of course, these premises misconceive the scope of the right to an impartially selected jury assured by the Fourteenth Amendment. That right does not entitle one accused of crime to a jury tailored to the circumstances of the particular case, whether relating to the sex or other condition of the defendant, or to the nature of the charges to be tried. It requires only that the jury be indiscriminately drawn from among those eligible in the community for jury service, untrammeled by any arbitrary and systematic exclusions. . . .

In the selection of jurors Florida has differentiated between men and women in two respects. It has given women an absolute exemption from jury duty based solely on their sex, no similar exemption obtaining as to men. And it has provided for its effectuation in a manner less onerous than that governing exemptions exercisable by men: women are not to be put on the jury list unless they have voluntarily registered for such service; men, on the other hand, even if entitled to an exemption, are to be included on the list unless they have filed a written claim of exemption as provided by law.

In neither respect can we conclude that Florida's statute is not "based on some reasonable classification," and that it is thus infected with unconstitutionality. Despite the enlightened emancipation of women from the restrictions and protections of bygone years, and their entry into many parts of community life formerly considered to be reserved to men, woman is still regarded as the center of home and family life. We cannot say that it is constitutionally impermissible for a State, acting in pursuit of the general welfare, to conclude that a woman should be relieved from the civic duty of jury service unless she herself determines that such service is consistent with her own special responsibilities. . . .

This case in no way resembles those involving race or color in which the circumstances shown were found by this Court to compel a conclusion of purposeful discriminatory exclusions from jury service. There is present here neither the unfortunate atmosphere of ethnic or racial prejudices which underlay the situations depicted in those cases, nor the long course of discriminatory administrative practice which the statistical showing in each of them evinced. . . .

Finding no substantial evidence whatever in this record that Florida has arbitrarily undertaken to exclude women from jury service, a showing which it was incumbent on appellant to make, we must sustain the judgment of the Supreme Court of Florida.

Affirmed. [unanimously]

ANY QUESTIONS?

How would you answer this question: Where is the best place to live?

_____

THINKERS

Drop It!

In Hawaii, if you drop a steel ball weighing 5 pounds from a height of 45 inches, will it fall more rapidly through water at 20 degrees Fahrenheit or water at 40 degrees Fahrenheit? Or will water temperature make no difference?

_____

Need a Hint?
Hawaii aside, what temperatures are we really talking about?

Journal Observations (see page 13)

SYNTHESIZING

1st Writing _____

_____

_____

_____

_____

_____

_____

_____

_____

_____

_____

_____

_____

2nd Writing _____

_____

_____

_____

_____

_____

_____

_____

_____

_____

_____

_____

_____

_____

3rd Writing _____

_____

_____

_____

_____

_____

_____

_____

_____

_____

READINGS

Advice to Young Men on Chastity

Sylvester Graham

All kinds of stimulating and heating substances; high-seasoned food; rich dishes; the free use of flesh; and even the excess of aliment; all, more or less,—and some to a very great degree—increase the concupiscent excitability and sensibility of the genital organs, and augment their influence on the functions of organic life, and on the intellectual and moral faculties. . . .

The convulsive paroxysms attending venereal indulgence, are connected with the most intense excitement, and cause the most powerful agitation to the whole system, that it is ever subject to. The brain, stomach, heart, lungs, liver, skin—and the other organs—feel it sweeping over them, with the tremendous violence of a tornado. The powerfully excited and convulsed heart drives the blood, in fearful congestion, to the principal viscera,—producing oppression, irritation, debility, rupture, inflammation, and sometimes disorganization;—and this violent paroxysm is generally succeeded by great exhaustion, relaxation, lassitude, and even prostration.

These excesses, too frequently repeated, cannot fail to produce the most terrible effects. The nervous system, even to its most minute filamentary extremities, is tortured into a shocking state of debility, and excessive irritability, and uncontrollable mobility, and aching sensibility: and the vital contractility of the muscular tissues throughout the whole system, becomes exceedingly impaired, and the muscles generally, become relaxed and flaccid; and consequently, all the organs and vessels of the body, even to the smallest capillaries, become extremely debilitated; and their functional power, exceedingly feeble. . . .

Though every young man, of any correct moral discipline, must consider a promiscuous and unrestrained commerce between the sexes, as equally destructive to sound morality, and social peace, and civil welfare; yet most young men are apt to think, that if it were not for the moral, and social, and civil disadvantages, such a state of lawless intercourse were exceedingly desirable. But they who entertain this sentiment, are not aware, that moral and civil laws, so far as they are right and proper, are only the verbal forms of laws which are constitutionally established in our nature. They do not consider, that, however destitute society might be, of all moral and civil restraints, in regard to sexual commerce; yet, there are fixed and permanent laws, established in their very constitutions, which they cannot violate, without inevitably incurring penalty;—and that, in the present depraved state of man's instinctive propensities, such a lawless commerce, would, with the certainty of necessity, lead to the most calamitous and loathsome diseases and sufferings, that human nature is capable of enduring! Many of the most terrible plagues which have swept over the earth, and threatened to depopulate it, have been connected with such excesses! . . .

Marriage—or a permanent and exclusive connexion of one man with one woman—is an institution founded in the constitutional nature of things, and inseparably connected with the highest welfare of man, as an individual and as a race! And so intimately associated are the animal and moral sensibilities and enjoyments of man, that, besides the physical and social evils which result from illicit commerce between the sexes, the chaste and delicate susceptibilities of the moral affections are exceedingly depraved, and the transgressor renders himself incapable of those pure and exalted enjoyments which are found in connubial life, where perfect chastity has been preserved. . . .

The mere fact that a man is married to one woman, and is perfectly continent to her, will by no means prevent the evils which flow from sexual excess, if his commerce with her exceeds the bounds of that connubial chastity which is founded on the real wants of the system. Beyond all question, an immeasurable amount of evil results to the human family, from sexual excess within the precincts of wedlock. Languor, lassitude, muscular relaxation, general debility and heaviness, depression of spirits, loss of appetite, indigestion, faintness and sinking at the pit of the stomach, increased susceptibilities of the skin and lungs to all the atmospheric changes, feebleness of circulation, chilliness, head-ache, melancholy, hypochondria, hysterics, feebleness of all the senses, impaired vision, loss of sight, weakness of the lungs, nervous cough, pulmonary consumption, disorders of the liver and kidneys, urinary difficulties, disorders of the genital organs, weakness of the brain, loss of memory, epilepsy, insanity, apoplexy,—and extreme feebleness and early death of offspring,—are among the too common evils which are caused by sexual excesses between husband and wife. . . .

It is, therefore, impossible to lay down a precise rule, which will be equally adapted to all men, in regard to the frequency of their connubial commerce. But as a general rule, it may be said, to the healthy and robust; it were better for you, not to exceed in the frequency of your indulgencies, the number of months in the year; and you cannot exceed the number of weeks in the year, without impairing your constitutional powers, shortening your lives, and increasing your liability to disease and suffering; if indeed, you do not thereby actually induce disease of the worst and most painful kind; and at the same time transmit to your offspring an impaired constitution, with strong and unhappy predispositions. . . .

Read and Respond

1. What surprises you about this 1833 article? Anything?

2. What part of this article is based on fact? What evidence, information, or data are presented? How believable do you think this article was in 1833? How believable is it today? What has happened during the past 165 years to affect the believability of the article?

3. What about the author's thinking as demonstrated in the article? Was it clear, logical, reasonable, consistent?

Petting and the Campus

Eleanor Wembridge
Survey, *July 1, 1925*

. . . [In 1924] I was at a student conference of young women comprised of about eight hundred college girls from the middle western states.

The subject of petting was very much on their minds, both as to what attitude they should take toward it with the younger girls (being upper-classmen themselves), and also how much renunciation of this pleasurable pastime was required of them. If I recall correctly, two entire mornings were devoted to discussing the matter, two evenings, and another overflow meeting.

So far as I could judge from their discussion groups, the girls did not advise younger classmen not to pet—they merely advised them to be moderate about it, not lose their heads, not go too far—in fact the same line of conduct which is advised for moderate drinking. Learn temperance in petting, not abstinence.

Before the conference I made it my business to talk to as many college girls as possible. I consulted as many, both in groups and privately, as I had time for at the conference. And since it is all to be repeated in another state this summer, I have been doing so, when opportunity offered, ever since. Just what does petting consist in? What ages take it most seriously? Is it a factor in every party? Do "nice" girls do it, as well as those who are not so "nice"? Are they "stringing" their elders, by exaggerating the prevalence of petting, or is there more of it than they admit? These are samples of the questions I have asked, and have heard them ask each other in the discussions where I have listened in.

One fact is evident, that whether or not they pet, they hesitate to have anyone believe that they do not. It is distinctly the *mores* of the time to be considered as ardently sought after, and as not too priggish to respond. As one girl said—"I don't particularly care to be kissed by some of the fellows I know, but I'd let them do it any time rather than think I wouldn't dare. As a matter of fact, there are lots of fellows I don't kiss. It's the very young kids that never miss a chance."

That petting should lead to actual illicit relations between the petters was not advised nor countenanced among the girls with whom I discussed it. They drew the line quite sharply. That it often did so lead, they admitted, but they were not ready to allow that there were any more of such affairs than there had always been. School and college scandals, with their sudden departures and hasty marriages, have always existed to some extent, and they still do. But only accurate statistics, hard to arrive at, can prove whether or not the sex carelessness of the present day extends to an increase of sex immorality, or whether since so many more people go to college, there is an actual decrease in the amount of it, in proportion to the number of students. The girls seemed to feel that those who went too far were more fools than knaves, and that in most cases they married. They thought that hasty and secret marriages, of which most of them could report several, were foolish, but after all about as likely to turn out well as any others. Their attitude toward such contingencies was disapproval, but it was expressed with a slightly amused shrug, a shrug which one can imagine might have sat well on the shoulders of Voltaire. In fact the writer was torn, in her efforts to sum up their attitude, between classifying them as eighteenth-century realists and as Greek nymphs existing before the dawn of history!

I sat with one pleasant college Amazon, a total stranger, beside a fountain in the park, while she asked if I saw any harm in her kissing a young man whom she liked, but whom she did not want to marry. "It's terribly exciting. We get such a thrill. I think it is natural to want nice men to kiss you, so why not do what is natural?" There was no embarrassment in her manner. Her eyes and her conscience were equally untroubled. I felt as if a girl from the Parthenon frieze had stepped down to ask if she might not sport in the glade with a handsome faun. Why not indeed? Only an equally direct forcing of twentieth century science on primitive simplicity could bring us even to the same level in our conversation, and at that, the stigma of impropriety seemed to fall on me, rather than on her. It was hard to tell whether her infantilism was real, or half-consciously assumed in order to have a child's license and excuse to do as she pleased. I am inclined to think that both with her and with many others, it is assumed. One girl said, "When I have had a few nights without dates I nearly go crazy. I tell my mother she must expect me to go out on a fearful necking party." In different parts of the country, *petting* and *necking* have opposite meanings. One locality calls necking (I quote their definition) "petting only from the neck up." Petting involves anything else you please. Another section reverses the distinction, and the girl in question was from the latter area. In what manner she announces to her mother her plans to neck, and in what manner her mother accepts the announcement, I cannot be sure. . . .

Read and Respond

1. Was it your impression—until you read this article—that petting and necking among young people were "modern" activities and that the college students of the 1920s did not commonly indulge in them? (at least not to the extent that this article seems to suggest)? If you had that impression, why did you have it? If you did not have that impression, what impression did you have about necking and petting among the young people of the 1920s? How was your impression formed?

2. What troublesome issues does this article raise? How would you characterize the attitudes toward necking and petting of the women informally surveyed in this article? What problems were raised related to necking and petting?

3. Compare and contrast the advice about petting given to "younger classmen" in 1924 with the advice commonly given to youth on the same topic today. Is it the same or different? What accounts for the similarity or difference?

4. What is the tone of this article? What words or sentences convey the tone? What does the tone of the writing tell you about the attitude of the writer toward the subject?

5. Is there any falling back upon issues of morality, values, or religion in this article? Just what point of view seems to be shaping the presentation of information?

ASKING CRITICAL QUESTIONS

After you read the article below, what critical questions come to mind? Everything you read will stir up your thinking if you read and question critically. What questions would you like to have answered in order for you to put the article in proper context and to completely understand what is being said or reported? *On the lines following the article, write three questions that, if answered, will help you understand what is really being said.*

An Apology

President Ronald Reagan

The Members of Congress and distinguished guests, my fellow Americans, we gather here today to right a grave wrong. More than 40 years ago, shortly after the bombing of Pearl Harbor, 120,000 persons of Japanese ancestry living in the United States were forcibly removed from their homes and placed in makeshift internment camps. This action was taken without trial, without jury. It was based solely on race, for these 120,000 were Americans of Japanese descent.

Yes, the Nation was then at war, struggling for its survival, and it's not for us today to pass judgment upon those who may have made mistakes while engaged in that great struggle. Yet we must recognize that the internment of Japanese-Americans was just that: a mistake. For throughout the war, Japanese-Americans in the tens of thousands remained utterly loyal to the United States. Indeed, scores of Japanese-Americans volunteered for our Armed Forces, many stepping forward in the internment camps themselves. The 442d Regimental Combat Team, made up entirely of Japanese-Americans, served with immense distinction to defend this nation, their nation. Yet back at home, the soldiers' families were being denied the very freedom for which so many of the soldiers themselves were laying down their lives.

Congressman Norman Mineta, with us today, was 10 years old when his family was interned. In the Congressman's words: "My own family was sent first to Santa Anita Racetrack. We showered in the horse paddocks. Some families lived in converted stables, others in hastily thrown together barracks. We were then moved to Heart Mountain, Wyoming, where our entire family lived in one small room of a rude tar paper barrack." Like so many tens of thousands of others, the members of the Mineta family lived in those conditions not for a matter of weeks or months but for 3 long years.

The legislation that I am about to sign provides for a restitution payment to each of the 60,000 surviving Japanese-Americans of the 120,000 who were relocated or detained. Yet no payment can make up for those lost years. So, what is more important in this bill has less to do with property than with honor. For here we admit a wrong. Here we reaffirm our commitment as a nation to equal justice under the law.

I'd like to note that the bill I'm about to sign also provides funds for members of the Aleut community who were evacuated from the Aleutian and Pribilof Islands after a Japanese attack in 1942. This action was taken for the Aleuts' own protection, but property was lost or damaged that has never been replaced.

And now in closing, I wonder whether you'd permit me one personal reminiscence, one prompted by an old newspaper report sent to me by Rose Ochi, a former internee. The clipping comes from the *Pacific Citizen* and is dated December 1945.

"Arriving by plane from Washington," the article begins, "General Joseph W. Stilwell pinned the Distinguished Service Cross on Mary Masuda in a simple ceremony on the porch of her small frame shack near Talbert, Orange County. She was one of the first Americans of Japanese ancestry to return from relocation centers to California's farmlands." "Vinegar Joe" Stilwell was there that day to honor Kazuo Masuda, Mary's brother. You see, while Mary and her parents were in an internment camp, Kazuo served as staff sergeant to the 442d Regimental Combat Team. In one action, Kazuo ordered his men back and advanced through heavy fire, hauling a mortar. For 12 hours, he engaged in a singlehanded barrage of Nazi positions. Several weeks later at Cassino, Kazuo staged another lone advance. This time it cost him his life.

The newspaper clipping notes that her two surviving brothers were with Mary and her parents on the little porch that morning. These two brothers, like the heroic Kazuo, had served in the United States Army. After General Stilwell made the award, the motion picture actress Louise Allbritton, a Texas girl, told how a Texas battalion had been saved by the 442d. Other show business personalities paid tribute—Robert Young, Will Rogers, Jr. And one young actor said: "Blood that has soaked into the sands of a beach is all of one color. America stands unique in the world: the only country not founded on race but on a way, an ideal. Not in spite of but because of our polyglot background, we have had all the strength in the world. That is the American way." The name of that young actor—I hope I pronounce this right—was Ronald Reagan. And, yes, the ideal of liberty and justice for all—that is still the American way.

Thank you, and God bless you. And now let me sign H.R. 442, so fittingly named in honor of the 442d.

Thank you all again, and God bless you all. I think this is a fine day.

My Critical Questions

1. _____

_____ ?

2. _____

_____ ?

3. _____

_____ ?

Generating Ideas

	ESSENTIAL THINKING SKILLS	
CHAPTER	**WHAT THEY'RE CALLED**	**WHAT THEY MEAN**
Chapter 3	**The Gathering Skills**	**Gathering all the information.**
	Observing	Actively seeking information through one or more senses.
	Questioning	Seeking information by asking questions.
Chapter 4	**The Organizing Skills**	**Organizing for the purpose of making sense.**
	Comparing and Contrasting	Noting similarities and differences between two or more things, events, or ideas.
	Classifying and Sequencing	Arranging things or concepts into categories and into sequential order.
	Identifying Cause and Effect	Recognizing the relationship between an effect and its cause.
Chapter 5	**The Generating Skills**	**Generating additional information.**
	Inferring	Making an assumption, stating a hypothesis, or coming to a conclusion based on limited information.
	Summarizing	Condensing the essence of the information accurately and efficiently.
	Synthesizing	Creating new information by combining two or more pieces of information.
	Generating Ideas	Creating new information, alternatives, or applications.
Chapter 6	**The Recognizing Skills**	**Recognizing what has been left unsaid.**
	Recognizing Purpose	Identifying a writer's or speaker's intention.
	Recognizing Fact and Opinion	Distinguishing between a statement of fact and a statement of opinion.
	Recognizing Tone	Identifying a sentiment or mood by assessing the writer's or speaker's choice of words.
	Recognizing Bias	Noting the presence and nature of a writer's or speaker's prejudice.
	Recognizing Organization	Identifying the organizational pattern of a thought, statement, passage, or plan.
	Recognizing Underlying Assumptions	Recognizing the suppositions that are taken for granted and are the foundation of a proposition, notion, or idea.
Chapter 7	**The Analyzing Skills**	**Analyzing for the purpose of coming to a conclusion.**
	Analyzing	Identifying and separating ideas, attributes, situations, and/or components in order to form a conclusion as to their relationship.
	Evaluating	Appraising something according to certain criteria and forming a judgment as to its worth or quality.
	Inducing	Analyzing individual facts or premises in order to derive a general conclusion.
	Deducing	Applying general principles or a broad framework to a situation in order to come to a conclusion about it.

"*Every new and good thing is liable to seem eccentric and dangerous at first glance.***"**
—Brewster Ghiselin

"*Discovery consists of seeing what everybody has seen and thinking what nobody has thought.***"**
—Albert von Szent-Gyorgyi

What questions am I going to have answered in this section on generating ideas?

1. What is the difference between having an idea and generating an idea?
2. What can we do to begin generating ideas about something?
3. What advantages does group brainstorming have over generating ideas individually?
4. Why are later ideas often better than immediate ideas?

GENERATING IDEAS:
Creating new information, alternatives, or applications

The need for new ideas never diminishes. Consequently, one of the most useful thinking skills is the skill of generating ideas. It is usually lumped into a category called "creative thinking" because it involves generating and developing new information by reusing "old" information in new ways. This means that you can stir up your thinking, look at what you already know, combine it in different ways, and generate new ideas worthy of further consideration.

"HAVING AN IDEA" IS NOT THE SAME THING

Generating an idea is different than *having an idea*. When you generate an idea, you maintain an attitude of flexibility and focus *actively* on creating new information, a new idea. When you have an idea, as we all do hundreds of times a day, you are thinking *passively* and not *actively* attempting to exercise your creative thinking.

THINK ABOUT THIS!

Crazy Predictions

Predicting the future is something we all like to do. It's also big business: just think about psychic telephone lines, betting on sports scores, buying lottery tickets with "special" numbers on them, or business and election "forecasting." Frequently, however, predictions are not just wrong, they are not even close. Following are some predictions from the past that we now know were really off the mark:

- *"Who the heck wants to hear actors talk?" (Harry M. Warner, of Warner Brothers Pictures, in 1927)*

- *"We might as well close the Patent Office. Everything that can be invented has been invented." (Charles Duell, Director of the U.S. Patent Office, in 1899)*

- *"Heavier than air flying machines are impossible." (Lord Kelvin, President, Royal Society, in 1895)*

- *"There is no likelihood man can ever tap the power of the atom." (Robert Millikan, winner of the 1923 Nobel Prize in physics)*

- *"Babe Ruth will never make it in baseball. He made a big mistake when he gave up pitching." (Tris Speaker, baseball player, in 1921)*

Making rational predictions is a great critical thinking activity. You are forced to employ many of your thinking abilities, such as synthesizing, analyzing, evaluating, deducing, and inducing. Stir up your thinking. On the lines below, make some predictions about the future (at least 50 years from now) that you really believe may come true.

_____

_____

_____

_____

_____

_____

_____

_____

COMMON WAYS WE GENERATE IDEAS

When we employ our idea generating skills, we do it in relationship to some problem, idea, or experience. What we are attempting to do is alter the way we think about something and create new ideas related to it. That "something" is the raw material that we can manipulate in order to generate new ideas. We can do any of the following things to it:

- *Break it into smaller parts and list ideas for each part.* We can divide it into pieces, functions, spaces, roles. Looking at the pieces/parts often stimulates ideas.

- *Combine it with something else.* We can combine ideas, uses, purposes and see what we come up with. What similarities does it share with other things or ideas?

- *Simplify, simplify, simplify.* We can make it streamlined, easier, more natural. What is suggested by this simplicity?

- *Substitute.* We try substituting other materials, power sources, approaches, ingredients, processes, people, places.

- *Subtract from it.* What's obsolete? What's no longer necessary? We can take away one part or several parts. We reduce the number.

- *Reverse it.* What are its opposites? We can look at it upside down, inside out, backwards. We can reverse roles, or transpose cause and effect.

- *Add to it.* What can we combine with this concept? How does this concept fit in with the rest of our knowledge? We can add other parts, ingredients, motion, color, flavor, functions, sounds, textures, odors.

- *Redesign it.* We can redesign the interior or the exterior, or both. We can make fun of it. We can change its symmetry, pace, shape, capacity, function.

- *Magnify it.* We can make it bigger, better. We can make multiples, add time, make it stronger, higher. We can exaggerate it, or make some parts bigger or more important.

- *Minimize it.* We can make it smaller, lower, lighter. We can understate it or condense it.

The story is told of an announcement tacked up on a company bulletin board that said, "John Roe is the proud papa of a bouncing, 8 lb. 3 oz. baby boy! Mama and baby are doing fine and resting comfortably at St. Joe's." Below it was an announcement of a "Name the Baby" contest. For the next two days, John Roe's colleagues posted their ideas on the bulletin board. Here are some of the names that were submitted. Notice how the contributors used techniques of building on, adding to, or adapting previous names on the list when they generated new ideas.

Zor Roe	Merrill Lynmon Roe
Henry David Thor Roe	Yermy Hee Roe
Scissor Roe	Meist Roe
A Long Hoad to Roe	Skid Roe
Phar Roe	Beg Steelerbar Roe
Wis Key Roe	Getcher Ducksina Roe
Wheel Bar Roe	Clarence Dar Roe
Kye Roe	Broken Air Roe
Fidel Cast Roe	Bone Mare Roe
Jeth Roe	Kilimanja Roe
A. Tennisp Roe	Sagua Roe
Figer Roe	Maha Gony Roe
Edward Armour Roe	Mike Roe
Af Roe	Velk Roe

Marymaryquitecontraryhowdoesyourgarden Roe

Withsilverbellsandcockleshellsandprettymaidsallina Roe

What other possibilities can you think of?

And then there is the fifth-grade teacher who asked her students to suggest different ways for them to line up when they left the room to go to the library. Here are some of the students' ideas:

We'd like to line up according to . . .
the number of freckles we have
our shoe sizes
the number of missing teeth we have
the number of cavities we have
the number of zippers on our clothes
our after-school activities
the length of our fingernails
the types of stuffed animals we own

our favorite places

our opinion of our intelligence

our opinion of our beauty

the teacher's opinion of our ugliness

the size of our noses

our future occupations

our favorite swim strokes

the colleges we want to attend

the colors of our bikes

how we're feeling today (happy, tired)

how clean our desks are

how much chocolate we can eat in 1 minute

INDIVIDUALS MAY GENERATE IDEAS, BUT . . .

It is frequently pointed out that generating ideas is a "different" kind of thinking, because generating ideas is usually an enjoyable experience (unlike other kinds of thinking?) that can occur when you are alone, in a crowd, dreaming, arguing, reading a book, taking a hike, or otherwise involved. In fact, idea generating can be so much fun that it has become a popular group activity. Idea generation frequently occurs at family and social get-togethers, wedding and baby showers, birthday parties, and anniversaries. On these occasions, the idea generating activities are called *games*. At work or in a classroom, idea generation is usually called *brainstorming* and occurs as a group process. In a typical brainstorming session, participants are prompted to suggest as many different ideas as they can, as quickly as they can. No judgment is rendered as to the quality of the ideas because this would inhibit people from suggesting ideas. Participants are encouraged to value the ideas of others and to build on them. Sometimes an idea that seems irrelevant at the time it is suggested will later prove valuable. This process of building new ideas on the foundation of others' reflects the way the majority of new inventions come into being. According to one estimate, 80 percent of the patents issued by the U.S. patent office are for improvements in existing things, rather than for new things. Even this book would not exist without other people's ideas. The insights and research of many scholars over several decades are reflected in the material printed on these pages. The very concept of a printed book is itself a collective idea. Apparently, Johann Gutenberg's idea for a printing press occurred to him after watching a friend use a winepress.

STIR IT UP 5.8 This exercise requires you to stir up your thinking and think as creatively as you can. First, think about some of the strong structures that you have seen. These might include buildings, bridges, and tall supporting posts, spheres, or cylindrical shapes. Jot down as many examples as you can. Then select one (or more, if you wish) of the design/construction projects from the list below and follow the building instructions. When finished, indicate where your final idea(s) for the project came from and how you arrived at your design decisions.

> *Limitations:* In each of the following projects, all you can use is one sheet of ordinary poster board and no more than 12 inches of masking tape.
>
> **Project 1.** Build a structure at least 12 inches tall that will support a textbook at least 1 inch thick.
>
> **Project 2.** Build the tallest structure you can that will stand by itself without anything or anybody holding it up.
>
> **Project 3.** Build a three-dimensional shape with the largest possible surface area. Measure the area using a mathematical formula.

Which project did you undertake? ⎯⎯⎯⎯⎯⎯⎯⎯⎯⎯

How did you arrive at your final design ideas? ⎯⎯⎯⎯⎯⎯⎯

⎯⎯⎯⎯⎯⎯⎯⎯⎯⎯⎯⎯⎯⎯⎯⎯⎯⎯⎯⎯⎯⎯

⎯⎯⎯⎯⎯⎯⎯⎯⎯⎯⎯⎯⎯⎯⎯⎯⎯⎯⎯⎯⎯⎯

ANY QUESTIONS?

You throw away the outside, cook the inside, eat the outside, and throw away the inside. What is it?

⎯⎯⎯⎯⎯⎯⎯⎯⎯⎯⎯⎯⎯⎯⎯⎯⎯⎯⎯⎯⎯

LATER IDEAS ARE BETTER IDEAS

The quality and quantity of ideas we generate will vary widely depending on things like our willingness to put forth effort, involve others, and postpone judgment, and how we stimulate our thinking. The good news is that the more we practice idea generating, the more prolific we get at it and the easier it becomes. When we generate ideas, we generally have *better* ideas the more we allow ourselves to think about our ideas and revise them or build on them. Our early ideas tend to be ordinary, while later ideas tend to be better. Similarly, the more people that are involved in generating ideas, the better the final ideas tend to be. Idea generation tends to be of better quality if more than one person is doing the generating and if ample time is spent in the process. It is reported that Ernest Hemingway came up with more than thirty titles for one novel before deciding on *For Whom the Bell Tolls*. Similarly, in the process of inventing the light bulb, Thomas Edison created many prototypes before finding a filament that didn't burn out.

You use your idea generating skill when you think about and answer questions like these:

• How many uses can you think of for a paper clip?

• The average new automobile tire loses about two pounds of rubber through use before it wears down—becomes "bald"—and is discarded. Where could all the rubber that is worn off millions of tires each year possibly go?

• Suggest three different titles for this painting (novel, sculpture, song, movie, poem).

STIR IT UP 5.9 Everyone knows what an airplane pilot is, and most people have a good idea of what a pilot does. And we all know what airports are, and what the ticket counter personnel (they don't count tickets!), skycaps, and air traffic controllers do at airports. But seventy-five years ago, before flying became common, these jobs and job titles did not exist. What jobs will there be seventy-five years from now that are not in existence today? Look at the following list of possible future job titles and see if you can write a brief description for each one. Then think up ten job titles that will exist seventy-five years from now and write them on the lines below. Give a brief description of each one you create. While you are doing this, pay attention to how you go about generating ideas.

Home spinner _____

Life-decision advisor _____

Host mother _____

Future shock therapist _____

Z-ray operator _____

Sea herder _____

Skysitter _____

Laser architect _____

Attendant watcher _____

Mechbrain analyst _____

Your job titles and job descriptions:

1. _____
2. _____
3. _____
4. _____
5. _____
6. _____
7. _____
8. _____
9. _____
10. _____

STIR IT UP 5.10 Ideas are not generated in a vacuum, they are "suggested" by other things, ideas, or experiences. For each of the inventions below, name the thing (that is, item, animal, plant, experience, or event) that you think might have given the inventor the idea for the invention. Notice how this exercise stimulates you to generate ideas.

Hammock	_____	Pliers	_____
Loom	_____	Fishing pole	_____
Sailboat	_____	Paper clip	_____
Hula-Hoop	_____	Bag swing	_____

Sparkplug	———————	Picture frame	———————
Band-Aid	———————	Revolving door	———————
Eyeglasses	———————	Snorkel	———————
Photo-gray sunglasses	———————		

THINKERS

Strange Poem!

T. Eliot top bard,
notes putrid tang emanating,
is sad. I'd assign it
a name: gnat
dirt upset on drab pot toilet.

What is the most unusual aspect of this verse?

Need a Hint?
Got a mirror?

STIR IT UP 5.11 Proficiency at generating ideas comes through experience thinking in unconventional terms. For example, assume that your eccentric aunt has died and left you ten million bricks (bricks, not dollars). You can use them in any way, except to build with. Compile a list of ways to use these bricks. Below are some suggestions—both serious and whimsical—to help you get started.

Ground down for eye shadow	Platform shoes
Brillo pads for the Jolly Green Giant's frying pan	Airmail stationery for people who can afford anything
Holding down clouds	Knife sharpeners
Earrings	Small tombstones
Rafts for suicidal roaches	Subjects of poems
Paperweights	Big dominoes

———————————————————————

———————————————————————

———————————————————————

STANDARDS FOR THINKING AND REASONING

Identify the three most important critical thinking standards to be applied to the skill of **generating ideas.**

Put a check (✔) next to your three choices. Be ready to explain your thinking. Why these three?

☐ Clear	☐ Specific	☐ Relevant
☐ Logical	☐ Significant	☐ Fair
☐ Precise	☐ Accurate	☐ Consistent
☐ Deep	☐ Complete	☐ Adequate

 Journal Observations (see page 13)

GENERATING IDEAS

1st Writing _____

_____

_____

_____

_____

_____

_____

_____

_____

_____

_____

_____

_____

2nd Writing _____

_____

_____

_____

_____

_____

_____

_____

_____

_____

_____

_____

3rd Writing _____

_____

_____

_____

_____

_____

_____

_____

_____

_____

_____

_____

_____

READINGS

Radioactive Waste Disposal

William R. Shine

One of the most controversial aspects of nuclear power is the disposal of spent fuel (long-half-life isotopes and fission products) from the reactors. The fuel consists of about 3% ^{235}U and 97% ^{238}U. During fission, ^{235}U falls to a level below 1%, and can no longer sustain fission.

Most of the ^{238}U remains unchanged; however, some is attacked by neutrons, followed by β decay, to form neptunium and plutonium. Both α and β decay, and neutron capture by many of these heavy isotopes form a whole series of isotopes of the actinide elements, actinium, thorium, americium, curium, and so on (see periodic table). They are all toxic, and some have very long half-lives. For example, plutonium-239, which forms in both light-water reactors and breeder reactors, has a half-life of 25,000 years; thus, waste disposal has repercussions for the very long term.

Fission products make up the remainder of spent fuel. For these products, γ radiation from ^{90}Sr and ^{137}Cs presents the greatest problem. In fact, after 5 years the decay of these isotopes is responsible for most of the heat released by radioactive waste. The isotopes have half-lives of 29 and 30 years, so that in 700 years less than one ten-millionth of their radioactivity will remain.

It has even been suggested that the burden of radioactive waste will actually become an asset in about 500 years. The γ emissions will be mostly gone then, and the remaining hazard will come from easily shielded α particle emissions from the actinide elements. The actinides can then be separated and used as reactor fuels or for other applications.

Of course, such a view assumes that the waste material can be safely stored for 500 years. Critics question the certainty of guaranteed continuous safe isolation from the environment. We appear to be placing a tremendous burden on future generations. The thought of safe storage for tens of thousands of years, while even the actinides decay, is hard to imagine. The danger of leaching into water supplies makes even the α emitters a cause for great concern, since they are biologically more damaging than γ emitters if they are ingested.

Nevertheless, much research is geared toward developing procedures for safe, permanent storage of nuclear waste. A multibarrier approach is favored, applying several techniques simultaneously so that if one component of the system fails, others will serve as backups. The most often mentioned candidate is deep burial in remote and geologically safe locations such as salt beds, domes, granite, and shale. Both remoteness and geology are barriers, however.

Burial in salt deposits seems ideal. The presence of solid salt deposits at locations in New Mexico (near Carlsbad) and elsewhere suggests that no water has been present in these places for some time, if ever. If it had, the salt would likely have washed away. Thus, the potential for leaching seems nonexistent. Salt also exhibits plastic flow under pressure, so that back-filling burial sites with crushed salt could result in self-sealing as the formation returns to a solid mass. Critics argue that the possibility of volcanic or seismic activity precludes the certainty that the geological environment will remain intact for the long time required for actinides to decay.

A third barrier might be a canister that could withstand even severe environmental conditions. A fourth barrier might be achieved by converting nuclear waste to a solid form that would itself be resistant to leaching. Almost 20 years of research has provided information on *vitrification,* which is conversion to glass. Conversion to a ceramic material is also under investigation. It has been suggested that radioactive waste could be propelled into outer space and forgotten forever. But the risks of getting the material safely off the earth are regarded as unacceptable.

Critics often argue that we do not know how to dispose of nuclear waste safely. A supportive view is that we have several choices and plenty of time to determine which approach is best and to develop better technologies. Meanwhile, spent fuel rods from nuclear reactors are merely stored in large pools of water, and the water absorbs the radiation and heat as the waste steadily decays.

Until the late 1970s it was assumed by many that spent fuel would be reprocessed. This means that the components of the spent fuel would be separated so that all fissionable isotopes (for example, ^{235}U and ^{239}Pu) and fertile isotopes (for example, ^{238}U) could be recovered and recycled into a reactor. One relevant sentiment has been phrased as, "Plutonium was born in a reactor; it has to die in a reactor." This statement argues for recovering the plutonium and returning it to a reactor to be disposed of by fission. In addition, there might be uses for some of the actinides, and the pure waste material that has no value could be concentrated and stored.

Various factors have prevented reprocessing from being developed for commercial use. The low price of uranium is one; it has made reprocessing economically uncompetitive. In addition, a serious concern always is the possible diversion of plutonium to unscrupulous individuals or governments. Plutonium is highly toxic and can be used to produce nuclear weapons.

Whether reprocessing ever becomes significant commercially in the United States remains to be seen. Political and environmental pressures against it make it highly unlikely for many years to come. Meanwhile, another approach may be developed for disposal of some dangerous isotopes. A technique known as accelerator transmutation of waste (ATW) is being studied. By this method, long-lived radioactive isotopes are bombarded by neutrons and undergo transmutation to form nonradioactive isotopes or short-lived radioisotopes that decay rapidly into a harmless form. The process is illustrated by the conversion of the fission product technetium 99, which has a half-life of 250,000 years, into nonradioactive ruthenium-100.

Read and Respond

1. This article is a bit technical for some people. The writer assumes that his readers will know the meaning of scientific terms such as *half-life* and *isotope*. Who would you assume is the intended audience for this piece?

2. The article describes several methods that have been suggested for the safe disposal of radioactive waste. List these suggestions, beginning with the one you like best and ending with the one you like least. Explain what you like or dislike about each suggestion and why you listed them the way you did.

3. What ideas do you have for radioactive waste disposal now that you have read this article? What are the implications of your idea? What is the most difficult part of attempting to conceive of a disposal method?

Critical Issues in American Policing

David R. Johnson

The original American model of a police founded on the principle of crime prevention had several failings aside from the fact that politics was to play so large a role in the departments. Three important problems confronted the first police officials in the early years of policing, between 1845 and 1860: 1) a controversy over the adoption of uniforms; 2) a concern about arming the police; 3) and the issue of appropriate force in making arrests. The uniform was an important issue for a variety of reasons. First, the lack of a uniform undermined one of the principal ideas associated with crime prevention. In theory, people would be deterred from committing crimes when they knew that an officer was nearby. This was the uniform's purpose—it made a patrolman visible. Without this visibility, so the theory went, people would be more inclined to commit crimes. Other considerations also affected the uniform issue. The victim of a crime, for example, usually wanted to find a policeman in a hurry. How was he to do so if the police dressed, and therefore, looked just like everyone else? . . . These, then, were some of the reasons why many people insisted that the police should be uniformed.

Policemen themselves had other ideas. A uniform smacked of subordination and tyranny to many of them. These officers denounced uniforms as un-American liveries which would destroy their sense of manliness and democracy. . . .

Opposition from the ranks thus made the uniform issue difficult to resolve. The tactics which eventually succeeded in uniforming the police varied from one city to another and depended upon the intensity of opposition as well as the means available to overcome it. Officials in New York took advantage of the fact that their police served four year terms of appointment. When those terms expired in 1853, the city's police commissioners announced that they would not rehire any man who refused to wear a uniform. The commissioners remained firm in their determination through a subsequent storm of protest, and New York became the first city with a uniformed police. . . . Both in Boston (1858) and in Chicago (1861) the police seemed less inclined to protest and uniforms were adopted in those cities with little incident.

Arming the police was a far more sensitive issue than the dispute over uniforms. The personal safety of officers and citizens alike was at stake, and problems could equal the threat of death for dramatic impact. . . .

However unhappy the critics of an armed police might be, they had to face one unavoidable fact. Americans, unlike the British, had a long tradition that every citizen had the right, even the duty, to own firearms. Guns were part of the American culture. Nativism, racism, and antagonisms among immigrant groups complicated the problem of gun use and control considerably. Beginning in the 1840s, people in cities began to use firearms against one another systematically for the first time. Street fights, riots among firemen, and various other sorts of social conflict became occasions for the use of pistols (and occasionally muskets). When the newly organized preventive police began patrolling the streets, they were armed only with nightsticks. During the late 1840s and early 1850s, newspapers began to carry stories about officers shot in the line of duty. A few of these incidents appear to have been ambushes, but most occurred when a policeman intervened in a fight in which one of the assailants was armed with a pistol.

The problem facing the police had now become critical. Patrolmen never could be sure when a rowdy might have a gun, yet the officer knew he had to intervene in disorder quickly or risk having a small dispute between a small number of people grow into a serious problem. Tactical considerations, such as when and how to use force, became more complicated in these circumstances. Officers who misjudged these questions could pay a severe penalty. The solution to these difficulties emerged during the 1850s as individual policemen began to carry firearms regardless of official orders and public opinion. In some cases, as in Philadelphia, the city councils authorized their police to carry pistols, but such authorization only recognized what was becoming standard, if informal practice. The public accepted an armed police because there appeared to be no other alternative at the time. One of the most significant changes in American policing thus developed from the conditions which officers confronted on the city streets.

One of the most admired characteristics of the London police was, and is, their restraint in using physical force to make arrests. American policemen, however, have been notorious for their readiness to use force, and this trait has attracted a great deal of criticism over the years. The attitudes toward, and the use of firearms in the United States helps explain our police's willingness to employ force, but the presence of guns does not completely account for it. There were at least two other reasons why policing in this country has often been so physical. The explanation for this behavior on the part of the police lies first in American attitudes toward law and law enforcement and second in the social turmoil of the mid-nineteenth century.

American attitudes toward law and law enforcement are full of contradictions. Many citizens believe that laws against certain kinds of behavior are necessary, but that those laws should not be enforced against them. (Traffic regulations are good examples of this attitude.) Some people want to use the law as a way to regulate conduct which they think is offensive; but there are others who oppose using the law in this manner because they are not offended by that same behavior. (Laws against drinking or keeping saloons open on Sundays are examples of controversial legislation.) In too many cases, then, there is no consensus that a particular law, or a group of laws, should be uniformly enforced. This becomes an extremely difficult problem for an officer who is, for instance, under orders to arrest drunks when he is patrolling a neighborhood where drinking and drunkenness are seen as normal activities. The officer knows that if he arrests a drunk who then resists him, he cannot rely on bystanders to assist him because they disapprove of his actions. But he cannot back down from making the arrest; such an act would make him look ridiculous to onlookers who are already inclined to disrespect him anyway. Faced with these circumstances many patrolmen in the mid-nineteenth century resorted to force as a means of establishing their personal authority over the people they policed. In effect, law enforcement was often reduced to a question of whether a particular officer had the physical strength to dominate a situation requiring his intervention.

The social turmoil of the era between 1840 and 1870 also helped explain the use of force. Violence had become commonplace, and many people who supported police reform did so in the expectation that a more effective police would reestablish order on the streets. These people did not always care overly much exactly how the police accomplished that goal. If a few heads got broken in the process, that was a cost they were willing to pay. . . .

Although no one probably intended it, the use of force became a permanent legacy once the police discovered how useful it was in solving many of their problems. Violence, after all, did decline, but it did not disappear in the social life of American cities. Uncertainty whether an offender was armed, and a continuing lack of consensus over the enforcement of some laws, perpetuated the policeman's need to rely on his physical prowess as a means of dealing with incidents on the streets.

Read and Respond

1. What questions did this article raise for you? Was this one of them: Why would anyone want to be a police officer back in the mid-nineteenth century? How would you answer that question?

2. You may not have been surprised that the issue of police officers carrying guns was a major controversy in the past, but were you surprised that the issue of uniforms was so controversial? Why was that such a surprise for you? What assumptions do many of us have about the police? Do most people, including minority groups, share these assumptions?

3. The article states that "American attitudes toward law and law enforcement are full of contradictions." Is this true? If so, what are some of these contradictions? Where do our attitudes toward law and law enforcement come from? Do we inherit them from parents

and family members, do we develop them from personal experiences, or do we acquire them from TV and movies?

ASKING CRITICAL QUESTIONS

After you read the article that follows, what critical questions come to mind? Everything you read will stir up your thinking if you read and question critically. What questions would you like to have answered in order for you to put the articles in proper context and to completely understand what is being said or reported? *On the lines following the article, write three questions that, if answered, will help you understand what is really being said.*

Earth First! Advocates Ecotage

Dave Foreman and Bill Howard

In early summer of 1977, the United States Forest Service began an 18-month-long inventory and evaluation of the remaining roadless and undeveloped areas on the National Forests and Grasslands of the United States. During this second Roadless Area Review and Evaluation (RARE II), the Forest Service identified 2,686 roadless areas of 5,000 acres or more totaling 66 million acres out of the 187 million acres of National Forest lands. Approximately 15 million acres of roadless areas were not included in RARE II because of sloppy inventory procedures or because they had already gone through land use planning after the first RARE program in the early '70s. All in all, there were some 80 million acres on the National Forests in 1977 retaining a significant degree of natural diversity and wildness (a total area equivalent in size to the state of New Mexico or a square 350 × 350 miles).

About the same time as the Forest Service began RARE II, the Bureau of Land Management (BLM) initiated a wilderness inventory as required by the Federal Land Planning and Management Act of 1976 (FLPMA) on the 189 million acres of federal land that they manage in the lower 48 states. In their initial inventory, BLM identified 60 million acres of roadless areas of 5,000 acres or more (a total area approximately the size of Oregon or a square 300 × 300 miles).

Along with the National Parks & Monuments, National Wildlife Refuges, existing Wilderness Areas and some state lands, these Forest Service and BLM roadless areas represent the remaining natural wealth of the United States. They are the remnant of natural diversity after the industrial conquest of the most beautiful, diverse and productive of all the continents of the Earth: North America. Turtle Island.

Only one hundred and fifty years ago, the Great Plains were a vast, waving sea of grass stretching from the Chihuahuan Desert of Mexico to the boreal forest of Canada, from the oak-hickory forests of the Ozarks to the Rocky Mountains. Bison blanketed the plains—it has been estimated that 60 million of the huge, shaggy beasts moved across the grass. Great herds of pronghorn and elk also filled this Pleistocene landscape. Packs of wolves and numerous grizzly bears followed the immense herds.

One hundred and fifty years ago, John James Audubon estimated that there were several *billion* birds in a flock of passenger pigeons that flew past him for several days on the Ohio River. It has been said that a squirrel could travel from the Atlantic seaboard to the Mississippi River without touching the ground, so dense was the deciduous forest of the East.

At the time of the Lewis and Clark Expedition, an estimated 100,000 grizzlies roamed the western half of what is now the United States. The howl of the wolf was ubiquitous. The condor dominated the sky from the Pacific Coast to the Great Plains. Salmon and sturgeon filled the rivers. Ocelots, jaguars, margay cats and jaguarundis roamed the Texas brush and Southwestern deserts and mesas. Bighorn sheep in great numbers ranged the mountains of the Rockies, Great Basin, Southwest and Pacific Coast. Ivory-billed woodpeckers and Carolina parakeets filled the steamy forests of the Deep South. The land was alive.

East of the Mississippi, giant tulip poplars, chestnuts, oaks, hickories and other trees formed the most diverse temperate deciduous forest in the world. On the Pacific Coast, redwood, hemlock, Douglas fir, spruce, cedar, fir and pine formed the grandest forest on Earth.

In the space of a few generations we have laid waste to paradise. The tall grass prairie has been transformed into a corn factory where wildlife means the exotic pheasant. The short grass prairie is a grid of carefully fenced cow pastures and wheat fields. The passenger pigeon is no more. The last died in the Cincinnati Zoo in 1914. The endless forests of the East are tame woodlots. The only virgin deciduous forest there is in tiny museum pieces of hundreds of acres. Six hundred grizzlies remain and they are going fast. There are only three condors left in the wild and they are scheduled for capture and imprisonment in the Los Angeles Zoo. Except in northern Minnesota and Isle Royale, wolves are known merely as scattered individuals drifting across the Canadian and Mexican borders (a pack has recently formed in Glacier National Park). Four percent of the peerless Redwood Forest remains and the monumental old growth forest cathedrals of Oregon are all but gone.

The tropical cats have been shot and poisoned from our southwestern borderlands. The subtropical Eden of Florida has been transformed into hotels and citrus orchards. Domestic cattle have grazed bare and radically altered the composition of the grassland communities of the West, displacing elk, moose, bighorn sheep and pronghorn and leading to the virtual extermination of grizzly, wolf, cougar, bobcat and other "varmints." Dams choke the rivers and streams of the land.

Nonetheless, wildness and natural diversity remain. There are a few scattered grasslands ungrazed, stretches of free-flowing river undammed and undiverted, thousand-year-old forests, Eastern woodlands growing back to forest and reclaiming past roads, grizzlies and wolves and lions and wolverines and bighorn and moose roaming the backcountry; hundreds of square miles that have never known the imprint of a tire, the bite of a drill, the rip of a 'dozer, the cut of a saw, the smell of gasoline.

These are the places that hold North America together, that contain the genetic information of life, that represent sanity in a whirlwind of madness.

In January of 1979, the Forest Service announced the results of RARE II: of the 80 million acres of undeveloped lands on the National Forests, only 15 million acres were recommended for protection against logging, road building and other "developments." In the big tree state of Oregon, for example, only 370,000 acres were proposed for Wilderness protection out of 4.5 million acres of roadless, uncut forest lands. Of the areas nationally slated for protection, most were too high, too dry, too cold, too steep to offer much in the way of "resources" to the loggers, miners and graziers. Those roadless areas with critical old growth forest values were allocated for the sawmill. Important grizzly habitat in the Northern Rockies was tossed to the oil industry and the loggers. Off-road-vehicle fanatics and the landed gentry of the livestock industry won out in the Southwest and Great Basin.

During the early 1980s, the Forest Service developed its DARN (Development Activities in Roadless Non-selected) list outlining specific projects in specific roadless areas. The implication of DARN is staggering. It is evidence that the leadership of the United States Forest Service consciously and deliberately sat down and asked themselves, "How can we keep from being plagued by conservationists and their damned wilderness proposals? How can we insure that we'll never have to do another RARE?" Their solution was simple and brilliant: get rid of the roadless areas. DARN outlines *nine thousand* miles of road, one and a half million acres of timber cuts, seven million acres of oil and gas leases in National Forest RARE II areas by 1987. In most cases, the damaged acreage will be far greater than the acreage stated because roads are designed to split areas in half and timber sales are engineered to take place in the center of roadless areas, thereby devastating the biological integrity of the entire area. The great roadless areas so critical to the maintenance of natural diversity will soon be gone. Species dependent upon old growth and large wild areas will be shoved to the brink of extinction.

But the situation on the National Forests is even worse than DARN indicated. After a careful review of Forest Service documents, Howie Wolke reported in the June 21, 1985, issue of *Earth First!* that more than 75,000 miles of road are proposed for construction in currently roadless areas on the National Forests over the next fifteen years. This immense road network (enough to encircle the planet three times) will cost the American taxpayer over 3 billion dollars to provide large timber corporations access to a mere 500 million dollars worth of timber.

The BLM wilderness review has been a similar process of attrition. It is unlikely that more than 9 million acres will be recommended for Wilderness out of the 60 million with which the review began. Again, it is the more spectacular but biologically less rich areas that will be proposed for protection.

During 1984, Congress passed legislation designating minimal National Forest Wilderness acreages for most states (generally only slightly larger than the pitiful RARE II recommendations and concentrating on "rocks and ice" instead of crucial forested lands). In the next few years, similar picayune legislation for National Forest Wilderness in the remaining states and for BLM Wilderness will probably be enacted. The other roadless areas will be eliminated from consideration. National Forest Management Plans emphasizing industrial logging, grazing, mineral and energy development, road building, and motorized recreation will be implemented. Conventional means of protecting these millions of acres of wild country will largely dissipate. Judicial and administrative appeals for their protection will be closed off. Congress will turn a deaf ear to requests for additional Wilderness so soon after disposing of the thorny issue. The effectiveness of conventional political lobbying by conservation groups to protect endangered wild lands will evaporate. And in half a decade, the saw, 'dozer and drill will devastate most of what is unprotected. The battle for wilderness will be over. Perhaps 3% of the United States will be more or less protected and it will be open season on the rest. Unless. . . .

Many of the projects that will destroy roadless areas are economically marginal. It is costly for the Forest Service, BLM, timber companies, oil companies, mining companies and others to scratch out the "resources" in these last wild areas. It is expensive to maintain the necessary infrastructure of roads for the exploitation of wild lands. The cost of repairs, the hassle, the delay, the down-time may just be too much for the bureaucrats and exploiters to accept if there is a widely-dispersed, unorganized, *strategic* movement of resistance across the land.

It is time for women and men, individually and in small groups, to act heroically and admittedly illegally in defense of the wild, to put a monkeywrench into the gears of the machine destroying natural diversity. This strategic monkeywrenching can be safe, it can be easy, it can be fun, and—most importantly—it can be effective in stopping timber cutting, road building, overgrazing, oil & gas exploration, mining, dam building, powerline construction, off-road-vehicle use, trapping, ski area development and other forms of destruction of the wilderness, as well as cancerous suburban sprawl.

But it must be strategic, it must be thoughtful, it must be deliberate in order to succeed. Such a campaign of resistance would follow these principles:

Monkeywrenching Is Non-Violent

Monkeywrenching is non-violent resistance to the destruction of natural diversity and wilderness. It is not directed toward harming human beings or other forms of life. It is aimed at inanimate machines and tools. Care is always taken to minimize any possible threat to other people (and to the monkeywrenchers themselves).

Monkeywrenching Is Not Organized

There can be no central direction or organization to monkeywrenching. Any type of network would invite infiltration, *agents provocateurs* and repression. It is truly individual action. Because of this, communication among monkeywrenchers is difficult and dangerous. Anonymous discussion . . . through the Dear Ned Ludd section of the *Earth First! Journal* seems to be the safest avenue of communication to refine techniques, security procedures and strategy.

Monkeywrenching Is Individual

Monkeywrenching is done by individuals or very small groups of people who have known each other for years. There is trust and a good working relationship in such groups. The more people involved, the greater are the dangers of infiltration or a loose mouth. Earth defenders avoid working with people they haven't known for a long time, those who can't keep their mouths closed, and those with grandiose or violent ideas (they may be police agents or dangerous crackpots).

Monkeywrenching Is Targeted

Ecodefenders pick their targets. Mindless, erratic vandalism is counterproductive. Monkeywrenchers know that they do not stop a specific logging sale by destroying any piece of logging equipment which they come across. They make sure it belongs to the proper culprit. They ask themselves what is the most vulnerable point of a wilderness-destroying project and strike there. Senseless vandalism leads to loss of popular sympathy.

Monkeywrenching Is Timely

There is a proper time and place for monkeywrenching. There are also times when monkeywrenching may be counterproductive. Monkeywrenchers generally should not act when there is a non-violent civil disobedience action (a blockade, etc.) taking place against the opposed project. Monkeywrenching may cloud the issue of direct action and the blockaders could be blamed for the ecotage and be put in danger from the work crew or police. Blockades and monkeywrenching usually do not mix. Monkeywrenching may also not be appropriate when delicate political negotiations are taking place for the protection of a certain area. There are, of course, exceptions to this rule. The Earth warrior always thinks: Will monkeywrenching help or hinder the protection of this place?

My Critical Questions

1. _____

_____ **?**

2. _____

_____ **?**

3. _____

_____ **?**

SOLUTIONS to Items in This Chapter

THINKERS (p. 159)

Ben likes only words that have the name of a bird or animal in them: *sc<u>owl</u>*, *g<u>rape</u>s*, *ka<u>yak</u>*, *<u>potter</u>*.

ANY QUESTIONS? (p. 163)

Here are some "possible" reasons:
1. The stores didn't start out as 24-hour-a-day operations.
2. The stores weren't always open 365 days a year.
3. The locks may be there in case of an emergency evacuation of the area.

THINKERS (p. 164)

The number 3. The number in a shape indicates the number of other shapes that border it.

THINK ABOUT THIS! (p. 182)

Chew the fat means "to chat for a long time." Before modern times, sailors preserved meat by packing it in barrels of brine. Salt beef was one of the few staples that could last through a long voyage, but the salting process made beef very tough to eat. Seamen had to chew it for a long time. They, therefore, had long periods of time to chew and talk.

A *ham actor* is one whose performance is overplayed. Theater in nineteenth-century America was very popular, but money was in short supply for the less talented actors and actresses. The cheapest way for them to remove greasepaint or makeup was with ham fat. Thus, bad performers came to be called *hamfatters* and later *ham actors*.

Lick into shape: Early humans believed animals were born in a formless manner and were licked into shape by their mothers. The notion was particularly associated with bears, who did not allow humans near their cubs. However, people could see the bear licking a bundle of fur.

THINKERS (p. 184)

204. Do you see them all?

THINKERS (p. 186)

If you literally cross out the letters found in the words *six letters,* you are left with the word *banana.*

ANY QUESTIONS? (p. 186)

Common sense is just ordinary thinking that is largely shaped by the culture in which we live. It's the kind of thinking that gets us through the day. The problem with common sense is that it can lead to wrong conclusions. Common sense has led people to think that sacrificing an animal was the best way to make it rain, that the earth was flat, that the sun revolved around the earth, that using leeches would cure disease, and that those mysterious stars in the heavens hid during the day.

THINKERS (p. 204)

How creative were you? There are at least three ways to turn IX into VI:
1. Draw a horizontal line through the middle of IX. Then cover the top half and turn your paper upside down.
2. Draw the "line" S in front of IX. It now reads SIX.
3. Add the "line" 6 after IX. It now reads I $\times$ 6: "one times six is six."

THINKERS (p. 206)

It will fall faster through water at 40°F. Since water freezes at 32°F, you will not be able to drop a steel ball through water that is 20°F. The water would be ice.

ANY QUESTIONS? (p. 206)

The best place to live is where your personal interests and abilities are challenged and encouraged. Living in such a place is more satisfying than living where the skiing, sailing, or socializing is great, but where you are not stimulated mentally and professionally.

ANY QUESTIONS? (p. 222)

How about corn on the cob? Or perhaps an egg (throw away the shell, fry the egg, eat the white, throw away the yolk). What others did you think of?

THINKERS (p. 226)

The verse reads the same forwards and backwards. It is an example of a *palindrome.* In fact, it is the longest palindrome in the English language to date.

Chapter 6

RECOGNIZING SKILLS

- ■ **Recognizing Purpose**
- ■ **Recognizing Fact and Opinion**
- ■ **Recognizing Tone**
- ■ **Recognizing Bias**
- ■ **Recognizing Organization**
- ■ **Recognizing Underlying Assumptions**

What has been left unsaid?

> "*A stand can be made against invasion by an army; no stand can be made against invasion by an idea.*"
> —Victor Hugo

> "*A word is not a crystal, transparent and unchanging, it is the skin of a living thought and may vary greatly in color and content according to the circumstances in which it is used.*"
> —Oliver Wendell Holmes

> "*Between the idea*
> *And the reality*
> *Between the motion*
> *And the act*
> *Falls the Shadow*"
> —T. S. Eliot, "The Hollow Men"

STIR UP YOUR THINKING BEFORE YOU START READING

Before you start reading this chapter, answer the questions below. Compare your answers with what you learn in this chapter.

What percentage of what we read and hear each day can we accept at face value, without suspecting a hidden bias or agenda? How much of what we read and hear contains hidden "persuaders"?

Recognizing Purpose

ESSENTIAL THINKING SKILLS		
CHAPTER	**WHAT THEY'RE CALLED**	**WHAT THEY MEAN**
Chapter 3	**The Gathering Skills**	**Gathering all the information.**
	Observing	Actively seeking information through one or more senses.
	Questioning	Seeking information by asking questions.
Chapter 4	**The Organizing Skills**	**Organizing for the purpose of making sense.**
	Comparing and Contrasting	Noting similarities and differences between two or more things, events, or ideas.
	Classifying and Sequencing	Arranging things or concepts into categories and into sequential order.
	Identifying Cause and Effect	Recognizing the relationship between an effect and its cause.
Chapter 5	**The Generating Skills**	**Generating additional information.**
	Inferring	Making an assumption, stating a hypothesis, or coming to a conclusion based on limited information.
	Summarizing	Condensing the essence of the information accurately and efficiently.
	Synthesizing	Creating new information by combining two or more pieces of information.
	Generating Ideas	Creating new information, alternatives, or applications.
Chapter 6	**The Recognizing Skills**	**Recognizing what has been left unsaid.**
	Recognizing Purpose	Identifying a writer's or speaker's intention.
	Recognizing Fact and Opinion	Distinguishing between a statement of fact and a statement of opinion.
	Recognizing Tone	Identifying a sentiment or mood by assessing the writer's or speaker's choice of words.
	Recognizing Bias	Noting the presence and nature of a writer's or speaker's prejudice.
	Recognizing Organization	Identifying the organizational pattern of a thought, statement, passage, or plan.
	Recognizing Underlying Assumptions	Recognizing the suppositions that are taken for granted and are the foundation of a proposition, notion, or idea.
Chapter 7	**The Analyzing Skills**	**Analyzing for the purpose of coming to a conclusion.**
	Analyzing	Identifying and separating ideas, attributes, situations, and/or components in order to form a conclusion as to their relationship.
	Evaluating	Appraising something according to certain criteria and forming a judgment as to its worth or quality.
	Inducing	Analyzing individual facts or premises in order to derive a general conclusion.
	Deducing	Applying general principles or a broad framework to a situation in order to come to a conclusion about it.

_____

_____

_____

_____

_____

_____

"Unsex me here, and fill me from the crown to the toe top full of direst cruelty; make thick my blood. Stop up the access and passage to remorse, that no compunctious visitings of nature shake my fell purpose."
—William Shakespeare, *Macbeth*

"The better shall my purpose work on him."
—William Shakespeare, *Othello*

What questions am I going to have answered in this section on recognizing purpose?

1. Why is it important to be able to recognize an author's or speaker's purpose?
2. What are the most common purposes of the books, publications, and lectures that we read and hear in college?
3. What are some easily recognized clues to a writer's or lecturer's purpose?

RECOGNIZING PURPOSE:
Identifying a writer's or speaker's intention

All speaking and writing has a purpose, and that purpose is tied very closely to the main point that the writer or speaker is attempting to make. The purpose is the reason for writing or speaking. Sometimes the purpose is identified by the speaker or writer, but frequently it is not. Instead, it is left up to the reader or the listener to recognize the purpose and then to use that knowledge to put what is said or written in proper perspective.

THINK ABOUT THIS!

Not Three Wishes, Three Choices

You are exploring a deep cave in the mountains near Punjabi (Where?), and you stumble across what appears to be an Aladdin-type magic lamp. Maybe you can get three wishes, you think, so naturally you rub the lamp. Smoke billows out and in seconds forms into a magical being, a genie. The genie looks at you with a lopsided grin and says, "I know what you are thinking, and that only happens in stories and movies. We genies don't give three wishes, we give three choices. And here are yours. Take them or leave them.

"Choice one: You can have twenty healthy years added to your life with the condition that another person that you don't know (and never will know) will have twenty years lopped off his or her life. Do you want the extra years?

"Choice two: You will receive $100,000 if you agree to have a permanent, never-to-be-removed-or-covered-up 5-inch Nazi swastika tattooed on your right arm. Would you take the money?

"Choice three: You can have a new skill or attribute if you give up a constructive skill or attribute. If you accept this choice, what skill or attribute do you choose and what do you give up?"

WRITING AND SPEAKING TO MANIPULATE

Nearly always, the purpose of spoken and written communication is obvious. Authors and speakers deliberately make their intentions clear. Frequently (as in this book), the purpose is to modify our attitudes, actions, thoughts, or knowledge in some way. In a real sense, spoken and written communication—everything from newspaper and television advertising to scholarly articles in research journals—is manipulative. The degree of manipulation and the purpose are determined by the author.

UNSOUND ARGUMENTS SOMETIMES FOOL US

Sometimes a writer's or speaker's purpose is hidden from us and we can be manipulated if we are not alert. Purpose can be hidden behind unsound arguments. Some common types are listed for you below. You probably have already run into these, and you are likely to meet them again. Recognizing *sound* reasoning is often fairly difficult to do.

Recognizing the common types of *unsound* reasoning (sometimes called *logical fallacies*) is fairly easy, once you are familiar with them. If you are aware of these fallacies and can spot them when you see or hear them, you will not be fooled by an unsound argument and a hidden purpose. Remember, your best tool for detecting unsound reasoning is always alertness on your part combined with your own common sense.

Common Logical Fallacies

1. *The stated conclusion is not necessarily a logical result of the facts presented. It is a* non sequitur *(Latin for "it doesn't follow").* Here is an example of this type of fallacy: "Joanne Benson has been an excellent high school principal, so she will make an excellent mayor for our city." If a person has been successful in one administrative position, it does not necessarily follow that the person will be successful in a different position. Common sense and your experience tell you that.

2. *An irrelevant point (a "red herring") is introduced to divert the reader's attention from the main issue.* The term *red herring* comes from the practice among escaping slaves or prisoners of dragging a smoked (reddish) herring or other strong-smelling fish across their trail to confuse the tracking dogs. If a writer is discussing the merits of a new novel and suddenly begins to condemn the sensationalism of tabloid newspapers, such a condemnation would be considered a red herring. The sensationalist newspapers have nothing to do with the novel.

3. *The writer evades the real issues by appealing to the reader's emotions. This is an argument* ad populum *("to the people").* The writer uses words that have become emotionally charged in either a positive or a negative way: for example, *liberal, communist, honesty, American,* and *freedom.* A writer who says, "Only a communist would see the merit in electing him to office" is avoiding discussion of the candidate's strengths and weaknesses and merely substituting an appeal to the emotions.

4. *An improper comparison is used as proof of a point. This is a faulty analogy.* Sometimes if you look closely at metaphors and extended comparisons you will see that the two things being compared are not really similar. An example of a faulty analogy would be arguing that a new law making it illegal to drink alcoholic beverages while piloting a boat is wrong because, if the state can prohibit that, it can just as easily make it illegal to drink alcoholic beverages while fishing from a dock. The two situations are not at all alike. Even though the analogy might suggest similarities (water, alcohol, law), it proves nothing.

5. *The writer attempts to convince the reader that the issue has only two sides—one right, one wrong. This is an either/or argument.* The statement "If you don't vote to build the nuclear power plant, you won't have any electricity" is irrational because it doesn't mention other ways of generating electricity. One of the best-known (and popularly accepted!) examples of an either/or oversimplification was the 1960s bumper-sticker slogan that appeared on thousands of cars during the Vietnam War: "America: Love It or Leave It." As we now see so clearly in hindsight, other choices were available.

6. *An argument is based on insufficient or unrepresentative evidence. This is a hasty generalization.* Suppose you have owned two parrots and both frequently bit you. If you declare that all parrots are vicious, you are making a hasty generalization, because thousands of parrots never bite anyone. If your generalization is based on an inadequate or unrepresentative sample (your own experience, for instance), it is invalid.

7. *An attempt is made to validate a point by saying something like "Everyone else believes this." This is called bandwagon appeal.* This technique is merely an attempt to evade discussing the issue itself. We are especially familiar with this tactic in advertising. "Discriminating men use POW! cologne." If "discriminating men" (like me, of course) use POW!, then it must be good, right? Wrong. Whether POW! is good or bad hasn't even been addressed.

8. *An attack is made on a person's character rather than on his or her argument. This is an argument* ad hominem *("to the man").* "Professor Goldsworthy can't be a good psychology teacher because he's divorced." This claim is invalid because, in itself, Professor Goldsworthy's marital status has nothing to do with his ability to teach psychology.

9. *Something is presented as truth that is supposed to be proven by argument. This is called begging the question, or circular thinking.* Take the statement "There aren't enough seats in the auditorium because there are too many students." In this case, the part of the statement that is supposed to prove the point simply repeats the point in different words. When a writer makes a point and offers "facts" to support it, without first proving the validity of the facts, the writer is using an invalid presentation. In the statement "All useless city property, such as the building on the corner of Ninth and Oak, should be sold," the writer has already decided that the building is useless but has not taken responsibility for proving the point.

10. *The writer implies that because one event follows another in time, the first event caused the second. This is called post hoc reasoning, from the Latin* post hoc ergo propter hoc *("after this, therefore because of this").* Occasionally we are fooled and mistake a time connection for a cause-and-effect connection. Lending your car to your roommate did not cause your water pump to quit; lending the car merely preceded the failure in time. If you had been driving your car at the time, the pump would still have given out. Rely heavily on your common sense.

11. *An abstract concept is used as if it were concrete reality. This is called hypostatization.* Be wary if a writer uses statements like "Sociology shows us . . .," "Literature illustrates . . .," or "Science proves . . ." The writer is attempting to suggest that the abstraction represents all the experts in the field, who here speak with one voice. Of course, that voice agrees with the argument the writer is making. On the contrary, experts in sociology, literature, and science hold varied and even contradictory opinions.

WHY EVEN WORRY ABOUT RECOGNIZING PURPOSE?

Often the writer's or speaker's purpose is innocent—perhaps simply to inform—but not always. Sometimes the speaker or writer has a different purpose—perhaps to persuade—and knowing this may affect your conclusions about what you are reading or hearing. Problems arise when a writer uses logical fallacies or other unsound reasoning, or fails to include a clear expression of purpose, and you believe the communication has one purpose when it really has a different one.

Being aware of the writer's or speaker's purpose *before, while,* and *after* reading or listening is a way of keeping ourselves from being fooled about the real message. In any communication, the author or speaker may or may not state his or her purpose outright, but it should always be discernible.

You develop skill in determining purpose when you regularly begin asking yourself questions like the following:

- Why did the writer write this, or why did the speaker say this?

- What was the writer of this passage trying to accomplish by telling us about this?

- Which words or terms best describe the writer's or speaker's purpose?

THINKERS

Limited Letters

Where do you see the following letters and no others?

C D E F L O P T Z

Need a Hint?
You've seen them before. They were just arranged differently.

THE MOST COMMON PURPOSES

Of the many purposes there are for writing and speaking, the ones you'll discover most frequently in your college experience are listed here. Just reminding yourself of them from time to time will help you spot them. The first four purposes (marked with asterisks) are the most common purposes for writing. Expect to run into them frequently.

*to inform	to suggest an alternative
*to describe	to defend
*to tell a story	to entertain
*to convince or persuade	to discuss
to state a problem	to define
to analyze	to compare
to classify	to evaluate
to offer a solution	to present new information
to achieve a combination	to criticize
of purposes	to move to action

CLUES TO IDENTIFYING PURPOSE

Identifying purpose is not as difficult as it may sound because often there are clues you can look for, such as the following:

1. *Statement of purpose.* Occasionally a writer or instructor will say something like "My purpose is . . ." Your responsibility then is to make certain as you read or listen that the stated purpose is the true purpose and not just a smoke screen. It is more likely, however, that the purpose will be implied, and you'll have to look for other clues.

2. *Word clues.* Words or phrases like "This discussion is focused on . . ." also point to purpose, though less explicitly.

3. *Author's tone.* The tone, or mood, of the passage may also give you a clue to a writer's or speaker's purpose. If the tone is humorous and lighthearted, then the author's purpose is not likely to be a serious one. Watch for emotion-laden words; they are good clues.

4. *Titles, headings, boldface, and italics.* In textbooks and other nonfiction publications, titles, headings, and subheadings often give a clue to the author's purpose. An article entitled "Recent Cognitive Research on Antisocial Juveniles" will probably have as its purpose to inform readers and not to entertain them. Boldface type and italics often give clues to purpose by signaling mood, tone, importance, or emphasis.

5. *Introductions, summaries, and conclusions.* Often an author's or instructor's purpose is clearly indicated in brief introductions, summaries, and conclusions. Special attention should be paid to all of these.

6. *Author's or speaker's background.* A writer's or speaker's background can signal purpose very effectively. Knowing that a writer is the Grand Wizard of the Ku Klux Klan can help make you aware that the article he wrote entitled "The Role of Minorities in Building Our Nation" may not be as objective as the title suggests.

7. *Publication date.* Yes, the times do put a different slant on things, and *when* something was written often is a clue to its purpose. An article written in the 1950s on investing government funds in Japan will certainly have a different purpose than one written today. The opinion and the circumstances prevailing at the time the article was written may have changed by the time you read the material.

STIR IT UP 6.1 What's the purpose? Read the brief article that follows, and then identify the writer's purpose from the selections given. Watch for clues in the article—the correct choice will be obvious. Be ready to explain the reason for your answer.

The Supply of Physicians
James R. Kearl

From the end of World War II until the mid-1960s, the proportion of active physicians in the population remained relatively stable. Since 1965, however, the physician–

THINKERS

The Bottle Problem

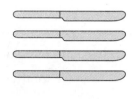

Can you build a platform on top of three bottles using only table knives? It can be done.

The rules: **(1)** Place each bottle upright at the corner point of a triangle having equal sides. **(2)** The distance between the bases of any two bottles must be *slightly more* than the length of a knife. **(3)** Use no more than four knives. **(4)** Knives may not touch the table or floor. Good luck.

Need a Hint?
You can't *think* your way through this, but you can *do* it. Get some bottles and try it. You'll be amazed at your inventive ability.

population ratio has risen from 1.4 to almost 2 per 1,000 population. Why the increase in supply?

Traditionally, the American Medical Association has carefully controlled entry into the medical profession by making it difficult for new medical schools to enter, limiting enrollment and expansion in existing medical schools, and working to ensure that states license only physicians who have graduated from AMA-accredited schools. As a consequence, incomes for physicians were high.

In the mid-1960s, federal and state governments began funding programs to encourage creation of new medical schools and expansion of old ones. At the same time, federal immigration laws were eased, making it easier for foreign doctors to enter the U.S. market. State licensing laws were relaxed. Finally, because of the high incomes, a fairly large number of U.S. students interested in studying medicine, but who could not get into U.S. medical schools, moved abroad to study (primarily to Mexico and places like Grenada).

As a result of these measures, it is estimated that there are 54,000 more physicians now than there would have been had pre-1965 conditions prevailed. Of these, 21,000 are foreigners who have benefited from easier immigration policies, 13,000 are foreigners who have entered because of relaxed licensing laws, and 20,000 are individuals who have benefited from medical school expansion. In addition, this increase in supply, reduced incomes for physicians by an estimated average of $23,000 in 1981 dollars.

_____ to convince, persuade	_____ to entertain
_____ to compare	_____ to criticize
_____ to analyze something	_____ to offer a solution
_____ to state a problem	_____ to evaluate

STIR IT UP 6.2   How can skill with words hide an author's purpose? Are some works so "well written" that readers don't know they are being manipulated? When does such manipulation occur? Is it acceptable? Under what conditions? Address these issues in a one- or two-page essay.

STIR IT UP 6.3   Writers have many purposes, some of which seem to predominate in the materials you are expected to read in college. List the three purposes that you think are the most common in your study reading.

_____

_____

_____

STIR IT UP 6.4   Are you aware of being manipulated by the ideas you are reading about *when you are reading*? Always? Sometimes? What determines your awareness during reading, and how do you respond? Where in your reading of a passage should you be able to make a judgment about the author's purpose? Must you wait until you have finished reading to make a judgment? Jot down some answers to these questions below. Be ready to discuss your answers with your classmates.

_____

_____

ANY QUESTIONS?

Sam the Thinker has a two-dollar bill and wants to buy a book that costs $3. What can he do to turn that two-dollar bill into $3 without borrowing the extra dollar or working for it? How many ways can you think of to accomplish this? In each case you think of for coming up with the extra dollar, who really ends up providing the extra dollar?

_____

_____

_____

Journal Observations (see page 13)

RECOGNIZING PURPOSE

1st Writing _____

_____

_____

_____

_____

_____

_____

_____

_____

_____

_____

_____

2nd Writing

3rd Writing

We Mustn't Open Drug-Use Floodgate

Dan Boatwright
Contra Costa Times, *December 10, 1989*

Hometown: Concord, California.

Occupation/credentials: State senator, chairman of Senate Committee on Bonded Indebtedness, member of Joint Committee on Prison Construction: former assemblyman and member of Legislature since 1972; former mayor of Concord; former deputy district attorney in Contra Costa County.

Education: Bachelor's degree in political science and law degree from UC–Berkeley, attended Vallejo Junior College.

Can you imagine walking into the local market with your children and seeing packages of cocaine marketed alongside cereal? How about grocery stores offering coupons—"Save $1 on your next quarter gram of nose candy!" Or picture drug manufacturers and distributors offering promotional prizes—"Enter our sweepstakes and win two weeks in Bogota!"

How about the corner crack cocaine peddler telling his customer, "That's $10, plus 73 cents tax. The county road tax and special earthquake tax have knocked the price up a little."

Is this the kind of society we might have if drugs were legalized? I don't know. But I do know I'm not anxious to increase drug usage, and legalizing drugs will do just that.

Frankly, it continues to amaze me that some people argue that we ought to legalize drugs at least for people who would "register" as drug users, and use the taxes to finance treatment programs. It makes me wonder what they have been smoking.

When methadone (a heroin substitute) was legalized in Great Britain, the heroin problem was not curtailed. Instead, they now have methadone addicts in addition to their heroin junkies.

Does anyone really believe that the legalization of drugs will take the profits out of the hands of drug traffickers, funneling them instead into drug prevention and treatment?

Are we to assume that people who wish to use drugs would "register" as drug users? (I'm sure an employer would love to know if he or she had a "registered user" on the payroll!) And those who didn't register—can we assume they wouldn't make any attempt to buy drugs? Of course not.

And, once drugs have been legalized, do you think we can count on producers to pay state and federal taxes, warehouses to remit their property taxes and street-corner dealers to forward sales taxes?

Even in a simplistic world, the legalization of drugs doesn't make sense. It will cause consumption to go way up. In 1980, West Virginia allowed table wine to be sold in grocery stores rather than state liquor stores. During the first year, wine sales increased by 700 percent.

In fact, every state that has changed policies to make liquor more accessible has experienced a huge increase in consumption. What makes any rational person think the same increase wouldn't hold true for drugs?

The National Institute on Drug Abuse estimates that 14.5 million, or 7 percent of the over-12 population, uses illicit drugs. Even if we make a conservative estimate of a 300 percent increase in consumption under legalization, it would mean that more than 20 percent of our population would be drug users. What would this mean for society? It could mean more car wrecks because of stoned drivers, more spousal abuse and child neglect by addicted parents, more accidents on the job, more babies born addicted to drugs, more deaths from drug overdoses, and more cases of AIDS from heroin users sharing needles.

It would also mean that more of society's resources would go into rehabilitation for addicts, new health programs and lost job productivity.

The Research Triangle Institute of North Carolina estimated in 1988 that the national cost of drug abuse is $100 billion. Approximately 30 percent of this amount, $30 billion, is spent on law enforcement.

Even if enforcement costs were saved by legalization, it is estimated that the doubling or tripling of the other social costs would still bring the price up to $140 billion to $210 billion.

Drug legalization won't lessen our crime problems. Organized crime and black markets will not disappear, nor will other problems such as prostitution or theft as a means to get drug money. In fact, crimes like reckless driving and abuse would surely increase.

Now is not the time to back down, especially since drug trafficking has been shifting toward the West.

Passage of the Crime Victim's Justice Reform Initiative on the June ballot will result in a more efficient, speedier criminal process, and will enable us to get convicted drug dealers into prison sooner. Longer prison terms will keep them off our streets. Confiscation of their personal property will deny them some of the tools of their trade.

We need to use all of our energies right now to fight drugs. We shouldn't be diverting our energies into conjuring up methods of legalization.

Progress has been made. Drug-awareness programs in the 1980s have helped to bring about a decrease in the number of people using drugs.

After spending years trying to convince our youngsters to "say no" to drugs, it would be devastating to suddenly tell them "it's OK after all."

I've personally seen too many victims of drugs. I don't care to hear another innocent infant, born to a drug-addicted mother, cry helplessly in the midst of a heroin withdrawal.

I don't want my children's children to grow up in a society where harmful drugs are marketed like candy. I don't think you do either.

Examine Your Thinking About What You Just Read

Pay attention to your thinking processes as you answer the following questions.

1. What is this author's conclusion concerning the legalization of drugs? Aside from the strong suggestion in the title, at what point in the article did you know what the conclusion was? How did you know?

2. Of the many arguments in this article for not legalizing the use of drugs, some are based on facts and some merely appeal to our emotions. In fact, if you were in favor of legalizing drug use, you might say that some of the arguments are fallacious, or at least weak. What are some of the weaker arguments in this article? What makes them weak? What would make them stronger?

3. If you were to attack this article and its conclusion, how would you go about it? How important is recognizing the author's underlying assumptions to successfully analyzing what is being stated?

4. Were you persuaded by the argument in this article? If so, were you easily persuaded? What is the strongest argument the author makes for not legalizing drug use? Is this argument made early or late in the article? Before reading the article, did you have an opinion concerning the legalization of drugs, or did the article help you to make a decision?

Write about this In a short essay, give your opinion concerning the legalization of drugs. Describe when and how you formed your opinion and what arguments most influenced your thinking. Also describe the conditions under which your opinion might change. Could there be some middle ground between the advocates on both sides of the issue?

To Be or Not to Be Single

Leslie Milne

Today's society presents a woman with the choice of whether to marry or remain single. Such a choice was not a practical option for women even one generation ago. It is worth examining the pros and cons of married versus single life for the modern young woman.

First impressions do much to recommend the single life. Freedom is, for many, the most attractive feature of singlehood. Your time is your own. You need answer to no one but yourself, in the form of your conscience. You are at liberty to take full advantage of opportunities in both career and romance when they arise. In addition, you may have as many sex partners as suits you at any given time.

As an independent, self-reliant person, you are in charge of your own life. You can be an assured, confident individual to whom others relate as such, rather than as "his other half." You can be secure in your ability to stand on your own two feet, rather than constantly worrying whether or not you could ever really manage without him.

As a single woman, there is less pressure on you to adhere to the role models ascribed by society. For instance, you don't have to cook, clean, have babies, and generally evolve your lifestyle to cater to the needs and desires of another. If you choose to live on pizza and TV dinners for a week, you can do it without affecting anyone else.

The single lady often holds mystery and allure for the attached male. Your friends' partners are apt to find you infinitely attractive and flirt outrageously with you. This is such a delightful ego-booster, and it tends to make you glow all the more appealingly.

Even if heavily involved with someone, as a single woman you retain the option of cutting loose, changing your mind, and resuming life on your own. That important escape route is always clear. You can avoid the stigma of divorce and all the damage which results from such a status move.

It certainly does seem that marriage would be rather a drag. Apart from all the hassle of making a commitment, there is the inevitably dull routine of it all. Also, for every one thing you adore about him, there are ten things that drive you nuts. How much better to enjoy the fun side of a relationship, and see a man on his best behavior, trying desperately to impress you on a date.

But wait! Is this a satisfactory way to live the rest of your life? Surely the flip side of the coin merits at least some examination. It may require the magical appearance in your life of the elusive Mr. Right, but somewhere down the line you are going to be confronted with at least the idea of marriage. It may be a friend who is taking the plunge, or perhaps your current partner is popping *the* question. Suddenly, life as a single girl is put into a whole new perspective.

In the middle of celebrating your treasured freedom, you realize that you are often lonely. You are tired of friends and colleagues taking advantage of you because you have freedom from family responsibilities. Why would it matter if *you* worked later or over the weekend? Such experiences in the past have made you become quite selfish about your own time. Do others consider you promiscuous for having more than one boyfriend, or for dating lots of men over the course of the past year? Worse yet, are you in risk of being infected with the AIDS virus?

Far from being regarded as self-reliant and independent, you seem to be coming across as a threat to potential partners who can't see what they could possibly offer you. As time goes on and you remain single into your late thirties, men may regard you as unable or unwilling to commit to a serious relationship, or may even believe that you are gay. All this undermines your confidence and sparks feelings of paranoia: What is wrong with me? Why are men avoiding me like the plague?

Not having to cater for anyone else is all very well, but with only yourself to cook and clean for, it is easy to let everything slide until you are suddenly and painfully aware that you look like a slob and live like a pig. Far from seeming attractive to the husbands and partners of your friends, you may come to be regarded as a "third wheel," a real nuisance who is always tagging along. Women suspect you of flirting, while men resent you for cramping their style with their own partners.

Avoidance of intimacy can lead to a string of superficial, nonprogressive relationships which evaporate after the first flush of lust is over. Unwillingness to commit to anyone signals fear of taking risks to many potential marriage partners.

Even after divorce, a once-married person often holds a lot of appeal. At least he or she tried, even if it didn't work out. Surveys reveal that the majority of divorced people do remarry at some stage. Surely these people are not "lemmings," repeatedly hurling themselves over the cliff to certain death. Marriage really must have a lot going for it.

There is no doubt that getting close enough to someone to recognize him—"warts and all"—leads to a deeper, truer, more meaningful love relationship. Such a union holds satisfaction, many rewards, and the real promise of enduring happiness. Wouldn't it be cozier to share your pizza or TV dinner with some less-than-perfect, but eminently familiar person? Dates are fun, but the continuity, security, true intimacy, and closeness resulting from a marriage partnership deserve serious consideration as cause to rethink your attitude toward that widely debated status.

While the single life may be infinitely more appealing to some, the benefits and long-term rewards of marriage provide, on balance, the greatest satisfaction for the majority of people.

Read and Respond

1. All writing has a purpose—at least all published writing. What would you say the purpose was for writing this article? Why do you think so? At what point did you first begin to sense that this was the purpose? At what point was that feeling confirmed?

2. Is this writing biased in any way, or would you characterize this article and the reasoning as basically objective? What evidence supports your conclusion?

3. Is what is written true? For example, how accurate would you consider this statement: "There is no doubt that getting close enough to someone to recognize him—'warts and all'—leads to a deeper, truer, more meaningful love relationship." Is this always true, sometimes true, or only true in movies? What about the other assertions? Are they accurate and fair?

4. Did the writer leave any arguments out? What are they?

5. What is your conclusion? Be objective, especially if you happen to be in love at the moment. Is it better to be married or single?

Why Do Japanese Workers Stay in Their Jobs Longer Than U.S. Workers Do?

James R. Kearl

Job turnover among Japanese workers in manufacturing industries is lower than it is for their counterparts in the United States. The monthly turnover in Japan is 0.9 percent of the manufacturing workforce; turnover in the United States is 3.5 percent. Some of the difference may be due to culture, but there are good economic reasons for the differences as well. Japanese turnover is low because Japanese workers receive much more on-the-job training than U.S. workers do. Much of this training is specific to the firms for which the workers are employed. That is, the training makes the worker more productive at a specific firm, but it does not enhance his or her productivity as much if he or she chooses to go to another firm. As a consequence, Japanese workers become attached to their firms. It has been estimated that 60 percent of the difference in turnover rates is caused by these differences in on-the-job training.

Why do the Japanese choose to provide this additional training? Since the early 1950s, the rate of technological change has been much greater in Japan than in the United States. This more rapid rate of change requires continuous training and retraining of workers. (In the period prior to World War II, when Japanese technology changed at a much slower rate than it did later, the turnover rate was considerably higher than it is today, and hence, much closer to that of the United States.)

It has also been found that Japanese workers who interrupt their careers for extended periods of time suffer larger wage declines than those in similar circumstances in the United States do. This suggests that there is more rapid obsolescence of skills in Japan, again because of rapid technological change.

Read and Respond

1. What questions are raised by this article? What inferences are made?

2. What is the real reason—that is, the reason *behind* the reasons given in the article—that Japanese workers don't leave their jobs?

3. Considering what you have just read and what you already know about the American job scene, what can you conclude about the opportunity for advancement in the Japanese manufacturing industry compared with that in the American manufacturing industry?

4. Do you find the Japanese training and employment practices described here a positive factor or a negative factor? What does your answer say about your values?

ASKING CRITICAL QUESTIONS

After you read the article that follows, what critical questions come to mind? Everything you read will stir up your thinking if you read and question critically. What questions would you like to have answered in order for you to put the article in proper context and to completely understand what is being said or reported? *On the lines following the article, write three questions that, if answered, will help you understand what is really being said.*

Invoice Costs and Prices

James R. Kearl

Consider the pricing problem of a jeweler when the price of gold fluctuates. Suppose, to simplify matters, that a jeweler has an inventory of rings, each weighing one ounce, each made of pure gold, and each purchased at a time when the price of gold was $350 per ounce. The jeweler has, for accounting and tax purposes, an invoice indicating the cost of acquiring her current inventory. The invoice indicates that each ring cost $350. What will happen to the price of rings if the world price of gold increases from $350 per ounce to $700 per ounce?

In approaching this kind of question, you ought to first ask what the opportunity costs are. To do so, you need to first determine what the opportunities are. In this case, the jeweler could sell rings either as jewelry or the rings could be melted and sold for their gold content. That is, if a jeweler sells rings to persons wanting jewelry, the jeweler gives up the opportunity of selling the gold in the ring on the world market at $700. Therefore, the opportunity cost of selling a ring for jewelry is $700, not $350. Even though the jeweler has not had to pay any additional amount of money for her inventory of rings, when the world price of gold increases, the jeweler's costs of operating the jewelry store increase, in this case quite substantially, and the price of rings should increase commensurate with the increase in cost.

Even though the jeweler has an invoice indicating that the cost per ring is $350, this invoice "cost" is not the opportunity cost of selling a ring. Costs are determined by *current* opportunities, not opportunities that were once available but which no longer can be chosen. Put differently, *opportunity costs are determined only by choices that can actually be made.* Choices that cannot actually be chosen cannot affect opportunity costs. The only opportunities currently facing the jeweler are to sell rings or to sell the gold in rings. Hence, the cost of selling rings is the best forgone opportunity, which is selling gold at $700.

The price of gold may, of course, decrease instead of increase. For instance, consider the jeweler's costs when the world price of gold declines to $200 per ounce. Once again, she can either sell the rings as gold on the world gold market *or* as jewelry. The cost of choosing to sell them as jewelry is now $200. The jeweler's opportunity cost has declined. The price of rings will also decline. Won't the jeweler lose money? Yes, but this does not affect the opportunity cost of selling rings. If the jeweler tries to sell rings for $350, she will be undersold by other individuals, because they can stock their inventories at $200 per ring. Therefore, the jeweler will confront the choice of selling no (or very few) rings for at least $350, or selling the entire inventory of rings priced at $200 per ounce, either as jewelry or as gold. Hence, less money will be lost by selling rings at $200 per ounce than if efforts were made to sell rings for something greater than $200.

My Critical Questions

1. _____
_____ ?

2. _____
_____ ?

3. _____
_____ ?

Recognizing Fact and Opinion

ESSENTIAL THINKING SKILLS

CHAPTER	WHAT THEY'RE CALLED	WHAT THEY MEAN
Chapter 3	**The Gathering Skills**	**Gathering all the information.**
	Observing	Actively seeking information through one or more senses.
	Questioning	Seeking information by asking questions.
Chapter 4	**The Organizing Skills**	**Organizing for the purpose of making sense.**
	Comparing and Contrasting	Noting similarities and differences between two or more things, events, or ideas.
	Classifying and Sequencing	Arranging things or concepts into categories and into sequential order.
	Identifying Cause and Effect	Recognizing the relationship between an effect and its cause.
Chapter 5	**The Generating Skills**	**Generating additional information.**
	Inferring	Making an assumption, stating a hypothesis, or coming to a conclusion based on limited information.
	Summarizing	Condensing the essence of the information accurately and efficiently.
	Synthesizing	Creating new information by combining two or more pieces of information.
	Generating Ideas	Creating new information, alternatives, or applications.
Chapter 6	**The Recognizing Skills**	**Recognizing what has been left unsaid.**
	Recognizing Purpose	Identifying a writer's or speaker's intention.
	Recognizing Fact and Opinion	Distinguishing between a statement of fact and a statement of opinion.
	Recognizing Tone	Identifying a sentiment or mood by assessing the writer's or speaker's choice of words.
	Recognizing Bias	Noting the presence and nature of a writer's or speaker's prejudice.
	Recognizing Organization	Identifying the organizational pattern of a thought, statement, passage, or plan.
	Recognizing Underlying Assumptions	Recognizing the suppositions that are taken for granted and are the foundation of a proposition, notion, or idea.
Chapter 7	**The Analyzing Skills**	**Analyzing for the purpose of coming to a conclusion.**
	Analyzing	Identifying and separating ideas, attributes, situations, and/or components in order to form a conclusion as to their relationship.
	Evaluating	Appraising something according to certain criteria and forming a judgment as to its worth or quality.
	Inducing	Analyzing individual facts or premises in order to derive a general conclusion.
	Deducing	Applying general principles or a broad framework to a situation in order to come to a conclusion about it.

"The world is not run by thought, nor by imagination, but by opinion."
—Elizabeth Drew

"Opinion is that exercise of the human will which helps us to make a decision without information."
—John Erskine

What questions am I going to have answered in this section on recognizing fact and opinion?

1. What is the most important difference between a fact and an opinion?
2. Under what circumstances is it possible for a fact to be incorrect?
3. What guidelines are there for differentiating between a fact and an opinion?
4. Is it possible to have a statement that is neither fact nor opinion, or that is both?

RECOGNIZING FACT AND OPINION:
Distinguishing between a statement of fact and a statement of opinion

In order for you to be as successful in college (and after college) as you can be, you will need to be able to determine the value of what you read and hear. You must be able to decide whether you should accept or reject new information, or seek additional information. In order to do this, you must develop habits of *questioning and evaluating* while reading and listening, and you must become adept at distinguishing between statements of fact and statements of opinion.

Students who do not think critically assume that because a statement appears in a textbook or journal article, or is spoken by a professor or by a "good" student, that statement is automatically a fact. This cannot be assumed to be the case. To be an efficient thinker and decision maker, you will need to know if you are being presented an opinion, a fact, or fact and opinion combined. Once you are able to differentiate in this way, you will be able to draw proper conclusions about what you have read or heard. As you study and learn, keep questions similar to the following in mind:

- Where can I check to see if this is really true?

- Is this a mixture of fact and opinion?

THINK ABOUT THIS!

What Was That Again?

Wise people, and even some not so wise, have said some wonderfully quotable things. Usually, however, they become so memorable because they are boiled down to their essence and may even be a bit difficult to really understand. Read the quotations below and then after you have thought about what was said, resay them in your own words. What are they *really* saying?

"It takes a very long time to become young." (Pablo Picasso)

"Freedom of will is the ability to do gladly that which I must do." (Carl Jung)

"The only way to get rid of temptation is to yield to it." (Oscar Wilde)

"Nothing comes of doing nothing." (William Shakespeare)

"Only the ephemeral is of lasting value." (Eugène Ionesco)

"There is nothing so unthinkable as thought unless it be the entire absence of thought." (Samuel Butler)

"Every decision you make is a mistake." (Edward Dahlberg)

"The word 'water' is itself undrinkable, and the formula H_2O will not float a ship." (Alan Watts)

- How is my judgment of a person's credibility affected if I know he or she is stating an opinion as if it were a fact?

THE IMPORTANT DIFFERENCE BETWEEN FACT AND OPINION

Determining the difference between fact and opinion is usually not difficult if you keep in mind two important guidelines:

1. *A fact is anything that can be validated or proved.* If a statement can be proved right *or* wrong by measurement or testing, it is a fact. The following statements are facts because they can be verified, frequently with one or more of our senses.

    The bird has an injured wing.

    It is 1,180 miles to Port Huron, Michigan, from Anna Maria Island, Florida.

    That delicious smell comes from baking cinnamon rolls.

2. *An opinion cannot be validated.* If no validation can be achieved, if no right *or* wrong can be established, the statement is an opinion. An opinion is what a person *believes.* A person may attempt to *justify* an opinion in some way or to *provide some degree of support* for it, but if a statement cannot be validated, it is still an opinion. A statement is an opinion when there is no way to check its accuracy.

STATEMENTS OF OPINION

Statements of opinion express an author's or speaker's *impressions, beliefs, and judgments* about something. *Opinions cannot be judged true or false, or right or wrong,* because they are a person's individual impressions about something. This truth gives rise to the familiar statement, "You have the right to your own opinion."

Keep in mind that an opinion is not necessarily *incorrect*—it just hasn't been proved. An opinion may seem true, in fact it may be exactly what you believe, but *if it can't be proved or hasn't yet been proved*, it is still an opinion.

The following are statements of opinion. Do you understand why?

- President Clinton's election angered more Americans than has any other election of a president.

- Checkers' baconburger with cheese is the best hamburger for the money in the country.

- Mickey the cat is much more loving than Annie the dog.

- Anna Maria Island has the best beaches in North America.

- People in California are more sophisticated thinkers than people in Florida.

- The school reform movement will never accomplish its goals.

These sentences present statements of opinion about real things, but they are unverifiable.

STATEMENTS OF FACT

Statements of fact present information without interpreting it. They imply neither judgment nor evaluation. Unlike statements of opinion, statements of fact can be verified in records or historical or scientific documents, or by means of tests or measurements.

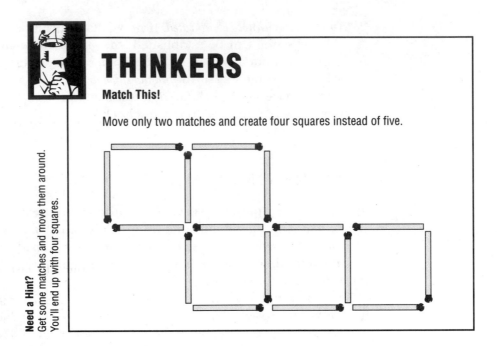

THINKERS

Match This!

Move only two matches and create four squares instead of five.

Need a Hint? Get some matches and move them around. You'll end up with four squares.

These are statements of fact. Do you understand why?

- Carmel, California, has twenty-four bed-and-breakfast inns located within one square mile.

- The temperature inside the car after one hour in the sun is 130 degrees.

- My grandchildren, Nicholas, Jaida, and Ryan, all have blue eyes.

- Over 300,000 people died in the Bosnian fighting during the final two years.

- The other Ben Jonson died in 1641.

- The sticker price of that car is $16,898, but you can buy it for $12,000.

You are able to *verify* the accuracy of each of these statements by going to source books, doing measurements, or consulting authorities. The statements are therefore statements of fact. Incidentally, even though these are all statements of fact, some of them contain *incorrect* information.

The following guidelines will help you determine what is a statement of fact.

1. Statements that can be proved or disproved are still statements of fact even when they are in error and proved false. A statement of

fact, then, is not always accurate or correct. It could very easily be an *incorrect* statement of fact: for example, "Three-hundred twenty-seven parents from twenty-two schools attended last night's school board meeting" (there were 342 parents from 21 schools, and the meeting was two nights ago).

2. Statements that present evaluations, attitudes, or probabilities are statements of opinion, because they cannot be proved true or false. Statements of opinion are often presented in an authoritative voice, and may be true, but they are still statements of opinion: for example, "Not enough people care about protecting the environment to ensure any positive change."

3. Statements dealing with persons, places, objects, occurrences, or processes that exist or did exist, and which can be proved or disproved, are statements of fact: for example, "In last night's class I showed a film about methods of teaching poetry at the middle school level."

4. Statements about future events are statements of opinion even when the events seem likely to occur: for example, "Eventually, there will be a cure for AIDS." (This probably will come to pass, but perhaps it won't. Because the statement deals with the future, it can't be validated in the present.)

5. Statements of fact often use concrete words referring to things, events, or measurable characteristics. Words such as *gallon, salt water, twenty-two years, 56 millimeters, cumulus clouds* are all concrete words.

6. Statements of opinion frequently rely on abstract words. Abstract words refer to things that can't be touched or measured, such as *faith, love, hope, courage, patriotism, health.* Because these words cannot be *specifically* defined and limited, people use them to mean different degrees of the same thing, or even to mean something completely different. As we all know from personal experience, the word *love* may mean one thing to one person and another thing to somebody else.

7. Watch for clue words and phrases in statements of opinion. Frequently you can spot value-judgment words such as *good, bad, unattractive, necessary, quality;* opinion phrases such as *I believe, it appears, we suggest;* or emotion-laden words such as *loving, generous, warm, honest, filthy, decadent, evil.* These words and phrases should tip you off to the probability that opinion, not fact, is being presented.

8. Cultivate a spirit of healthy skepticism about what you read and hear in college. Start asking yourself, or others, questions like, Where's

the proof? Who says? and even, What is the significance of that? if the answers are not apparent.

9. Beware of expert opinion disguised as fact. Don't be unduly impressed by what experts say. The opinions of experts in any field may be more valuable and credible than opinions by nonexperts, and they need to be taken seriously, but without validation they are still opinions.

STATEMENTS OF FACT *AND* OPINION

Frequently what we read and hear is a *mixture* of fact and opinion, as illustrated by the following example: "I failed my biology quiz today, and I will fail it again tomorrow." "I failed my biology quiz today" is a statement of *fact* that can be verified. "I will fail it again tomorrow" is a statement of *opinion* that cannot be verified because tomorrow hasn't come.

STIR IT UP 6.5　Now that you know that statements of fact can be objectively verified in a number of ways, determine which of the statements below are state-

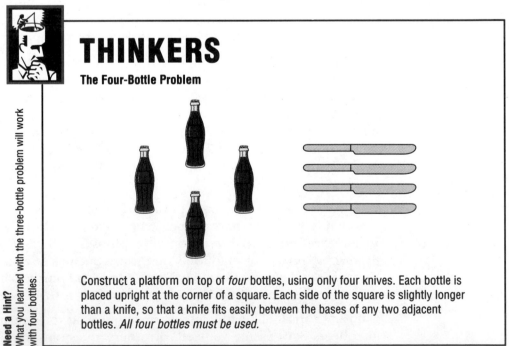

THINKERS

The Four-Bottle Problem

Construct a platform on top of *four* bottles, using only four knives. Each bottle is placed upright at the corner of a square. Each side of the square is slightly longer than a knife, so that a knife fits easily between the bases of any two adjacent bottles. *All four bottles must be used.*

Need a Hint?
What you learned with the three-bottle problem will work with four bottles.

ments of fact. For each statement of fact, indicate how you could go about verifying it. For each statement of opinion, briefly indicate why it would be impossible to verify. If a statement contains both fact and opinion, indicate which part of the statement is which.

1. Orchids are the most beautiful flowers in the world.

_____

2. Construction workers are better protected from injury than children at playgrounds.

_____

3. The production of electromagnetic waves with frequencies greater than radio waves is accomplished by molecular excitation, but the process is hard to duplicate.

_____

4. On any given night, an estimated 735,000 people in the United States are homeless and without hope.

_____

5. By and large, drug use among teens is limited to a few types of drugs. Use of other drugs may occur sporadically, but it does not usually last long. What is curious is that the most widely used drug, alcohol, is often viewed with the least alarm by adults.

_____

STIR IT UP 6.6   What do statements of opinion that are presented as if they were statements of fact suggest to you? Clearly explain what you think by giving examples where possible.

_____

_____

_____

_____

_____

_____

_____

_____

STIR IT UP 6.7   Relate a sad or amusing anecdote in which you believed a statement was fact and found out it was opinion. Jot down the "facts" of that story below and be ready to share it with the class.

_____

_____

_____

STIR IT UP 6.8   Think about this and then write your conclusions below. What do you do when you read? Discuss what you think occurs that gets the meaning of the words on a page turned into meaning in your mind. Is the meaning in your mind the same as the author's intended meaning? How and why does the meaning stay in your memory?

_____

_____

_____

_____

_____

_____

STIR IT UP 6.9   Give short answers (where possible) to the following questions:

1. Are opinions ever valuable, or are facts the only things worth reading and remembering?

   _____

   _____

2. Do opinions ever become facts? If so, under what circumstances?

   _____

   _____

3. What three things did you read in this book so far that you think you _should_ remember? What did you learn that is so important that you _want_ to remember it always?

   _____

   _____

   _____

❓ ANY QUESTIONS?

"All religions are equally correct." This statement may be politically correct, but what is wrong with it?

_____

_____

_____

Journal Observations (see page 13)

RECOGNIZING FACT AND OPINION

1st Writing _____

_____

_____

_____

_____

_____

_____

_____

_____

_____

2nd Writing _____

_____

3rd Writing _____

READINGS

Welfare as a Women's Issue

Johnnie Tillmon
Liberation News Service, *February 26, 1972*

I'm a woman. I'm a black woman. I'm a poor woman. I'm a fat woman. I'm a middle-aged woman. And I'm on welfare.

In this country, if you're any one of those things—poor, black, fat, female, middle-aged, on welfare—you count less as a human being. If you're all those things, you don't count at all. Except as a statistic.

I am a statistic.

I am 45 years old. I have raised six children.

I grew up in Arkansas, and I worked there for fifteen years in a laundry, making about $20 or $30 a week, picking cotton on the side for carfare. I moved to California in 1959 and worked in a laundry there for nearly four years. In 1963 I got too sick to work anymore. Friends helped me to go on welfare.

They didn't call it welfare. They called it A.F.D.C.—Aid to Families with Dependent Children. Each month I got $363 for my kids and me. I pay $128 a month rent; $30 for utilities, which include gas, electricity, and water; $120 for food and nonedible household essentials; $50 for school lunches for the three children in junior and senior high school who are not eligible for reduced-cost meal programs.

There are millions of statistics like me. Some on welfare. Some not. And some, really poor, who don't even know they're entitled to welfare. Not all of them are black. Not at all. In fact, the majority—about two-thirds—of all the poor families in the country are white.

Welfare's like a traffic accident. It can happen to anybody, but especially it happens to women.

And that is why welfare is a women's issue. For a lot of middle-class women in this country, Women's Liberation is a matter of concern. For women on welfare it's a matter of survival.

Forty-four percent of all poor families are headed by women. That's bad enough. But the *families* on A.F.D.C. aren't really families. Because 99 percent of them are headed by women. That means there is no man around. In half the states there really can't be men around because A.F.D.C. says if there is an "able-bodied" man around, then you can't be on welfare. If the kids are going to eat, and the man can't get a job, then he's got to go. So his kids can eat.

The truth is that A.F.D.C. is like a supersexist marriage. You trade in a man for *the* man. But you can't divorce him if he treats you bad. He can divorce you, of course, cut you off anytime he wants. But in that case, *he* keeps the kids, not you.

The man runs everything. In ordinary marriage, sex is supposed to be for your husband. On A.F.D.C., you're not supposed to have any sex at all. You give up control of your own body. It's a condition of aid. You may even have to agree to get your tubes tied so you can never have more children just to avoid being off welfare.

The man, the welfare system, controls your money. He tells you what to buy, what not to buy, where to buy it, and how much things cost. If things—rent, for instance—really cost more than he says they do, it's just too bad for you.

There are other welfare programs, other kinds of people on welfare—the blind, the disabled, the aged. (Many of them are women too, especially the aged.) Those others make up just over a third of all the welfare caseloads. We A.F.D.C. are two-thirds.

But when the politicians talk about the "welfare cancer eating at our vitals," they're not talking about the aged, blind, and disabled. Nobody minds them. They're the "deserving poor." Politicians are talking about A.F.D.C. Politicians are talking about us—the women who head up 99 percent of the A.F.D.C. families—and our kids. We're the "cancer," the "undeserving poor." Mothers and children.

In this country we believe in something called the "work ethic." That means that your work is what gives you human worth. But the work ethic itself is a double standard. It applies to men and to women on welfare. It doesn't apply to all women. If you're a society lady from Scarsdale and you spend all your time sitting on your prosperity paring your nails, well, that's okay.

The truth is a job doesn't necessarily mean an adequate income. A woman with three kids—not twelve kids, mind you, just three kids—that woman earning the full federal minimum wage of $2.00 an hour, is still stuck in poverty. She is below the Government's own official poverty line. There are some ten million jobs that now pay less than the minimum wage, and if you're a woman, you've got the best chance of getting one.

The President keeps repeating the "dignity of work" idea. What dignity? Wages are the measure of dignity that society puts on a job. Wages and nothing else. There is no dignity in starvation. Nobody denies, least of all poor women, that there is dignity and satisfaction in being able to support your kids through honest labor.

We wish we could do it.

The problem is that our country's economic policies deny the dignity and satisfaction of self-sufficiency to millions of people—the millions who suffer everyday in underpaid dirty jobs—and still don't have enough to survive.

People still believe that old lie that A.F.D.C. mothers keep on having kids just to get a bigger welfare check. On the average, another baby means another $35 a month—barely enough for food and clothing. Having babies for profit is a lie that only men could make up, and only men could believe. Men, who never have to bear the babies or have to raise them and maybe send them to war.

There are a lot of other lies that male society tells about welfare mothers; that A.F.D.C. mothers are immoral, that A.F.D.C. mothers are lazy, misuse their welfare checks, spend it all on booze and are stupid and incompetent.

If people are willing to believe these lies, it's partly because they're just special versions of the lies that society tells about all women. . . .

On TV, a woman learns that human worth means beauty and that beauty means being thin, white, young and rich.

She learns that her body is really disgusting the way it is, and that she needs all kinds of expensive cosmetics to cover it up.

She learns that a "real woman" spends her time worrying about how her bathroom bowl smells; that being important means being middle class, having two cars, a house in the suburbs, and a minidress under your maxicoat. In other words, an A.F.D.C. mother learns that being a "real woman" means being all the things she isn't and having all the things she can't have.

Either it breaks you, and you start hating yourself, or you break it.

There's one good thing about welfare. It kills your illusions about yourself, and about where this society is really at. It's laid out for you straight. You have to learn to fight, to be aggressive, or you just don't make it. If you can survive being on welfare, you can survive anything. It gives you a kind of freedom, a sense of your own power and togetherness with other women.

Maybe it is we poor welfare women who will really liberate women in this country. We've already started on our welfare plan.

There would be no "categories"—men, women, children, single, married, kids, no kids—just poor people who need aid. You'd get paid according to need and family size only—$6,500 for a family of four (which is the Department of Labor's estimate of what's adequate), and that would be upped as the cost of living goes up.

If I were president, I would solve this so-called welfare crisis in a minute and go a long way toward liberating every woman. I'd just issue a proclamation that "women's" work is *real* work.

In other words, I'd start paying women a living wage for doing the work we are already doing—child-raising and house-keeping. And the welfare crisis would be over, just like that. Housewives would be getting wages, too—a legally determined percentage of their husband's salary—instead of having to ask for and account for money they've already earned.

For me, Women's Liberation is simple. No woman in this country can feel dignified, no woman can be liberated, until all women get off their knees. That's what N.W.R.O. is all about—women standing together, on their feet.

Along with other welfare recipients, we have organized together so we can have some voice. Our group is called the National Welfare Rights Organization (N.W.R.O.). We put together our own welfare plan, called Guaranteed Adequate Income (G.A.I.), which would eliminate sexism from welfare.

Read and Respond

1. Have you had any experience with welfare, or do you know people who have had to depend on some form of welfare? If so, how do your or their experiences relate to the experiences described in this article? Are they similar or different?

2. How valid is the opinion expressed in this article? How good is the evidence? Does your agreement with the opinion have anything to do with your own values? Explain your answer.

3. What do you think about the suggestion to pay women for being mothers and homemakers? Would this end welfare, extend welfare, or do something else? Is it even possible?

4. This article is crammed with information, some in the form of fact and some in the form of opinion. Go back over the article. As you do so, write the letter *F* at the end of lines that contain statements of fact and the letter *O* at the end of lines that contain statements of opinion. Where both are present, put both *O* and *F.* Does this article include more fact or more opinion? Do you have an opinion as to whether or not most of the statements of fact are correct or incorrect?

Reinforcing Good Health Habits with Money

James R. Kearl

In the past few years, many firms have built gyms at factories and business sites, provided "healthy heart" alternatives in cafeterias, and put scales in washrooms—all to encourage more healthful lifestyles among their employees. Now, however, a number of firms are providing a straightforward incentive for good health: money.

By not smoking, agreeing to buckle their seatbelts, and participating in health-promotion workshops, employees of the Bank of Delaware receive $6 per month. This amount increases to $9 per month for employees who are willing to get a fitness evaluation or follow a prescribed exercise plan, and to $12 per month for employees who participate in both programs. U-Haul employees can earn up to $130 dollars per year for specified healthful behavior. Similar programs at Baker-Hughes net employees $120 per year; at ICH, $180 per year, at Southern California Edison, $120 per year. Gosnell Builders' employees can earn from $96 to $552 per year, and Coors offers a 5 percent reduction in coinsurance payments.

Since 1988, the state of Kansas has reduced health insurance premiums by $10 per month for employees who pledge not to smoke for one year. Southern California Edison's program sets standards for weight, blood pressure, cholesterol, blood sugar, and lung carbon monoxide. Those who meet the standards—or who pledge to work toward meeting the standards—receive $10 per month. The payoff for Southern California Edison? Employees who met the standards had average health bills of $1,273 in 1989, while those at risk in three of the areas had health bills of $2,284.

Of course, incentives can be both enticements and penalties. Although it had previously paid all health insurance premiums, Texas Instruments decided to charge employees and their dependents $10 per month for health insurance (up to $30 per family) if they use any form of tobacco. An internal study indicated that health claims of tobacco users were 50 percent higher than those of nonusers.

Read and Respond

1. Is there a conclusion stated in this article, or is the article simply a listing of data? If there is a stated conclusion, underline it.

2. Is the conclusion implied but not stated? If so, what is it?

3. What are the reasons, illustrations, or evidence supporting the conclusion?

4. Are there any underlying assumptions in the article? Does the writer perhaps assume that readers will understand the relationship between money and health? What might the writer assume?

5. Go back over the article, and write F at the end of lines that contain statements of fact and O at the end of lines that contain statements of opinion. Are there more statements of fact or statements of opinion? Do you get a feel for whether or not most of the statements of fact are correct or incorrect? Are the statements of opinion persuasive? If so, what makes them persuasive?

ASKING CRITICAL QUESTIONS

After you read the articles that follow, what critical questions come to mind? Everything you read will stir up your thinking if you read and question critically. What questions would you like to have answered in order for you to put the articles in proper context and to completely understand what is being said or reported? *On the lines following each article, write three questions that, if answered, will help you understand what is really being said.*

Fight Until Complete Victory!

Ho Chi Minh

Compatriots and fighters throughout the country!
The barbarous U.S. imperialists have unleashed a war of aggression in an attempt to conquer our country, but they are sustaining big defeats.

They have rushed an expeditionary corps of about 300,000 men into the southern part of our country. They have used a puppet administration and a mercenary army fostered by them as instruments of their aggressive policy. They have resorted to extremely savage means of warfare—toxic chemicals, napalm bombs, and so forth. With such crimes they hope to subdue our southern compatriots.

But under the firm and wise leadership of the NFLSV [National Front for the Liberation of South Vietnam, or NLF], the South Viet-Nam army and people, closely united and fighting heroically, have scored very glorious victories and are determined to struggle until complete victory with a view to liberating the South, defending the North, and subsequently achieving national reunification.

The U.S. aggressors have brazenly launched air attacks on North Viet-nam in an attempt to get out of the quagmire in the South and to impose negotiations on us on their terms.

But North Viet-Nam will not falter. Our army and people have shown redoubled eagerness in the emulation to produce and fight heroically. So far we have blasted out of the skies more than 1,200 aircraft. We are determined to defeat the enemy's war of destruction and at the same time to extend all-out support to our dear compatriots in the South.

Of late the U.S. aggressors hysterically took a very serious step further in the escalation of the war: They launched air attacks on the suburbs of Hanoi and Haiphong. That was an act of desperation comparable to the agony convulsions of a grievously wounded wild beast.

Johnson and his clique should realize this: They may bring in 500,000 troops, 1 million, or even more to step up the war of aggression in South Viet-Nam. They may use thousands of aircraft for intensified attacks against North Viet-Nam. But never will they be able to break the iron will of the heroic Vietnamese people to fight against U.S. aggression, for national salvation. The more truculent they are, the further they will aggravate their crime. The war may still last ten, twenty years, or longer. Hanoi, Haiphong, and other cities and enterprises may be destroyed, but the Vietnamese people will not be intimidated! Nothing is more precious than independence and freedom. When victory day comes, our people will rebuild our country and endow it with bigger and more beautiful construction.

It is common knowledge that each time they are about to step up their criminal war, the U.S. aggressors always resort to their peace talks swindle in an attempt to fool world opinion and blame Viet-Nam for unwillingness to enter into peace talks!

President Johnson! Reply publicly to the American people and the peoples of the world: Who has sabotaged the Geneva Agreements which guarantee the sovereignty, independence, unity, and territorial integrity of Viet-Nam? Have Vietnamese troops invaded the United States and massacred Americans: Is it not the U.S. Government which has sent U.S. troops to invade Viet-Nam and massacre the Vietnamese?

Let the United States end its war of aggression in Viet-Nam, withdraw from this country all U.S. and satellite troops, and peace will return here at once. . . .

The Vietnamese people cherish peace, genuine peace, peace in independence and freedom, not sham peace, American peace.

For the defense of the independence of the fatherland and for the fulfillment of our obligation to the peoples struggling against U.S. imperialism, our people and army, united as one man, will resolutely fight until complete victory, whatever the sacrifices and hardships may be. In the past we defeated the Japanese fascists and the French colonialists in much more difficult junctures. Today the conditions at home and abroad are more favorable; our people's struggle against U.S. aggression for national salvation is sure to win a total victory.

My Critical Questions

1. _____

_____ **?**

2. _____

_____ **?**

3. _____

_____ **?**

The Evacuation of Saigon (1975)

Al Santoli

The evacuation of Saigon, the whole thing, was called Operation New Wind or Fresh Wind or Fresh Breeze or something like that. We got to the aircraft carrier *Midway,* and as soon as we got off the helicopter—since I was a surgical tech, my hair was always under a cap and it was rather long, about halfway down my ears—the CO [commanding officer], who was up in the tower, comes down and says, "Get those guys down for haircuts." So right away he gets on us for haircuts. The *Midway* was our base of operations. Our surgical equipment, all the green crates, never did catch up to us. That's known throughout the military, that they never catch up with you, and the *Midway* didn't have an operating room. This is about April 10 or 11.

We were real close to shore at that time, right off Saigon. We heard that we were taking on a whole bunch of civilians. We would be flying in and out with refugees, with American personnel, with reporters. The Tan Son Nhut airport was being bombed with big rockets. You could see the explosions from the sea. We were flying in and taking on refugees, and they were flying out whatever they could. With the refugees there were worms, women going into labor, TB and wounded lying on the choppers because there were a lot of shells coming in. There were a couple dead or dying on the chopper whom we couldn't save. We were landing in Tan Son Nhut. That was our staging point, where everybody was loading.

There were people coming out in boats, half-sinking boats. There were people who had their own airplanes who were flying out. There were all these choppers we had left there; they were using these to fly out, the Vietnamese. The flight deck was so full of choppers that we had to push them overboard because there was no room, we couldn't get our own choppers in. We were flying the big medevac choppers. We had an overload, packing in about twenty-five at a time, both Vietnamese and American. It was total chaos. The Purple Heart Trail, the road that came into Saigon from the paddies west of the city, was so jammed, from the air I could see columns of people that were at least twenty miles long. A lot of children crying. Some had clothes they picked off dead bodies. Most were barefoot. There were oxcarts and they were hauling what they had. There were wounded men on both sides of the road with battle dressings on. The NVA was lobbing these rockets all over the place, they were wiping out civilians . . . There were piles of wounded on the back of ambulances. They were dropping the rockets right into crowds of fleeing people. There were trucks, buses, anything they could get into. Saigon was the last stand, the capital, where the American embassy was.

A lot of American Marines were activated and had put up a perimeter guard around Tan Son Nhut. The NVA was still lobbing these rockets in. In fact, when I took off we were also flying out from the American embassy—a lot of people had been told to go there instead of Tan Son Nhut. It was really a mess. These rockets are lobbing in and a C-130 took off full of people going out to one of the aircraft carriers and it was blown out of the sky . . . that was all over the runway. There were corpses, there were burned-out tanks that people had used to come in, there were pieces of bodies lying in the fields and on the streets. It was just bananas, total chaos. It was one mess of humanity being pushed to where people were being trampled. People screaming, "I want a place on this chopper!" and not being able to communicate because of the language barrier and because they would not listen.

They were raiding the American Exchange. The image I have is this one guy holding up one of those ten-packs of Kellogg's cereal and he's waving it. They were throwing American money up in the air . . . totally berserk . . . total chaos. We were trying to get the wounded first. They were piled in these old ambulances. The refugees were coming up from the Delta as well as from the North. We were trying to get the wounded out first and a lot of them we just couldn't.

Each time we went in, a bunch of Marines would get out and cover the landing zone as we tried to get the wounded on first, but sometimes they were just overwhelmed. They had orders to shoot if they couldn't maintain order. They shot mostly over the heads. I didn't see any of the Marines shoot any civilians. The Marines set up a defensive perimeter and would return fire at the enemy, but like the rest of the war, you never saw the NVA. The ARVN were running, they were coming in, they were bypassing civilians, shooting civilians, trying to get out first all the time. The best way to describe it was every man for himself. There were pregnant women going into labor right there on the goddam landing zone. I delivered a baby right on the chopper. And I also delivered two more on the ships. It was just bananas.

We ended up with three thousand civilians aboard the *Midway*. We had taken all of our squadrons off because they had been there for offensive purposes. The civilians all stayed where the squadrons used to be. There were people sleeping on the floors, all over. Of course, they didn't know what a bathroom was. They were packed in, I'll tell you that. So we'd all take turns walking duty and if someone was puking or if someone had diarrhea or worms, we'd treat that.

On April 30 Saigon fell. South Vietnam had fallen. The Vice-President, Ky, flew out to the *Midway* in his own Cessna. Ky had with him an immense amount of gold bars. A lot of these people, some of the higher-ups in the ARVN and so on, had with them a lot of American money. We confiscated everything from civilians when they came on board. There were pounds and pounds of pure heroin, pounds and pounds of nice marijuana, which I really wanted to sample. People had little cherry-bomb grenades. We picked up guns. A lot of canned fish had to be tossed out. A lot of fever, they had a lot of malaria. So we had these three thousand people packed in there. That was the best we could do.

My Critical Questions

1. _____

_____ **?**

2. _____

_____ **?**

3. _____

_____ **?**

Recognizing Tone

ESSENTIAL THINKING SKILLS		
CHAPTER	**WHAT THEY'RE CALLED**	**WHAT THEY MEAN**
Chapter 3	**The Gathering Skills**	**Gathering all the information.**
	Observing	Actively seeking information through one or more senses.
	Questioning	Seeking information by asking questions.
Chapter 4	**The Organizing Skills**	**Organizing for the purpose of making sense.**
	Comparing and Contrasting	Noting similarities and differences between two or more things, events, or ideas.
	Classifying and Sequencing	Arranging things or concepts into categories and into sequential order.
	Identifying Cause and Effect	Recognizing the relationship between an effect and its cause.
Chapter 5	**The Generating Skills**	**Generating additional information.**
	Inferring	Making an assumption, stating a hypothesis, or coming to a conclusion based on limited information.
	Summarizing	Condensing the essence of the information accurately and efficiently.
	Synthesizing	Creating new information by combining two or more pieces of information.
	Generating Ideas	Creating new information, alternatives, or applications.
Chapter 6	**The Recognizing Skills**	**Recognizing what has been left unsaid.**
	Recognizing Purpose	Identifying a writer's or speaker's intention.
	Recognizing Fact and Opinion	Distinguishing between a statement of fact and a statement of opinion.
	Recognizing Tone	Identifying a sentiment or mood by assessing the writer's or speaker's choice of words.
	Recognizing Bias	Noting the presence and nature of a writer's or speaker's prejudice.
	Recognizing Organization	Identifying the organizational pattern of a thought, statement, passage, or plan.
	Recognizing Underlying Assumptions	Recognizing the suppositions that are taken for granted and are the foundation of a proposition, notion, or idea.
Chapter 7	**The Analyzing Skills**	**Analyzing for the purpose of coming to a conclusion.**
	Analyzing	Identifying and separating ideas, attributes, situations, and/or components in order to form a conclusion as to their relationship.
	Evaluating	Appraising something according to certain criteria and forming a judgment as to its worth or quality.
	Inducing	Analyzing individual facts or premises in order to derive a general conclusion.
	Deducing	Applying general principles or a broad framework to a situation in order to come to a conclusion about it.

> **"**Take the tone of the company that you are in.**"**
> —Lord Chesterfield

> **"**Don't look at me, Sir, with—ah—in that tone of voice.**"**
> —Punch

What questions am I going to have answered in this section on recognizing tone?

1. What is tone in writing and speaking?
2. Why is recognizing tone such an important thinking skill?
3. What are some common words used to convey tone?

RECOGNIZING TONE:
Identifying a sentiment or mood by assessing the writer's or speaker's choice of words

---

The ability to recognize a speaker's or writer's tone is a critical thinking skill that is not difficult to master. Your professors often ask you questions about assigned readings or talks, such as, "What is the tone (or mood, or feeling) the writer or speaker creates in his or her statements?" or simply, "What is the tone of this work?" Your professors expect you to be able to recognize the *attitude* the writer or speaker takes toward the material he or she discusses. That attitude can be anything: lighthearted or malicious, ironic or gentle, or any number of others.

For example, when I set out to write this book, I knew that it had to be serious in tone because I wanted students to take it seriously. I knew that I wasn't going to be writing a funny book (although the book would include some humorous things) or a scary book (there is nothing scary about this book—I hope). Also, I didn't want the book to have a heavy, "textbookish" tone. Therefore, I have attempted to keep the tone of this book light enough to encourage continued easy (even enjoyable) reading but serious enough to convey the importance of the subject matter. When writing, rewriting, and editing, I measured what I was writing against my desired tone.

You want to develop your ability to recognize tone so that you routinely ask and answer questions like these about what you read and hear:

THINK ABOUT THIS!

"Did you hear the one about . . .?"

Because you are in college you are accustomed to serious discussions with serious people about serious subjects. However, at times humor can stir up your thinking just as effectively as serious critical thinking. In fact, in order to even find humor in a joke, you are required to use many of your critical thinking skills. Humor forces you to look at things in a new light or from a different point of view. Your curiosity is aroused, you look for multiple levels of meaning, and you reject the literal meaning of words and statements. "Funny" people are frequently described as being spontaneous, unconventional, playful, and flexible—important characteristics also found in the most creative thinkers.

Even bad humor makes you think. It may not make you laugh, but it stirs up your thinking. In order to even recognize bad humor, you must be able to look beyond the literal meaning of words. For example:

Why did the orange stop in the middle of the road? It ran out of juice.

I know that a train just passed because I can see its tracks.

"I was shot in the arm." "Have a scar?" "No thanks, I don't smoke."

The atomic scientist told his friends he was going on vacation to do some fission.

Do you have cold winters in Arkansas? No, just Hot Springs.

How do ghosts like their eggs? Terrifried.

Did you know that *smiles* is the longest word in the English language? There is a mile between the first and last letters.

"I just married a fine Irish lad." "Oh, really?" "No, O'Reilly."

Stir up your critical thinking skills by creating more atrocious humor. Don't just restate something you've heard before. Create something new. Perhaps your instructor will offer a reward to the student who can create the worst joke.

_____

_____

_____

_____

_____

_____

- Is this talk or piece of writing disapproving, angry, or mocking?

- What mood was the writer of this passage in when she or he wrote it?

WHY IS RECOGNIZING TONE IMPORTANT?

Identifying authors' and speakers' attitudes about what they say can tell you a great deal about their *purpose.* The feelings and attitudes of speakers and writers toward the ideas they express greatly influence word choice and emphasis. You, as listener or reader, should be aware of how the author or speaker feels so that you can read or listen critically and objectively, putting the ideas, facts, and opinions expressed in perspective. If the tone in a statement is one of ridicule and irony, the author or speaker may be trying to turn you against the person, event, or idea that is being discussed. If the tone is earnest, formal, or sympathetic, then perhaps the author intends to encourage your support of some cause or idea.

Tone Is a Clue to Purpose

The two short paragraphs that follow illustrate different tones and show how tone is an important clue to an author's or speaker's purpose.

> The school board's policy on absenteeism has proved to be as liberal and unthinking as it was when it traded choice land to corporations and industrialists rather than preserve it as sites for future schools.

> The school board has an established policy to trade or sell large sections of valuable land to manufacturing and industrial corporations in exchange for commitments to provide future school sites and fund the building of schools located in planned growth areas of the county.

In the first paragraph, the author uses a condemning tone in discussing the school board's policy. The words *liberal* and *unthinking* are meant to create an unfavorable attitude in the reader.

In the second paragraph, the words *established, commitments,* and *planned* create a positive and accepting tone, clearly designed to encourage the reader to approve of what is said.

DON'T LET TONE CONFUSE YOU

The idea of tone often puts students off because they may think it hard to define. You ought to think of tone merely as the impression you have of the author's or speaker's attitude toward his or her subject. Tone in a written passage is similar to tone in music. The same words you use to

Need a Hint?
How's your spelling?

THINKERS

Make a Man

Add two lines to the numbers below and make a man.

I I 0 3 0

describe the mood created by a piece of music (sad, intimate, light-hearted, uneasy) are the same words you use to describe the tone in a reading passage or spoken address.

COMMON TONE WORDS

You face no real difficulties in learning to identify tone in a reading. The most difficult task is coming up with a word or phrase that fits the tone as you recognize it. One good way (and about the only way) to become more proficient at recognizing the author's tone is to become familiar with a lot of "tone words."

The following list contains a selection of common tone words. Place a check mark next to any word whose meaning you are not sure of, and look up the words in a dictionary. Doing so will increase your vocabulary of tone words and will help you appraise the tone in a passage more accurately.

Tone Words

disapproving	frustrated	awestruck	distressed
cruel	melancholy	wondering	sensational
serious	formal	ridiculous	ironic
vindictive	playful	intimate	gentle
amused	intense	hard	detached
malicious	reverent	impassioned	irreverent
farcical	sympathetic	mocking	reticent
prayerful	righteous	pathetic	cynical

loving	solemn	outspoken	ambivalent
optimistic	condescending	arrogant	indignant
evasive	objective	obsequious	critical
angry	apathetic	satiric	cheerful
joyous	nostalgic	outraged	grim
condemning	celebratory	incredulous	uneasy

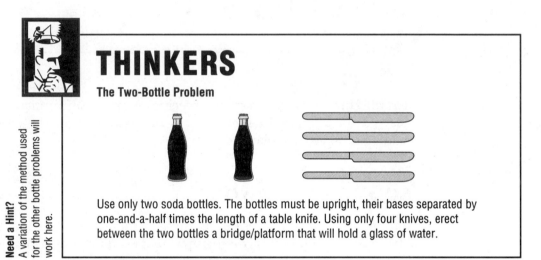

THINKERS

The Two-Bottle Problem

Use only two soda bottles. The bottles must be upright, their bases separated by one-and-a-half times the length of a table knife. Using only four knives, erect between the two bottles a bridge/platform that will hold a glass of water.

Need a Hint?
A variation of the method used for the other bottle problems will work here.

STIR IT UP 6.10 Can you think of contemporary slang or colloquial tone words that are not included in the preceding list? What are they, and what do they express? How about *nerdy*? Think of others. What words, if any, did they replace?

_____

_____

_____

_____

_____

STIR IT UP 6.11 Think about the tone of your college reading materials. Does the tone vary from one text to another, or is it about the same? Are there any materials in which the tone seems to change periodically, maybe even drastically? List your classes, and indicate (1) the general tone of the class, (2) the tone or tones of the textbook or textbooks.

_____

_____

_____

_____

_____

STIR IT UP 6.12   What is the tone of this chapter? Of this book so far?

_____

_____

STIR IT UP 6.13   If you were asked to explain as clearly as possible just what tone is, what would you say?

_____

_____

_____

_____

_____

STIR IT UP 6.14   Identify the three most important pieces of information this chapter should include on the thinking skill of identifying tone. Write one sentence for each piece of information.

a. _____

_____

b. _____

_____

c. _____

_____

Journal Observations (see page 13)

RECOGNIZING TONE

1st Writing _____

_____

_____

_____

_____

_____

_____

_____

_____

_____

_____

_____

_____

2nd Writing _____

_____

_____

_____

_____

_____

_____

_____

_____

_____

_____

_____

_____

3rd Writing _____

_____

_____

_____

_____

_____

_____

_____

_____

_____

I Just Wanna Be Average

READINGS

Mike Rose

Students will float to the mark you set. I and the others in the vocational classes were bobbing in pretty shallow water. Vocational education has aimed at increasing the economic opportunities of students who do not do well in our schools. Some serious programs succeed in doing that, and through exceptional teachers—like Mr. Gross in *Horace's Compromise*—students learn to develop hypotheses and troubleshoot, reason through a problem, and communicate effectively—the true job skills. The vocational track, however, is most often a place for those who are just not making it, a dumping ground for the disaffected. There were a few teachers who worked hard at education; young Brother Slattery, for example, combined a stern voice with weekly quizzes to try to pass along to us a skeletal outline of world history. But mostly the teachers had no idea of how to engage the imagination of us kids who were scuttling along at the bottom of the pond.

And the teachers would have needed some inventiveness, for none of us was groomed for the classroom. It wasn't just that I didn't know things—didn't know how to simplify algebraic fractions, couldn't identify different kinds of clauses, bungled Spanish translations—but that I had developed various faulty and inadequate ways of doing algebra and making sense of Spanish. Worse yet, the years of defensive tuning out in elementary school had given me a way to escape quickly while seeming at least half alert. During my time in Voc. Ed., I developed further into a mediocre student and a somnambulant problem solver, and that affected the subjects I did have the wherewithal to handle: I detested Shakespeare; I got bored with history. My attention flitted here and there. I fooled around in class and read my books indifferently—the intellectual equivalent of playing with your food. I did what I had to do to get by, and I did it with half a mind.

But I did learn things about people and eventually came into my own socially. I liked the guys in Voc. Ed. Growing up where I did, I understood and admired physical prowess, and there was an abundance of muscle here. There was Dave Snyder, a sprinter and halfback of true quality. Dave's ability and his quick wit gave him a natural appeal, and he was welcome in any clique, though he always kept a little independent. He enjoyed acting the fool and could care less about studies, but he possessed a certain maturity and never caused the faculty much trouble. It was a testament to his independence that he included me among his friends—I eventually went out for track, but I was no jock. Owing to the Latin alphabet and a dearth of *R*s and *S*s, Snyder sat behind Rose, and we started exchanging one-liners and became friends.

There was Ted Richard, a much-touted Little League pitcher. He was chunky and had a baby face and came to Our Lady of Mercy as a seasoned street fighter. Ted was quick to laugh and he had a loud, jolly laugh, but when he got angry he'd smile a little smile, the kind that simply raises the corner of the mouth a quarter of an inch. For those who knew, it was an eerie signal. Those who didn't found themselves in big trouble, for Ted was very quick. He loved to carry on what we would come to call philosophical discussions: What is courage? Does God exist? He also loved words, enjoyed picking up big ones like *salubrious* and *equivocal* and using them in our conversations—laughing at himself as the word hit a chuckhole rolling off his tongue. Ted didn't do all that well in school—baseball and parties and testing the courage he'd speculated about took up his time. His textbooks were *Argosy* and *Field and Stream*, whatever newspapers he'd find on the bus stop—from the *Daily Worker* to pornography—conversations with uncles or hobos or businessmen he'd meet in a coffee shop, *The Old Man and the Sea*. With hindsight, I can see that Ted was developing into one of those rough-hewn intellectuals whose sources are a mix of the learned and the apocryphal, whose discussions are both assured and sad.

And then there was Ken Harvey. Ken was good-looking in a puffy way and had a full and oily ducktail and was a car enthusiast . . . a hodad. One day in religion class, he said the sentence that turned out to be one of the most memorable of the hundreds of thousands I heard in those Voc. Ed. years. We were talking about the parable of the talents, about achievement, working hard, doing the best you can do, blah-blah-blah, when the teacher called on the restive Ken Harvey for an opinion. Ken thought about it, but just for a second, and said (with studied, minimal affect), "*I just wanna be average.*" That woke me up. Average?! Who wants to be average? Then the athletes chimed in with the clichés that make you want to laryngectomize them, and the exchange became a platitudinous melee. At the time, I thought Ken's assertion was stupid, and I wrote him off. But his sentence has stayed with me all these years, and I think I am finally coming to understand it.

Ken Harvey was gasping for air. School can be a tremendously disorienting place. No matter how bad the school, you're going to encounter notions that don't fit with the assumptions and beliefs that you grew up with—maybe you'll hear these dissonant notions from teachers, maybe from the other students, and maybe you'll read them. You'll also be thrown in with all kinds of kids from all kinds of backgrounds, and that can be unsettling—this is especially true in places of rich ethnic and linguistic mix, like the L.A. basin. You'll see a handful of students far excel you in courses that sound exotic and that are only in the curriculum of the elite: French, physics, trigonometry. And all this is happening while you're trying to shape an identity, your body is changing, and your emotions are running wild. If you're a working-class kid in the vocational track, the options you'll have to deal with this will be constrained in certain ways: You're defined by your school as "slow"; you're placed in a curriculum that isn't designed to liberate you but to occupy you, or, if you're lucky, train you, though the training is for work the society does not esteem; other students are picking up the cues from your school and your curriculum and interacting with you in particular ways. If you're a kid like Ted Richard, you turn your back on all this and let your mind roam where it may. But youngsters like Ted are rare. What Ken and so many others do is protect themselves from such suffocating madness by taking on with a vengeance the identity implied in the vocational track. Reject the confusion and frustration by openly defining yourself as the Common Joe. Champion the average. Rely on your own good sense. Fuck this bullshit. Bullshit, of course, is everything you—

and the others—fear is beyond you: books, essays, tests, academic scrambling, complexity, scientific reasoning, philosophical inquiry.

The tragedy is that you have to twist the knife in your own gray matter to make this defense work. You'll have to shut down, have to reject intellectual stimuli or diffuse them with sarcasm, have to cultivate stupidity, have to convert boredom from a malady into a way of confronting the world. Keep your vocabulary simple, act stoned when you're not or act more stoned than you are, flaunt ignorance, materialize your dreams. It is a powerful and effective defense—it neutralizes the insult and the frustration of being a vocational kid and, when perfected, it drives teachers up the wall, a delightful secondary effect. But like all strong magic, it exacts a price.

Read and Respond

1. How would you describe the author's tone in this article? What tone does he use when he describes his vocational education teachers? Who is the author writing for? Is the intended audience people who went to vocational schools? Or, perhaps, is the intended audience people who are highly educated?

2. What is the author's attitude toward his vocational education teachers? What is his attitude toward the other students?

3. Is this author mentally deficient in any way? Does he appear to have been socially troublesome in his earlier education? What led to his "not knowing things" and ending up in vocational education classes?

Clinical Trial of Azidothymidine (AZT) in the Treatment of AIDS

Joseph Levine and Kenneth Miller

Hypothesis

The drug azidothymidine (AZT) is effective in the treatment of acquired immune deficiency syndrome (AIDS).

Background

AIDS is caused by a virus that cripples the body's ability to fight disease. . . . Most people infected with this virus die of *opportunistic infections,* diseases that the body normally fights off but that ravage people with

AIDS. Once afflicted with full-blown AIDS (as defined at the time), patients have no hope of survival without treatment. AZT first showed promise by interfering with the reproduction of the causative virus in test-tube experiments. Preliminary trials in seriously ill patients were not conclusive.

Experimental Design

This experiment, sponsored by the manufacturer of AZT, was a double-blind, randomized, placebo-controlled study. Obviously, researchers did not inject healthy individuals with the virus; persons already infected by the virus were asked to volunteer. A computer-generated code randomly assigned each subject to receive either AZT or a placebo. Neither the subjects nor the researchers evaluating their condition knew which patients received AZT. The placebo itself was designed to look and taste just like AZT. Subjects were asked not to take any other medications without the permission of the researchers. No other treatment to prevent or control opportunistic infections was permitted to either experimental or control subjects during the course of the study. Data were rigorously analyzed by advanced statistical methods to determine whether differences between experimentals and controls could have been due to chance alone. . . .

Ethical considerations weighed heavily in experimental design. The study was approved by committees at each of 12 participating medical centers across the country. An additional independent board was established to review the study data on a regular basis. It was this group's responsibility to protect the subjects if it appeared that AZT was causing unacceptable toxic side effects. This board also kept watch for any sign that the drug was clearly benefiting those who received it. Every subject signed a consent form certifying that he or she understood the risks and benefits of the procedure. (Imagine the courage of these participants; they knew that half of them were voluntarily forgoing treatment that might save or prolong their lives. They did so in order to help produce evidence about whether or not the drug worked.)

Results

Because many of the data from this experiment deal with complex phenomena that we will not cover until later, we will present only the most basic results here. Figure 1.14(a) and (b) show the number of patients who developed opportunistic infections during the treatment period. Figure 1.14(a) shows results among those people with full-blown AIDS;

Figure 1.14(b) shows similar information for subjects with the less severe illness then called AIDS-related complex (ARC). Note that in both groups subjects receiving AZT had a lower rate of opportunistic infections than did those receiving the placebo. Table 1.2 shows that AZT recipients also had significantly higher chances of surviving the 24-week treatment period. Additional data indicated that AZT caused side effects of varying severity in different subjects. Side effects ranged from muscle aches, insomnia, and nausea to serious anemia and the loss of certain classes of white blood cells.

Conclusions

This study indicated that AZT produced the best short-term results of any medication available for AIDS treatment at the time it was conducted. Researchers therefore recommended the use of AZT in the treatment of AIDS and AIDS-related complex (ARC) in patients who could tolerate its side effects.

Read and Respond

1. Does the conclusion stated necessarily follow from the design and results of this experiment? Why or why not?

2. How would you summarize the ethical concerns at the heart of this study?

3. What do you think the subjects with full-blown AIDS were thinking when they agreed to participate in this study? Could they have been thinking several things? What are the possibilities?

4. What might the subjects with AIDS-related complex have been thinking about their participation in this study?

5. What makes you think that this study is a valid, reliable, genuine study and not just something that the author of this text made up?

ASKING CRITICAL QUESTIONS

After you read the article that follows, what critical questions come to mind? Everything you read will stir up your thinking if you read and question critically. What questions would you like to have answered in order for you to put the article in proper context and to completely understand what is being said or reported? *On the lines following the article, write three questions that, if answered, will help you understand what is really being said.*

A Few Kind Words About Creative Strategy

Howard Shank (Advertising Executive)

I t seems to be in the nature of creative people to chafe at those little pieces of paper entitled "Creative Strategy."

To watch a lot of creative people react, you'd think those documents were really headed, "Creative Straitjacket." Or, "Arsenic. Take full strength. Do not dilute."

There is, to be sure, some reason for this revulsion. It is not unheard of for writers and art directors to be asked to execute something that should really be called an "*un*creative strategy."

The authors of these papers have been known to be neither creative nor strategic in their thinking and to mask a certified non-idea behind formularized words. If you execute such a non-idea, what you are bound to have is a noncompelling advertisement. No matter how cleverly you write and visualize.

Which is too bad for all concerned.

Especially the client (who may be expected, if presented with too many nonthoughts, to become a *non*client).

Basic truth, you folks: the highest form of creativity in advertising is the setting of *real* creative strategies.

We must never forget it.

It's what built this business.

It's where your future and my future lie.

It's where at least half the joy in our business is found.

It's also where the hardest work is found, I'll admit. But don't forget, you always love hard work. Afterwards.

If you're still with me, I'd like to tell you what a real creative strategy is.

But first, I'll suggest to you some of the things it is *not*.

It is not just a sentence that says, "The advertising will convince people that our product is the (tastiest) (freshest) (mildest) (hardest-working) (classiest) (fastest) product in the store."

It is not the product of logic and analysis alone—although they're part of how you get there.

It is not the province of the client or the account man—although they should be heavily involved.

It is not a jail for creative execution. Rather, if you've got a real creative strategy, it will inspire you to write and visualize at the height of your powers.

It is not aimed at robots but at human beings with hearts and guts as well as brains.

The last sentence is the crux of the matter.

The real creative strategy is the one that relates product to yearnings. Formula to life style. Performance to passions.

If you can look at a thinner cigarette and see it not only as a special cigarette for women but also as a symbol of equality for women, you can create real creative strategies.

If you can look at a bar of soap with pumice in it and see not only an efficient hand washer but also the solution to the problem of "Public Dirt," you can create real creative strategies.

If you can look at a glass of chocolate milk and see it not as just a yummy thirst-quencher or a hunger-fighter but as a cure for a kid's "thungries," you can create real creative strategies. (Some of our smart people did that just the other day.)

In all truth, the process that leads to real creative strategies is the process that leads to inventions.

It involves the seeing of old facts in new relationships.

It involves the discovery of needs and wants in people that even the people may not have discovered in themselves. (Hardly anyone knew he needed a telephone until A. G. Bell came along.)

It also involves hard work. As I said before.

When you have a creative strategy problem on your plate, you are confronted by a need to know everything you can get your hands on. About the product itself. About competitive products. About the market: its habits, its attitudes, its demographics. About the advertising history of the category.

You need to study all the research you can get your hands on.

You need to ask questions until people hate to see you coming.

You need, in short, to dig, dig, dig.

The dismal truth is that your chances of finding a compelling creative strategy are in direct proportion to how much information you stuff your head with.

If you are working on a new coffee, say, you will wind up knowing more about coffee than you ever thought you wanted to know.

There is a very good reason why you must do this human sponge act if you are to invent real creative strategies.

Your subconscious mind—where a very important part of the invention process goes on—needs a richly-stocked data bank to do its best work.

The job of your subconscious is to review and re-review everything you know about a subject. It searches, even during your sleep, for new relationships between people and products; searches, as I suggested earlier, for new combinations of old ideas; searches for the new insight that can give even a very old product the right to ask for new attention in the market.

If you stint your subconscious on the input side, it will surely stint you on the output.

Creative strategy goes around in the world under several pseudonyms: basic concept, basic selling idea, product positioning, basic selling proposition.

But whatever the name, the purpose of real creative strategizing is simple and vital: the invention of a big idea.

I said earlier that *this* kind of creative strategy work is the highest form of creativity in advertising.

I believe it wholeheartedly.

I also believe wholeheartedly in the power of brilliant execution.

What I believe in most of all is the synergism you create when you couple a big idea with brilliant words and pictures.

When you can do that regularly, you can't help getting rich and famous. Not to mention happy in your work.

One final thought. If you don't have the habit already, make close business friends of every client, every client service man, every research man you can. Pick their brains. Push them for information. Involve them heavily in your invention work.

Their input can—and very likely will—make all the difference in your output.

My Critical Questions

1. _____

_____ **?**

2. _____

_____ **?**

3. _____

_____ **?**

Recognizing Bias

ESSENTIAL THINKING SKILLS		
CHAPTER	**WHAT THEY'RE CALLED**	**WHAT THEY MEAN**
Chapter 3	**The Gathering Skills**	**Gathering all the information.**
	Observing	Actively seeking information through one or more senses.
	Questioning	Seeking information by asking questions.
Chapter 4	**The Organizing Skills**	**Organizing for the purpose of making sense.**
	Comparing and Contrasting	Noting similarities and differences between two or more things, events, or ideas.
	Classifying and Sequencing	Arranging things or concepts into categories and into sequential order.
	Identifying Cause and Effect	Recognizing the relationship between an effect and its cause.
Chapter 5	**The Generating Skills**	**Generating additional information.**
	Inferring	Making an assumption, stating a hypothesis, or coming to a conclusion based on limited information.
	Summarizing	Condensing the essence of the information accurately and efficiently.
	Synthesizing	Creating new information by combining two or more pieces of information.
	Generating Ideas	Creating new information, alternatives, or applications.
Chapter 6	**The Recognizing Skills**	**Recognizing what has been left unsaid.**
	Recognizing Purpose	Identifying a writer's or speaker's intention.
	Recognizing Fact and Opinion	Distinguishing between a statement of fact and a statement of opinion.
	Recognizing Tone	Identifying a sentiment or mood by assessing the writer's or speaker's choice of words.
	Recognizing Bias	Noting the presence and nature of a writer's or speaker's prejudice.
	Recognizing Organization	Identifying the organizational pattern of a thought, statement, passage, or plan.
	Recognizing Underlying Assumptions	Recognizing the suppositions that are taken for granted and are the foundation of a proposition, notion, or idea.
Chapter 7	**The Analyzing Skills**	**Analyzing for the purpose of coming to a conclusion.**
	Analyzing	Identifying and separating ideas, attributes, situations, and/or components in order to form a conclusion as to their relationship.
	Evaluating	Appraising something according to certain criteria and forming a judgment as to its worth or quality.
	Inducing	Analyzing individual facts or premises in order to derive a general conclusion.
	Deducing	Applying general principles or a broad framework to a situation in order to come to a conclusion about it.

> **"***I can promise to be frank. I cannot promise to be impartial.***"**
> —Johann Wolfgang von Goethe

> **"***Bias and prejudice are attitudes to be kept in hand, not attitudes to be avoided.***"**
> —Charles Curtis

What questions am I going to have answered in this section on recognizing bias?

1. What is bias, and why is it important to be able to recognize it in writing and speaking?
2. What are five common signs that bias is present?
3. How do I *bring* bias to what I hear, read, and study?

RECOGNIZING BIAS:
Noting the presence and nature of a writer's or speaker's prejudice

---

Probably now more than ever before in this century, we are bombarded by propaganda of all sorts. Radio and television personalities have made a career out of being biased. Is there any question as to the political loyalties and biases of Ross Perot, Rush Limbaugh, Newt Gingrich, or Jesse Jackson? They are aware of the truth of the advertising maxim, "It's not just *what* you say, it's also *how* you say it." Politicians and public relations experts are adept at molding public opinion on political and social issues.

By the time we get to college we are generally aware that the public media are "loaded" with bias, that is, with a predisposition, prejudice, or prejudgment. We see bias especially in such things as commercials, political speeches, and even pep talks by religious and charitable fundraisers. They are loaded with words and phrases that play upon our emotions in order to move our thinking—and thus our actions—in a specific direction. The task for the careful thinker is to be aware of the word choices and to avoid being unthinkingly moved by their persuasive power.

The presence of bias has become routine in much of what we read and hear. In fact, we take bias so much for granted that we usually don't even think about its presence unless our emotions are strongly touched in some way, and then we *may* question the cause. It is important for us as thinkers to realize that what we see, hear, and read all through life is usually *not* fair and unbiased—even in college.

THINK ABOUT THIS!

Even Menus Make You Think

What we eat and drink reflects more than just what tastes good to us. What we eat and drink also reflects important social customs. People ate different things during different historical periods. As you read the following menu that was reported in a Paris newspaper on December 4, 1870, try to imagine the conditions or events that might make such a menu possible. Write down some of the possibilities. According to the newspaper, these foods were eaten at a banquet for the leading figures of French society. That certainly makes you think, doesn't it?

- Consommé of horse with birdseed
- Skewered dog liver, maitre d'hôtel
- Minced cat's back, mayonnaise sauce
- Shoulder of dog, tomato sauce
- Dog cutlets with peas
- Ragout of rats Robert
- Dog leg flanked by ratlets
- Escarole salad
- Elephant's ear au jus
- Plum pudding with horse marrow
- Dessert and wines

Possible circumstances:

_____

_____

_____

_____

_____

Check the end of this chapter for the circumstances that led to this menu.

And, while you're at it, try creating a "diet for the twenty-first century." What will we be eating?

_____

_____

_____

_____

THINKERS

Even if you don't know a word of Latin, you should be able to read and understand the following poem:

O sibili, si ergo,
Fortibus essen ero.
Ono sed bili themis trux.
Sivat sinem, causor dux.

Need a Hint?
Read the poem slowly out loud to someone. What did your listener hear?

BIAS IN TEXTBOOKS, LECTURES, AND LIFE

We seldom think of questioning statements that we hear in lectures or read in textbooks or journals. We seldom wonder if the professor or author is unbiased in presenting facts. We should be more questioning, because it is possible that bias in a lecture, journal article, or textbook may negate its value.

We need to pay close attention not only to the ideas and facts presented, but also to the words used to express them. Being sensitive to the language in a presentation matters just as much as being aware of the facts presented and the logic behind them. Often a writer's or speaker's words reveal a bias that springs from an attempt to influence the reader or listener. The writer or speaker may be trying to get people to like or dislike, agree or disagree with, support or refute a cause. In the relatively innocent questions that follow, do you notice the particular *slant* that is designed to bring about a particular response?

- Do you really believe that the state government has a right to invade your private life by requiring that you fill in and return that questionnaire?

- Do you approve of making the community suffer by depriving it of a place to dump waste, just to protect a moth?

- Wouldn't you really rather trust a think tank than a group of politicians?

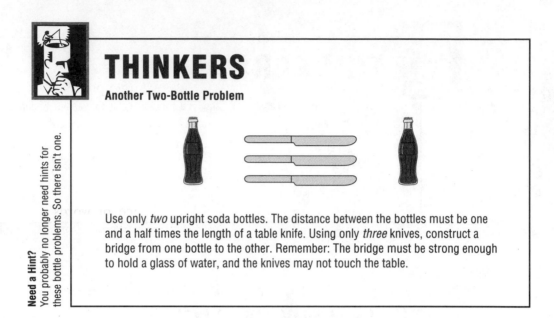

Need a Hint? You probably no longer need hints for these bottle problems. So there isn't one.

THINKERS

Another Two-Bottle Problem

Use only *two* upright soda bottles. The distance between the bottles must be one and a half times the length of a table knife. Using only *three* knives, construct a bridge from one bottle to the other. Remember: The bridge must be strong enough to hold a glass of water, and the knives may not touch the table.

In some reading matter, such as newspapers and magazines, writers attempt to influence our thinking and behavior in overt ways. Some newspapers and magazines, as well as some journalists, have widely recognized reputations for being biased, primarily because of the liberal or conservative stands they take on issues. Nothing is wrong with this "fixed" bias unless you allow yourself to be unknowingly influenced. Being unable to tell that bias lurks in college lectures and assigned readings is a severe handicap. Accepting every bit of information and interpretation without question will result in confusion.

THE NEED TO DETECT BIAS

In order to be skillful and efficient thinkers we need to be able to detect bias and allow for it when we evaluate what is written or said. We ought to develop an attitude that routinely causes us to raise questions similar to these:

- Did the writer of this piece seem to like the social worker, the police officer, the single parent, or the child best?

- Which is more likely to be fair and objective, this newspaper or my psychology textbook?

- What makes me feel that the instructor is biased in her presentation of the events?

- Is the sample in this study representative? Does it have the same characteristics in the same proportion as the target population?

- Are these experts affiliated with any interest groups? Do they subscribe to a cause?

HOW TO RECOGNIZE BIAS

Bias is often present when a writer's choice of words arouses the reader's emotions, but it is *always* there when the material includes one or more of these elements:

1. *Name-calling* (for example, "The military officer was not able to continue speaking because of irresponsible interruptions by several ill-mannered, unkempt weirdos.")

2. *Contradictions* (for example, "Our charitable organization is in no trouble at all. The recent scandal will blow over, and people will resume their donations.")

3. *Highly emotional, even inflammatory statements* (for example, "We all feel the same way: let them go back where they came from and stop causing trouble in our community. They don't belong here with normal people.")

4. *False assumptions based on weak or inaccurate information* (for example, "Asian refugees have a hard time adjusting to Western society because they are used to being told when to do everything, and in this country people are free to do whatever they want to do.")

5. *Stereotyping, often with inaccurate overgeneralizations* (for example, "Everyone knows that men make much better airline pilots than women.")

   Keep in mind that biased writing may be very interesting to read and biased speaking may be very interesting to listen to because of the colorful, emotional language designed to sway you. This doesn't mean you should be suspicious of all interesting speaking and writing, but you should heighten your sensitivity to bias.

STIR IT UP 6.15 Find several examples of possible bias in books, magazines, television or radio programs, or newspaper articles and bring them to class for discussion. (Don't use editorials—that's too easy.) Look closely at your textbooks and note examples that seem to support a particular viewpoint. Many television "news magazines" are considered to have a conservative or liberal bias.

STIR IT UP 6.16 It is time to write. Pick an issue of your choice and create two viewpoints about it. For example, you might try writing two brief paragraphs about the use of marijuana, one from the viewpoint of a user and one from the viewpoint of a police officer, parent, doctor, or politician. See how subtly you can express each bias.

STIR IT UP 6.17 Remember the O. J. Simpson trial? It provides an excellent example for the following assignment. Dig back into the published records of the trial for this exercise, or find some other case in which expert testimony was contradicted by equally expert testimony. Check the editorial pages of publications (for example, local newspapers or the debate page in *USA Today*) or programs such as "Nightline" and "Newshour with Jim Lehrer." Find examples of reporting that are biased toward each side. Identify the basic disagreements and the reasons given for each side's support. Which side do you agree with? Why? Is there a third side?

 *Journal Observations* (see page 13)

RECOGNIZING BIAS

1st Writing _____

_____

_____

_____

_____

_____

2nd Writing _____

3rd Writing _____

READINGS

The Differences Between Men and Women

Phyllis Schlafly

The first requirement for the acquisition of power by the Positive Woman is to understand the differences between men and women. Your outlook on life, your faith, your behavior, your potential for fulfillment, all are determined by the parameters of your original premise. The Positive Woman starts with the assumption that the world is her oyster. She rejoices in the creative capability within her body and the power potential of her mind and spirit. She understands that men and women are different, and that those very differences provide the key to her success as a person and fulfillment as a woman.

The women's liberationist, on the other hand, is imprisoned by her own negative view of herself and of her place in the world around her. This view of women was most succinctly expressed in an advertisement designed by the principal women's liberationist organization, the National Organization for Women (NOW), and run in many magazines and newspapers and as spot announcements on many television stations. The advertisement showed a darling curlyheaded girl with the caption: "This healthy, normal baby has a handicap. She was born female."

This is the self-articulated dog-in-the-manger, chip-on-the-shoulder, fundamental dogma of the women's liberation movement. Someone— it is not clear who, perhaps God, perhaps the "Establishment," perhaps a conspiracy of male chauvinist pigs—dealt women a foul blow by making them female. It becomes necessary, therefore, for women to agitate and demonstrate and hurl demands on society in order to wrest from an oppressive male-dominated social structure the status that has been wrongfully denied to women through the centuries.

By its very nature, therefore, the women's liberation movement precipitates a series of conflict situations—in the legislatures, in the courts, in the schools, in industry—with man targeted as the enemy. Confrontation replaces cooperation as the watchword of all relationships. Women and men become adversaries instead of partners.

The second dogma of the women's liberationists is that, of all the injustices perpetuated upon women through the centuries, the most oppressive is the cruel fact that women have babies and men do not. Within the confines of the women's liberationist ideology, therefore, the abolition of this overriding inequality of women becomes the primary goal. This goal must be achieved at any and all costs—to the woman herself, to the baby, to the family, and to society. Women must be made equal to men in their ability *not* to become pregnant and *not* to be expected to care for babies they may bring into the world.

This is why women's liberationists are compulsively involved in the drive to make abortion and child-care centers for all women, regardless of religion or income, both socially acceptable and government-financed. Former Congresswoman Bella Abzug has defined the goal: "to enforce the constitutional right of females to terminate pregnancies that they do not wish to continue."

If man is targeted as the enemy, and the ultimate goal of women's liberation is independence from men and the avoidance of pregnancy and its consequences, then lesbianism is logically the highest form in the ritual of women's liberation. Many, such as Kate Millett, come to this conclusion, although many others do not.

The Positive Woman will never travel that dead-end road. It is self-evident to the Positive Woman that the female body with its baby-producing organs was not designed by a conspiracy of men but by the Divine Architect of the human race. Those who think it is unfair that women have babies, whereas men cannot, will have to take up their complaint with God because no other power is capable of changing that fundamental fact. . . .

The third basic dogma of the women's liberation movement is that there is no difference between male and female except the sex organs, and that all those physical, cognitive, and emotional differences you *think* are there, are merely the result of centuries of restraints imposed by a male-dominated society and sex-stereotyped schooling. The role imposed on women is, by definition, inferior, according to the women's liberationists.

The Positive Woman knows that, while there are some physical competitions in which women are better (and can command more money) than men, including those that put a premium on grace and beauty, such as figure skating, the superior physical strength of males over females in competitions of strength, speed, and short-term endurance is beyond rational dispute. . . .

Does the physical advantage of men doom women to a life of servility and subservience? The Positive Woman knows that she has a complementary advantage which is at least as great—and, in the hands of a skillful woman, far greater. The Divine Architect who gave men a superior strength to lift weights also gave women a different kind of superior strength.

The women's liberationists and their dupes who try to tell each other that the sexual drive of men and women is really the same, and that it is only societal restraints that inhibit women from an equal desire, an equal enjoyment, and an equal freedom from the consequences, are doomed to frustration forever. It just isn't so, and pretending cannot make it so. The differences are not a woman's weakness but her strength. . . .

The new generation can brag all it wants about the new liberation of the new morality, but it is still the woman who is hurt the most. The new morality isn't just a "fad"—it is a cheat and a thief. It robs the woman of her virtue, her youth, her beauty, and her love—for nothing, just nothing. It has produced a generation of young women searching for their identity, bored with sexual freedom, and despondent from the loneliness of living a life without commitment. They have abandoned the old commandments, but they can't find any new rules that work.

The Positive Woman recognizes the fact that, when it comes to sex, women are simply not the equal of men. The sexual drive of men is much stronger than that of women. That is how the human race was designed in order that it might perpetuate itself. The other side of the coin is that it is easier for women to control their sexual appetites. A Positive Woman cannot defeat a man in a wrestling or boxing match, but she can motivate him, inspire him, encourage him, teach him, restrain him, reward him, and have power over him that he can never achieve over her with all his muscle. How or whether a Positive Woman uses her power is determined solely by the way she alone defines her goals and develops her skills.

The differences between men and women are also emotional and psychological. Without woman's innate maternal instinct, the human race would have died out centuries ago. There is nothing so helpless in all earthly life as the newborn infant. It will die within hours if not cared for. Even in the most primitive, uneducated societies, women have always cared for their newborn babies. They didn't need any schooling to teach them how. They didn't need any welfare workers to tell them it is their social obligation. Even in societies to whom such concepts as "ought," "social responsibility," and "compassion for the helpless" were unknown, mothers cared for their new babies.

Why? Because caring for a baby serves the natural maternal need of a woman. Although not nearly so total as the baby's need, the woman's need is nonetheless real.

The overriding psychological need of a woman is to love something alive. A baby fulfills this need in the lives of most women. If a baby is not available to fill that need, women search for a baby-substitute. This is the reason why women have traditionally gone into teaching and nursing careers. They are doing what comes naturally to the female psyche.

The schoolchild or the patient of any age provides an outlet for a woman to express her natural maternal need. . . .

Finally, women are different from men in dealing with the fundamentals of life itself. Men are philosophers, women are practical, and 'twas ever thus. Men may philosophize about how life began and where we are heading; women are concerned about feeding the kids today. No woman would ever, as Karl Marx did, spend years reading political philosophy in the British Museum while her child starved to death. Women don't take naturally to a search for the intangible and the abstract. The Positive Woman knows who she is and where she is going, and she will reach her goal because the longest journey starts with a very practical first step.

Read and Respond

1. What are some of the issues raised in this article?

2. From what point of view is the writer reasoning? How effective, how persuasive is her argument? Does it lead you to any thinking about your life, your beliefs, or your attitude toward women's issues?

3. Are the issues raised *really* important to society? Why? What other social issues do they relate to? Are the issues important to you ? Why?

4. What bias do you find in this article, and how is it expressed?

Sexing Chickens

Richard DeWitt

Not surprisingly, it is important, within the poultry business, to distinguish between male and female chickens. As such, the poultry business employs a fair number of people whose primary job is the sexing of chickens. Chicken sexers are able to discriminate the sex of a chicken with apparent ease, yet when queried as to how they tell a boy from girl chicken, they are typically unable to specify any particular procedure. Learning this talent proceeds by hanging around an experienced chicken sexer until the novice begins to make the same judgments as the experienced sexer. Eventually the trainees are able to look at a chicken and reliably distinguish whether it is male or female, but apparently without the conscious use of any particular procedure. In short, they can do it, but they cannot say exactly how.

Read and Respond

1. This paragraph is a small portion of a longer essay. What point is the author trying to get across? How important is it for us to know this information?

2. Assume that the paragraph following this one begins: "As is the case with the skill of chicken sexing . . ." How would you finish this sentence?

3. Do you believe this paragraph, or is the author playing a trick on you? Do you think that there really are chicken sexers? And if there are, is this really how you become one? What makes you think that in this high-tech age there are people standing around sexing chickens? What features of this paragraph make you believe or disbelieve? How can you validate the author's claims?

ASKING CRITICAL QUESTIONS

After you read the article that follows, what critical questions come to mind? Everything you read will stir up your thinking if you read and question critically. What questions would you like to have answered in order for you to put the article in proper context and to completely understand what is being said or reported? *On the lines following the article, write three questions that, if answered, will help you understand what is really being said.*

The Abandonment of the Jews

David S. Wyman

Between June 1941 and May 1945, five to six million Jews perished at the hands of the Nazis and their collaborators. Germany's control over most of Europe meant that even a determined Allied rescue campaign probably could not have saved as many as a third of those who died. But a substantial commitment to rescue almost certainly could have saved several hundred thousand of them, and done so without compromising the war effort. The record clearly shows, though, that such a campaign would have taken place only if the United States had seized the initiative for it. But America did not act at all until late in the war, and even then, though it had some success, the effort was a very limited one. . . . Why did America fail to carry out the kind of rescue effort that it could have?

In summary form, these are the findings that I regard as most significant:

1. The American State Department and the British Foreign Office had no intention of rescuing large numbers of European Jews. On the contrary, they continually feared that Germany or other Axis nations might release tens of thousands of Jews into Allied hands. Any such exodus would have placed intense pressure on Britain to open Palestine and on the United States to take in more Jewish refugees, a situation the two great powers did not want to face. Consequently, their policies aimed at obstructing rescue possibilities and dampening public pressures for government action.

2. Authenticated information that the Nazis were systematically exterminating European Jewry was made public in the United States in November 1942. President Roosevelt did nothing about the mass murder for fourteen months, then moved only because he was confronted with political pressures he could not avoid and because his administration stood on the brink of a nasty scandal over its rescue policies.

3. The War Refugee Board, which the President then established to save Jews and other victims of the Nazis, received little power, almost no cooperation from Roosevelt or his administration, and grossly inadequate government funding. (Contributions from Jewish organizations, which were necessarily limited, covered 90 percent of the WRB's costs.) Through dedicated work by a relatively small number of people, the WRB managed to help save approximately 200,000 Jews and at least 20,000 non-Jews.

4. Because of State Department administrative policies, only 21,000 refugees were allowed to enter the United States during the three and one-half years the nation was at war with Germany. That amounted to 10 percent of the number who could have been legally admitted under the immigration quotas during that period.

5. Strong popular pressure for action would have brought a much fuller government commitment to rescue and would have produced it sooner. Several factors hampered the growth of public pressure. Among them were anti-Semitism and anti-immigration attitudes, both widespread in American society in that era and both entrenched in Congress; the mass media's failure to publicize Holocaust news, even though the wire services and other news sources made most of the information available to them; the near silence of the Christian churches and almost all of their leadership;

the indifference of most of the nation's political and intellectual leaders; and the President's failure to speak out on the issue.

6. American Jewish leaders worked to publicize the European Jewish situation and pressed for government rescue steps. But their effectiveness was importantly diminished by their inability to mount a sustained or unified drive for government action, by diversion of energies into fighting among the several organizations, and by failure to assign top priority to the rescue issue.

7. In 1944 the United States War Department rejected several appeals to bomb the Auschwitz gas chambers and the railroads leading to Auschwitz, claiming that such actions would divert essential airpower from decisive operations elsewhere. Yet in the very months that it was turning down the pleas, numerous massive American bombing raids were taking place within fifty miles of Auschwitz. Twice during that time large fleets of American heavy bombers struck industrial targets in the Auschwitz complex itself, not five miles from the gas chambers.

8. Analysis of the main rescue proposals put forward at the time, but brushed aside by government officials, yields convincing evidence that much more could have been done to rescue Jews, if a real effort had been made. The record also reveals that the reasons repeatedly invoked by government officials for not being able to rescue Jews could be put aside when it came to other Europeans who needed help.

9. Franklin Roosevelt's indifference to so momentous an historical event as the systematic annihilation of European Jewry emerges as the worst failure of his presidency.

10. Poor though it was, the American rescue record was better than that of Great Britain, Russia, or the other Allied nations. This was the case because of the work of the War Refugee Board, the fact that American Jewish organizations were willing to provide most of the WRB's funding, and the overseas rescue operations of several Jewish organizations. . . .

What could the American government have achieved if it had really committed itself to rescue? The possibilities were narrowed by the Nazis' determination to wipe out the Jews. War conditions themselves also made rescue difficult. And by mid-1942, when clear news of the systematic murder reached the West, two million Jews had already been massacred and the killing was going forward at a rapid rate. Most likely,

it would not have been possible to rescue millions. But without impeding the war effort, additional tens of thousands—probably hundreds of
thousands—could have been saved. What follows is a selection of twelve
programs that could have been tried. All of them, and others, were proposed during the Holocaust.

1. Most important, the War Refugee Board should have been established in 1942. And it should have received adequate government
   funding and much broader powers.

2. The U.S. government, working through neutral governments or the
   Vatican, could have pressed Germany to release the Jews. If nothing
   else, this would have demonstrated to the Nazis—and to the world—
   that America was committed to saving the European Jews. It is worth
   recalling that until late summer 1944, when the Germans blocked
   the Horthy offer, it was far from clear to the Allies that Germany
   would not let the Jews out. On the contrary, until then the State
   Department and the British Foreign Office feared that Hitler might
   confront the Allies with an exodus of Jews, a possibility that they
   assiduously sought to avoid.

   In a related area, ransom overtures might have been much more
   thoroughly investigated. The use of blocked funds for this purpose
   would not have compromised the war effort. Nor, by early 1944,
   would payments of limited amounts of currency have hurt the
   progress of the war. . . .

3. The United States could have applied constant pressure on Axis
   satellites to release their Jews. By spring 1943, the State Department
   knew that some satellites, convinced that the war was lost, were seeking favorable peace terms. Stern threats of punishment for mistreat-
   ing Jews or allowing their deportation, coupled with indications that
   permitting them to leave for safety would earn Allied goodwill, could
   have opened the way to the rescue of large numbers from Rumania,
   Bulgaria, Hungary, and perhaps Slovakia. Before the Germans took
   control of Italy, in September 1943, similar pressures might have
   persuaded the Italian government to allow its Jews to flee, as well as
   those in Italian-occupied areas of Greece, Yugoslavia, and France.

4. Success in setting off an exodus of Jews would have posed the problem of where they could go. Strong pressure needed to be applied
   to neutral countries near the Axis (Spain, Portugal, Turkey,
   Switzerland, and Sweden) to take Jews in. To bypass time-consuming
   immigration procedures, these nations could have been urged to set
   up reception camps near the borders. In return, the Allies should

have offered to fund the operations, supply food, and guarantee removal of the refugees. At the same time, havens of refuge outside Europe were essential to accommodate a steady movement of Jews out of the neutral countries. Thus the routes would have remained open and a continuing flow of fugitives could have left Axis territory.

5. Locating enough outside havens, places beyond continental Europe where refugees could safely await postwar resettlement, would have presented difficulties. The problems encountered in finding havens for the limited numbers of Jews who did get out during the war pointed up the callousness of the Western world. But an American government deeply concerned about the Jews and willing to share the burden could have used its prestige and power to open doors. If a camp existence was all that was offered, that was still far preferable to deportation and death.

   Ample room for camps was available in North Africa. In the United States, the immigration quotas were almost untouched; in addition, a government committed to rescue would have provided several camps besides Fort Ontario. A generous response by the United States would have put strong pressure on the Latin American nations, Canada, the British dominions, and Palestine. Instead, other countries used American stinginess as an excuse for not accepting Jews. For instance, in Jerusalem on his 1942 trip around the world, Wendell Willkie confronted the British leadership with the need to admit large numbers of Jews into Palestine. The British high commissioner replied that since the United States was not taking Jews in even up to the quota limits, Americans were hardly in a position to criticize.

6. Shipping was needed to transfer Jews from neutral countries to outside havens. Abundant evidence (summarized later in this chapter) proves that it could have been provided without interfering with the war effort.

   The preceding steps, vigorously pursued, might have saved scores or even hundreds of thousands. Instead, important opportunities were lost by default. Early in 1943, the United States turned its back on the Rumanian proposal to release 70,000 Jews. It was a pivotal failure; seizure of that chance might have led to other overtures by Axis satellites.

   At the same time, Switzerland was willing to accept thousands of children from France if it had assurance of their postwar removal. After refusing for more than a year, the State Department furnished the guarantee. But by then the main opportunity had passed.

During the summer of 1943, the way opened for evacuating 500 children from the Balkans. But a boat had to be obtained within a month. The State Department responded with bureaucratic delays. Allied actions, instead of encouraging neutral countries to welcome fleeing Jews, influenced them to do the opposite. For instance, it took more than a year to move a few hundred refugees out of Spain to the long-promised camp in North Africa. With a determined American effort, these failures, and others, could have been successes.

7. A campaign to stimulate and assist escapes would have led to a sizable outflow of Jews. Once the neutral nations had agreed to open their borders, that information could have been publicized throughout Europe by radio, airdropped leaflets, and underground communications channels. Local currencies could have been purchased in occupied countries, often with blocked foreign accounts. These funds could have financed escape systems, false documentation, and bribery of lower-level officials. Underground movements were willing to cooperate. (The WRB, in fact, carried out such operations on a small scale.) Even without help, and despite closed borders, tens of thousands of Jews attempted to escape to Switzerland, Spain, Palestine, and other places. Thousands succeeded. With assistance, and assurance of acceptance into neutral nations, those thousands could have been scores of thousands.

8. Much larger sums of money should have been transferred to Europe. After the WRB was formed, the earlier, tiny trickle of funds from the United States was increased. But the amounts were still inadequate. Besides facilitating escapes, money would have helped in hiding Jews, supplying food and other essentials, strengthening Jewish undergrounds, and gaining the assistance of non-Jewish forces.

9. Much more effort should have gone into finding ways to send in food and medical supplies. The American government should have approached the problem far sooner than it did. And it should have put heavy pressure on the International Red Cross and British blockade authorities on this issue.

10. Drawing on its great prestige and influence, the United States could have applied much more pressure than it did on neutral governments, the Vatican, and the International Red Cross to induce them to take earlier and more vigorous action. By expanding their

diplomatic missions in Axis countries, they would have increased the numbers of outside observers on the scene and perhaps inhibited actions against Jews. More important, the measures taken by Raoul Wallenberg [a Swedish diplomat who saved thousands of Hungarian Jews by giving them Swedish protection papers] in Budapest should have been implemented by all neutral diplomatic missions and repeated in city after city throughout Axis Europe. And they should have begun long before the summer of 1944.

The United States could also have pressed its two great allies to help. The Soviet Union turned away all requests for cooperation, including those from the WRB. An American government that was serious about rescue might have extracted some assistance from the Russians.

Britain, though more responsive, still compiled an abysmal record. Until 1944, Roosevelt and the State Department let the British lead in setting policy regarding European Jews. Even when the United States finally took the initiative, Roosevelt did not press for British cooperation. British officials resented the WRB, dismissed it as an election-year tactic, and tried to obstruct its work. The situation did not have to develop that way. An American president strongly committed to rescue could have insisted on a more helpful British response.

11. Some military assistance was possible. The Air Force could have eliminated the Auschwitz killing installations. Some bombing of deportation railroads was feasible. The military could have aided in other ways without impeding the war effort. It was, in fact, legally required to do so by the executive order that established the WRB.

12. Much more publicity about the extermination of the Jews should have been disseminated through Europe. Allied radio could have beamed the information for weeks at a time, on all possible wavelengths, as the Germans did regarding the alleged Russian massacre of Polish officers at the Katyn forest. This might have influenced three groups: the Christian populations, the Nazis, and the Jews. Western leaders and, especially, the Pope could have appealed to Christians not to cooperate in any way with the anti-Jewish programs, and to hide and to aid Jews whenever possible.

Roosevelt, Churchill, and the Pope might have made clear to the Nazis their full awareness of the mass-murder program and their severe condemnation of it. If, in addition, Roosevelt and Churchill had threatened punishment for these crimes and offered asylum to the Jews, the Nazis at least would have ceased to believe that the West did not care what they were doing to the Jews. That might possibly have slowed the killing. And it might have hastened the decision of the SS, ultimately taken in late 1944, to end the extermination. Even if top Nazis had brushed the threats aside, their subordinates might have been given pause.

The European Jews themselves should have been repeatedly warned of what was happening and told what the deportation trains really meant. (With good reason, the Nazis employed numerous precautions and ruses to keep this information from their victims.) Decades later, Rudolf Vrba, one of the escapees who exposed Auschwitz to the outside world, remained angry that the Jews had not been alerted. "Would anybody get me alive to Auschwitz if I had this information?" he demanded. "Would thousands and thousands of able-bodied Jewish men send their children, wives, mothers to Auschwitz from all over Europe, if they knew?" Roosevelt, Churchill, other Western leaders, and major Jewish spokesmen should have warned Jews over and over against the steps that led to deportation and urged them to try to hide or flee or resist. To help implement these actions, the Allies could have smuggled in cadres of specially trained Jewish agents.

None of these proposals guaranteed results. But all deserved serious consideration, and those that offered any chance of success should have been tried. There was a moral imperative to attempt everything possible that would not hurt the war effort. If that had been done, even if few or no lives had been saved, the moral obligation would have been fulfilled. But the outcome would not have been anything like that barren. The War Refugee Board, a very tardy, inadequately supported, partial commitment, saved several tens of thousands. A timely American rescue effort that had the wholehearted support of the government would have achieved much more.

A commitment of that caliber did not materialize. Instead, the Roosevelt administration turned aside most rescue proposals. In the process, government officials developed four main rationalizations for inaction. The most frequent excuse, the unavailability of shipping, was a fraud. When the Allies wanted to find ships for nonmilitary projects, they located them. In 1943, American naval vessels carried 1,400 non-Jewish Polish refugees from India to the American West Coast. The State and War departments arranged to move 2,000 Spanish Loyalist refugees to Mexico using military shipping. In March 1944, blaming the shipping shortage, the British backed out of an agreement to transport 630 Jewish refugees from Spain to the Fedala camp, near Casablanca. Yet at the same time, they were providing troopships to move non-Jewish refugees by the thousands from Yugoslavia to southern Italy and on to camps in Egypt.

When it was a matter of transporting Jews, ships could almost never be found. This was not because shipping was unavailable but because the Allies were unwilling to take the Jews in. In November 1943, Breckinridge Long told the House Foreign Affairs Committee that lack of transportation was the reason the State Department was issuing so few visas. "In December 1941," he explained, "most neutral shipping disappeared from the seas. . . . There just is not any transportation." In reality, ample shipping existed. Neutral vessels crossed the Atlantic throughout the war. Three Portuguese liners, with a combined capacity of 2,000 passengers, sailed regularly between Lisbon and U.S. ports. Each ship made the trip about every six weeks. Most of the time, because of the tight American visa policy, they carried only small fractions of their potential loads. Two dozen other Portuguese and Spanish passenger ships crossed the Atlantic less frequently but were available for fuller service. In addition, several score neutral cargo vessels could have been obtained and refitted to transport refugees.

American troopships and lend-lease and other cargo vessels could also have carried thousands of refugees across the Atlantic, clearing neutral European countries of fugitives and opening the way for a continuing exodus from Axis territory. War and State department correspondence shows that returning military transports could have performed this mission without hampering the war effort. In fact, U.S. Army authorities in North Africa offered in 1943 to take refugees to the United States on returning military ships. But the State and War departments blocked the plan.

In spring 1944, Roosevelt himself informed Pehle that the Navy could bring refugees to the United States on returning troopships. The War Shipping Administration believed that Liberty ships could also have transported refugees effectively. While the State Department was claiming that transportation for refugees was unavailable, Liberty ships were having difficulty finding ballast for the return trips from North Africa.

The United States and Britain leased Swedish ships to carry food from the Western Hemisphere to Greece. Sweden readily furnished replacements and additions to this fleet. Despite repeated pleas, however, the two great Allies never managed to provide a single boat to ferry Jews from the Balkans to Turkey or to shuttle Jews across the Mediterranean to safety. Yet the War Department admitted to the War

Refugee Board in spring 1944 that it had "ample shipping" available for evacuating refugees; the problem, it agreed, was to find places where they could go.

Another stock excuse for inaction was the claim that Axis governments planted agents among the refugees. Although this possibility needed to be watched carefully, the problem was vastly overemphasized and could have been handled through reasonable security screening. It was significant that Army intelligence found not one suspicious person when it checked the 982 refugees who arrived at Fort Ontario. Nevertheless, potential subversion was continually used as a reason for keeping immigration to the United States very tightly restricted. Turkey, Latin American nations, Britain, and other countries used the same exaggerated argument. It played an important part in blocking the channels of rescue.

A third rationalization for failing to aid European Jews took the high ground of nondiscrimination. It asserted that helping Jews would improperly single out one group for assistance when many peoples were suffering under Nazi brutality. Equating the genocide of the Jews with the oppression imposed on other Europeans was, in the words of one of the world's foremost churchmen, Willem Visser 't Hooft, "a dangerous half-truth which could only serve to distract attention from the fact that no other race was faced with the situation of having every one of its members . . . threatened by death in the gas chambers."

The Roosevelt administration, the British government, and the Intergovernmental Committee on Refugees regularly refused to acknowledge that the Jews faced a special situation. One reason for this was to avoid responsibility for taking special steps to save them. Such steps, if successful, would have confronted the Allies with the difficult problem of finding places to put the rescued Jews.

Another reason was the fear that special action for the Jews would stir up anti-Semitism. Some asserted that such action would even invite charges that the war was being fought for the Jews. Emanuel Celler declared years later that Roosevelt did nearly nothing for rescue because he was afraid of the label "Jew Deal"; he feared the political effects of the accusation that he was pro-Jewish. The Jews, according to artist Arthur Szyk, were a skeleton in the democracies' political closet, a matter they would rather not mention. "They treat us as a pornographical subject," he wrote, "you cannot discuss it in polite society."

The fourth well-worn excuse for rejecting rescue proposals was the claim that they would detract from the military effort and thus prolong the war. This argument, entirely valid with regard to projects that actually would have hurt the war effort, was used almost automatically to justify inaction. Virtually none of the rescue proposals involved enough infringement on the war effort to lengthen the conflict at all or to increase the number of casualties, military or civilian.

Actually, the war effort was bent from time to time to meet pressing humanitarian needs. In most of these instances, it was non-Jews who were helped. During 1942, 1943, and 1944, the Allies evacuated large numbers of non-Jewish Yugoslavs, Poles, and Greeks to safety in the Middle East, Africa, and elsewhere. Difficulties that constantly ruled out the rescue of Jews dissolved. Transportation somehow materialized to move 100,000 people to dozens of refugee camps that sprang into existence. The British furnished transport, supplies, much of the camp staffing, and many of the campsites. The United States contributed lend-lease materials and covered the bulk of the funding through UNRRA. Most of these refugees had been in desperate straits. None, though, were the objects of systematic annihilation.

Between November 1943 and September 1944, 36,000 Yugoslavs escaped to southern Italy. Most crossed the Adriatic by boat, thousands on British naval craft. Some even came out in American troop planes. The aircraft, sent mainly to evacuate wounded partisans, in many cases returned with civilians, including hundreds of orphaned babies. Using troopships, the British moved most of the Yugoslavs from Italy to camps in Egypt.

About 120,000 Poles, mostly men of military age and their dependents, came out of Russia during 1942 and passed into British-controlled camps in Iran. They were part of the remnant of a million and a half Poles the Soviets had deported to Siberia after the seizure of eastern Poland in September 1939. The Soviets released these thousands to join the British armed forces. Two-thirds of them did; the other 40,000 became refugees. Iran did not want them, supplying them was difficult, and conditions at the camps were bad. Most were moved out, mainly on British troopships, between August 1942 and August 1943. Ultimately, about 35,000 went to camps in Africa, India, Mexico, and the Middle East. The greatest numbers were placed in British colonies in East Africa, where camps were made available by shifting thousands of prisoners of war to the United States.

Despite the demands of war, the United States, with British support, extended significant help to the Greek people. Food for Greece moved freely through the blockade, and ships to carry it were located without trouble. American lend-lease funds paid for the project.

The Allies also helped thousands of Greeks to flee Nazi control and provided sanctuary for them in the Middle East and Africa. By 1944, 25,000 Greeks had been evacuated. The largest numbers, reported at between 9,000 and 12,000, were taken to Palestine—most to a former army installation at Nuseirat, near Gaza. Palestine also sheltered 1,800 of the non-Jewish Polish refugees. While the British, intent on keeping the small White Paper quota from being filled, turned back endangered Jews, they generously welcomed these other victims of the storm.

In all, Britain and the United States rescued 100,000 Yugoslav, Polish, and Greek refugees from disastrous conditions. Most of them traveled by military transport to camps where the Allies maintained them at considerable cost in funds, supplies, and even military staff. In contrast, the United States (with minimal cooperation from the British) evacuated fewer than 2,000 Jews to the three camps open to *them.* . . .

It was not a lack of workable plans that stood in the way of saving many thousands more European Jews. Nor was it insufficient shipping, the threat of infiltration by subversive agents, or the possibility that rescue projects would hamper the war effort. The real obstacle was the absence of a strong desire to rescue Jews. A month before the Bermuda Conference, the Committee for a Jewish Army declared:

> *We, on our part, refuse to resign ourselves to the idea that our brains are powerless to find any solution. . . . In order to visualize the possibility of such a solution, imagine that the British people and the American nation had millions of residents in Europe. . . . Let us imagine that Hitler would start a process of annihilation and would slaughter not two million Englishmen or Americans, not hundreds of thousands, but, let us say, only tens of thousands. . . . It is clear that the governments of Great Britain [and] the United States would certainly find ways and means to act instantly and to act effectively.*

But the European Jews were not Americans and they were not English. It was their particular misfortune not only to be foreigners but also to be Jews.

My Critical Questions

1. _____

_____ **?**

2. _____

_____ **?**

3. _____

_____ **?**

Recognizing Organization

ESSENTIAL THINKING SKILLS

CHAPTER	WHAT THEY'RE CALLED	WHAT THEY MEAN
Chapter 3	**The Gathering Skills**	**Gathering all the information.**
	Observing	Actively seeking information through one or more senses.
	Questioning	Seeking information by asking questions.
Chapter 4	**The Organizing Skills**	**Organizing for the purpose of making sense.**
	Comparing and Contrasting	Noting similarities and differences between two or more things, events, or ideas.
	Classifying and Sequencing	Arranging things or concepts into categories and into sequential order.
	Identifying Cause and Effect	Recognizing the relationship between an effect and its cause.
Chapter 5	**The Generating Skills**	**Generating additional information.**
	Inferring	Making an assumption, stating a hypothesis, or coming to a conclusion based on limited information.
	Summarizing	Condensing the essence of the information accurately and efficiently.
	Synthesizing	Creating new information by combining two or more pieces of information.
	Generating Ideas	Creating new information, alternatives, or applications.
Chapter 6	**The Recognizing Skills**	**Recognizing what has been left unsaid.**
	Recognizing Purpose	Identifying a writer's or speaker's intention.
	Recognizing Fact and Opinion	Distinguishing between a statement of fact and a statement of opinion.
	Recognizing Tone	Identifying a sentiment or mood by assessing the writer's or speaker's choice of words.
	Recognizing Bias	Noting the presence and nature of a writer's or speaker's prejudice.
	Recognizing Organization	Identifying the organizational pattern of a thought, statement, passage, or plan.
	Recognizing Underlying Assumptions	Recognizing the suppositions that are taken for granted and are the foundation of a proposition, notion, or idea.
Chapter 7	**The Analyzing Skills**	**Analyzing for the purpose of coming to a conclusion.**
	Analyzing	Identifying and separating ideas, attributes, situations, and/or components in order to form a conclusion as to their relationship.
	Evaluating	Appraising something according to certain criteria and forming a judgment as to its worth or quality.
	Inducing	Analyzing individual facts or premises in order to derive a general conclusion.
	Deducing	Applying general principles or a broad framework to a situation in order to come to a conclusion about it.

> *"I always have two things in my head—I always have a theme and the form. The form looks for the theme, theme looks for the form, and when they come together you're able to write."*
> —W. H. Auden

> *"Art is the imposing of a pattern on experience, and our aesthetic enjoyment is recognition of the pattern."*
> —Alfred North Whitehead

What questions am I going to have answered in this section on recognizing organization?

1. Of what value is being able to recognize the organization of what I read or hear?
2. What are the most common patterns of organization, and how do they differ?
3. What are the clue words that signal the presence of a specific pattern of organization?

THINK ABOUT THIS!

Three Sexes?

What if there were three sexes instead of two? How would families change? What would dating be like? Would there be more or less gender discrimination? What would the third sex wear? Which sex would be the most powerful? Jot down your ideas about how life would change.

_____

_____

_____

_____

_____

_____

_____

_____

_____

RECOGNIZING ORGANIZATION:
Identifying the organizational pattern of a thought, statement, passage, or plan

Sometimes we begin to read something or listen to someone speaking and we lose the train of thought. The book or talk no longer makes sense, and we get so frustrated that sometimes we just quit listening or reading. This happens because we can't tell how the author or speaker is developing the ideas or we can't identify the overall pattern of organization of what is being said. Recognizing the organization of what we read and hear assists us in figuring out what is relevant, important, and timely.

The way authors and speakers arrange their material to best accomplish their purpose and to express their ideas clearly is called the pattern of organization. You need to be aware of this organization because it helps you to follow a speaker's or author's train of thought. You can think along with him or her, and you are less likely to lose sight of the main point, get frustrated, waste time, be tricked, or quit reading or listening.

TYPES OF PROSE WRITING AND SPEAKING

Nonfiction writing and most lecturing can generally be divided into four broad types.

1. *Narration.* The most easily recognized kind of writing and lecturing you'll encounter in college is called *narration.* The writer or speaker narrates events, either real or imagined, in chronological order and in much the same way a storyteller might. Typically, the writer or speaker starts at the beginning of some event and tells what happens until the event is concluded.

2. *Description.* The purpose of descriptive writing and speaking is to *describe* a specific person, thing, or place. The writer or speaker attempts to paint a mental picture using sensory words, that is, words that appeal to the reader's or listener's senses. Descriptive writing and speaking abound in concrete details of shape, color, sight, sound, smell, and taste.

3. *Persuasion.* The purpose of persuasive writing and speaking is to *persuade* you of something, to change your mind. The writer or speaker

attempts to make you believe what he or she is saying and act on it. We see persuasive writing in editorials and advertisements, and we are barraged with it at election time when the candidates present their views. Persuasive speaking and writing relies heavily on both appeals to reason and appeals to the emotions. A related type of organization is *argumentation*, which refers to writing that sets up logically valid arguments in support of a specific viewpoint.

4. *Exposition.* Expository writing and speaking is the most common type of writing and speaking that you will encounter in college. Exposition is an attempt to lay out information, to explain something, to *expose* something as clearly as possible. It is factual writing and speaking. Expository organization may contain elements of narration, description, and persuasion, but its overwhelming objective is to present information.

A variety of organizational patterns is possible within each of these four major types of writing and speaking. It is important to be able to recognize the patterns.

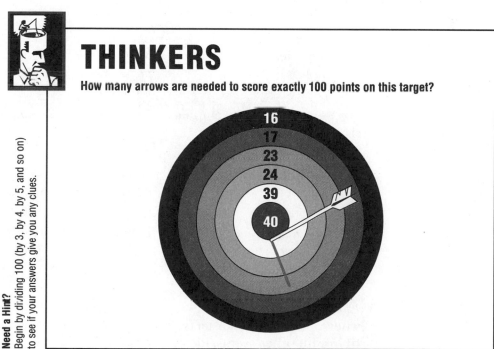

THINKERS

How many arrows are needed to score exactly 100 points on this target?

16
17
23
24
39
40

Need a Hint?
Begin by dividing 100 (by 3, by 4, by 5, and so on) to see if your answers give you any clues.

COMMON OVERALL PATTERNS OF ORGANIZATION AND THEIR CLUE WORDS

Most of the material college students are required to read and most of the lectures they will listen to are *expository,* that is, intended to inform or to explain. Several different patterns of organization can be used in expository writing. In well-thought-out lectures or reading, the organization is recognizable. The pattern of organization in most textbooks and lectures is likely to be either cause and effect (showing how something occurs because of other factors); comparison and contrast (pointing out likenesses and differences among ideas and events); time order (putting facts and events into a chronological sequence); statement and classification (statement of a fact or problem followed by discussion or solution); or simple listing (enumeration, in order, of facts, events, and ideas). Other patterns too are used. To improve your comprehension of the works you read and the lectures you hear, become aware of the twelve common organizational patterns described in the following chart. Also, notice the clue words that help you identify an organizational pattern.

Patterns of Organization and Their Clue Words

Pattern of Organization	Clue Words
1. *Time order:* discussion of events or ideas in relation to passing time	*after, afterward, at last, at that time, before, during, immediately, now, presently, shortly, since, thereupon, until, while*
2. *Simple listing / Process:* emphasis on the order in which something occurs	*next, then, first, second, third, last*
3. *Definition:* emphasis on the meaning of a word, phrase, or idea	*means, can be defined as, the same as, like, is*
4. *Statement and clarification:* statement of fact with discussion intended to make that statement clear	*words, obviously, of course, too*
5. *Classification:* analysis of where events, ideas, or facts fit in with other events, ideas, and facts	*category, field, rank, group, various elements, characteristics, some feature, types, parts*

6. *Summary:* condensed statement of the principal points in a larger statement or idea

in brief, in conclusion, in short, on the whole, to sum up, to summarize

7. *Comparison:* discussion of similarities in two or more ideas, events, or things

also, likewise, in like manner, similarly, similar to, compared with

8. *Contrast:* discussion of the differences in two or more ideas, events, or things

although, however, but, conversely, nevertheless, yet, on the contrary, on one hand . . . on the other hand, at the same time

9. *Generalization and example:* statement with examples designed to illustrate or clarify the statement

for example, e.g., for instance, that is, thus, to illustrate, as demonstrated

10. *Cause and effect:* a reason or condition and the subsequent effect or conclusion

accordingly, affect, as a result, and, because, consequently, hence, in short, may be due to, reasons, results, then, therefore, thus

11. *Addition:* emphasis on providing more information

again, also, and, besides, equally important, finally, further, furthermore, in addition, last, likewise, moreover

12. *Location / Spatial order:* emphasis on whereabouts of a thing or things

above, adjacent to, below, beyond, then, close by, elsewhere, inside, nearby, next to, opposite, within, without

MIXED PATTERNS

Although writers and speakers generally follow one overall organization when they write and speak, they occasionally mix patterns in order to accomplish their objectives more efficiently. Mixing *comparison* and *contrast* is very common, as is mixing *definition* and *classification*. Don't be alarmed if you notice an author or a speaker moving from one pattern to a different one, or combining two patterns. This just means that you have mastered the technique of recognizing organization. It doesn't matter which pattern of organization an author or speaker employs as long as *you* recognize it.

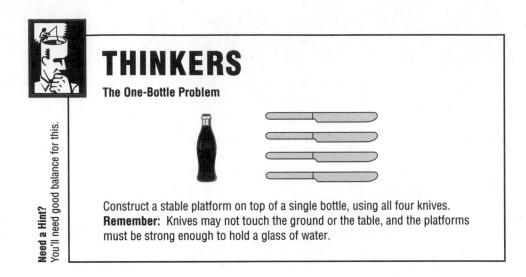

THINKERS
The One-Bottle Problem

Construct a stable platform on top of a single bottle, using all four knives.
Remember: Knives may not touch the ground or the table, and the platforms must be strong enough to hold a glass of water.

Need a Hint? You'll need good balance for this.

STIR IT UP 6.18   Write a brief statement (three or four paragraphs) setting forth your feelings about illegal drug use, but write it according to a preselected pattern of organization. Be ready to discuss the ease or difficulty of doing this exercise.

STIR IT UP 6.19   On the lines provided, explain why it is important to be able to answer the following three questions as you do your reading assignments.

    a. Do I understand this material?

    b. Could I restate this material?

    c. Where does all this writing lead?

_____

_____

_____

_____

_____

_____

_____

_____

Journal Observations (see page 13)

RECOGNIZING ORGANIZATION

1st Writing _____

_____

_____

_____

_____

_____

_____

_____

_____

_____

2nd Writing _____

_____

_____

_____

_____

_____

_____

_____

_____

_____

_____

_____

3rd Writing _____

_____

_____

_____

_____

_____

_____

_____

_____

_____

READINGS

The Testimony of a Detroit Sniper

Ray Rogers
New York Post, *July 29, 1967*

A teenage Negro who identified himself as one of the elusive Detroit snipers says "the war" will not be over until "they kill all of us."

But, he insisted yesterday, his activities were not organized.

"When the thing broke out me and my main man were out there helping. We threw some cocktails. But after a while we got tired of that so we decided to go home and get our pieces," he explained.

"Get One or Two"

"We had them ——— cops so scared that first night they were shooting at one another. I know I got one or two of them, but I don't think I killed them. I wish I had, the dirty ———."

The young man explained that he went and got his "piece" after he and his buddy had looted a liquor store.

"We drank a little. And after a while—boom, just like that we decided to do some shootin'."

Did he realize he could be killed?

"I'm not crazy—I'm not crazy to be killed. I'm just gettin' even for what they did to us. Really. That's where it's at."

"Man, they killed Malcolm X just like that. So I'm gonna take a few of them with me. They may get me later on, but somebody else will take my place—just like that."

He explained that he avoided the area patrolled by the airborne troops because of the intensity with which they returned fire.

"They got a lot of soul brothers in their outfit too and I'm not trying to waste my own kind. I am after them honkies . . ." he said.

Mother Died

His mother had died years ago, leaving him and his sister in a dilapidated apartment, he said.

"Man, that place was so bad that I hated to come home at night. My sister became a hustler for a guy I grew up with." He said he had heard that she had been shot Wednesday night while looting a store.

"That makes me mad. Why they have to shoot somebody for takin' something out of a store during a riot? These white mothers are something else," he said angrily as he rubbed his long, powerful fingers together.

He said he wished he had a better weapon than the U.S. M1 automatic carbine because it lacked range and fire power. Thus he could not fire more than one or two rounds at most before National Guardsmen laid down a heavy barrage.

"But I know I got two of them. I saw them mothers fall.

"One was a honky-tonk cop with a big belly and he couldn't run too fast. And when I hit him he hollered and hit the pavement.

"And them stupid mothers fired all over the place except the place where I was—I was laying among some bricks in a burnt-out store. It was beautiful, baby, so beautiful I almost cried with joy."

He said he never carried the carbine with him and he hid it in a different place after each time he used it.

He laughed and said:

"Twice they had their hands on me and searched me but they let me go. That's why I say that the war ain't over until they put all of us in jail or kill us. . . . I mean all of us soul brothers. But they can't do that because there's too many of us."

Suddenly he began talking about his early life.

"I went to school just like you did. I believed in all that oakie-doak and then I woke up one day and said later for that stuff because that stuff would just mess up my mind, just mess up my mind. I hustled and did a little bit of everything to stay alive.

"I got a couple of kids by some sister on the other side of town but I never see them. What can I say to them?"

He said that he and his buddy paid his 10-year-old cousin to watch for National Guard patrols while they were staked out on roofs. They communicated with him by a toy walkie-talkie.

"It was funny for a while because all they could do was lay there and holler at one another. Man, it was beautiful. We controlled the scene.

"We were just like guerrillas—real ones."

Read and Respond

1. What criteria can you use to evaluate the sniper's reasoning in this article? Is there any reasoning present? If so, what is it? Are there any fallacies in the reasoning?

2. Are there other causes, not identified, for the sniper's behavior?

3. What would you predict for the future of this sniper? Why? What is your prediction based on?

Who Benefits?

James R. Kearl

In 1986, when Congress passed the Tax Reform Act, it also slipped in another piece of legislation that could mean a great deal more to both employers and employees than tax reform ever will. As a matter of fact, any tax simplification achieved by tax reform could well be wiped out by the headaches created by Section 89.

The story behind Section 89 is one of good intentions. The Congress wanted to make sure that the bosses won't be treated substantially better than the workers when employee benefits are passed out. At first glance, this may seem like a great idea, especially if you're a worker. But take a closer look at Section 89 in action.

The provision that probably affects you as a college student most directly compels companies to give essentially the same benefit package to all part-time employees working over 17.5 hours per week that it gives to its full-time employees. Put yourself into the position of the owner of the Sleeping Beauty Motel chain. You have 100 full-time employees, all in managerial positions, each earning $30,000 per year in addition to a benefit package costing $2,000. You also have 1,000 part-time employees working 20 hours per week and earning minimum wage, or about $3,500 per year. What are your choices under the new law? You can extend full-time benefits to all of your part-time employees, essentially increasing their compensation by nearly 60 percent and your labor costs by 20 percent. Or you can cut the hours of your part-time employees to the maximum allowable by law before you must offer benefits, reducing their incomes by 12.5 percent and requiring you to hire and train an additional 140 employees. Or you can stop hiring part-time employees altogether. If you pursue this last option, you will have to let 500 employees go and your labor costs will still increase by 10 percent. Finally, you can quit giving employee benefits entirely and opt instead to give your full-time employees a $2,000 raise.

Although this example is a bit extreme, it shows that there may be tremendous costs involved in extending benefit packages to all part-time employees, costs that profit-maximizing owners will not want to (and may not be able to) absorb. So, rather than ensuring equal benefits for everyone, the law will likely reduce benefits for many and make them harder to get for many more. An employee who is looking for a good benefit package to help pay for braces for his or her children may find it hard to get one because many employers will merely pare down everyone's benefits to comply with the law. This may be a small matter, however, compared with the problems faced by individuals who want to work something like 30 hours per week. They will either have to work two jobs (at less than 17.5 hours each) or work full-time, if they are to work at all.

Read and Respond

1. What are the implications of Section 89 of the Tax Reform Act for you personally? Are you working part-time? Are you receiving any benefits? Why not? If you are working part-time and not receiving any benefits, what does that suggest about the information in this article?

2. What conflicts are present in the values that come into play when employers comply with Section 89?

3. What would happen if every employer decided to stop hiring part-time workers so that there were only full-time workers? What would be the implications for the economy?

Recognizing Underlying Assumptions

ESSENTIAL THINKING SKILLS

CHAPTER	WHAT THEY'RE CALLED	WHAT THEY MEAN
Chapter 3	**The Gathering Skills**	**Gathering all the information.**
	Observing	Actively seeking information through one or more senses.
	Questioning	Seeking information by asking questions.
Chapter 4	**The Organizing Skills**	**Organizing for the purpose of making sense.**
	Comparing and Contrasting	Noting similarities and differences between two or more things, events, or ideas.
	Classifying and Sequencing	Arranging things or concepts into categories and into sequential order. .
	Identifying Cause and Effect	Recognizing the relationship between an effect and its cause.
Chapter 5	**The Generating Skills**	**Generating additional information.**
	Inferring	Making an assumption, stating a hypothesis, or coming to a conclusion based on limited information.
	Summarizing	Condensing the essence of the information accurately and efficiently.
	Synthesizing	Creating new information by combining two or more pieces of information.
	Generating Ideas	Creating new information, alternatives, or applications.
Chapter 6	**The Recognizing Skills**	**Recognizing what has been left unsaid.**
	Recognizing Purpose	Identifying a writer's or speaker's intention.
	Recognizing Fact and Opinion	Distinguishing between a statement of fact and a statement of opinion.
	Recognizing Tone	Identifying a sentiment or mood by assessing the writer's or speaker's choice of words.
	Recognizing Bias	Noting the presence and nature of a writer's or speaker's prejudice.
	Recognizing Organization	Identifying the organizational pattern of a thought, statement, passage, or plan.
	Recognizing Underlying Assumptions	Recognizing the suppositions that are taken for granted and are the foundation of a proposition, notion, or idea.
Chapter 7	**The Analyzing Skills**	**Analyzing for the purpose of coming to a conclusion.**
	Analyzing	Identifying and separating ideas, attributes, situations, and/or components in order to form a conclusion as to their relationship.
	Evaluating	Appraising something according to certain criteria and forming a judgment as to its worth or quality.
	Inducing	Analyzing individual facts or premises in order to derive a general conclusion.
	Deducing	Applying general principles or a broad framework to a situation in order to come to a conclusion about it.

"Until we can understand the assumptions in which we are drenched we cannot know ourselves."
—Adrienne Rich

"The meaning of a proposition is the method of its verification."
—Moritz Schlick

What questions am I going to have answered in this section on recognizing underlying assumptions?

1. In what ways might our values shape our position in an argument or shape our reaction to world events?
2. Why do we frequently examine our assumptions only when a problem develops?
3. What are the two types of underlying assumptions, and how are they different?

> **RECOGNIZING UNDERLYING ASSUMPTIONS:**
> **Recognizing the suppositions that are taken for granted and that are the foundation of a proposition, notion, or idea**

I just went to the store and purchased two candy bars for a total of $1.00. How much did each candy bar cost?

"Fifty cents," you quickly answer.

"Wrong," I say. "One candy bar cost 40 cents and the other, bigger candy bar cost 60 cents."

"No fair," you reply. "You tricked me. Most candy bars are the same price. I assumed that both candy bars you were talking about were the same size. You should have told me they were different sizes."

"You made an incorrect assumption."

What's the point of this story? In every situation where a conclusion is called for, even the most simple, there are underlying assumptions. Not to consider these assumptions is to increase the likelihood of responding incorrectly to the situation.

ASSUMPTIONS ARE PART OF OUR LIVES

Everything we think, reason, say, or do is based on assumptions, things we believe are true. Assumptions are those unstated beliefs that we take for granted and upon which we base our actions or rest our arguments.

THINK ABOUT THIS!

Ludicrous Laws

Laws reflect people's thinking at certain times in history. A law originates because people in a certain locale at a certain point in time feel the need to legislate a particular type of behavior. As time passes, some laws may no longer be needed, and they are changed to reflect the current times or they are dropped. However, some laws are never changed because of legislative inertia. Contemplating these outdated laws provides us with an opportunity to examine the thinking process of people in the past. Consider the following examples of "ludicrous laws" that are still on the books, and attempt to figure out why these laws were originally legislated. Record your explanations on the lines.

- In Brooklyn, New York, it is against the law to let an animal go to sleep in your bathtub.

_____

_____

- In Spades, Indiana, it is illegal to open a can of food by firing a revolver at it.

_____

_____

- In Connecticut, it is against the law to walk your pet bear along the highway.

_____

_____

- In California, you need a hunting license to capture mice.

_____

_____

- In Garfield County, Montana, people are forbidden to draw cartoons or funny faces on their window shades.

_____

_____

Which of our current laws do you think would be ludicrous or incomprehensible to people living in 1800? List a few.

_____

_____

_____

_____

For example, perhaps at the age of 18 you take your first college course. In class you find that nearly everyone looks to be about the same age. After a few weeks, you ask the friendly, attractive student sitting next to you to go out with you. The student says, "Thank you, but I'm married." Oops! You acted on at least one false assumption. You assumed that because the other students in the class appeared to be your age, they were also unmarried. What you didn't do was identify your assumptions and check their validity before acting on them. It is easy for you to identify your assumption now because it led to some embarrassment for you. This is frequently the case with assumptions. We identify them only when it is too late and they have caused us problems.

Assumptions differ from person to person, but they all tend to become deeply ingrained over time in our thinking. We seldom examine them or check them for appropriateness or consistency until we are confronted by conflicting ideas. Until then, assumptions are simply *there* and not thought about. In any discussion, debate, or presentation of an argument, assumptions are usually left unstated, but they are still present. They determine not just what we say but what we really mean.

WHY SEEK HIDDEN ASSUMPTIONS?

The ability to identify hidden assumptions is an important critical thinking skill for life as well as college. Knowing that everything we learn in college is based on a variety of assumptions, and realizing that all people have assumptions on which they base their thinking and decision making, will help us be more aware of our thinking, reasoning, and actions. As we identify hidden assumptions in ourselves and others, as we assess and correct our assumptions, we can use our growing knowledge to understand what writers and speakers *really* mean. This will help keep us from faulty reasoning and poor decisions. Other people's assumptions are frequently wrong—or at least different from our own—and any argument, proposition, or idea based on those faulty assumptions will also be faulty. Reasoning is only as sound as the assumptions it is based on. That is why it is important to examine, question, and understand underlying assumptions. We need to be certain we are not accepting good arguments based on nonexistent or misunderstood "facts." If we do not understand what the underlying assumptions are for a particular idea, we will have very little chance at recognizing the truth or merit of the idea.

Finding underlying assumptions is a "collecting" process. You collect hints from the things people say and then make guesses about what they believe but don't say. These hidden assumptions then can be examined in order to interpret or explain what is really meant and why it is being said.

THINKERS

On a Corner . . .

The first modern one appeared on a corner on Euclid Avenue in Cleveland, Ohio, in 1914. What was it?

Need a Hint?
What can be found on street corners, and what "modern" thing came into wide use about 1914?

TWO KINDS OF ASSUMPTIONS

There are two main categories of assumptions: *value assumptions* and *reality assumptions.*

Value assumptions are beliefs (ideals really) that we accept and hold about the way things ought to be. These assumptions are based on the values communicated to us by such people as family members, religious leaders, and people we associate with. The values we absorb and accept as we mature form the basis of our opinions. Some values are so universally accepted that we assume that everyone holds them. For example, murder, rape, and other forms of violence against individuals is wrong; helping the weak, sick, and poor is right. However, not all values that we may hold are held by other people, or are held as strongly as we hold them. We may believe that gambling, drugs, and prostitution do no harm and should be legalized, but we find that many people don't share our values and disagree with us. In many cases, arguments and conflicts occur because the opposing sides have different values. It is common to hear the words "You're assuming that I . . ." when two people disagree.

Reality assumptions are beliefs (perceptions really) that we hold about the way things are. They are assumptions that we make and hold about what happened or what exists or how something works. In any criminal trial, the two sides, prosecution and defense, base their trial arguments on reality assumptions—what each thinks really happened during the crime. The evidence that is presented, the witnesses that are called, the arguments that are raised—all are determined by each side's reality assumptions. Whether the two sides and the jury believe a person guilty or not guilty has to do with their assumptions concerning reality—what they believe really happened. When two cars collide at a busy intersection, the two drivers usually have different reality assumptions. In fact, their perceptions of what happened may differ dramatically. It is not surprising that police officers and insurance agents frequently must rely on detached, unemotional observers to determine what really occurred.

STIR IT UP 6.20   What are the assumptions behind the statements below? Several assumptions can usually be seen at work in each case. Where do you think the assumptions came from? Under what conditions might they have been formed? Are they value assumptions or reality assumptions? Who is making these statements?

1. The person I want to hire for the position of senior engineer should be very experienced. He should have exceptional references.

   _____

2. I don't care if you are going to the beach, you are not wearing that bathing suit.

   _____

3. Growing, selling, and smoking marijuana should be legalized.

   _____

4. Radios are as necessary in cars as airbags.

   _____

5. The sheer number of professional and amateur boxing matches proves that Americans prefer violent sports.

   _____

6. At their ages, they should live together for a while before they get married.

   _____

7. You're going to love this shirt I bought you.

   _____

8. If you care about the poor, you'll support Proposition 22.

   _____

9. That bottled mineral water is of superior quality; it comes from Europe.

_____

10. I was really surprised—and a bit horrified—when I learned that she went out with him.

_____

STIR IT UP 6.21   There are several assumptions underlying each of the following accounts. What are they?

1. The lights were low, the room was crowded, the conversation was loud, and the music was even louder. He walked up to me, slowly looked me over from head to toe—spending more time on parts of my anatomy then others—and asked, "What's a nice girl like you doing in a place like this?"

2. I think it is a real shame that Native Americans are not forced to leave reservation lands when they are children and go to school in communities with public schools. Unless this occurs, Native Americans will never make any major contribution to society.

3. The man walking back and forth in front of the Planned Parenthood clinic was wearing a homemade sandwich board that said, "The wages of sin is death."

4. The main reason there is so much juvenile crime is that there are no mothers at home anymore during those early formative years. They have put the children in 'holding pens' in daycare centers.

STIR IT UP 6.22   When is the thinking skill of recognizing underlying assumptions especially important? See how many additional occasions you can add to the following list.

1. When reading anything in newspapers or magazines.

2. When analyzing contractual agreements.

3. When negotiating a change in job responsibilities.

4. When reading my world history textbook.

5. _____

6. _____

7. _____

8. _____
9. _____
10. _____
11. _____
12. _____
13. _____
14. _____
15. _____

STIR IT UP 6.23 Identify at least one possible underlying assumption for each of the situations you listed in Stir It Up 6.22.

1. _____
2. _____
3. _____
4. _____
5. _____
6. _____
7. _____
8. _____

THINKERS

By moving only the minus sign (–) in the number below, create nine-fifty.

$$- \quad I0I0I0$$

Need a Hint? This isn't a math problem; it is an "appea'ance" problem. Take time to look at it closely.

9. _____

10. _____

11. _____

12. _____

13. _____

14. _____

15. _____

STIR IT UP 6.24   What assumptions do you have about your college education? What assumptions do you have about your professors, about your textbooks, about the purpose of your assignments, about the difficulty of the work, about the amount of studying required? List some of your assumptions below. What assumptions do you or did you have about dormitory life, dating at college, the ease of making friends? Next to each assumption, indicate how you can check its validity.

1. _____

2. _____

3. _____

4. _____

5. _____

6. _____

7. _____

8. _____

9. _____

10. _____

STIR IT UP 6.25   What do you assume when you see a newspaper advertisement that boldly proclaims, "All new cars being sold at below dealer cost"? Identify some of your assumptions below.

_____

_____

_____

_____

_____

_____

_____

_____

_____

_____

_____

_____

Standards for Thinking and Reasoning

Identify the three most important critical thinking standards to be applied to the skill of **recognizing underlying assumptions.** Put a check (✓) next to your three choices. Be ready to explain your thinking. Why these three?

☐ Clear ☐ Specific ☐ Relevant
☐ Logical ☐ Significant ☐ Fair
☐ Precise ☐ Accurate ☐ Consistent
☐ Deep ☐ Complete ☐ Adequate

ANY QUESTIONS?

How many different ways can you write 1999 in Roman numerals?

_____

_____

_____

_____

Journal Observations (see page 13)

RECOGNIZING UNDERLYING ASSUMPTIONS

1st Writing _____

_____
_____
_____
_____
_____
_____
_____
_____
_____

2nd Writing _____

_____
_____
_____
_____
_____
_____
_____
_____
_____
_____

3rd Writing _____

_____

_____

_____

_____

_____

_____

_____

_____

_____

Choosing Healthier Foods?

READINGS

James R. Kearl

In late 1991, the U.S. government announced new regulations, to be implemented gradually, governing the labeling of food. Some 80,000 types of food and almost 300,000 food labels will come under a common set of regulations. Terms such as "fresh," "low calorie," "fat free," "low in cholesterol," "light," "less," "reduced," and "more" will have specific, consistent meanings on all labels. Nutrition labeling will be mandatory on processed foods but voluntary, at least initially, for raw fruits, vegetables, meat, poultry, and seafood. Health claims will be allowed only if they can be supported by scientific evidence. The government will also regulate serving sizes. Implementation costs (new labels, standardized packaging, and so on) for manufacturers are estimated to be $1.7 billion over 20 years.

One purpose of the regulations is to better inform consumers of the nutrients in foods they purchase. Since words and labels will be consistent across products, the regulations should reduce the cost to consumers of gathering useful information. Better informed consumers, it is hoped, will make more healthful food consumption decisions.

Standardized serving sizes will allow consumers to see price changes more clearly. (In the past, price changes could be hidden partially by changes in serving sizes.)

A second purpose of the regulations is to provide incentives for firms to get a competitive edge by providing more healthful food products. If producers assume that consumers make choices based on the health-fulness of the product, then, consumer advocates argue, firms will have the appropriate incentives to produce more healthful products.

There is evidence that firms do respond to their belief that the public will be more critical. That is, incentives of this sort make a difference. In late 1991, a survey of 421 companies found that 70 percent were developing new reduced-fat and reduced-calorie products. Moreover, the number of products with health-related marketing claims increased to 10,301 in 1990, up from 9,192 in 1989 and 8,183 in 1988.

Read and Respond

1. What are some of the underlying assumptions on the part of the government, businesses, and consumers that are behind the decisions and actions described in this article?

2. Is "health labeling" an important issue to society? Is this issue important to you? Why or why not?

3. Two purposes are given for the labeling regulations. Are there others, perhaps ones which may not be quite as publicly acceptable? What are they?

The Great Railway Competition

Jack Chen

On the plains, the Chinese worked in tandem with all the Indians Crocker could entice to work on the iron rails. They began to hear of the exploits of the Union Pacific's "Irish terriers" building from the east. One day, the Irish laid six miles of track, they were told. The Chinese of the Central Pacific topped this with seven. "No Chinaman is going to beat us," growled the Irish, and the next day, they laid seven and a half miles of track. They swore that they would outperform the competition no matter what it did.

Crocker taunted the Union Pacific that his men could lay ten miles of track a day. Durant, president of the rival line, laid a $10,000 wager that it could not be done. Crocker took no chances. He waited until the day before the last sixteen miles of track had to be laid and brought up all needed supplies for instant use. Then he unleashed his crews. On April 28, 1869, while Union Pacific checkers and newspaper reporters looked on, a combined gang of Chinese and eight picked Irish rail handlers laid ten miles and 1,800 feet more of track in twelve hours. This record was never surpassed until the advent of mechanized track laying. Each Irishman that day walked a total distance of ten miles, and their combined muscle handled sixty tons of rail.

So keen was the competition that when the two lines approached each other, instead of changing direction to link up, their builders careered on and on for 100 miles, building lines that would never meet. Finally, the government prescribed that the linkage point should be Promontory [Point], Utah.

Competition was keen, but there seems to be no truth in the story that the Chinese and Irish in this phase of work were trying to blow each other up with explosives. It is a fact, however, that when the two lines were very near each other, the Union Pacific blasters did not give the Central Pacific men timely warning when setting off a charge, and several Chinese were hurt. Then a Central Pacific charge went off unannounced and several Irishmen found themselves buried in dirt. This forced the foremen to take up the matter and an amicable settlement was arranged. There was no further trouble.

On May 10, 1869, the two lines were officially joined at Promontory [Point], north of Ogden in Utah. A great crowd gathered. A band played. An Irish crew and a Chinese crew were chosen to lay the last two rails side by side. The last tie was made of polished California laurel with a silver plate in its center proclaiming it "The last tie laid on the completion of the Pacific Railroad, May 10, 1869." But when the time came it was nowhere to be found. As consternation mounted, four Chinese approached with it on their shoulders and they laid it beneath the rails. A photographer stepped up and someone shouted to him "Shoot!" The Chinese only knew one meaning for that word. They fled. But order was restored and the famous ceremony began; Stanford drove a golden spike into the last tie with a silver hammer. The news flashed by telegraph to a waiting nation. But no Chinese appears in that famous picture of the toast celebrating the joining of the rails.

Crocker was one of the few who paid tribute to the Chinese that day: "I wish to call to your minds that the early completion of this railroad we have built has been in large measure due to the poor, despised class of laborers called the Chinese, to the fidelity and industry they have shown." No one even mentioned the name of Judah.

The building of the first transcontinental railway stands as a monument to the union of Yankee and Chinese-Irish drive and know-how. This was a formidable combination. They all complemented each other. Together they did in seven years what was expected to take at least fourteen.

In his book on the building of the railway, John Galloway, the noted transportation engineer, described this as "without doubt the greatest engineering feat of the nineteenth century," and that has never been disputed. David D. Colton, then vice-president of the Southern Pacific, was similarly generous in his praise of the Chinese contribution. He was asked, while giving evidence before the 1876 congressional committee, "Could you have constructed that road without Chinese labor?" He replied, "I do not think it could have been constructed so quickly, and with anything like the same amount of certainty as to what we were going to accomplish in the same length of time."

And, in answer to the question, "Do you think the Chinese have been a benefit to the State?" West Evans, a railway contractor, testified, "I do not see how we could do the work we have done, here, without them; at least I have done work that would not have been done if it had not been for the Chinamen, work that could not have been done without them."

It was heroic work. The Central Pacific crews had carried their railway 1,800 miles through the Sierra and Rocky mountains, over sagebrush desert and plain. The Union Pacific built only 689 miles, over much easier terrain. It had 500 miles in which to carry its part of the line to a height of 5,000 feet, with another fifty more miles in which to reach the high passes of the Black Hills. With newly recruited crews, the Central Pacific had to gain an altitude of 7,000 feet from the plain in just over 100 miles and make a climb of 2,000 feet in just 20 miles.

All this monumental work was done before the age of mechanization. It was pick and shovel, hammer and crowbar work, with baskets for earth carried slung from shoulder poles and put on one-horse carts.

For their heroic work, the Chinese workmen began with a wage of $26 a month, providing their own food and shelter. This was gradually raised to $30 to $35 a month. Caucasians were paid the same amount of money, but their food and shelter were provided. Because it cost $0.75 to $1.00 a day to feed a white unskilled worker, each Chinese saved the Central Pacific, at a minimum, two-thirds the price of a white laborer (1865 rates). Chinese worked as masons, dynamiters, and blacksmiths and at other skilled jobs that paid white workers from $3 to $5 a day. So, at a minimum, the company saved about $5 million by hiring Chinese workers.

Did this really "deprive white workers of jobs" as anti-Chinese agitators claimed. Certainly not. In the first place, experience had proved that white workers simply did not want the jobs the Chinese took on the railroad. In fact, the Chinese created jobs for white workers as straw bosses, foremen, railhandlers, teamsters, and supervisors.

The wages paid to the Chinese were, in fact, comparable to those paid unskilled or semiskilled labor in the East (where labor was relatively plentiful), and the Chinese were at first satisfied. Charles Nordhoff estimated that the frugal Chinese could save about $13 a month out of those wages. The *Alta California* estimated their savings at $20 a month and later, perhaps, as wages increased, they could lay aside even more. With a bit of luck, a year and a half to two years of work would enable them to return to China with $400 to buy a bit of land and be well-to-do farmers.

But the Chinese began to learn the American way of life. On one occasion in June 1867, 2,000 tunnelers went on strike, asking for $40 a month, an eight-hour day in the tunnels, and an end to beating by foremen. "Eight hours a day good for white man, all same good for Chinese," said their spokesman in the pidgin English common in the construction camps. But solidarity with the other workers was lacking, and after a week the strike was called off when the Chinese heard that Crocker was recruiting strikebreakers from the eastern states.

When the task was done, most of the Chinese railwaymen were paid off. Some returned to China with their hard-earned savings, and the epic story of building the Iron Horse's pathway across the continent must have regaled many a family gathering there. Some returned with souvenirs of the great work, chips of one of the last ties, which had been dug up and split up among them. Some settled in the little towns that had grown up along the line of the railway. Others took the railway to seek adventure further east and south. Most made their way back to California and took what jobs they could find in that state's growing industries, trades, and other occupations. Many used their traditional and newly acquired skills on the other transcontinental lines and railways that were being swiftly built in the West and Midwest. This was the start of the diaspora of the Chinese immigrants in America.

The Union and Central Pacific tycoons had done well out of the building of the line. Congressional investigation committees later calculated that, of $73 million poured into the Union Pacific coffers, no more than $50 million could be justified as true costs. The Big Four and their associates in the Central Pacific had done even better. They had made at least $63 million and owned most of the CP stock worth around $100 million and 9 million acres of land grants to boot.

Ironically, the great railway soon had disastrous results for the Chinese themselves. It now cost only $40 for an immigrant to cross the continent by rail and a flood of immigrants took advantage of the ease and cheapness of travel on the line the Chinese had helped to build. The labor shortage (and resulting high wages) in California turned into a glut. When the tangled affairs of the Northern Pacific line led to the stock market crash of Black Friday, September 19, 1873, and to financial panic, California experienced its first real economic depression. There was devastating unemployment, and the Chinese were made the scapegoats.

Read and Respond

1. What was at the heart of the competition described in this article? How did the competition begin? Was it a "healthy" competition? Why or why not?

2. Summarize the life of a Chinese railroad worker of the 1860s.

Execution of a Witch at Sea

Account of Father Francis Fitzherbert's Voyage to Maryland

Four ships sailed together from England, which a fearful storm overtook, when carried beyond the Western Isles, and the ship in which the Father was carried, the violent waves so shattered, that, springing a leak by the continued violence of the sea, it almost filled its hold. But in carrying away and exhausting the water, the men, four at a time, not only of the ship's crew but of the passengers, every one in his turn, sweated at the great pump in ceaseless labor, day and night.

Wherefore, having changed their course, their intention was to make sail towards the island, which the English call Barbados; but it could be accomplished by no art, by no labor; then the design was, having abandoned the ship and its freight, to commit themselves to the long boat. But the sea, swelling with adverse winds, and the huge mountainous waves, forbade. Many a form of death presenting itself to the minds of all, the habit of terror, now grown familiar, had almost excluded the fear of death. The tempest lasted two months in all, whence the opinion arose, that it was not raised by the violence of the sea or atmosphere, but was occasioned by the malevolence of witches. Forthwith they seize a little old woman suspected of sorcery; and after examining her with the strictest scrutiny, guilty or not guilty, they slay her, suspected of this very heinous sin. The corpse, and whatever belonged to her, they cast into the sea. But the winds did not thus remit their violence, or the raging sea its threatenings. To the troubles of the storm, sickness was added, which having spread to almost every person, carried off not a few. Nevertheless, the Father remained untouched by all the contagion, and unharmed, except that in working and exercising at the pump too laboriously, he contracted a slight fever of a few days' continuance. Having passed through multiplied dangers, at length, by the favor of God, the ship, contrary to the expectation of all, reached the port of Maryland.

The Testimonies of Two Witnesses

The Deposition of mr Henry Corbyn of London Merchant aged about 25 years, Sworne and Examined in the Province of Maryland before the Governour & Councell there (whose Names are hereunto Subscribed) the 23th day of June Anno Domini 1654. Saith

That at Sea upon his this Deponents Voyage hither in the Ship called the Charity of London m^r John Bosworth being Master and about a fortnight or three weeks before the Said Ships arrivall in this Province of Maryland, or before A Rumour amongst the Seamen was very frequent, that one Mary Lee then aboard the Said Ship was a witch, the Said Seamen Confidently affirming the Same upon her own deportment and discourse, and then more Earnestly then before Importuned the Said Master that a tryall might be had of her which he the Said Master, m^r Bosworth refused, but resolved (as he Expressed to put her ashore upon the Barmudoes) but Cross winds prevented and the Ship grew daily more Leaky almost to desparation and the Chiefe Seamen often declared their Resolution of Leaving her if an opportunity offered it Self which aforesaid Reasons put the Master upon a Consultation with m^r Chipsham and this Deponent, and it was thought fitt, Considering our Said Condition to Satisfie the Seamen in a way of trying her according to the Usuall Custome in that kind whether She were a witch or Not and Endeavoured by way of delay to have the Commanders of other Ships aboard but Stormy weather prevented, In the Interime two of the Seamen apprehended her without order and Searched her and found Some Signall or Marke of a witch upon her, and then calling the Master m^r Chipsham and this Deponent with others to See it afterwards made her fast to the Capstall betwixt decks, And in the Morning the Signall was Shrunk into her body for the Most part, And an Examination was thereupon importuned by the Seamen which this Deponent was desired to take whereupon She confessed as by her Confession appeareth, And upon that the Seamen Importuned the

Said Master to put her to Death which as it Seemed he was unwilling to doe, and went into his Cabbinn, but being more Vehemently pressed to it, he tould them they might doe what they would and went into his Cabbinn, and Sometime before they were about that Action he desired this depon[t] to acquaint them that they Should doe no more then what they Should Justifie which they Said they would doe by laying all their hands in generall to the Execution of her, All which herein before Expressed or the Same in Effect this Depon[t] averreth upon his oath to be true, And further Sayth not

William Stone   Sworne before us the   Henry Corbyne
Tho: Hatton   day and year above written
Job Chandler

The Deposition of ffrancis Darby Gent Aged about 39 yeares Sworne and Examined in the Province of Maryland before the Governour and Councell there whose Names are hereunto Subscribed the 23 day of June Anno Domini 1654, Saith

That at Sea upon the Voyage hither about a fortnight or three weeks before the Arrivall of the Ship called the Charity of London in this Province of Maryland, whereof m[r] John Bosworth was then Master and upon the Same day that one Mary Lee was put to Death aboard the Said Ship as a witch he the Said m[r] Bosworth Seeing him this Deponent backward to Assist in the Examination of her asked this Depon[t] why? and tould him that he was perplext about the busieness Seeing he did not know how he might doe it by the Law of England afterwards this deponent being present in the Round house heard the Said m[r] Bosworth give Order that nothing Should be done concerning the Said Mary Lee without Speaking first with him, and after She was put to Death or Executed to the best of this Deponents remembrance he Said he knew nothing of it, And this Deponent Saith that the Said Bosworth was in the inner room of the Roundhouse, he this deponent being in the next room at the time they treated about the busieness And this Depon[t] could not perceive any thing either by word or Deed whereby he gave order for her Execution or putting to Death and after this he Commanded they Should doe Nothing without his Order and alsoe after the Execution, expressed he knew not of it for that this Deponent hearing these words (She is dead) ran out and asked who was dead, and it was replyed the witch then this Deponent Entred the next Room and Said they have hanged her and he the Said Bosworth thereupon as it were Speaking with trouble in a high Voyce replyed he knew not of it All which herein before Expressed or the Same in Effect this Deponent averreth upon his oath to be true, And further Sayth not.

Sworne before us the day and   Francis Darby
Yare abovewritten
  William Stone
  Tho: Hatton
  Job Chandler

Read and Respond

1. These three accounts describe from different perspectives the killing of an old woman thought to be a witch. There seems to be some confusion in the accounts as to who was responsible for making the decision to have her executed. Reconstruct as best you can the circumstances that resulted in the execution. Who did what? How do you account for the different perspectives? Is one account more accurate than the others? How much do you have to rely on inference in order to reconstruct what you believe occurred?

2. What evidence is cited for the conclusion that the old woman was a witch? From your perspective, how much of this "evidence" can be explained away? Why couldn't the people on the ship explain the evidence away? Weren't there alternatives to execution available?

3. Do we encounter similar reasoning and behavior today about anything?

ASKING CRITICAL QUESTIONS

After you read the article that follows, what critical questions come to mind? Everything you read will stir up your thinking if you read and question critically. What questions would you like to have answered in order for you to put the article in proper context and to completely understand what is being said or reported? *On the lines following the article, write three questions that, if answered, will help you understand what is really being said.*

Human Intelligence: Are There Genes for IQ?

Joseph Levine and Kenneth Miller

E very person is an individual with unique capacities, abilities, strengths, and weaknesses. Just as individuals differ in physical characteristics, they differ in mental characteristics too. In 1903 Alfred

Binet, a French social scientist, introduced a test to measure intelligence—the *IQ test*. The premise of the test was simple. Just as all people have a physical age, Binet reasoned, they have a mental age. He also assumed that an *intelligence quotient (IQ)* could be computed by dividing the mental age by the physical age and multiplying by 100. A child of 10 with a mental age of 9 would have an IQ of 90, for example, whereas a child of the same age with a mental age of 11 would score 110 on the test.

Intelligence quotient scores differ widely among the human population. However, the claim that IQ tests measure intelligence has been challenged by many investigators, some of whom have charged that the tests are flawed by hidden racial and ethnic bias. We will leave those questions unanswered and instead will ask a question that is a bit more biological. Are individual differences in IQ scores the result of genetic differences between individuals or the result of differences in the individual environments that children experience in their formative years? In short, are there genes for IQ?

The answer to this question is emotionally charged for a number of reasons. One of them is finding that average IQ scores of American blacks are about 15 points lower than average IQ scores of American whites. Some scholars, including Arthur Jensen and William Shockley (the latter is one of the inventors of the transistor), have cited this as proof that differences in average academic performance between white and black children are biological and cannot be eliminated by improved schooling. There is substantial evidence that the ability to score well on an IQ test may indeed be inherited to some degree. Identical twins, whether they are reared together or apart, are more likely to have similar IQ scores than nonidentical siblings reared together. Unrelated children who are adopted into the same home, by contrast, do not show any strong similarity of scores.

However, the situation is not as simple as these statistics may make it appear. Studies of children adopted from orphanages have shown that adoption itself may raise the adopted child's IQ score by as much as 10 points, and there is a very high correlation of IQ level with social and economic status. Individual IQ is now known to be variable, which is to say that it can be changed by study and a positive learning environment, and it may be dramatically affected by self-image (what a child thinks of himself or herself). Therefore, many other social scientists have cautioned that the prevalence of social and economic inequality is not entirely the *result* of differences in IQ scores between different racial groups but rather acts as one of the *causes* of such differences. At this point, there is little doubt that intelligence is shaped by both genetic and environmental factors, but there is little scientific support for the notion that biological differences will undermine the positive effects of improved schooling for any children.

My Critical Questions

1. _____

_____ **?**

2. _____

_____ **?**

3. _____

_____ **?**

SOLUTIONS to Items in This Chapter

THINKERS (p. 249)

On a doctor's eye chart:

THINKERS (p. 251)

The easiest solution requires only three knives, not four.

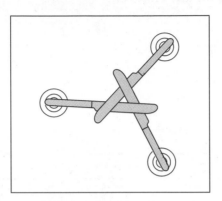

ANY QUESTIONS? (p. 253)

Of course Sam the Thinker could steal the extra dollar, but let's assume he doesn't. Here is one possible way to get the extra dollar: He takes the two-dollar bill to a pawn-shop, where he pawns it for $1.50. He then meets a stranger to whom he offers to sell the $1.50 pawn ticket (that will get the stranger $2 at the pawn shop) for $1.50. The stranger thinks getting $2 for $1.50 is a good deal and gives him $1.50. Sam the Thinker now has $3. Who is out the extra dollar? The stranger. When he takes the pawn ticket to the pawn shop, *he has to pay $1.50 to redeem the $2.* Thus, he spends a total of $3 to acquire $2.

THINKERS (p. 268)

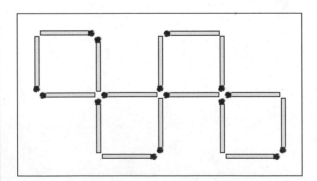

THINKERS (p. 270)

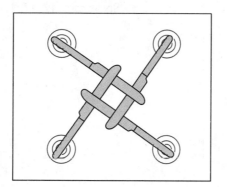

ANY QUESTIONS? (p. 273)

All religions can't be equally correct. It is an impossibility—unless, of course, they are equally incorrect!

THINKERS (p. 289)

THINKERS (p. 290)

Think About This! (p. 304)

This menu was drawn up when Paris was under siege by the Prussian army during the Franco-Prussian War. Normal food supplies had been used up. How close to this reason were your ideas?

THINKERS (p. 305)

When you read the poem aloud, a listener should hear:

"Oh see, Billy, see 'er go,
Forty buses in a row."
"Oh no," said Billy, "them is trucks.
See what's in 'em, cows or ducks."

THINKERS (p. 306)

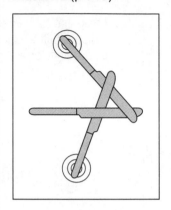

THINKERS (p. 332)

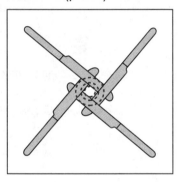

THINKERS (p. 345)

(Ten to ten is nine-fifty on the clock.)

THINKERS (p. 329)

Six arrows: 17, 17, 17, 17, 16, 16.

THINKERS (p. 342)

A traffic light with red, yellow, and green lights.

Any Questions? (p. 347)

Here are a few ways:
1. MDCCCCLXXXXVIIII(1000 + 500 + 100 + 100 + 100 + 100 + 50 + 10 + 10 + 10 + 10 + 5 + 1 + 1 + 1 + 1)
2. MCMXCIX (The "subtractive" method: 1000 + 900 + 90 + 9)
3. MCMLXXXXIX
4. MCMIC
5. MIM
6. IMM
Are any of these ways "more correct" than others? Who says?

Chapter 7

ANALYZING SKILLS

- ■ **Analyzing**
- ■ **Evaluating**
- ■ **Inducing**
- ■ **Deducing**

My conclusion is . . .

"The human race's favorite method for being in control of facts is to ignore them."
—Celia Green

"Examine for a moment an ordinary mind on an ordinary day."
—Virginia Woolf

"To live is to have problems, and to solve problems is to grow intellectually."
—J.P. Guildford

"It's simple. This is how it works—I think."
—Anyone explaining how to work a VCR

"The pellet with the poison's in the vessel with the pestle. The chalice from the palace has the brew that is true."
—Norman Panama and Melvin Frank, *The Court Jester*

What questions am I going to have answered in this section on analyzing?

1. What kind of thinking do I do when I analyze?
2. What are the five steps to analyzing an argument?
3. Doesn't everyone analyze as part of their ordinary thinking behavior?

Analyzing

ESSENTIAL THINKING SKILLS		
CHAPTER	**WHAT THEY'RE CALLED**	**WHAT THEY MEAN**
Chapter 3	**The Gathering Skills**	**Gathering all the information.**
	Observing	Actively seeking information through one or more senses.
	Questioning	Seeking information by asking questions.
Chapter 4	**The Organizing Skills**	**Organizing for the purpose of making sense.**
	Comparing and Contrasting	Noting similarities and differences between two or more things, events, or ideas.
	Classifying and Sequencing	Arranging things or concepts into categories and into sequential order.
	Identifying Cause and Effect	Recognizing the relationship between an effect and its cause.
Chapter 5	**The Generating Skills**	**Generating additional information.**
	Inferring	Making an assumption, stating a hypothesis, or coming to a conclusion based on limited information.
	Summarizing	Condensing the essence of the information accurately and efficiently.
	Synthesizing	Creating new information by combining two or more pieces of information.
	Generating Ideas	Creating new information, alternatives, or applications.
Chapter 6	**The Recognizing Skills**	**Recognizing what has been left unsaid.**
	Recognizing Purpose	Identifying a writer's or speaker's intention.
	Recognizing Fact and Opinion	Distinguishing between a statement of fact and a statement of opinion.
	Recognizing Tone	Identifying a sentiment or mood by assessing the writer's or speaker's choice of words.
	Recognizing Bias	Noting the presence and nature of a writer's or speaker's prejudice.
	Recognizing Organization	Identifying the organizational pattern of a thought, statement, passage, or plan.
	Recognizing Underlying Assumptions	Recognizing the suppositions that are taken for granted and are the foundation of a proposition, notion, or idea.
Chapter 7	**The Analyzing Skills**	**Analyzing for the purpose of coming to a conclusion.**
	Analyzing	Identifying and separating ideas, attributes, situations, and/or components in order to form a conclusion as to their relationship.
	Evaluating	Appraising something according to certain criteria and forming a judgment as to its worth or quality.
	Inducing	Analyzing individual facts or premises in order to derive a general conclusion.
	Deducing	Applying general principles or a broad framework to a situation in order to come to a conclusion about it.

THINK ABOUT THIS!

Vital Learning

Many things we learn in life are worth passing on to our children and grandchildren. Interestingly, these valuable things are learned when we are young, not when we are old. What have you learned so far that you would want to pass down to your grandchildren? List five of the most important things.

1. _____

   _____

2. _____

   _____

3. _____

   _____

4. _____

5. _____

   _____

ANALYZING:
Identifying and separating ideas, attributes, situations, and/or components in order to form a conclusion as to their relationship

It is impossible to go through a single hour in a day without calling on your analyzing skills many times. We are informally, almost instinctively, analyzing all the time. When we are asked questions like the following, we depend on our analyzing skills to help us find correct answers:

- Which of the following reasons for being late to class and not having completed the assigned paper is your professor going to accept?

- Which one of the westward islands has a good elevation, is protected from the wind, has fresh water, and is isolated from navigational traffic?

- Which of the following statements is an unverified assumption on the part of the city council?

- What are some logical reasons for supporting a balanced-budget amendment?

- How would you describe the positions taken by both sides in this conflict?

We constantly analyze what we take in with our senses—situations, ideas, things that we read or hear. When we analyze, we attempt to identify the separate components of the situation or thing so that we can form a conclusion as to the relationship between those components.

THINKERS

There is a word in the English language in which the first two letters signify a male, the first three signify a female, the first four signify a great man, and the whole word, a great woman. What is the word?

Need a Hint?
Break this into parts. Take it step by step. What two letters signify a male? What three letters signify a female? And so on.

QUICK! TELL ME WHAT THIS MEANS

Whenever we try to figure something out, we follow a pattern of thinking that helps us separate the thing into understandable parts so that we can make sense of it. The step-by-step procedure we follow is probably different for everyone, but there are some basics that we all employ:

1. We establish our purpose. Why are we doing this? What are we trying to find out? Determining the purpose shapes the direction and the limits of our thinking.

2. We examine the situation, material, or idea and look for its separate pieces, reasons, or assumptions.

3. We examine the separate parts in light of our purpose.

4. We form conclusions about the parts and about what the sum total of those parts means.

WHY IS A PENCIL DESIGNED THE WAY IT IS?

Put your powers of analysis to work on the following problem. Follow the preceding four steps and see how they lead you to a logical conclusion based on analysis of the problem.

Problem: Why is a pencil designed the way it is?

1. *Establish your purpose.* What are you trying to figure out? The purpose here is to determine why a pencil is made the way it is.

2. *Look over the item being analyzed.* A pencil consists of a wooden case holding a piece of graphite, which makes marks on paper. Some pencils have erasers attached.

3. *Examine the separate parts in light of your purpose.* What about the material? The wooden case is lightweight, easy to hold and to sharpen. Lead is soft, dark, easy to mark with. Both wood and graphite are cheap. What about the shape? The six-sided shape makes the pencil easy to grip and to pack in boxes, and the pencil won't roll off a surface easily. It's about 20 centimeters long, so it won't wear out quickly.

4. *Form your conclusions based on your observations of the parts.* A pencil is made the way it is because it is cheap to make and buy, and easy to use.

Would you have come to the same conclusion about why pencils are made the way they are without using this four-step guide? Probably (after all, this was a very simple problem), but in all likelihood not as quickly. Notice how using this four-step process of analyzing seems to organize your thinking. Your thinking focuses on specifics and doesn't get stuck on related but unimportant facts (for example, the traditional color of pencils, or their similarity around the world), as so often happens when you don't use the four-step process.

ANALYZING AN ARGUMENT SEEMS A BIT TOUGHER

For many college students, the prospect of analyzing an argument or an idea that they encounter in their studies sounds considerably more difficult than analyzing the design of a pencil. That is simply because in high school many students become used to accepting what they are told and what they read without critically examining ideas and arguments. But now, things are different. In college you are expected to critically analyze everything you read and hear. What this means is that you are expected to look at things closely and selectively, interpreting what you see.

HOW TO ANALYZE AN IDEA OR AN ARGUMENT

The process of analyzing ideas or arguments has five separate and distinct steps.

1. *Determine your purpose.* What are you trying to find out? You analyze for many different reasons. Do you want to identify the structure of the argument, clarify the reasoning, check the validity of what is said, classify what is being said into logical categories, or simply seek understanding? Your purpose determines how you proceed with your analysis.

2. *Divide the issue or argument into its component parts.* What is the nature of the parts, and what are the parts? Search the material piece by piece, keeping your purpose in mind.

3. *Interpret the relationship of these parts to one another (that is, find the pattern).* What is the relationship of the elements to one another? What is the structure? In what way are these parts connected? Is that connection reasonable and valid?

4. *State the results of your analysis.* What do you conclude? What is the organizational connection of the elements to the whole?

5. *Identify the questions you still have about the issue or argument.* Are there any components left that don't fit? What conclusions does this lead you to? Is there another way of looking at this issue or argument? Are there any examples? Are there some inconsistencies? Is there an alternative?

STIR IT UP 7.1   Select a short story from a literature text or a chapter from a novel and analyze the psychology of one or more of the characters. Explore your character's mind in a one- or two-page essay. Suggest a compatible background for your character that includes a plausible childhood and other events that may account for his or her actions and thoughts. Rely heavily on your inferring skills. In short, answer this question: "Why is this character behaving the way he or she is behaving?"

STIR IT UP 7.2   Analyze your country's foreign policy. How? Professional foreign policy analysts attempt to understand world events as the (usually) purposive acts of government policy makers. They look carefully at events and then work backwards to explain why a government chose the action in question. They are thus able to determine what a government's policy is. Check today's newspaper for articles describing some action or actions of the U.S. government toward another country or group of countries, and then attempt to explain the government's policy or intention concerning that country or group of countries. Identify the country, the incident, and your basic conclusions below. Be ready to explain your thinking.

_____

_____

_____

_____

ANY QUESTIONS?

You've probably been frustrated by the following riddle before. Read it again, but this time analyze it with the purpose of determining what makes it impossible to solve as it is stated.

Three people shared a hotel room. The room charge was $30, so each person paid $10. Later, the desk clerk discovered that she had charged $5 too much for the room, so she handed the bellhop 5 one dollar bills and told him to return the money to the three people. The bellhop secretly put $2 in his pocket and then gave each person $1. Here's the problem: The three people originally paid $10 each, but each received $1 back, so they've now paid a total of $27 for the room. Add to that the $2 that the bellhop stole, and you have a total expenditure of $29 instead of $30. What happened to the other dollar?

_____

_____

_____

_____

_____

STIR IT UP 7.3 Check with your friends, family members, and professors to see if any of them know by what process decisions are made in a political campaign, government agency, corporation, or school. Ask them how key decisions are made. Are there attempts at analyzing situations to determine policy? How important is the ability to analyze situations to top-level people? Be prepared to discuss your findings in class.

STIR IT UP 7.4 If you aren't already familiar with the punk rock scene, research it by using the library, interviews, the Internet, and other sources. Then write an essay analyzing the current state of the punk rock movement, especially the place of violence in the movement. At the end of the essay, project the punk rock movement's future over the next ten years.

STIR IT UP 7.5 On college tests, you will frequently read directions like the following: "Analyze the trends in economic development since 1945." Analyze that statement and explain what exactly you think the professor is asking you to do.

_____

_____

_____

_____

_____

_____

THINKERS

Time Flies

The day before yesterday, Suzie was nine years old. Next year she will be twelve. How is this possible?

Need a Hint?
Leap year isn't involved, and this isn't as tricky as it seems. Think about having a birthday at the end of a year or the beginning of a year.

Journal Observations (see page 13)

ANALYZING

1st Writing _____

_____

_____

_____

_____

_____

_____

_____

_____

_____

_____

2nd Writing _____

_____

_____

_____

_____

_____

_____

_____

_____

_____

_____

_____

_____

3rd Writing _____

_____
_____
_____
_____
_____
_____
_____
_____
_____
_____
_____

READINGS

America's Addiction to Addictions

Art Levine
U.S. News and World Report, *February 5, 1990*

When District of Columbia Mayor Marion Barry tearfully announced that he had "weaknesses" and entered a Florida treatment program recently, he and his aides were also launching a political and legal strategy. Barry wanted to portray his addiction problems as a disease—something beyond his control and thus politically less damaging.

By going into treatment for chemical dependency, he stood to gain public sympathy and, he and his advisers hoped, prosecutorial leniency. But Barry's downfall and speedy resort to treatment also raise basic questions about the nature and causes of addictions and the role of individual willpower in curbing excessive behavior.

Most medical experts today view alcoholism and drug addiction as chronic diseases with biological, and perhaps genetic, underpinnings. But it was not that long ago that even these excesses were seen as evidence of moral turpitude rather than medical conditions.

What worries some addiction experts is society's willingness to expand the definition of addictive behavior beyond substance abuse to include a host of excessive behaviors—ranging from shopping to promiscuity—and clinicians' readiness to treat what may be social and willpower problems as medical disorders instead.

Helpless and Sick?

Addiction was once seen primarily as a physical dependence on a drug that created severe physical symptoms when the drug was withdrawn. But that view is changing.

"The drug is necessary but not sufficient to cause addiction," says Jack Henningfield, chief of the clinical pharmacology branch of the National Institute of Drug Abuse. He and others point to the clear effects of social conditions on drug use: for example, the ability of 90 percent of addicted Vietnam veterans to kick their heroin habits once free of the stress of battle. By contrast, three-fourths of other heroin addicts who try to quit fail.

It is this sort of wide variation in addictive patterns that, in part, prompts some critics to question whether substance abuse is truly a disease with an inevitable course if untreated. Furthermore, they argue, the disease model sends a harmful message to abusers. It not only excuses irresponsibility but "indoctrinates them with the idea they're helpless and sick," says Herbert Fingarette, an addiction expert at UC—Santa Barbara.

Medical authorities generally dismiss these criticisms, noting that other well accepted diseases, such as diabetes, lack a simple pattern while still having a physical component. They also argue that disease-oriented treatment programs don't absolve patients of responsibility for their habits, though they have biological roots.

"Once a behavior becomes an addiction, it involves a biological component," points out Dr. Frederick K. Goodwin, a psychiatrist and administrator of the Alcohol, Drug Abuse and Mental Health Administration. But "it starts as a voluntary act, then becomes reflexive and automatic."

Can any behavior become reflexive and automatic—in effect, an addiction? Some experts are inclined to see addiction in any pleasurable behavior that turns compulsive, despite the problems that can cause.

In part because of this looser definition, addiction chic is everywhere: There are now more than 2,000 meetings each week of groups catering to self-styled sex and love addicts, up at least 20 percent in the past year; there are more than 200 national Alcoholics Anonymous–style groups in the country, including Messies Anonymous; and there are inpatient therapy programs and self-help groups for those people—called "codependents"—whose main problem is that they remain with, and worry too much about, destructive mates.

Whether it is excesses in drug taking or even TV watching, Harvey Milkman, a professor of psychology at Metropolitan State College in Denver and co-author of *Craving for Ecstasy,* argues, "The disease concept may be applied to the entire spectrum of compulsive problem behaviors."

But the prospect of less personal responsibility concerns critics of the would-be addictions. "Creating a world of addictive diseases may mean creating a world in which anything is excusable," says psychologist Stanton Peele, author of the new book *Diseasing of America.* Even some addiction researchers are questioning whether the boom in addiction treatments has gone too far.

"It is vogue now to call any excessive behavior an addiction, and, frankly, the professions are too quick to turn a dollar on this," says Howard J. Shaffer, director of the Center for Addiction Studies at Harvard Medical School and Cambridge Hospital. And none of the often expensive treatments offered for the alleged behavioral addictions has proved effective, experts say.

Yet researchers exploring the disease models of addiction are often genuinely seeking to understand the underpinnings of some self-destructive, repetitive behaviors that trouble individuals—and baffle scientists. How do we explain someone who buys more pairs of shoes than could ever possibly be worn or gambles away the family home and life savings?

The idea of an addictive-personality type has been proposed, but the science is inconclusive. "There is no single characteristic or constellation of traits that is inevitably associated with addiction," notes psychologist Alan Lang of Florida State University, who contributed a chapter on personality to a National Research Council report on habitual behavior. At the same time, his research review points to such predisposing traits as a sense of alienation, impulsivity and a need for instant gratification.

Despite the controversies over addictions, they have made their way into the legal system as defenses. Defendants claiming "diminished capacity" because of their addictions sometimes succeed: one Vietnam veteran accused of drug running was acquitted after a defense expert argued that he was a victim of the "action-addict syndrome." "Is every problem a disease?" asks sociologist Martin Levine of Bloomfield College in New Jersey.

It sometimes seems that way. A leading "sex addiction" theorist, Minnesota psychologist Patrick Carnes, has designed the country's first Sexual Dependency Unit at Golden Valley Health Center in Minnesota.

It has offered both inpatient and outpatient treatment to more than 1,000 people since 1984. The roughly four-week, $16,000 treatment includes an AA style 12-step program, group therapy and celibacy pledges. The critics of the sex-addiction movement view it more as a moralistic crusade than as a genuine medical effort.

Biological Hints

But for many who consider themselves sex addicts, the damage in their lives can be quite real, even if there is no agreement on what causes their problems. Jamie, a Minneapolis member of Sex Addicts Anonymous, says he lost a few jobs because of his constant search for new sex partners.

"Everything else got in the way," he says. And there are some hints of a biological basis for such behavior. New York City psychologist William Wedin recalls one patient, a well-paid executive who began spending thousands of dollars a week on prostitutes and joined a 12-step sex-addict program.

It wasn't until he collapsed on the street one day that doctors diagnosed him as a victim of a stroke, suggesting that an organic brain disorder had probably spurred his flings. Other experts are using anti-depressants to successfully treat sexual compulsives.

Compulsive gambling may pose the greatest theoretical challenge for addiction researchers. Unlike alcoholism and drug addiction, it involves no toxic substance that might directly affect brain chemistry and lead to physical craving. Yet it is well accepted by such groups as the American Psychiatric Association as an addictive syndrome.

The Department of Veterans Affairs offers inpatient and outpatient treatment for gambling at four medical centers. And there may even be a biological factor: In 1988, researchers at the National Institute on Alcohol Abuse and Alcoholism found higher levels of the brain chemical norepinephrine in gamblers, that could signal a mood-regulation disturbance that spurs them to seek greater thrills. It is theoretically possible that others seek the same kinds of rewards through compulsive shopping and sex.

For those who work with such troubled people, the causes are still ultimately mysterious, but Dr. Sheila Blume, who heads the alcohol, chemical-dependency and compulsive-gambling programs at South Oaks Hospital in Amityville, N.Y., says, "I'm hopeful a final pathway in the brain will be found." Until the biology of excessiveness is better understood, America's addiction to addiction will no doubt continue.

Examine Your Thinking About What You Just Read

Pay close attention to your thinking processes as you answer the following questions.

1. Did you notice the many comparisons and contrasts that this writer set up throughout the article? Relying only on your memory, identify a few of the comparisons and contrasts. Then go over the article and put a check mark in the margin wherever a comparison or contrast is made. How many did you find? Why so many? What was the author trying to accomplish by including so many similar or contradictory expert opinions? How does the use of comparisons and contrasts in this article make you feel about the subject?

2. In general, does the use of comparisons and contrasts build credibility in conversations and in writing, or doesn't it matter because credibility rests on something quite different?

3. What are your own views about overindulgence in such things as drugs, sex, shopping, sunbathing, TV watching, eating, and church-going? Can overindulgence in any of these things become an addiction? How important to your definition of *addiction* is the presence of a physical or biological component of some sort?

4. Compare (and contrast) the idea of an addictive-personality type with the idea of a biologically caused addiction. Which is more reasonable? Which is more desirable in terms of social acceptance and treatment?

5. Can an addiction be a good thing? Under what conditions?

Write about this In a brief essay, compare and contrast your ideas on addiction with those of some older person you know well, a parent, a grandparent, or even your employer. For example, how would you characterize your attitudes toward addictions of all types compared to the other person's attitude? Can you agree on what constitutes an addiction? What is the nature of the disagreement? How do you account for the disagreement on the definition of an addiction? How much of this disagreement is a generational thing, or a male-female thing?

Should the Reclamation Project Be Completed?

James R. Kearl

S uppose that the initial cost of a large system of dams and canals to capture water from melting snow in the mountains and move it closer to a population center was estimated to be $10 billion. Because the benefits, say $15 billion, were thought to be greater than this amount, the project was started. After spending $5 billion, the project comes to the Congress for the appropriation necessary to finish it. Congresspeople from the state where the project is being built provide the following data:

Money already spent	$5 billion
Benefits already obtained	$12 billion
Total benefits to be obtained if project is finished	$15 billion

Would you vote to approve the expenditure (assuming there were no competing uses for the money)?

Suppose, instead, these data were presented:

Money already spent	$5 billion
Benefits already obtained	$5 billion
Total benefits to be obtained if project is finished	$9 billion

Would you vote to approve the expenditure?

Finally, suppose that, instead of either of the above, the following data were presented:

Money already spent	$5 billion
Benefits already obtained	$2 billion
Total benefits to be obtained if project is finished	$9 billion

Would you vote to approve the expenditure?

In the first case, the congresspeople from the state argue that having invested $5 billion in the project with the aim of getting $15 billion in benefits, "we can't waste the $5 billion already spent." They note that the benefits haven't changed from the initial estimates and argue that by spending $10 billion overall, $15 billion in benefits can be obtained. In the second and third cases, congresspeople from other states argue that the overall benefits are now only $9 billion and that spending $10 billion to get $9 billion in benefits is foolish.

In each case, you should begin by asking what *additional* benefit can be obtained from additional spending—that is, you should find the marginal benefit and the marginal cost. In the first case, the expenditure of an additional $5 billion results in only an additional $3 billion in benefits. In the second case, spending an additional $5 billion results in an additional $4 billion in benefits. In the third case, spending an additional $4 billion results in $7 billion in benefits. Marginal benefits exceed marginal costs only in the last case. It only "makes sense" to spend additional money in this case.

How should you respond to these arguments?

a. "We don't want to waste the $5 billion already spent."

b. "Overall, we would be spending $10 billion to get only $9 billion in benefits."

c. "Overall, we would be spending only $10 billion to get $15 billion in benefits."

The answer is that sunk costs are irrelevant! To see why, note that, in the first case, the net benefit if no additional money is spent is $12 billion minus the $5 billion already spent or $7 billion. Completing the project, however, reduces the net benefit from $7 to $5 billion. In the second case, the net benefits if the project is not funded further are $0 ($5 billion minus $5 billion). Completing the project reduces the net benefits to −$1 billion. In the third case, by contrast, the net benefits now are −$3 billion, but if the project is completed, the losses will only be −$1 billion.

Read and Respond

1. In this article, what information is left out of the calculations that might have an influence on the spending decision? Are decisions on projects like this one always made on the basis of a budget? Should they be?

2. How might the calculations be deceptive? What is being assumed or taken for granted?

3. Is the reasoning for each scenario clear, precise, accurate, relevant, consistent, logical, broad, fair, and so forth? If it lacks one of these qualities, what effect does that have on the conclusion?

Story of a Lithuanian

Anonymous

[After I arrived in the United States] Everything got quicker—worse and worse—till then at last I was in a boarding house by the stockyards in Chicago with three Lithuanians, who knew my father's sisters at home.

That first night we sat around in the house and they asked me, "Well, why did you come?" I told them about that first night and what the ugly shoemaker said about "life, liberty and the getting of happiness." They all leaned back and laughed. "What you need is money," they said. "It was all right at home. You wanted nothing. You ate your own meat and your own things on the farm. You made your own clothes and had your own leather. The other things you got at the Jew man's store and paid him with sacks of rye. But here you want a hundred things. Whenever you walk out you see new things you want, and you must have money to buy everything."

Then one man asked me, "How much have you?" and I told him $30. "You must buy clothes to look rich, even if you are not rich," he said. "With good clothes you will have friends."

The next morning three of these men took me to a store near the stockyards to buy a coat and pants. . . . "You stand still. That is all you have to do," they said. So the Jew man kept putting on coats and I moved my arms and back and sides when they told me. We stayed there till it was time for dinner. Then we bought a suit. I paid $5 and then I was to pay $1 a week for five weeks. . . .

The next night they took me for a walk down town. We would not pay to ride, so we walked so long that I wanted to take my shoes off, but I did not tell them this. When we came there I forgot my feet. We stood by one theater and watched for half an hour. Then we walked all around a store that filled one whole block and had walls of glass. Then we had a drink of whiskey, and this is better than vodka. We felt happier and looked into cafes. We saw shiny carriages and automobiles. I saw men with dress suits, I saw women with such clothes that I could not think at all. Then my friends punched me and I turned around and saw one of these women, and with her was a gentleman in a fine dress suit. I began looking harder. It was the Jew man that sold me my suit. . . . Then we walked home and I felt poor and my shoes got very bad. . . .

The next morning my friends woke me up at five o'clock and said, "Now, if you want life, liberty and happiness," they laughed, "you must push for yourself. You must get a job. Come with us." And we went to the yards. Men and women were walking in by thousands as far as we could see. We went to the doors of one big slaughter house. There was a crowd of about 200 men waiting there for a job. They looked hungry and kept watching the door. At last a special policeman came out and began pointing to men, one by one. Each one jumped forward. Twenty-three were taken. Then they all went inside, and all the others turned their faces away and looked tired. I remember one boy sat down and cried, just next to me, on a pile of boards. Some policemen waved their clubs and we all walked on. I found some Lithuanians to talk with, who told me they had come every morning for three weeks. Soon we met other crowds coming away from other slaughter houses, and we all walked around and felt bad and tired and hungry.

That night I told my friends that I would not do this many days, but would go some place else. "Where?" they asked me, and I began to see then that I was in bad trouble, because I spoke no English. Then one man told me to give him $5 to give the special policeman. I did this and the next morning the policeman pointed me out, so I had a job. I have heard some big talk since then about my American freedom of contract, but I do not think I had much freedom in bargaining for this job with the Meat Trust. My job was in the cattle killing room. I pushed the blood along the gutter . . . One Lithuanian who worked with me, said, "They get all the blood out of those cattle and all the work out of us men." This was true, for we worked that first day from six in the morning till seven at night. The next day we worked from six in the morning till eight at night. The next day we had no work. So we had no good, regular hours. It was hot in the room that summer, and the hot blood made it worse.

I held my job six weeks, and then I was turned off. I think some other man had paid for my job, or perhaps I was too slow. The foreman in that room wanted quick men to make the work rush, because he was paid more if the work was done cheaper and quicker. . . .

The Republican boss in our district, Jonidas, was a saloon keeper. A friend took me there. Jonidas shook hands and treated me fine. He taught me to sign my name, and the next week I went with him to an office and signed some paper, and then I could vote. I voted as I was told, and then they got me back into the yards to work, because one big politician owns stock in one of the houses. Then I felt that was getting in beside the game. I was in a combine like other sharp men. Even when work was slack I was all right, because they got me a job in the street cleaning department. I felt proud, and I went to the back room in Jonidas's saloon and got him to write a letter to Alexandra to tell her she must come soon and be my wife.

But this was just the trouble. All of us were telling our friends to come soon. Soon they came—even thousands. The employers in the yard liked this, because those sharp foremen are inventing new machines and the work is easier to learn, and so these slow Lithuanians and even green girls can learn to do it, and then the Americans and Germans and Irish are put out and the employer saves money, because the Lithuanians work cheaper. This was why the American labor unions began to organize us all just the same as they had organized the Bohemians and Poles before us.

. . . I had been working hard in the cattle killing room and I had a better job. I was called a cattle butcher now and I joined the Cattle Butchers' Union. This union is honest and it has done me a great deal of good. . . .

With more time and more money I live much better and I am very happy. So is Alexandra. She came a year ago and has learned to speak English already. Some of the women go to the big store the day they get here, when they have not enough sense to pick out the clothes that look right, but Alexandra waited three weeks till she knew, and so now she looks the finest of any woman in the district. We have four nice rooms, which she keeps very clean, and she has flowers growing in boxes in the two front windows. We do not go much to church, because the church seems to be too slow. But we belong to a Lithuanian society that gives two picnics in summer and two big balls in winter, where we have a fine time. I go one night a week to the Lithuanian Concertina Club. On Sundays we go on the trolley out into the country.

But we like to stay at home more now because we have a baby. When he grows up I will not send him to the Lithuanian Catholic school. They have only two bad rooms and two priests who teach only in Lithuanian from prayer books. I will send him to the American school, which is very big and good. The teachers there are Americans and they belong to the Teachers' Labor Union, which has three thousand teachers and belongs to our Chicago Federation of Labor. I am sure that such teachers will give him a good chance.

Read and Respond

1. This testimony of a Lithuanian immigrant contains a wealth of information about life in Chicago one hundred years ago. How was life for newly arrived immigrants different then than it is now? What makes you believe that there are *any* differences in opportunity or living conditions other than those brought about by the passing of

time? For example, what differences in opportunity are created by marrying "the boss's daughter"?

2. What do you think about having to pay someone for a job? Is that fair, right, moral? Was it something that the Lithuanian immigrant seemed to have any problem with?

3. What does the author's refusal to send his children to the Lithuanian Catholic school and his loyalty to labor unions say about the changing values and perceptions of immigrants?

ASKING CRITICAL QUESTIONS

After you read the article that follows, what critical questions come to mind? Everything you read will stir up your thinking if you read and question critically. What questions would you like to have answered in order for you to put the article in proper context and to completely understand what is being said or reported? *On the lines following the article, write three questions that, if answered, will help you understand what is really being said.*

Why the Sky Is Blue and Sunsets Are Red

James T. Shipman, Jerry D. Wilson, and Aaron W. Todd

The gas molecules of the air account for most of the scattering in the visible region of the spectrum. In the visible spectrum the wavelength increases from violet to red. The blue end is therefore scattered more than the red end. (The colors of the visible spectrum—and the rainbow—may be remembered with the help of the name of ROY G. BIV—red, orange, yellow, green, blue, indigo, and violet.)

As the sunlight passes through the atmosphere, the blue end of the spectrum is preferentially scattered. Some of this scattered light reaches Earth, where we see it as blue skylight. Keep in mind that all colors are present in skylight, but the dominant wavelength or color lies in the blue. You may have noticed that the skylight is more blue directly overhead or high in the sky and less blue toward the horizon, becoming white just above the horizon. You see these effects because there are fewer scatterers along a path through the atmosphere overhead than toward the horizon, and multiple scattering along the horizon path mixes the colors to give the white appearance. If Earth had no atmosphere the sky would appear black, other than in the vicinity of the Sun.

Because Rayleigh scattering is greater the shorter the wavelength, you might be wondering why the sky isn't violet, since this color has the shortest wavelength in the visible spectrum. Violet light is scattered, but the eye is more sensitive to blue light than to violet light; also, sunlight contains more blue light than violet light. The greatest color component is yellow-green, and the distribution generally decreases toward the ends of the spectrum.

The scattering of sunlight by the atmospheric gases *and* small particles give rise to red sunsets. One might think that because sunlight travels a greater distance through the atmosphere to an observer at sunset, most of the shorter wavelengths would be scattered from the sunlight and only light in the red end of the spectrum would reach the observer. However, the dominant color of this light, were it due solely to molecular scattering, would be orange. Hence additional scattering by small particles in the atmosphere must shift the light from the setting (or rising) Sun toward the red. Foreign particles (natural or pollutants) in the atmosphere are not necessary to give a blue sky, and even detract from it. Yet they are necessary for deep red sunsets and sunrises.

The beauty of red sunrises and sunsets is often made more spectacular by layers of pink-colored clouds. The cloud color is due to the reflection of red light.

Larger particles of dust, smoke, haze, and those from air pollution in the atmosphere may preferentially scatter long wavelengths. These scattered wavelengths, along with the scattered blue light due to Rayleigh scattering, can cause the sky to have a milky blue appearance—white being the presence of all colors. Hence the blueness of the sky gives an indication of atmospheric purity. Cloud droplets and raindrops scatter even longer wavelengths. This fact is used in the principle of weather radar, which is an important means of weather monitoring.

My Critical Questions

1. _____
   _____ **?**

2. _____
   _____ **?**

3. _____
   _____ **?**

Evaluating

ESSENTIAL THINKING SKILLS

CHAPTER	WHAT THEY'RE CALLED	WHAT THEY MEAN
Chapter 3	**The Gathering Skills**	**Gathering all the information.**
	Observing	Actively seeking information through one or more senses.
	Questioning	Seeking information by asking questions.
Chapter 4	**The Organizing Skills**	**Organizing for the purpose of making sense.**
	Comparing and Contrasting	Noting similarities and differences between two or more things, events, or ideas.
	Classifying and Sequencing	Arranging things or concepts into categories and into sequential order.
	Identifying Cause and Effect	Recognizing the relationship between an effect and its cause.
Chapter 5	**The Generating Skills**	**Generating additional information.**
	Inferring	Making an assumption, stating a hypothesis, or coming to a conclusion based on limited information.
	Summarizing	Condensing the essence of the information accurately and efficiently.
	Synthesizing	Creating new information by combining two or more pieces of information.
	Generating Ideas	Creating new information, alternatives, or applications.
Chapter 6	**The Recognizing Skills**	**Recognizing what has been left unsaid.**
	Recognizing Purpose	Identifying a writer's or speaker's intention.
	Recognizing Fact and Opinion	Distinguishing between a statement of fact and a statement of opinion.
	Recognizing Tone	Identifying a sentiment or mood by assessing the writer's or speaker's choice of words.
	Recognizing Bias	Noting the presence and nature of a writer's or speaker's prejudice.
	Recognizing Organization	Identifying the organizational pattern of a thought, statement, passage, or plan.
	Recognizing Underlying Assumptions	Recognizing the suppositions that are taken for granted and are the foundation of a proposition, notion, or idea.
Chapter 7	**The Analyzing Skills**	**Analyzing for the purpose of coming to a conclusion.**
	Analyzing	Identifying and separating ideas, attributes, situations, and/or components in order to form a conclusion as to their relationship.
	Evaluating	Appraising something according to certain criteria and forming a judgment as to its worth or quality.
	Inducing	Analyzing individual facts or premises in order to derive a general conclusion.
	Deducing	Applying general principles or a broad framework to a situation in order to come to a conclusion about it.

> **"**We all think we are evaluating, *but most of the time we are only 'opinionating.'***"**
> —No one special

> **"**Hear everything and judge for yourself.**"**
> —George Eliot, *Middlemarch*

What questions am I going to have answered in this section on evaluating?

1. What are we doing when we evaluate, and how is this different from forming an opinion?
2. Why can't we evaluate if we have not established evaluation criteria?
3. How much evaluation is there in most advertisements and in book, concert, music, and movie reviews?

> **EVALUATING:**
> Appraising something according to certain criteria and forming a judgment as to its worth or quality

When we employ the thinking skill of evaluation, we are expressing our conclusions about such things as the appropriateness of underlying assumptions, the accuracy of reporting, the credibility of sources, the authority of someone or some idea, and the relevancy, consistency, appropriateness, and value of evidence. In the process, we are also giving clues to our preferences, our attitudes, our likes and dislikes, our values. What sets evaluation apart from opinion is the *foundation of criteria* on which the evaluation rests and which is missing when we merely express our opinion or attitude.

In order for evaluation to be evaluation, *justifiable criteria* must be offered for the evaluations made, and all evaluations must be set forth *in the light of those criteria*. It is not sufficient in evaluation to say, "The play is bad"; "That book is great"; "The solution is inadequate." We must also indicate our criteria for such judgments. It is a sign of immaturity in thinking for students to make statements like these and then, when asked why, to answer, "Because . . . just because." It is always important to know—and sometimes to indicate—the standards or criteria that are being used for an evaluation. Otherwise, the evaluation may be simply "opinionating" and lack value or authority.

THINK ABOUT THIS!

Mental Fitness

Sometimes we need to encourage ourselves to begin thinking critically because we tend to function most of the time in an unthinking, basic response mode. Real learning in college requires that we be ready to think critically all the time, not just occasionally. So, how do we keep ourselves mentally fit?

One way is to raise one or more questions each day that require us to use our many different thinking abilities. For example, starting your day with a glass of orange juice (Is it really orange, or should it be called yellow juice?) and a provocative question that you attempt to answer—or find the answer to—will do wonders for your mental muscles over a period of time.

Try questions like these:

Why do whitecaps form on bodies of water, and why are they white?

Why does a piece of chalk produce a terrible squeal if you hold it in a certain way?

Does a Frisbee have to be spinning to work?

Why do fish travel in schools?

Why does the moon seem larger near the horizon?

How do microwave ovens cook meat?

What questions of your own (and better than these, of course) can you suggest for keeping mentally fit? Where can you find more entertaining, thought-provoking questions?

_____

_____

_____

_____

_____

_____

_____

_____

_____

_____

We are faced with the need to evaluate in all parts of our daily lives. Note the need for establishing or knowing specific evaluation criteria when called upon to answer ordinary questions like these:

- What kind of puppy should we choose if we want to select the right puppy for our family?

- How do age, condition, and mileage affect the value of an automobile?

- How should the state of Florida proceed in its nuclear energy development program in light of the potential risks to the environment discussed in paragraph 3 on page xxx?

ESTABLISHING EVALUATION CRITERIA

We continually evaluate people, ideas, objects, plans, experiences, relationships, and everything else in life. It is through the thinking skill of evaluation that we determine what is worthwhile and what we want to make a part of our lives and of our thinking. Every time we evaluate something we evaluate it against one or more criteria that we have established. It would be nice if we could use the same set of criteria for evaluating everything, but we can't. Different kinds of evaluation require different evaluation criteria. It is the careful establishment of evaluation criteria that allows the evaluation process to work. Consequently, whenever we are called upon to evaluate, we must follow essentially the same steps:

1. Determine exactly what we are going to evaluate.

2. Identify the criteria to be used in the evaluation. (We can use an existing set of criteria or create our own.)

3. Illustrate these criteria by descriptive limits or examples.

4. Examine the situation or information against each criterion.

5. Determine the extent to which the situation or information matches the criteria.

6. State a judgment.

THINKERS

If these two sets of numbers were added up, which sum would you estimate to be greater, the one on the left or the one on the right? Why?

987654321	123456789
87654321	12345678
7654321	1234567
654321	123456
54321	12345
4321	1234
321	123
21	12
1	1
_____	_____

Need a Hint?
What does the arrangement of the numbers have to do with the sum of the numbers?

STIR IT UP 7.6   Follow the steps outlined on page 387 and establish evaluation criteria for each of the following tasks. Be ready to describe the thinking that led to your criteria selection. How reasonable and appropriate are your criteria in each case?

1. Task: selecting a boyfriend/girlfriend

   Criteria: _____

   _____

   _____

   _____

   _____

2. Task: selecting a college major/vocation

   Criteria: _____

   _____

_____

_____

_____

3. Task: selecting a used car

Criteria: _____

_____

_____

_____

_____

4. Task: determining what is "art"

Criteria: _____

_____

_____

_____

_____

_____

? ANY QUESTIONS?

Is there any way to gauge a person's intellectual ability without subjecting him or her to a battery of "intelligence" tests?

_____

_____

_____

_____

_____

_____

_____

_____

STIR IT UP 7.7   Assume that you are now able to purchase your first house. First, establish your criteria for evaluating any house to determine if it fits your needs. After you have written down your criteria on the lines below, go to any real estate office in your area, or pick up one of those free publications that show pictures of houses for sale. Select one or more houses that meet your criteria, and bring pictures of the house(s) to class for discussion. Be ready to discuss how easy or difficult it was to stick to your criteria.

Criteria: _____

_____

_____

_____

_____

_____

———————————————————

Journal Observations (see page 13)

EVALUATING

1st Writing _____

_____

_____

_____

_____

_____

_____

_____

_____

_____

2nd Writing _____

3rd Writing _____

READINGS

Substituting Gasoline Purchased in the Suburbs for Gasoline Purchased in the City

James R. Kearl

In August 1980, city officials in Washington, D.C., imposed a 6 percent excise tax on gasoline in an effort to generate tax revenues. It was assumed that the price of gasoline would increase by about 6 percent but that the amount of gasoline sold wouldn't change by much. It was also assumed that the price increase would directly accrue to the city as tax revenues. By November 1980, however, the amount of gasoline sold in the city had fallen by 33 percent. A 6 percent price increase together with a 33 percent quantity decrease is equivalent to a price elasticity of demand of 5.5! And this was only a short-run response to the price change. Because of the decline in sales, tax revenues did not increase. Gasoline dealers in the city were hurt as well.

An elasticity of 5.5 suggests massive substitution. But what would be a good substitute for gasoline? It was the gasoline sold in the neighboring Virginia and Maryland suburbs. Thus, as gasoline stations in the District attempted to increase price in order to cover the new tax, they provided an incentive for individuals to find lower-priced substitutes for their gasoline. Since a larger portion of the automobiles driven in Washington, D.C., are driven into the city each day by commuters from neighboring Maryland and Virginia, substitutes were readily available. Drivers apparently purchased gasoline before they left for D.C. in the morning, after they returned to the suburbs in the evening, or on weekends.

The tax was repealed in December 1980, just months after it was imposed. During the discussion about its repeal, a D.C. councilman observed:

> We tend to think of ourselves here in the District as an
> island to ourselves. But we've got to realize that we're not.
> We've got to realize that Maryland and Virginia are right out
> there, and there's nothing to stop people from crossing over
> the line.

The mayor, when announcing the repeal of the tax, suggested that there was overwhelming evidence the tax had not worked. Rather, it had caused undue hardships both for consumers of gas and for those who operate retail gas businesses.

Read and Respond

1. What was the reasoning that led to the 6 percent excise tax on gasoline? What was wrong with the reasoning? What wasn't taken into consideration?

2. What could the D.C. officials have done to check their assumptions and reasoning before implementing the tax?

Diary of an Unknown Aviator (1918)

Anonymous

We've lost a lot of good men. It's only a question of time until we all get it. I'm all shot to pieces. I only hope I can stick it. I don't want to quit. My nerves are all gone and I can't stop. I've lived beyond my time already.

It's not the fear of death that's done it. I'm still not afraid to die. It's this eternal flinching from it that's doing it and has made a coward out of me. Few men live to know what real fear is. It's something that grows on you, day by day, that eats into your constitution and undermines your sanity. I have never been serious about anything in my life and now I know that I'll never be otherwise again. But my seriousness will be a burlesque for no one will recognize it. Here I am, twenty-four years old, I look forty and I feel ninety. I've lost all interest in life beyond the next patrol. No one Hun will ever get me and I'll never fall into a trap, but sooner or later I'll be forced to fight against odds that are too long or perhaps a stray shot from the ground will be lucky and I will have gone in vain. Or my motor will cut out when we are trench strafing or a wing will pull off in a dive. Oh, for a parachute! The Huns are using them now. I haven't a chance, I know, and it's this eternal waiting around that's killing me. I've even lost my taste for licker. It doesn't seem to do me any good now. I guess I'm stale. Last week I actually got frightened in the air and lost my head. Then I found ten Huns and took them all on and I got one of them down out of control. I got my nerve back by that time and came back home and slept like a baby for the first time in two months. What a blessing sleep is! I know now why men go out and take such long chances and pull off such wild stunts. No discipline in the world could make them do what they do of their own accord. I know now what a brave man is. I know now how men laugh at death and welcome it. I know now why Ball went over and sat above a Hun airdrome and dared them to come up and fight with him. It takes a brave man to even experience real fear. A coward couldn't last long enough at the job to get to that stage. What price salvation now?

War is a horrible thing, a grotesque comedy. And it is so useless. This war won't prove anything. All we'll do when we win is to substitute one sort of Dictator for another. In the meantime we have destroyed our best resources. Human life, the most precious thing in the world, has become the cheapest. After we've won this war by drowning the Hun in our own blood, in five years' time the sentimental fools at home will be taking up a collection for these same Huns that are killing us now and our fool politicians will be cooking up another good war. Why shouldn't they? They have to keep the public stirred up to keep their jobs and they don't have to fight and they can get soft berths for their sons and their friends' sons. To me the most contemptible cur in the world is the man who lets political influence be used to keep him away from the front. For he lets another man die in his place.

The worst thing about this war is that it takes the best. If it lasts long enough the world will be populated by cowards and weaklings and their children. And the whole thing is so useless, so unnecessary, so terrible! . . .

The devastation of the country is too horrible to describe. It looks from the air as if the gods had made a gigantic steam roller, forty miles wide and run it from the coast to Switzerland, leaving its spike holes behind as it went. . . .

I've lost over a hundred friends, so they tell me—I've seen only seven or eight killed—but to me they aren't dead yet. They are just around the corner, I think, and I'm still expecting to run into them any time. I dream about them at night when I do sleep a little and sometimes I dream that some one is killed who really isn't. Then I don't know who is and who isn't. I saw a man in Boulogne the other day that I had dreamed I saw killed and I thought I was seeing a ghost. I can't realize that any of them are gone. Surely human life is not a candle to be snuffed out. . . .

Read and Respond

1. This is a gripping piece of reading. But what was it that gripped you? Was it the despair, the knowing that the aviator would in all likelihood be killed soon? Was it the courage? Was it the questioning of the war itself? What was it?

2. The writer had some pretty pointed things to say about courage, fear, cowards, politicians, and even about the future population of the world. How much of what he said do you agree with? How much

of your agreement is based on what you believed before you read this article, and how much of your agreement is based on emotions inspired by the article?

3. How would you characterize the writer's psychological and emotional state of mind? Support your answer with reasons and examples. On what do you base your inferences?

4. Did the writer make it back alive? How do you know?

ASKING CRITICAL QUESTIONS

After you read the article that follows, what critical questions come to mind? Everything you read will stir up your thinking if you read and question critically. What questions would you like to have answered in order for you to put the article in proper context and to completely understand what is being said or reported? *On the lines following the article, write three questions that, if answered, will help you understand what is really being said.*

Rose Schneiderman and the Triangle Fire

Bonnie Mitelman

On Saturday afternoon, March 25, 1911, in New York City's Greenwich Village, a small fire broke out in the Triangle Waist Company, just as the 500 shirtwaist employees were quitting for the day. People rushed about, trying to get out, but they found exits blocked and windows to the fire escape rusted shut. They panicked.

As the fire spread and more and more were trapped, some began to jump, their hair and clothing afire, from the eighth and ninth floor windows. Nets that firemen held for them tore apart at the impact of the falling bodies. By the time it was over, 146 workers had died, most of them young Jewish women.

A United Press reporter, William Shepherd, witnessed the tragedy and reported, "I looked upon the heap of dead bodies and I remembered these girls were the shirtwaist makers. I remembered their great strike of last year in which these same girls had demanded more sanitary conditions and more safety precautions in the shops. These dead bodies were the answer."

The horror of that fire touched the entire Lower East Side ghetto community, and there was a profuse outpouring of sympathy. But it was

Rose Schneiderman, an immigrant worker with a spirit of social justice and a powerful way with words, who is largely credited with translating the ghetto's emotional reaction into meaningful, widespread action. Six weeks following the tragedy, and after years of solid groundwork, with one brilliant, well-timed speech, she was able to inspire the support of wealthy uptown New Yorkers and to swing public opinion to the side of the labor movement, enabling concerned civic, religious, and labor leaders to mobilize their efforts for desperately needed safety and industrial reforms.

The Triangle fire, and the deaths of so many helpless workers, seemed to trigger in Rose Schneiderman an intense realization that there was absolutely nothing or no one to help working women except a strong union movement. With fierce determination, and the dedication, influence, and funding of many other people as well, she battled to regulate hours, wages, and safety standards and to abolish the sweatshop system. In so doing, she brought dignity and human rights to all workers.

The dramatic "uprising of the 20,000" of 1909–10, in which thousands of immigrant girls and women in the shirtwaist industry had endured three long winter months of a general strike to protest deplorable working conditions, had produced some immediate gains for working women. There had been agreements for shorter working hours, increased wages, and even safety reforms, but there had not been formal recognition of their union. At Triangle, for example, the girls had gained a 52 hour week, a 12–15 percent wage increase, and promises to end the grueling subcontracting system. But they had not gained the only instrument on which they could depend for lasting change: a viable trade union. This was to have disastrous results, for in spite of the few gains that they seemed to have made, the workers won no rights or bargaining power at all. In fact, "The company dealt only with its contractors. It felt no responsibility for the girls."

There were groups as well as individuals who realized the workers' impotence, but their attempts to change the situation accomplished little despite long years of hard work. The Women's Trade Union League [WTUL] and the International Ladies' Garment Workers' Union, through the efforts of Mary Dreier, Helen Marot, Leonora O'Reilly, Pauline Newman, and Rose Schneiderman, had struggled unsuccessfully for improved conditions: the futility that the union organizers were feeling in late 1910 is reflected in the WTUL minutes of December 5 of that year.

A scant eight months after their historic waistmakers' strike, and three months before the deadly Triangle fire, a Mrs. Malkiel (no doubt

Theresa Serber Malkiel, who wrote the legendary account of the strike, *The Diary of a Shirtwaist Striker: A Story of the Shirtwaist Makers' Strike in New York*) is reported to have come before the League to urge action after a devastating fire in Newark, New Jersey, killed twenty-five working women. Mrs. Malkiel attributed their loss to the greed and negligence of the owners and the proper authorities. The WTUL subsequently demanded an investigation of all factory buildings and it elected an investigation committee from the League to cooperate with similar committees from other organizations.

The files of the WTUL contain complaint after complaint about unsafe factory conditions; many were filled out by workers afraid to sign their names for fear of being fired had their employers seen the forms. They describe factories with locked doors, no fire escapes, and barred windows. The New York *Times* carried an article which reported that fourteen factories were found to have no fire escapes, twenty-three that had locked doors, and seventy-eight that had obstructed fire escapes. In all, according to the article, 99 percent of the factories investigated in New York were found to have serious fire hazards.

Yet no action was taken.

It was the Triangle fire that emphasized, spectacularly and tragically, the deplorable safety and sanitary conditions of the garment workers. The tragedy focused attention upon the ghastly factories in which most immigrants worked; there was no longer any question about what the strikers had meant when they talked about safety and sanitary reform, and about social and economic justice.

The grief and frustration of the shirtwaist strikers were expressed by one of them, Rose Safran, after the fire: "If the union had won we would have been safe. Two of our demands were for adequate fire escapes and for open doors from the factories to the street. But the bosses defeated us and we didn't get the open doors or the better fire escapes. So our friends are dead."

The families of the fire victims were heartbroken and hysterical, the ghetto's *Jewish Daily Forward* was understandably melodramatic, and the immigrant community was completely enraged. Their Jewish heritage had taught them an emphasis on individual human life and worth; their shared background in the *shtetl* [Jewish village in Eastern Europe] and common experiences in the ghetto had given them a sense of fellowship. They were, in a sense, a family—and some of the most helpless among them had died needlessly.

The senseless deaths of so many young Jewish women sparked within these Eastern Europeans a new determination and dedication. The fire had made reform absolutely essential. Workers' rights were no longer just socialist jargon: They were a matter of life and death.

The Triangle Waist Company was located on the three floors of the Asch Building, a 10-story, 135-foot-high structure at the corner of Greene Street and Washington Place in Greenwich Village. One of the largest shirtwaist manufacturers, Triangle employed up to 900 people at times, but on the day of the fire, only about 500 were working.

Leon Stein's brilliant and fascinating account of the fire, entitled simply *The Triangle Fire,* develops and documents the way in which the physical facilities, company procedures, and human behavior interacted to cause this great tragedy. Much of what occurred was ironic, some was cruel, some stupid, some pathetic. It is a dramatic portrayal of the eternal confrontation of the "haves" and the "have-nots," told in large part by those who survived.

Fire broke out at the Triangle Company at approximately 4:45 P.M. (because time clocks were reportedly set back to stretch the day, and because other records give differing times of the first fire alarm, it is uncertain exactly what time the fire started), just after pay envelopes had been distributed and employees were leaving their work posts. It was a small fire at first, and there was a calm, controlled effort to extinguish it. But the fire began to spread, jumping from one pile of debris to another, engulfing the combustible shirtwaist fabric. It became obvious that the fire could not be snuffed out, and workers tried to reach the elevators or stairway. Those who reached the one open stairway raced down eight flights of stairs to safety; those who managed to climb onto the available passenger elevators also got out. But not everyone could reach the available exits. Some tried to open the door to a stairway and found it locked. Others were trapped between long working tables or behind the hordes of people trying to get into the elevators or out through the one open door.

Under the work tables, rags were burning; the wooden floors, trim, and window frames were also afire. Frantically, workers fought their way to the elevators, to the fire escape, and to the windows—to any place that might lead to safety.

Fire whistles and bells sounded as the fire department raced to the building. But equipment proved inadequate, as the fire ladders reached only to the seventh floor. And by the time the firemen connected their hoses to douse the flames, the crowded eighth floor was completely ablaze.

For those who reached the windows, there seemed to be a chance for safety. The New York *World* describes people balancing on window sills, nine stories up, with flames scorching them from behind, until firemen arrived: "The nets were spread below with all promptness. Citizens were commandeered into service, as the firemen necessarily gave their attention to the one engine and hose of the force that first arrived. The catapult force that the bodies gathered in the long plunges made the nets utterly without avail. Screaming girls and men, as they fell, tore the nets from the grasp of the holders, and the bodies struck the sidewalks and lay just as they fell. Some of the bodies ripped big holes through the life nets."

One reporter who witnessed the fire remembered how,

> A young man helped a girl to the window sill on the ninth floor. Then he held her out deliberately, away from the building, and let her drop. He held out a second girl the same way and let her drop. He held out a third girl who did not resist. They were all as unresisting as if he were helping them into a street car instead of into eternity. He saw that a terrible death awaited them in the flames and his was only a terrible chivalry. He brought around another girl to the window. I saw her put her arms around him and kiss him. Then he held her into space—and dropped her. Quick as a flash, he was on the window sill himself. His coat fluttered upwards—the air filled his trouser legs as he came down. I could see he wore tan shoes.

Those who had rushed to the fire escape found the window openings rusted shut. Several precious minutes were lost in releasing them. The fire escape itself ended at the second floor, in an airshaft between the Asch Building and the building next door. But too frantic to notice where it ended, workers climbed onto the fire escape, one after another until, in one terrifying moment, it collapsed from the weight, pitching the workers to their death.

Those who had made their way to the elevators found crowds pushing to get into the cars. When it became obvious that the elevators could no longer run, workers jumped down the elevator shaft, landing on the top of the cars, or grabbing for cables to ease their descent. Several died, but incredibly, some did manage to save themselves in this way. One man was found, hours after the fire, beneath an elevator car in the basement of the building, nearly drowned by the rapidly rising water from the firemen's hoses.

Several people, among them Triangle's two owners, raced to the roof, and from there were led to safety. Others never had that chance. "When Fire Chief Croker could make his way into the [top] three floors," states one account of the fire, "he found sights that utterly staggered him. . . .

He saw as the smoke drifted away bodies burned to bare bones. There were skeletons bending over sewing machines."

The day after the fire, the New York *Times* announced that "the building was fireproof. It shows hardly any signs of the disaster that overtook it. The walls are as good as ever, as are the floors: nothing is worse for the fire except the furniture and 141 [*sic*] of the 600 men and girls that were employed in its upper three stories."

The building *was* fireproof. But there had never been a fire drill in the factory, even though the management had been warned about the possible hazard of fire on the top three floors. Owners Max Blanck and Isaac Harris had chosen to ignore these warnings in spite of the fact that many of their employees were immigrants who could barely speak English, which would surely mean panic in the event of a crisis.

The New York *Times* also noted that Leonora O'Reilly of the League had reported Max Blanck's visit to the WTUL during the shirtwaist strike, and his plea that the girls return to work. He claimed a business reputation to maintain and told the Union leaders he would make the necessary improvements right away. Because he was the largest manufacturer in the business, the League reported, they trusted him and let the girls return.

But the improvements were never made. And there was nothing that anybody could or would do about it. Factory doors continued to open in instead of out, in violation of fire regulations. The doors remained bolted during working hours, apparently to prevent workers from getting past the inspectors with stolen merchandise. Triangle had only two staircases where there should have been three, and those two were very narrow. Despite the fact that the building was deemed fireproof, it had wooden window frames, floors, and trim. There was no sprinkler system. It was not legally required.

These were the same kinds of conditions which existed in factories throughout the garment industry; they had been cited repeatedly in the complaints filed with the WTUL. They were not unusual nor restricted to Triangle; in fact, Triangle was not as bad as many other factories.

But it was at Triangle that the fire took place.

The *Jewish Daily Forward* mourned the dead with sorrowful stories, and its headlines talked of "funerals instead of weddings" for the dead young girls. The entire Jewish immigrant community was affected, for it seemed there was scarcely a person who was not in some way touched by the fire. Nearly everyone had either been employed at Triangle themselves, or had a friend or relative who had worked there at some time or another. Most worked in factories with similar conditions, and so everyone identified with the victims and their families.

Many of the dead, burned beyond recognition, remained unidentified for days, as searching family members returned again and again to wait in long lines to look for their loved ones. Many survivors were unable to identify their mothers, sisters, or wives; the confusion of handling so many victims and so many survivors who did not understand what was happening to them and to their dead led to even more anguish for the community. Some of the victims were identified by the names on the pay envelopes handed to them at quitting time and stuffed deeply into pockets or stockings just before the fire. But many bodies remained unclaimed for days, with bewildered and bereaved survivors wandering among them, trying to find some identifying mark.

Charges of first- and second-degree manslaughter were brought against the two men who owned Triangle, and Leon Stein's book artfully depicts the subtle psychological and sociological implications of the powerful against the oppressed, and of the Westernized, German-Jewish immigrants against those still living their old-world, Eastern European heritage. Ultimately, Triangle owners Blanck and Harris were acquitted of the charges against them, and in due time they collected their rather sizable insurance.

The shirtwaist, popularized by Gibson girls, had come to represent the new-found freedom of females in America. After the fire, it symbolized death. The reaction of the grief-stricken Lower East Side was articulated by socialist lawyer Morris Hillquit:

> The girls who went on strike last year were trying to readjust the conditions under which they were obliged to work. I wonder if there is not some connection between the fire and that strike. I wonder if the magistrates who sent to jail the girls who did picket duty in front of the Triangle shop realized last Sunday that some of the responsibility may be theirs. Had the strike been successful, these girls might have been alive today and the citizenry of New York would have less of a burden upon its conscience.

For the first time in the history of New York's garment industry there were indications that the public was beginning to accept responsibility for the exploitation of the immigrants. For the first time, the establishment seemed to understand that these were human beings asking for their rights, not merely troublemaking anarchists.

The day after the Triangle fire a protest meeting was held at the Women's Trade Union League, with representatives from twenty leading labor and civic organizations. They formed "a relief committee to cooperate with the Red Cross in its work among the families of the victims, and another committee . . . to broaden the investigation and research on fire hazards in New York factories which was already being carried on by the League."

The minutes of the League recount the deep indignation that members felt at the indifference of a public which had ignored their pleas for safety after the Newark fire. In an attempt to translate their anger into constructive action, the League drew up a list of forceful resolutions that included a plan to gather delegates from all of the city's unions to make a concerted effort to force safety changes in factories. In addition, the League called upon all workers to inspect factories and then report any violations to the proper city authorities and to the WTUL. They called upon the city to immediately appoint organized workers as unofficial inspectors. They resolved to submit the following fire regulations suggestions: compulsory fire drills, fireproof exits, unlocked doors, fire alarms, automatic sprinklers, and regular inspections. The League called upon the legislature to create the Bureau of Fire Protection and finally, the League underscored the absolute need for all workers to organize themselves at once into trade unions so that they would never again be powerless.

The League also voted to participate in the funeral procession for the unidentified dead of the Triangle fire.

The city held a funeral for the dead who were unclaimed. "More than 120,000 of us were in the funeral procession that miserable rainy April day," remembered Rose Schneiderman. "From ten in the morning until four in the afternoon we of the Women's Trade Union League marched in the procession with other trade-union men and women, all of us filled with anguish and regret that we had never been able to organize the Triangle workers."

Schneiderman, along with many others, was absolutely determined that this kind of tragedy would never happen again. With single-minded dedication, they devoted themselves to unionizing the workers. The searing example of the Triangle fire provided them with the impetus they needed to gain public support for their efforts.

They dramatized and emphasized and capitalized on the scandalous working conditions of the immigrants. From all segments of the community came cries for labor reform. Stephen S. Wise, the prestigious reform rabbi, called for the formation of a citizens' committee. Jacob H. Schiff, Bishop David H. Greer, Governor John A. Dix, Anne Morgan (of *the* Morgans) and other leading civic and religious leaders collaborated in a mass meeting at the Metropolitan Opera House on May 2 to protest factory conditions and to show support for the workers.

Several people spoke at that meeting on May 2, and many in the audience began to grow restless and antagonistic. Finally, 29-year-old Rose Schneiderman stepped up to the podium.

In a whisper barely audible, she began to address the crowd.

> I would be a traitor to these poor burned bodies, if I came here to talk good fellowship. We have tried you good people of the public and we have found you wanting. The old Inquisition had its rack and its thumbscrews and its instruments of torture with iron teeth. We know what these things are today: the iron teeth are our necessities, the thumbscrews the high-powered and swift machinery close to which we must work, and the rack is here in the fire-proof structures that will destroy us the minute they catch on fire.
>
> This is not the first time girls have burned alive in the city. Every week I must learn of the untimely death of one of my sister workers. Every year thousands of us are maimed. The life of men and women is so cheap and property is so sacred. There are so many of us for one job it matters little if 140-odd are burned to death.
>
> We have tried you, citizens; we are trying you now, and you have a couple of dollars for the sorrowing mothers and daughters and sisters by way of a charity gift. But every time the workers come out in the only way they know to protest against conditions which are unbearable, the strong hand of the law is allowed to press down heavily upon us.
>
> Public officials have only words of warning to us—warning that we must be intensely orderly and must be intensely peaceable, and they have the workhouse just back of all their warnings. The strong hand of the law beats us back when we rise into the conditions that make life bearable.
>
> I can't talk fellowship to you who are gathered here. Too much blood has been spilled. I know from my experience it is up to the working people to save themselves. The only way they can save themselves is by a strong working-class movement.

Her speech has become a classic. It is more than just an emotional picture of persecution; it reflects the pervasive sadness and profound understanding that comes from knowing, finally, the cruel realities of life, the perspective of history, and the nature of human beings.

The devastation of that fire and the futility of the seemingly successful strike that had preceded it seemed to impart an undeniable truth to Rose Schneiderman: They could not fail again. The events of 1911 seemed to have made her, and many others, more keenly aware than they had ever been that the workers' fight for reform was absolutely essential. If they did not do it, it would not be done.

In a sense, the fire touched off in Schneiderman an awareness of her own responsibility in the battle for industrial reform. This fiery socialist worker had been transformed into a highly effective labor leader.

The influential speech she gave did help swing public opinion to the side of the trade unions, and the fire itself had made the workers more aware of the crucial need to unionize. Widespread support for labor reform and unionization emerged. Pressure from individuals, such as Rose Schneiderman, as well as from groups like the Women's Trade Union League and the International Ladies' Garment Workers' Union, helped form the New York State Factory Investigating Commission, the New York Citizens' Committee on Safety, and other regulatory and investigatory bodies. The League and Local 25 (the Shirtwaist Makers' Union of the ILGWU) were especially instrumental in attaining a new Industrial Code for New York State, which became "the most outstanding instrument for safeguarding the lives, health, and welfare of the millions of wage earners in New York State and . . . in the nation at large."

It took years for these changes to occur, and labor reform did not rise majestically, Phoenix-like, from the ashes of the Triangle fire. But that fire, and Rose Schneiderman's whispered plea for a strong working-class movement, had indeed become the loud clear call for action.

My Critical Questions

1. _____

_____ **?**

2. _____

_____ **?**

3. _____

_____ **?**

Inducing

ESSENTIAL THINKING SKILLS		
CHAPTER	**WHAT THEY'RE CALLED**	**WHAT THEY MEAN**
Chapter 3	**The Gathering Skills**	**Gathering all the information.**
	Observing	Actively seeking information through one or more senses.
	Questioning	Seeking information by asking questions.
Chapter 4	**The Organizing Skills**	**Organizing for the purpose of making sense.**
	Comparing and Contrasting	Noting similarities and differences between two or more things, events, or ideas.
	Classifying and Sequencing	Arranging things or concepts into categories and into sequential order.
	Identifying Cause and Effect	Recognizing the relationship between an effect and its cause.
Chapter 5	**The Generating Skills**	**Generating additional information.**
	Inferring	Making an assumption, stating a hypothesis, or coming to a conclusion based on limited information.
	Summarizing	Condensing the essence of the information accurately and efficiently.
	Synthesizing	Creating new information by combining two or more pieces of information.
	Generating Ideas	Creating new information, alternatives, or applications.
Chapter 6	**The Recognizing Skills**	**Recognizing what has been left unsaid.**
	Recognizing Purpose	Identifying a writer's or speaker's intention.
	Recognizing Fact and Opinion	Distinguishing between a statement of fact and a statement of opinion.
	Recognizing Tone	Identifying a sentiment or mood by assessing the writer's or speaker's choice of words.
	Recognizing Bias	Noting the presence and nature of a writer's or speaker's prejudice.
	Recognizing Organization	Identifying the organizational pattern of a thought, statement, passage, or plan.
	Recognizing Underlying Assumptions	Recognizing the suppositions that are taken for granted and are the foundation of a proposition, notion, or idea.
Chapter 7	**The Analyzing Skills**	**Analyzing for the purpose of coming to a conclusion.**
	Analyzing	Identifying and separating ideas, attributes, situations, and/or components in order to form a conclusion as to their relationship.
	Evaluating	Appraising something according to certain criteria and forming a judgment as to its worth or quality.
	Inducing	Analyzing individual facts or premises in order to derive a general conclusion.
	Deducing	Applying general principles or a broad framework to a situation in order to come to a conclusion about it.

"If the cycle goes over a bump and the engine misfires, and then goes over another bump and the engine misfires, and then goes over a long smooth stretch of road and there is no misfiring, and then goes over a fourth bump and the engine misfires again, one can logically conclude that the misfiring is caused by the bumps. That is induction. . . ."
—Robert M. Pirsig

"In our human state, there are very few issues that can be proven beyond a shadow of a doubt. Even our court system only asks that a conclusion be proven 'beyond a reasonable *doubt.' That means the evidence does point to the conclusion with the reservation that there may be an* unusual *exception."*
—Sherry Diestler

What questions am I going to have answered in this section on inducing?

1. How is inductive thinking useful?
2. How does inductive thinking relate to the scientific method, and why is it sometimes called causal thinking?
3. Isn't inductive thinking just logical thinking?

THINK ABOUT THIS!

Start Now!

You are captured by a mad scientist, who gives you two hourglasses. One measures exactly four minutes, the other measures exactly seven minutes. The mad scientist (who values critical thinking and problem solving puzzles) says you must tell when exactly nine minutes have passed. If you can do this, you may go free. If you can't, you will be forced to wash test tubes for the rest of your life.

The mad scientist yells, "Start now!"

What must you do *immediately* in order to stand a chance of surviving? Record your answer here before reading any further.

_____

What you must do immediately is turn the hourglasses over. If you don't, you will miss your chance to solve the problem because some time will slip away before you do. Even if you figure out in a couple of minutes how to solve the problem, you can't make up those two minutes. When the mad scientist said "now," he meant now. While the sand is dropping, you can use the time to think and to solve the problem.

Now, figure out how to use the hourglasses to measure exactly nine minutes. You can do it.

INDUCING:
Analyzing individual facts or premises in order to
derive a general conclusion

When we reason inductively we start with specific premises, evidence, details, and facts. Then we use these specifics in our thinking process to formulate inferences and conclusions of a broad and general nature. Much of the learning you do in all subject areas in college is strongly dependent on inductive thinking. You go from observations to inferences. Without thinking inductively, all you do in college is learn isolated premises, memorize facts, and rely on memorization and recall for answers to factual questions and solutions to factual problems. Inductive reasoning is a way of obtaining information. We reason inductively when we arrive at a conclusion about a broad group after we have examined a sample of the group. When it is impossible to examine all the data, we extrapolate from the data that we have. With inductive thinking, we can take limited evidence about some members of a class or about the facts of a problem in order to form a conclusion about all members of the class or to arrive at a probable solution for the problem.

In reasoning inductively, scientists work from a collection of *particular* events to formulate *general* principles. In other words, they use unifying concepts to link events that were previously not seen as related to one another. Thus, they try to establish a logical completion for the sentence "All these things happen as they do because ———."

THINKERS

What five-letter word becomes shorter when you add two letters to it? There is only one possibility.

Need a Hint?
A trick question, but also a *literal* question.

WE START WITH OBSERVATION

We start by observing something, by acquiring and understanding the basics, the premises, facts, details, and specific information about it.

Then we move to arranging and combining the individual pieces of information so that we can see a pattern, draw inferences, and come to a conclusion, understand a situation or event, or formulate a principle or a rule. In the practice of medicine, doctors rely heavily on inductive thinking. They look at the evidence—the symptoms—in order to come to a conclusion—a diagnosis. The diagnosis is the *general* principle formulated from the *particular* symptoms. Inducing is a way of accounting for and understanding how the specifics go together in order to produce the whole.

Inducing broad truths, observations, or conclusions from individual facts permits us to answer questions like the following. (Remember, though, that if the facts are in error, anything we induce from them may be in error.)

- After hearing what the weather forecaster said about conditions outside, will you need to bring your umbrella, your bathing suit, or your mittens?

- Given the conditions described in the reading selection, which diseases are likely to thrive?

- From your observations of them, can you tell which of those four people is likely to be the owner of the gold coins, the diamonds, the rare paintings, and the expensive cars?

- A poll reported that 82 percent of the people surveyed disliked people smoking near them while they were eating. What does that suggest to you about the feasibility of having more nonsmoking sections in restaurants?

- If the three interviewers got conflicting descriptions of the robber from the three witnesses, what is the likelihood that the authorities will ever get an accurate or usable description?

You will note that in each case, these questions depend for their answers on inferring, on combining specific facts so as to arrive at a broad conclusion that encompasses more than the facts or premises stated. Frequently we see this inductive thinking at work when people interpret polls or new product surveys. Pollsters and marketers ask selected individuals specific questions. Their answers are then used to predict the success of a product or the outcome of an election. Inductive thinking occurs regularly during televised election-day voting coverage. Network experts predict the winners after interviewing a limited number of voters. This representative sampling of voters allows for an inference, a prediction, as to the winner of the race. It is important that these inferences be probable, not improbable, and arise out of the facts of a situation. Because inductive thinking relies on probable inferences, our conclusions can be probable, but they are seldom totally certain.

STIR IT UP 7.8   In forming inferences, we need to be responsible in our interpretations. Read the following brief scenario and then take the quiz to see if you can distinguish between what is *definitely* true or false (a fact) from what is *probably* true or false (an inference).

Heidi and Alice are driving when they see an older model car pulled over at the side of the road. The rear end of the car is smashed in and a side window is broken. There is a man in front of the car. He is doubled over, swaying slightly, violently ill. He stands up straight as they pass, watching them, but doesn't indicate any need for help. "Obviously a drunk," says Alice. "I hope he makes it home safely," says Heidi.

1. In brief, this story is about observing a car and driver at the side of the road.   T ☐ F ☐?

2. The wrecked car was undrivable.   T ☐ F ☐?

3. The wrecked car had no passengers.   T ☐ F ☐?

4. The driver was drunk.   T ☐ F ☐?

5. Heidi was driving; Alice was the passenger.   T ☐ F ☐?

6. There were no other cars on the road.   T ☐ F ☐?

7. The man standing in front of the car was the driver.   T ☐ F ☐?

8. Heidi was concerned for the driver; Alice wasn't.   T ☐ F ☐?

9. Heidi and Alice stopped at a pay phone and called the police.   T ☐ F ☐?

10. The scene at the side of the road upset Heidi and Alice.   T ☐ F ☐?

Look at your answers. Were you able to differentiate between what was clearly a fact and what was an inference? Were there some *unlikely* inferences, that is, statements that were possibly true but probably not true?

WHY DID THAT HAPPEN?

Another common form of inductive thinking (sometimes called *causal* thinking or reasoning) occurs when we ask questions such as, Why did

ANY QUESTIONS?

You come to a fork in the road on the way to Hana and meet two men. One man is from Hana and the other is from Anah. You know that one man always tells the truth and the other always lies. But you don't know who is the liar and who is the truth teller. To get to Hana, you can ask only one question of the men. What should that question be?

_____

_____

_____

_____

that happen? Why did that accident occur? Why did the clothes dryer stop working? Why do I have such a bad headache? Why did the fish stop biting? Why are our winters much colder in recent years? We frequently observe (or experience) an event, a happening of some sort, a problem, and then attempt to determine the cause. The procedure we follow is the process of inductive thinking. We compile data related to the problem, analyze and evaluate the data in light of the question raised, and then infer or conclude the answer. As with all inductive thinking, the process moves from gathering and analyzing individual facts to forming a general conclusion based on them.

When we attempt to state why something happened, the correctness of our conclusion depends on whether or not we can answer yes to the following questions:

1. Are all the related facts or events known?

2. Are these facts or events sufficient to arrive at a conclusion or inference that answers the question "Why did that happen?"

3. Does the conclusion or inference arrived at (the answer to the question) arise naturally and logically from the facts or events?

THE SCIENTIFIC METHOD

Inductive thinking is the foundation for much thinking that has helped us understand and live in our complex world. Early in our education most of us were introduced in our science classes to the *scientific method*. This is a systematic procedure that relies on inductive thinking in order to discover causal relationships. The steps in the scientific method are as follows. A real-life problem is used to illustrate the thinking that takes place.

1. *Identify the event or events to be investigated.* Example: The fish have not been biting for the last month in the Gulf waters near my home.

2. *Gather information about the event or events.* I use lures, not live bait. The water is very warm. I fish in the early evenings, after work. No one else usually fishes at that time. In past months I often used to catch fish.

3. *Develop a theory or hypothesis (a conclusion derived from inductive reasoning) to explain what is happening.* Possible explanations for not catching fish are: I'm using the wrong bait.
   The water is too warm.
   I'm fishing at the wrong time of day for this season.

4. *Test the theory or hypothesis through experimentation.* Of the possible explanations listed above, I can rule out the bait because I used the same bait in the past and caught fish. It's probably not water temperature because it is only a few degrees warmer than it was a few months ago when I caught fish. Perhaps I'm fishing at the wrong time of day for the season. That seems the most reasonable theory to test. It can be tested a couple of ways. I'll ask other people when they fish and when the fish are biting best, and I'll go fishing at different times of the day.

5. *Evaluate the theory or hypothesis.* The theory that I was fishing at the wrong time of the day was correct. I evaluated the theory by going fishing several times earlier in the day, and each time I caught something.

As you can see from these steps, and as you may remember from your experiences in school, the scientific method leads thinkers step by step in inducing causal relationships, first analyzing individual facts or premises, then deriving a general conclusion, and then testing the accuracy of the conclusion.

STIR IT UP 7.9   Select one of the following situations and analyze it by working through the steps of the scientific method described above.

You drove to school, parked your car, and went to class, but now your car won't start. What's wrong?

You are having a hard time passing the quizzes and exams in one of your courses. What's wrong?

Some of your clothes seem to be missing from your dormitory room closet. What is happening?

Step 1: Describe the situation. _____

_____

_____

_____

_____

Step 2: Gather information. (Details? Possible causes?) _____

_____

_____

_____

_____

Step 3: What's your theory about what's happening? (What is the likely reason?) _____

_____

_____

_____

_____

Step 4: Test your theory. (How can you test your theory?) _____

_____

_____

_____

_____

Step 5: Evaluate your theory. (Results? Do you accept or reject your theory?) _____

_____

_____

_____

Journal Observations (see page 13)

INDUCING

1st Writing _____

_____
_____
_____
_____
_____
_____
_____
_____
_____

2nd Writing _____

_____
_____
_____
_____
_____
_____
_____
_____
_____
_____

3rd Writing _____

_____

_____

_____

_____

_____

_____

_____

_____

READINGS ## Our Daily Life Is Not a Pleasant One

Anonymous

I am thirty-five years old, married, the father of four children, and have lived in the coal region all my life. Twenty-three of these years have been spent working in and around the mines. My father was a miner. He died ten years ago from "miners' asthma [black lung disease]."

Three of my brothers are miners; none of us had any opportunities to acquire an education. We were sent to school (such a school as there was in those days) until we were about twelve years of age, and then we were put into the screen room of a breaker to pick slate. From there we went inside the mines as driver boys. As we grew stronger we were taken on as laborers, where we served until able to call ourselves miners. We were given work in the breasts and gangways. There were five of us boys. One lies in the cemetery—fifty tons of top rock dropped on him. He was killed three weeks after he got his job as a miner—a month before he was to be married.

In the fifteen years I have worked as a miner I have earned the average rate of wages any of us coal heavers get. To-day I am little better off than when I started to do for myself. I have $100 on hand; I am not in debt; I hope to be able to weather the strike without going hungry.

I am only one of the hundreds you see on the street every day. The muscles on my arms are no harder, the callous on my palms no deeper than my neighbor's whose entire life has been spent in the coal region. By years I am only thirty-five. But look at the marks on my body; look at the lines of worriment on my forehead; see the gray hairs on my head and in my mustache; take my general appearance, and you'll think I'm ten years older.

You need not wonder why. Day in and day out, from Monday morning to Saturday evening, between the rising and the setting of the sun, I am in the underground workings of the coal mines. From the seams water trickles into the ditches along the gangways; if not water, it is the gas which hurls us to eternity and the props and timbers to a chaos.

Our daily life is not a pleasant one. When we put on our oil soaked suit in the morning we can't guess all the dangers which threaten our lives. We walk sometimes miles to the place—to the man way or traveling way, or to the mouth of the shaft on top of the slope. And then we enter the darkened chambers of the mines. On our right and on our left we see the logs that keep up the top and support the sides which may crush us into shapeless masses, as they have done to many of our comrades.

We get old quickly. Powder, smoke, after-damp, bad air—all combine to bring furrows to our faces and asthma to our lungs.

I did not strike because I wanted to; I struck because I had to. A miner—the same as any other workman—must earn fair living wages, or he can't live. And it is not how much you get that counts. It is how much what you get will buy. I have gone through it all, and I think my case is a good sample.

I was married in 1890, when I was 23 years old—quite a bit above the age when we miner boys get into double harness [married]. The woman I married is like myself. She was born beneath the shadow of a dirt bank; her chances for school weren't any better than mine; but she did have to learn how to keep house on a certain amount of money. After we paid the preacher for tying the knot we had just $185 in cash, good health and the good wishes of many friends to start us off.

Our cash was exhausted in buying furniture for housekeeping. In 1890 work was not so plentiful, and by the time our first baby came there was room for much doubt as to how we would pull out. Low wages, and not much over half time in those years, made us hustle. In 1890–91, from June to May, I earned $368.72. That represented eleven months' work, or an average of $33.52 per month. Our rent was $10 per month; store not less than $20. And then I had my oil suits and gum boots to pay for. The result was that after the first year and a half of our married life we were in debt. Not much, of course, and not as much as many of my neighbors, men of larger families, and some who made less money, or in whose case there had been sickness or accident or death. These are all things which a miner must provide for.

I have had fairly good work since I was married. I made the average of what we contract miners are paid; but, as I said before, I am not much better off than when I started.

In 1896 my wife was sick eleven weeks. The doctor came to my house almost every day. He charged me $20 for his services. There was medicine to buy. I paid the drug store $18 in that time. Her mother nursed her, and we kept a girl in the kitchen at $1.50 a week, which cost me $15 for ten weeks, besides the additional living expenses.

In 1897, just a year afterward, I had a severer trial. And mind, in those years, we were only working about half time. But in the fall of that year one of my brothers struck a gas feeder. There was a terrible explosion. He was hurled downward in the breast and covered with the rush of coal and rock. I was working only three breasts away from him and for a moment was unable to realize what had occurred. Myself and a hundred others were soon at work, however, and in a short while we found him, horribly burned over his whole body, his laborer dead alongside of him.

He was my brother. He was single and had been boarding. He had no home of his own. I didn't want him taken to the hospital, so I directed the driver of the ambulance to take him to my house. Besides being burned, his right arm and left leg were broken, and he was hurt internally. The doctors—there were two at the house when we got there—said he would die. But he didn't. He is living and a miner today. But he lay in bed just fourteen weeks, and was unable to work for seven weeks after he got out of bed. He had no money when he was hurt except the amount represented by his pay. All of the expenses for doctors, medicine, extra help and his living were borne by me, except $25, which another brother gave me. The last one had none to give. Poor work, low wages and a sickly woman for a wife had kept him scratching for his own family.

It is nonsense to say I was not compelled to keep him, that I could have sent him to a hospital or the almshouse. We are American citizens and we don't go to hospitals and poorhouses. . . .

Read and Respond

1. What qualities of character, what values do you see in the coal miner who wrote this article? What does he mean when he says, "We are American citizens and we don't go to hospitals and poorhouses"?

2. What does the writer seem to take for granted about his life?

Public Lands and Harvesting Trees

James R. Kearl

There are more trees in forests in the United States today than there were in 1920. There are three reasons: First, oil and gas replaced fireplaces and stoves. Second, cars, trucks, and tractors replaced horses—one-third of agricultural land was used to feed the horses and much of that land has since been converted back into forest land. Third, advances in seeds and fertilizers mean that less land is needed for growing food and, again, much of the land that is no longer used now grows trees once more.

About 72 percent of the timberland in the United States is privately owned. The remainder is managed by the U.S. Forest Service, which sells millions of trees from 122 national forests, but loses as much as $200 million each year. For the most part, national forests are in areas where costs are higher to harvest timber. Then why is this land logged? The reason is that the Forest Service sells the timber at prices below the cost of harvesting on private lands. Critics claim that the Forest Service hides the true costs in several ways:

1. Although roads last for 25 years, it amortizes them over 100 years or more. (One road in Alaska was amortized over 1,800 years, leading one critic to note that if this were true, the current Italian government would still be paying for the Appian Way.)

2. It does not include the $110 million payroll for Forest Service employees.

3. It omits the costs of land surveys and road work.

4. It pays money to local governments in lieu of taxes, but does not deduct these expenditures from the income it receives from selling trees.

Including these costs turns the Forest Service's estimated $630 million net revenue into a $120 million net revenue loss (critics' estimate).

Although the Forest Service does admit that not all national forest timber sales result in positive net revenue, it argues that jobs would be lost if it were to cease below-cost sales. Critics respond that because the demand for wood will not change, the jobs will simply be relocated to private timberland.

Read and Respond

1. What issue is addressed in this article? State your answer in fewer than ten words. Explain why you think your answer is correct.

2. What evidence, information, or data are presented? Does the information help clarify the arguments set forth in this article? If not, why not?

3. The article suggests that the Forest Service hides the true costs of selling timber by citing four examples. Look at the sequence of the examples. Are they arranged in any special order? If so, what impact is the sequence supposed to have? What other sequence might be used for the same examples? What would be the intended effect if you arranged them differently? Explain your thinking.

4. How does the information in this article correspond to your beliefs about our nation's timber resources and about the activities of the Forest Service?

ASKING CRITICAL QUESTIONS

After you read the articles that follow, what critical questions come to mind? Everything you read will stir up your thinking if you read and question critically. What questions would you like to have answered in order for you to put the articles in proper context and to completely understand what is being said or reported? *On the lines following each article, write three questions that, if answered, will help you understand what is really being said.*

The Gaia Hypothesis

Joseph Levine and Kenneth Miller

James Lovelock, a British biochemist, and his American colleague Lynn Margulis do not believe that long-term constancy in Earth's temperature and the life-sustaining levels of oxygen in the atmosphere have arisen incidentally.

Life's influence on planetary conditions struck Lovelock as so powerful and so precisely regulated that he proposed the *Gaia hypothesis*. According to Lovelock, "the physical and chemical condition of the earth's surface of the atmosphere, and of the oceans has been and is actively made fit and comfortable by the presence of life itself."

His hypothesis rests on evidence that living organisms *interact* with, and powerfully affect, Earth's atmosphere and geochemical cycles. Lovelock goes further, however; he proposes that all life on Earth has evolved into a global superorganism—Gaia—whose parts monitor and manipulate carbon dioxide concentration, oxygen levels, and other environmental parameters. He argues that only this active monitoring and correction keep global conditions within the narrow margins essential for life.

In this view, Gaia's atmosphere and oceans act like a global circulatory system, carrying compounds across the globe and dumping them where necessary. Plants and animals living and dead process and store such critical compounds as oxygen and carbon dioxide, releasing them as necessary to control Earth's temperature and atmospheric composition.

Homeostasis is the term physiologists use to describe an organism's maintenance of stable internal conditions in the face of a changing external environment. Lovelock was bold enough to propose that this global superorganism has actively maintained planetary homeostasis over the 3.5 billion years it has been alive.

The Gaia hypothesis is controversial, but it is extremely useful as an alternative point of view. It reminds us that though we tend to think of Earth as stable, we as living organisms have altered it in many ways. What will come of those changes no one knows. In the meantime, Lovelock's ideas can help us view the evolution of life and the physical evolution of Earth not as two separate series of events but as a single, tightly integrated process.

My Critical Questions

1. _____
   _____ **?**

2. _____
   _____ **?**

3. _____
   _____ **?**

Income and Substitution Effects and the Design of Public Policy

James R. Kearl

When OPEC reduced the supply of oil to the United States in 1974, a number of policies directed at reducing United States dependence on imported oil were proposed. One proposal was a tax on gasoline. Such a tax was thought to be politically unpopular because it would further increase the price of gasoline and reduce real income. To offset this political problem, the proponents of the tax increase suggested that the full amount of the tax revenue received by the government be rebated to gasoline consumers. Consumers would pay higher prices for gasoline but would receive the tax they paid back from the government. This appears to be nonsense because, from the consumers' perspective, it appears to be a wash—more money in total is spent on gasoline on the one side, reducing demand, but the same amount of money comes back on the other side, increasing demand. Can any sense be made of this proposal?

It turns out that because of income and substitution effects, the effect of the tax would probably be different than the effect of the tax rebate. The tax would increase the relative price of gasoline. As a consequence, individuals would use less gasoline. This would reduce the reliance on imported oil—an objective of the policy. The rebate would increase money income. If a mechanism could be worked out to ensure that each consumer would receive exactly what he or she paid in gasoline taxes, the average consumer could afford to purchase just as much gasoline. Yet because gasoline would be relatively more expensive, most consumers would use part or all of the rebate for other things, not gasoline.

My Critical Questions

1. _____
   _____ **?**

2. _____
   _____ **?**

3. _____
   _____ **?**

Deducing

ESSENTIAL THINKING SKILLS		
CHAPTER	**WHAT THEY'RE CALLED**	**WHAT THEY MEAN**
Chapter 3	**The Gathering Skills**	**Gathering all the information.**
	Observing	Actively seeking information through one or more senses.
	Questioning	Seeking information by asking questions.
Chapter 4	**The Organizing Skills**	**Organizing for the purpose of making sense.**
	Comparing and Contrasting	Noting similarities and differences between two or more things, events, or ideas.
	Classifying and Sequencing	Arranging things or concepts into categories and into sequential order.
	Identifying Cause and Effect	Recognizing the relationship between an effect and its cause.
Chapter 5	**The Generating Skills**	**Generating additional information.**
	Inferring	Making an assumption, stating a hypothesis, or coming to a conclusion based on limited information.
	Summarizing	Condensing the essence of the information accurately and efficiently.
	Synthesizing	Creating new information by combining two or more pieces of information.
	Generating Ideas	Creating new information, alternatives, or applications.
Chapter 6	**The Recognizing Skills**	**Recognizing what has been left unsaid.**
	Recognizing Purpose	Identifying a writer's or speaker's intention.
	Recognizing Fact and Opinion	Distinguishing between a statement of fact and a statement of opinion.
	Recognizing Tone	Identifying a sentiment or mood by assessing the writer's or speaker's choice of words.
	Recognizing Bias	Noting the presence and nature of a writer's or speaker's prejudice.
	Recognizing Organization	Identifying the organizational pattern of a thought, statement, passage, or plan.
	Recognizing Underlying Assumptions	Recognizing the suppositions that are taken for granted and are the foundation of a proposition, notion, or idea.
Chapter 7	**The Analyzing Skills**	**Analyzing for the purpose of coming to a conclusion.**
	Analyzing	Identifying and separating ideas, attributes, situations, and/or components in order to form a conclusion as to their relationship.
	Evaluating	Appraising something according to certain criteria and forming a judgment as to its worth or quality.
	Inducing	Analyzing individual facts or premises in order to derive a general conclusion.
	Deducing	Applying general principles or a broad framework to a situation in order to come to a conclusion about it.

> *"If, from reading the hierarchy of facts about the machine, the mechanic knows the horn of the cycle is powered exclusively by electricity from the battery, then he can logically infer that if the battery is dead the horn will not work. That is deduction."*
> —Robert M. Pirsig

> *"I always voted at my party's call,*
> *And I never thought of thinking for myself at all."*
> —W.S. Gilbert, *H.M.S. Pinafore*

What questions am I going to have answered in this section on deducing?

1. What is the difference between inducing and deducing?

2. In simple terms, how would one explain or define the thinking process of deduction?

3. What makes deducing effective?

> **DEDUCING:**
> **Applying general principles or a broad framework to a situation in order to come to a conclusion about it**

You have just read about the thinking skill of inducing. You learned that when thinking inductively about specifics, you can infer broad conclusions, generalizations, and principles. Deducing is related, but different. Deducing is a particularly useful analyzing skill that is a kind of mirror image of inducing. When deducing, you move from an understanding of the general principle to conclusions about related specifics. Deductive reasoning can be employed to make predictions from the general statements, principles, or hypothesis believed to be true. You will soon see that a broad conclusion, generalization, or principle reached through inducing can be used as the general premise in deductive applications.

ISN'T THIS ANOTHER NAME FOR FORMAL ARGUMENTATION?

Deductive thinking is frequently associated with the study of logic, especially the several forms of *formal argumentation* that demonstrate

THINK ABOUT THIS!

There's Guessing, and Then There's Educated Guessing

In order to encourage his university students to think, Enrico Fermi, winner of the Nobel Prize for his work in elementary particle physics, conducted the following discussion based on making educated guesses.

"How many piano tuners are there in Chicago?"

Silence in the room.

"OK, then how many people live in Chicago?"

"Three million."

"How many people in an average family in Chicago?"

"Say an average of four."

"How many families own pianos?"

"One out of three."

"How many pianos, then, in Chicago?"

"Approximately 250,000."

"How often would each piano be tuned?"

"Once every ten years. Thus, 25,000 pianos are being tuned each year."

"How many pianos can a tuner tune in a day?"

"Four."

"How many working days are there each year?"

"About 250."

"How many pianos can one piano tuner tune in one year?"

"Four times 250 working days per year means that each piano tuner could tune 1,000 pianos a year."

"How many piano tuners can make a living tuning pianos in Chicago?"

"With 25,000 tunings available per year, this would mean that there should be approximately 25 piano tuners working at any one time in Chicago."

A check of the Chicago Yellow Pages showed that number to be very close to the number of tuners listed.

Why did this procedure work, even though the answer arrived at was only an approximation? What made students end up with the "correct" answer? What was Fermi trying to show his students?

_____

_____

_____

ANY QUESTIONS?

Sometimes the solution to a problem can seem obvious when it is not. Now, having read that, answer the following question: If it takes London's Big Ben 30 seconds to chime six o'clock, how long does it take to chime twelve o'clock?

_____

_____

_____

_____

THINKERS

What's Next?

What is the next letter in the following sequence?

O T T F F S S

Need a Hint?
This is really a math problem.

reasoning. In formal argumentation the focus is on the basic patterns of deductive argumentation, with their complex system of rules.

You will be glad to know that we are not going to get into formal argumentation here. Instead, we are going to focus on the application of *informal* deductive thinking to everyday conversations, experiences, and readings. That should be a relief to those of you who have had experience with formal deductive argumentation.

APPLYING THE GENERAL TRUTH TO PARTICULAR CASES

When we use the thinking skill of deduction, what we are reasoning from broad, general awareness or from overarching concepts and principles. In brief, we are reasoning from the general to the specific.

Simply put, in deducing we are stipulating the truth of a general statement and applying that truth to one or more related particular cases. The challenge in deductive thinking is to be certain that the general truth or statement actually applies to the particular cases and to avoid the many thinking fallacies that are associated with deductive thinking.

In the following list there is a principle or general concept stated or implied, and then a specific question is asked that requires you to apply that principle or information to a particular case. Do you see how each item is a valid application of a general truth applied to a specific situation?

- Sweet foods with lots of sugar in them are not good for you. Which of the foods listed below are not good for you? (In this case, the particular foods must each be measured against the "lots of sugar" condition to determine which foods on the list are not good for you.)

- The First Amendment to the Constitution guarantees free speech. In which of the following situations would the speaker be protected by this amendment? (Each situation must be analyzed in light of the free speech guarantee.)

- If radiation can cause cancer, as indicated by extensive research, then which of the following illnesses best justifies the use of radiation? (Since we accept the truth of the statement that radiation can cause cancer, we must look at the specific illnesses to see which illness is already so serious that the potential benefit of the treatment outweighs the threat of cancer.)

TO DEDUCE YOU RELY ON WHAT YOU ALREADY KNOW

Most of us already reason deductively for situations we encounter every day. We have broad frameworks of understanding—things we "know"—against which we measure new situations. For example, our inductive thinking process works something like this:

Broad framework: The majority of high school students who get called to the office during class are in trouble or have an emergency at home.

Specific situation: Tiffany, a student in class, got called to the office.

Specific situation: Tiffany has never been called out of class before.

Specific situation: Tiffany never gets into trouble in school.

Deductive conclusion: Tiffany probably has a family emergency.

NOW FIGURE THIS OUT

Since we already make use of our deductive thinking skills, why is deducing included in this book? You can figure out the answer to this question by simple deduction:

Broad framework: The book discusses only the things we don't know well or don't know well enough.

Specific situation: We already make use of the deductive thinking skill.

Specific situation: This book discusses deduction.

Deductive conclusion: We must not know or use our deducing skills well enough.

STIR IT UP 7.10   A Sock in the Dark

You wake up for an early morning class. It is still dark, and you don't want to wake your roommate by turning on the light. You need to get a pair of socks from your sock drawer, which has six pairs of socks in it. The problem is that the socks are all white with different color borders, and it is too dark to see if you are pulling out a matching pair. Two pairs have red borders, two pairs have green borders, and two pairs have blue borders. How many socks must you take out of the drawer (and then take to the bathroom where you can close the door and turn on the light) in order to be sure that you have one matching pair? Use your deducing skills to figure this out. Then read on.

Broad framework: We need one sock more than the number of possible color combinations in order to have one matched pair.

THINKERS
Words in a Word

"Therein lies the secret," Shakespeare (or somebody) said. "For you see, there is a seven-letter word in the English language in which you can find nine words without rearranging any of its letters." What is the word?

Need a Hint?
The answer is in the statement of the question.

Specific situation: The number of socks doesn't matter.

Specific situation: There are only three different colored borders.

Deductive conclusion: We need take only four socks in order to guarantee a match with another sock. If the first three socks pulled out each had a different color border, the fourth sock would match one of the three.

Standards for Thinking and Reasoning

Identify the three most important critical thinking standards to be applied to the skill of **deducing.** Put a check (✓) next to your three choices. Be ready to explain your thinking. Why these three?

☐ Clear	☐ Specific	☐ Relevant
☐ Logical	☐ Significant	☐ Fair
☐ Precise	☐ Accurate	☐ Consistent
☐ Deep	☐ Complete	☐ Adequate

Journal Observations (see page 13)

DEDUCING

1st Writing _____

_____

_____

_____

_____

_____

_____

2nd Writing

3rd Writing

Plants and Medicine

Joseph Levine and Kenneth Miller

A young leukemia patient resting peacefully in a cancer ward is thousands of miles away from the exotic island of Madagascar, which lies off the eastern coast of Africa. She and her hopeful parents, who have been told that the odds are good she will recover from the deadly cancer, may not know the location of that island, and they may not have heard of the Madagascar periwinkle (*Catharanthus rosea*), a plant with white and pink flowers native to the island. Nonetheless, the little girl may owe her life to this flower and to a compound extracted from it known as *vincristine*. Vincristine is a cellular poison that breaks down the mitotic spindle and makes it impossible for cells to complete cell division. Cancer cells, which divide rapidly, are particularly vulnerable to vincristine, and in the past decade or so the drug has become a powerful weapon in the medical arsenal with which patients are winning battle after battle in the war against childhood cancer.

Vincristine is just one example of a human dependence on plants that is much less obvious than our dependence on plants as sources of food. Plants are one of our most valuable sources of medicines, old and new. In many cases, well-known drugs are responsible for the effectiveness of folk remedies. Hindu folk medicine has made wide use of *Rauwolfia serpentina,* the snakeroot plant, as a treatment for circulatory and nervous disorders. From a careful analysis of the effects of this plant, researchers extracted *reserpine,* a drug often essential to the treatment of high blood pressure. The use of willow bark as a pain remedy is effective because the plant contains a close chemical relative of aspirin. The flowering foxglove contains *digitalis,* one of the most effective heart medicines known. It is estimated that more than 25 percent of the drugs prescribed for use in the United States contain plant materials as their active ingredients, and that percentage would be much larger if synthetic chemicals first discovered in plants were included in the total.

The possibilities of plants in medicine are almost limitless. For years, biologists have collected rare plant species from around the world with the hope of finding new medicines. The search has been long and costly, but it has also been rewarding. Sometimes success in that search comes from the commonplace: the polyacetylene poisons in marigolds hold great promise as antitumor drugs. But just as frequently, it comes from the exotic, as with *curare,* a potent muscle relaxant derived from the plant poisons used by Amazon natives on their blowgun darts.

Ironically, just as we develop the biochemical techniques to make the most of these botanical gifts, we may be on the verge of destroying the world's greatest storehouses of plant chemicals. The tropical rain forests, including the Amazon, are vanishing at an astonishing rate. As one acre after another is cleared for the quick gain of timber or for cultivation, the wild forests become ever smaller and the chances for discovery of rare plant species diminish. Sadly, the land beneath the forest is of little use for farming. So much of its nutrient content is tied up in vegetation that once it has been cleared, the land will support farming for no more than a few years. Recent estimates are that more than half the land cleared for the Amazon forest has now been abandoned. The farms and ranches come and go, but once a plant species has been lost, its potential for medical application is gone forever.

Read and Respond

1. You have heard and read much about the vanishing rain forests and the loss of plant and animal species. Let's assume that nothing is being done to stop this loss. What are the implications for this generation? What are the implications for the next generation?

2. Is the loss of rain forests and valuable species important to society? Why do you think that? What is your proof that anyone even cares?

An Irish Laborer Confronts Hardship in San Francisco

Anonymous
[April, 1875]

I began work on the 12th instant in the Pacific Works. Ed Jones [is] foreman. What my wages is, I don't yet know and may not for some 6 weeks yet. If I could have what is coming to me each week, as it [is] earned, in a very little time I would have things all O.K. But, while I want money very badly, I cannot afford to forfeit my job. I have asked Lowell for the loan of some money which he has promised to let me have today. And, if he does, it will help to straighten matters a little. I must have money this coming week, come from where it may, because I have no fuel, and that alone is most indispensable. . . .

I am now indebted $3.25 for wood and coal, $15.00 for groceries and milk, $1 for bread, $5 on [the] stove, and $1 borrowed, making a total of $26.25. I have drawn $10 on my 1st weeks payment which is now due. Two [are] being kept back. This will render it impossible for me to settle up all I could wish, but still I shall struggle through as well as I can. I shall have another month's rent to pay and probably $5 more for groceries which makes $48.25, not to speak of meat and other little eccteras. I shall then have only coming to me on the 15th [of] May [wages] for 14 days and $6\frac{1}{2}$ hours.

May, 1875

Sunday [the] 2nd is the molders' picnic. Would like to go but cannot for want of funds. Lowell is to call on that day, and [I] may get some money from him. [I] rely upon him but may again be disappointed. . . .

My wife's anticipated sickness (parturition) is not yet arrived which will leave me better prepared for the event when it does take place. Though, even then, I won't be as well off for her sake as I could wish, but, as it is, God be thanked for what we have. . . .

June, 1875

Business still continues to get dull, and but very little prospects of it being much better.

On the 17th my wife was confined, and at 7:15 A.M. another boy was born. Everything turned out all right. Mrs. McDevitt is evidently both skillful and considerate as a midwife.

Joe Whalley from Omaha called upon me on the 19th on his way to Seattle, W.T. [He] gives very discouraging accounts of that place and hopes largely from his new home. Since then, two molders, [the] Tenny brothers, have gone to Seattle, but Wharburton gives very discouraging accounts from that place. . . .

July, 1875

Moved to another house, No. 225 Perry St., owned by a man named Murphy. Rent $17.00. I got laid off at the "Pacific" and began work in the "City" Iron Works. . . .

The crowds on the streets of persons from Salt Lake City would give me the impression of it being a doomed city.

It seems as if this climate was not going to agree with me. The variety of weather one gets in San Francisco in a day is enough to satisfy the most fastidious for almost a season.

I want still another change and again think it is for the better. Of one thing I am satisfied. Moulding is not the business for me to follow. While out of it, I can always do without drinking. And [I] can, too, for a time after returning to it. But, gradually, the feeling grows upon me, and I again begin to taste. I want to quit that practice if possible. And the only remedy I know of is to secure a position outside of the business altogether. . . .

August, 1875

Moved to No. 3 Margaret Place; rent $13 per month.

Was laid off in [the] City foundry. I disliked the place all the time I was in it most thoroughly. . . .

During the month of August I did nothing, but [I] made $11.50 on the election. This, with some credit and $10 from Charley Butterfield, carried me through. . . .

September, 1875

Borrowed $5 from A. Sloan, $10 from G. McClelland, and $10 from C. Lowell, also $1 from E. Jones. Began work on Friday afternoon [the] 10th. . . .

On the last of the month, contrary to all expectations, [I] was laid off. . . .

[9] December, 1875

. . . With this month ends a year I had hoped from its auspicious beginning to terminate in a far different manner. But, while we hope still for the silver lining to the dark cloud of adversity, and as we think, we hope and work and toil for it, yet as time revolves on his unerring axis and brings not the mildest tinge of our fancyful lining, our hopes become tinctured with despair. . . . And, with the beginning of another year, [so also] does our hopes ascend till perhaps, by patient, constant toiling [and] hopeful, steady perseverance [which is] never wholly subdued by any obstacle, there comes a day in some bright year when we may gaze back on our labor and enter into the enjoyment of their results.

I began the year with very mild expectations, that of being out of debt by this time and of having my family, still increasing, better provided for. But, instead of clearing off my past indebtedness, I have added to it. And, while I still hope that another year will see me clearly out of debt, I confess I am somewhat doubtful. . . .

January, 1876

2nd In order to begin the New Year in a lucky, if not a more Christian manner, my wife insisted upon getting both Willie and the baby Christened today. Accordingly, I accompanied her to St. Mary's

Cathedral for that purpose and accomplished it notwithstanding it was very cold for this climate and rained exceedingly. On our return home, we ate dinner and really felt happier than we had done for some[time] notwithstanding our poverty. The names given are William John and Edward Alfred.

3rd, 4th, and 5th Attended the Odd Fellows' Employment Office each day with no result.

6th & 7th Met Mr. Douglas, [the] freight agent [of the] Southern Pacific Railroad, who sent me to work at the Company's wharf where I helped to load cars with coal from noon till Friday night and earned $5. . . .

13th and 14th No success thus far. As usual, I have visited those shops where I might reasonably hope to get a job, but the ill fortune which has persistently followed me for 25 months still clings to me as tenaciously as ever.

While I regret my circumstances, I am aware [that] others are a good deal worse off. I still keep house. Of course, in a poor fashion, but yet I manage to eat some and secure enough warmth and sleep. But, my wife and children [are] pent up from week to week, without a sufficiency of warmth or of warm clothing. They feel the effects of this mode of living, and it begins to tell upon them.

20th Began work this day in the Union Iron Works. I was afraid I was not going to begin work, but after a little [while], the foreman came to me and told me [that], if I wanted to work for $3.50 a day, I could start. And, further, [he said] that he had orders to start no new men at any higher price. And so, I started. Worked the full day of 9 hours and all night and next day till quitting time. . . .

23rd Sunday. A most disagreeably wet day. I could not have gone out if I had to in consequence of my boots being very bad. In fact, both my wife and children as well as myself are [at] a very low ebb in clothing. During all of this day, [I] felt generally well pleased and, of course, was in good humor. [This was] the result of being employed and having some prospect ahead of not only being out of debt but being in a position to save a little money. My wife also feels in better condition than I have seen her for a long time from the same cause. I believe, or at least sincerely hope, she will pull with me [so] that, by the end of the year, we may have begun some provision for our children. . . .

31st Worked today 10 hours and made two pipes weighing about 700 lbs. The month of January terminates this day and has been productive of some benefit. I hope it is the precursor of better times than I have experienced in a long time. . . .

February, 1876

16th I have been suffering for 3 weeks past with a severe cold and have had a terrible cough. But today, I have had an intense pain in my left lung which may, if it continues, render it necessary for me to take a rest to recuperate if it don't assume a more serious character which, with God's help, I hope not for the sake of my young family. Worked 10 hours and produced 1,000 lbs. . . .

29th . . . This records the second month of this Centennial Year of Grace 1876, during which I have earned $84.50 and produced 15 tons, averaging clear profit to the proprietors [of] $450. . . .

March, 1876

. . . *19th* Sunday. Visited Maguire's Opera House last night with the wife and today being a beautiful day took the family out to 26th St. on the horse car. . . .

Read and Respond

1. What difficulties did this Irish laborer face in attempting to live and work in San Francisco? Why didn't he leave and go to some other community where more jobs were available? Are there any people in the United States today who are facing similar difficulties? Are there more ways available to them to deal with these problems than were available to the Irish laborer?

2. Describe what life was like for this Irish laborer and his family as you imagine it. What are the implications and consequences of that kind of life?

3. Do things appear to be getting better for the Irish laborer by the end of the article? Support your answer with details from the article.

Dietary Rules and Meatless Fridays

James R. Kearl

Species	Percentage change in price
Sea scallops	−17
Yellowtail flounder	−14

Species	Percentage change in price
Large haddock	−21
Scrod	− 2
Cod	−10
Ocean perch	−10
Whiting	−20
Average	−12.5

For hundreds of years, Roman Catholics were required to abstain from eating meat on Fridays. Traditionally, they ate fish instead. In February 1966, Pope Paul VI issued a decree that allowed local bishops to lift the requirement, except for those Fridays during Lent. The ban was lifted for American Catholics in December 1966. Did this change in nonmonetary incentives change behavior? Or, put differently, had the ban on meat actually affected behavior? In a study of the northeastern United States, where 45 percent of the population was Roman Catholic, one economist estimated that, after the ban on Friday consumption of meat had been lifted, the demand for fish changed, lowering the price by 12.5 percent, on average.

For seven different species of fish, the results were as shown in the table above.

Estimating these changes is not a simple matter. A study of this sort must account for the quantity of a particular fish caught; the quantity of a particular fish imported from other areas; the quantity of a particular fish already in storage and therefore available to be supplied to the market; personal income, and the price of meat and poultry. Nevertheless, the ban on meat had clearly affected fish consumption, because lifting the ban reduced demand.

Read and Respond

1. When the American Council of Bishops decided that American Catholics could eat meat on Friday except for those Fridays in Lent, the council in other countries did not issue the same decree for the rest of the world. Why do you think "meatless Fridays" remained for non-Americans? What do you suppose the thinking was behind the council's decision? Does this suggest that the Catholic Church treats different people around the world differently?

2. What inferences are made in this article?

3. Can you suggest reasons for the drop in market price of fish that have nothing to do with "meatless Fridays," reasons that might better explain the price drop?

ASKING CRITICAL QUESTIONS

After you read the article that follows, what critical questions come to mind? Everything you read will stir up your thinking if you read and question critically. What questions would you like to have answered in order for you to put the article in proper context and to completely understand what is being said or reported? *On the lines following the article, write three questions that, if answered, will help you understand what is really being said.*

The Wilderness Transformed

Carolyn Merchant

By the late seventeenth century, much of New England was still covered by a vast forest, and thousands of settlers were clearing the woodlands, killing rattlesnakes, and building traps to catch the wolves that were destroying cattle. Even where the dangerous animals had been driven out, there were still "vast numbers of Frogs, toads, owls, batts, and other Vermin" at the edge of the uncleared land. But a short distance from the frontier—and especially in Boston—there were strects "full of Girles and Boys sporting up and downe, with a continued concourse of people," and crafts that depended on timber products were thriving.

The shipbuilders of Boston were producing over half the shipping tonnage launched in New England, and shipbuilding had created a prosperous local trade in white and black oak, chestnut, larch, and red cedar framing timbers, in spruce and white pine trees for masts, and in pitch and tar. (Unlike their English counterparts, who were often forced to purchase timber abroad, Boston shipwrights could easily obtain even specially shaped trees for stems, sterns, and ribs.) Shipbuilding encouraged the development of a number of specialized woodworking industries as well—to build superstructures, install fittings, and decorate the vessels.

Cooperage also thrived in Boston and other seacoast towns. Because vast amounts of staves were collected at Boston for shipment overseas, it was never a problem to procure supplies there, and coopers made thousands of casks each year for shipbuilders, brewers, distillers, fishermen, and merchants. They also made wooden pails, churns, tubs, and other utensils for foreign markets and for the settlers.

As a meat-packing center and the major port of entry for hides from the West Indies, Boston was the tanning center of New England. The bark of young white oak trees was preferred for tanning cowhides, and although large numbers of such oaks could not be found everywhere in New England, enough tanbark was available in the coastal regions, especially south of Boston.

. . . By the end of the century, over half a million acres of woodland had been cleared for farming. In some regions sheep grazed on peaceful meadows reminiscent of the gentle English countryside, and English fruits, grains, and vegetables grew where dank, murky forests or swamps had been. In the open areas, such English plants as the daisy, buttercup, clover, chickory, hawkweed, and dandelion had replaced the native wild flowers, which, no longer protected by the trees, died from exposure to the sun.

The forest was the greatest obstacle to the expansion of agriculture, but it was also the source of timbers for houses, outbuildings, and fences—and of firewood, the ashes of which served as a fertilizer. And in many settlements farmers supplemented their meager incomes by producing timbers, staves, hoops, and shingles for the artisans and merchants of the port towns. They also made feeding troughs from elm logs, and plows, harrows, shovels, flails, and pitchforks of ash and oak. Ink was made from oak galls, and dyes from many species, among them the sumac, hickory, butternut, hemlock, ash, sassafras, dogwood, alder, birch, oak, and maple. Maple sugar and honey were also taken from the forest, for West Indian sugar was expensive. Wild cherries, wild plums, blueberries, and currants added variety to the settlers' diet. From the forest, too, came the bark and wood of the walnut, spruce, birch, and sassafras for making beer; nut oils for purgatives; the bark of the willow, oak, alder, and birch for suppuratives; cherry bark for cough remedies; and the sap of the white pine and hemlock for astringents.

On the edge of the forest there was good hunting, and game was part of the New England diet. The passenger pigeons and blackbirds that often attacked the cornfields were killed and eaten in large numbers, and in Connecticut so many deer were killed by 1698 that the General Court limited the hunting season. Whereas in England most people were forbidden to hunt with a gun, marksmanship was essential for survival in the New England forest. . . .

Pollution of the environment and waste of natural resources are often considered consequences of the Judeo-Christian belief that man should have dominion over all nature. And indeed, before John Winthrop set out for the American colonies, he wrote: "The whole earth is the Lords garden, and he hath given it to the sonnes of men, and with a gen[eral] Commission: Gen: 1:28: increace and multiplie, and replenish the earth and subdue it." But the seventeenth-century colonists' attitude toward nature was not as simple as that. Town records show that south of the Merrimack, where settlers were not wholly dependent on the sale of timber products they themselves could make, the cutting of timber trees was restricted by various laws. The system of land ownership in the early New England towns encouraged preservation of timber, for townships were granted to groups of men known as proprietors, who distributed land among themselves and other settlers but had the sole right to large tracts of common, or undivided, land held in reserve. Although the proprietors of a town allowed all of its inhabitants to take some building timber, fuel, and other essential wood from the common land, much of the valuable timber was reserved for the proprietors.

. . . Late in the seventeenth century, and even in the eighteenth century, after hundreds of thousands of acres of timberland had been destroyed, New Englanders seem to have noticed only a few of the many significant changes that resulted from the clear-cutting of the forests: drier air, stronger winds, the disappearance of small streams, and a decline in the number of wolves, bears, and other wild animals. They considered most of these changes beneficial.

My Critical Questions

1. _____

_____ **?**

2. _____

_____ **?**

3. _____

_____ **?**

SOLUTIONS to Items in This Chapter

THINKERS (p. 366)

Heroine.

ANY QUESTIONS? (p. 369)

There is no missing dollar. The original $30 is divided like this: the desk clerk has $25, the three guests have $3, and the bellhop has $2. **Why is the problem so hard to figure out?** The way the problem is stated is misleading (and not good math or good accounting). Expenses and assets are added together to come up with an apparently missing $1. An asset ($2 kept by the bellhop) was added to an expense ($27) rather than to the other assets ($25 kept by the hotel and $3 kept by the guests).

THINKERS (p. 370)

The statement was made on January 1. Suzie's birthday is December 31. She was nine on December 30 (the day before yesterday). She was ten on December 31 (yesterday). She will be eleven later this year. She will be twelve next year.

THINKERS (p. 388)

The two sums are equal.

ANY QUESTIONS? (p. 389)

Gauging intellectual ability is difficult at best, but one way is to observe over a period of time what people know. If a person knows *what* happens, he or she likely has average intellectual ability; if a person knows *how* things happen, he or she has superior ability; if a person knows *why* things happen, he or she probably has exceptional intellectual ability.

THINKERS (p. 407)

The word is *short*. When you add two letters (*er*) to *short*, it becomes *shorter*.

ANY QUESTIONS? (p. 410)

While pointing down one road, ask this question: "If I were to ask you if this is the correct way to Hana, would you answer yes?" The two men will end up giving you the same answer, "Yes," for the correct route to Hana. Are there any other questions that would work just as well?

THINKERS (p. 425)

The next letter is E. The complete sequence: O (one), T (two), T (three), F (four), F (five), S (six), S (seven), E (eight).

ANY QUESTIONS? (p. 425)

It takes 66 seconds—not 60 seconds. When Big Ben strikes six o'clock, there are five intervals between the first bell and the last bell. Each interval is 6 seconds (one-fifth of 30 seconds) long. When Big Ben strikes twelve o'clock, there are eleven intervals between the first and the last gong. Six seconds times eleven intervals equals 66 seconds.

THINKERS (p. 427)

The word is *therein*, which contains *the, there, he, here, her, herein, rein, ere, in*.

Part Three

THINKING THAT APPLIES THINKING

Chapter 8 STUDYING AND THINKING CRITICALLY

> **"***My dear friend, clear your mind of cant. . . .
> You may talk in this manner; it is a mode of
> talking in Society; but don't think foolishly.***"**
> —Samuel Johnson

Chapter 8

STUDYING AND THINKING CRITICALLY

"The proper study of mankind is books."
—Aldous Huxley

"The original owner had highlighted the entire book—literally. Every line on every page had been drawn through with a bright green Magic Marker. It was a terrifying example of a mind that had lost all power of discrimination."
—Florence King

Please note: This chapter is crammed with instructions for applying critical thinking skills to college studies. It is also loaded with plain good advice. But unless you absorb the information and then make every effort to apply it, your reading will be wasted. You don't learn and get good grades by simply *reading* about how to study. Therefore, the intention of this chapter is to assist you in applying what you learn in this chapter to the textbooks that you are required to read for your other classes. As you learn from this chapter, apply what you are learning to your classes and textbooks for those classes. (A word to the wise student?)

STUDYING AND THINKING CRITICALLY ARE NOT THE SAME AS STUDYING AND THINKING

There is immediate value in working hard, doing well, and achieving academic success. In order to do well in any of your classes and get good grades, you must *learn* the material covered, not just read it. It is not enough merely to read the required pages passively and then put the book aside until the next reading assignment. Instead, you must read the assigned materials with a questioning mind and then think carefully

THINK ABOUT THIS!

What Motivates Us to Learn?

Giving yourself a reason to learn tends to make you progress faster. A good way to encourage learning is to put yourself in a situation where you *must* progress. Do something small that forces you to learn something big. It could be signing up and paying for a course that has essays, tests, and final exams. Or it could be buying a book that tells you how to do something that you want or need to do and feeling that you must read it. Necessity is the mother of learning. (Curiosity is probably the father of learning.)

My friend Jim tried everything to stop smoking. Finally he decided to give his lawyer several registered letters that outlined all the nasty, embarrassing things that Jim had ever done. If Jim didn't stop smoking by a certain date, the lawyer was instructed to send the letters to Jim's friends and coworkers. The fear that his dirty laundry would get aired publicly was enough to make Jim quit smoking.

So, what does It take to motivate you to learn and learn well? Write down what would be for you the equivalent of Jim's arrangement with his lawyer. Describe at least one position in which you could put yourself to guarantee your top performance in college.

_____

_____

_____

_____

_____

_____

and deeply about what you have read. You must study critically so that you, in effect, study pages in a history book the way a historian would, study pages in an English book the way a writer would, or study pages in a biology book the way a biologist would. You must approach what you study from the perspective of the professionals who work in that field. You must be able to think critically about what you read. This, in turn, makes you smarter. A lot smarter.

SO, WHAT'S THE PLAN?

It's all in the mindset. If you intend to study critically, you will begin to study critically. You should begin in the following manner.

Get Moving

No amount of planning, thinking, or discussing ever accomplished anything unless it was followed by some action. So get started studying something—read an assignment, begin the rough draft of a composition, or start the library research for a term paper. The only way to accomplish what you want in college is to take action now. Do not delay.

Do Your Assignments with a Questioning Mind

Instructors give assignments during the course of the term, and they expect them to be completed to the best of your ability and turned in on time. These assignments provide practice for skills you are learning, and they provide the instructor with an idea of how well you are progressing. If they are not completed, not completed well, or not turned in on time, your instructor will begin to regard you as a student who is less than serious about getting an education.

When it comes to your assignments, always apply the following rules:

- Know what is required of you.

- Begin work on assignments as soon as they are assigned.

- Do each assignment carefully and thoroughly, frequently asking yourself if you are focused on what is important in what you are assigned to do.

- Do all assignments.

- Before submitting an assignment, reread it, and ask for a peer's opinion.

- Turn in assignments when they are due, if not before.

- Keep a copy of each paper you write.

Use Study Aids

The following foundational study aids will help you immediately begin to develop sound study habits.

1. *Set a specific time to study for each class.* And don't let anything interfere.

2. *Study in a specific place every day.* Associate a specific spot with studying. Then when you sit there, you will slip more easily into a studious frame of mind.

3. *Eliminate distractions when you study, including the radio.* No, you cannot study better with the radio on. If you are aware of what is playing on the radio, then your concentration is decreased by the degree of that awareness. If your goal is to learn and retain as efficiently and quickly as possible, why disrupt that concentration by dividing your attention? Studies do indicate, however, that relatively unfamiliar, quiet, soothing background music ("elevator music") *without lyrics* often has a soothing, calming effect and is an aid to studying and retention. But if you know the words and tend to sing along, the music hinders efficient learning.

4. *Adjust your study schedule periodically to match the requirements of different classes.* Yes, some classes are easier than others, so don't foolishly spend the same amount of study time on easy classes that you do on difficult ones. Think. Question. Evaluate. Adjust.

Use Helpful People

You will find many helpful people on campus, including classmates, who will help you succeed in a problem course. Many students form study groups and assist each other in mastering difficult material or in preparing for exams. *Academic counselors* and *peer tutors* are available through the learning assistance services office and the student support center. And don't forget the professor of the course. She or he wants you to understand and keep up. Making an appointment to discuss your questions or confusions about the class and assignments can only lead to improvement.

HOW DO I DEAL WITH ALL THOSE READING ASSIGNMENTS?

You will need to rethink how you do your reading. There will be thousands of pages to read each semester—a challenge for the fastest speed reader—and chances are that you are not a particularly fast and efficient reader. What can you do?

Read with a Purpose

Have at least one *purpose* for everything you read. If you don't, you will read slowly and inefficiently. Purpose gives meaning to your reading. It

THINKERS

Statues of heroes on horseback show the horses in different positions. What is the significance of the following positions?

1. All four hooves on the ground.
2. One hoof raised.
3. Two hooves raised.

Need a Hint?
Have fun with this one. Speculate. The *real* answer has to do with how the hero on the horse died.

is never good enough merely to intend to read pages 79–103 for class tomorrow. What you are really saying is that your purpose is to get from page 79 to page 103. In reading those pages your purpose might be to learn information contained there in preparation for a quiz or a major exam, to identify the main points, to find five good illustrations, or to analyze the style of writing. Think deeply about the assignment, then determine your purpose and keep that purpose in mind. This will help keep you from being distracted and from slowing down.

Adjust Your Reading Rate

Think about it. You can never answer the question How fast do you read? Why not? Because you don't have one reading speed—you have many. Your reading speed depends on the difficulty of the material, your prior knowledge of it, and your purpose for reading. You read light fiction quickly and technical books probably half as fast. When you read easy material, you naturally speed up. When you read difficult, unfamiliar material, you are forced to read more slowly, perhaps taking notes often or rereading difficult passages. Your speed varies according to the difficulty of the material. With more difficult material, you should *expect* your speed to decrease.

Different kinds of materials ought to be read at different speeds. For instance, you may read a novel at 250 words per minute and a philosophy book at 125 words per minute. But if you double your reading rate for one, you will probably double it for the other. Faster reading techniques can still be utilized no matter how difficult the material, and you ought to attempt to be as flexible as possible in applying your new skills to all types of reading. With increased practice comes increased efficiency.

You will even have different rates of reading for the same page. You may be reading an unfamiliar, difficult section that is suddenly followed by a familiar, narrative-style illustration that is easy to read. Do you keep reading at the same slow speed? No, of course not. You speed up until you have finished the narrative and then slow down as you move back into the difficult text.

Perhaps your purpose is to get a quick overview of a difficult chapter that you would normally read slowly. So you speed up, moving quickly through the pages as your purpose requires. Thus, along with the level of difficulty of subject and style and the level of familiarity with the subject, purpose is very important in determining reading speed.

Don't Always Read Everything— Skim, Scan, Glance, and Skip

It may sound a bit surprising at first, but you don't always need to read everything when you are studying. Sometimes you can skip some material and still be able to complete the study assignment *thoroughly*. As a result, you will be able to read a lot faster, because you are able to cut out some of the reading.

There are four techniques that will help you improve your reading rate by eliminating reading. They can enable you to dramatically decrease the time it takes to complete a study assignment. The techniques are skimming, scanning, glancing, and skipping.

Skimming   This is a very simple but effective means of identifying the main idea of a passage. You *read only the first sentence of each paragraph* in order to get the central idea of the entire passage. Often the first sentence is the topic sentence. Skimming takes only a few seconds, but it provides an overview of the passage and often identifies the main idea. Later, when you read the entire passage, you will have a framework within which to slot the details and make sense of them. This overview also helps you read faster because the passage seems familiar when you read the entire paragraphs. Later you can locate information you need in order to answer a question without reading the entire passage.

Scanning   This technique allows you to look for a word, a phrase, a number, or other *detail* (unlike skimming, where you look for a main idea). In order to scan, you must know what you are looking for. You move your hand or pen in a steady zigzag pattern from the beginning of the paragraph to the end. At the same time, silently repeat to yourself the word or phrase you are looking for. This repetition will heighten your visual perception. As you pass near the word you are looking for, it will seem to jump out at you. You will be passing words—not reading—at a very high speed.

Glancing This skill will be useful for reading and for taking tests. Glancing involves flicking your eyes over a passage in no particular pattern in order to get an impression of the internal structure or organization of the passage. Glancing is useful when you have to determine whether the passage is organized according to a time sequence, cause and effect, or some other organizational pattern. Often a glance will

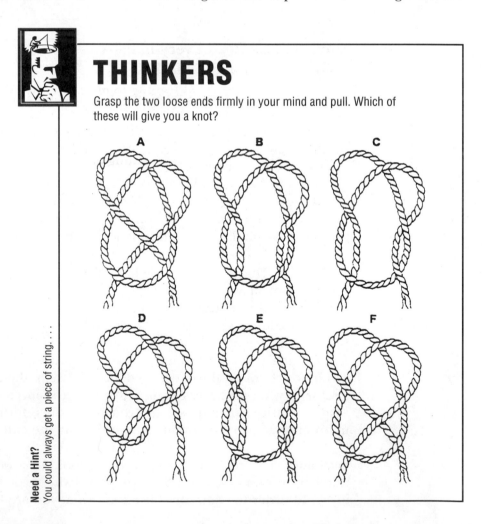

THINKERS

Grasp the two loose ends firmly in your mind and pull. Which of these will give you a knot?

A   B   C

D   E   F

Need a Hint?
You could always get a piece of string. . . . .

enable you to spot words such as *first, second, third,* or *Monday, Wednesday, Friday*—organizational pattern indicators.

Skipping   You will be able to skip some portions of your reading assignments altogether. Perhaps you are very familiar with something and don't need to review. Save time. Skip it. At other times, your instructor may have indicated that material is outdated or unimportant. Skip it. And you will find other kinds of reading that will be safe to skip—sometimes paragraphs, sometimes chapters. When time to study is at a premium, make use of this important reading acceleration technique.

Prereading and Postreading Techniques

Prereading before you begin reading sometimes can be a useful technique. Before reading the material, take five to ten seconds to glance at each page, using a pacing motion to guide your eyes down the page. This will give you a preview, an overview or suggestion, of what you are about to read. You should be able to glimpse such things as the main ideas, the thesis, the style, and the illustrations.

The effect of prereading is a feeling of confidence and assurance that will increase your speed and comprehension. You feel as if you were covering familiar territory. Prereading also enables you to identify and discard useless material without wasting time reading it for detail.

Prereading is essential in defining your purpose in reading a particular work. It helps you identify content that is familiar, irrelevant to your purpose, or too technical for you to handle, and that can therefore be safely skipped.

Prereading and reading should always be followed by *postreading*. Postreading is simply reviewing after you have finished reading. Its purpose is to note for a second time the important points that were covered during the reading. Taking a couple of minutes to review the contents reinforces the key points of the reading and aids retention.

USE A READING-STUDY SYSTEM THAT WORKS

Reading a college-level textbook is usually more difficult for most of us than other reading. Textbook assignments seem to take a long time and to need a lot of rereading and reviewing if we want to remember the important points. Students often wonder if there isn't a better way to absorb and retain information than just to reread it several times. And there is. There is a highly efficient way to read and study textbooks that takes some of the work out of reading and studying. It involves using a *critical reading-study system.*

What Is a Critical Reading-Study System?

A reading-study system is a step-by-step *method* for identifying, reading, studying, retaining, and recalling the most important information in a textbook chapter. Using a reading-study system can help focus your concentration on important information, assist you in acquiring and retaining the information, and aid you in recalling the information at a later time.

A Variety of Reading-Study Systems Exist

You probably have already been introduced to some of the techniques used in reading-study systems: reading the preface of a book; noting headings, charts, and graphs; reading introductions, conclusions, and summaries; reading study questions first; and much more. And you have been encouraged to do all this before reading the chapter. All you have to do is put these techniques into a step-by-step program, and you will be on your way to using a study system.

You can choose a reading-study system from a great many that exist. You are probably familiar with some of these systems, because they have been in use for thirty or forty years. Some of the most widely used are listed here.

Reading-Study System	Emphasis
SQ3R	Survey–Question–Read–Recite–Review
SQ4R	Survey–Question–Read–Recite–"Rite"–Review
POINT	Purpose–Overview–Interpret–Note–Test
OK4R	Overview–Key ideas–Read–Recite–Review–Reflect
OKSR	Overview–Key ideas–Read–Record–Recite–Review–Reflect
PQRST	Preview–Question–Read–Summarize–Test
RSVP	Review–Study–Verbalize–Preview
EARTH	Explore–Ask–Read–Tell–Harvest

OARWET	Overview–Ask–Read–Write–Evaluate–Test
PANORAMA	Purpose–Adaptability–Need to question–Overview–Read–Annotate–Memorize–Assess
PARS	Set a purpose–Ask questions re purpose–Read for answer–Summarize
SQRQCQ (for math)	Survey–Question–Read–Question–Compute–Question

Which is the best reading-study system? There has not been, and probably will not be, a clear indication that one system is better than another, but any system is better than no system at all. Any system you choose will be better than simply reading and rereading.

Characteristics of Reading-Study Systems

As you can see from looking at the list of reading-study systems, they all have six techniques in common.

1. *Look over the material before you read it.* Previewing (also called *overview, survey, review, explore*) allows you to get a good idea of what the subject is and how difficult the material may be to read.

2. *Establish your purpose.* This step (also called *question, ask*) forces you to focus on what you want to learn from the chapter. Having previewed the chapter, you are probably now able to raise questions about the material in the chapter. Perhaps there are even study questions in the chapter that you can try to answer as you read. Establishing a purpose enables you to focus your reading and helps keep your mind from wandering.

3. *Read.* Actively seek information as you read the chapter.

4. *Recall what you have just read.* Recall (also called *recite, tell, verbalize, write, compute, summarize*) the material by stating the content of the chapter in your own words. This reinforces your learning.

5. *Review periodically.* Reviewing (also termed *test, assess*) forces you to test your memory periodically to determine if you still retain the important information. This ensures long-term recall.

6. *Focus on the system's strength.* Each of these systems has its strength in that it usually emphasizes one of the following areas: (1) locating information, (2) organizing information, (3) interpreting information, (4) applying/using information.

Comprehension Monitoring

Most reading-study systems have been around for many years, and although they are still effective, recent research indicates that these basic systems could be still more effective if they incorporated an additional type of critical thinking: comprehension monitoring.

Learning skills researchers now know that a student's ability to monitor his or her comprehension is essential for effective mastery of content-area reading, especially in college, where students read independently.

You must have a method for being aware of and monitoring your comprehension as you read so that you can continually adjust to different types of academic reading. At any time you need to be aware of whether or not your comprehension levels are acceptably high. Therefore, comprehension monitoring must be added to whichever reading-study system you prefer to use if that system is to be as effective as possible.

Comprehension monitoring consists of five basic activities in which the reader engages *during silent reading:* (1) summarizing, (2) clarifying, (3) rereading, (4) questioning, (5) predicting.

Summarizing is simply stopping periodically and telling yourself in abbreviated fashion what you have read. *Clarifying* is asking yourself, "Do I understand this? Is this clear?" *Rereading* is carefully reading again any passages that were not clear, or that perhaps were clear but did not fit in with the rest of the text. *Questioning* is asking yourself teacher-type questions that might come up on a test about the passage. *Predicting* is trying to tell yourself what is likely to come next in the passage you are about to read.

Comprehension monitoring is that simple, but the difference it will make in your reading comprehension is gigantic.

The "Doing It Right" Reading-Study System

But where does comprehension monitoring fit into the typical reading-study system? It is *concurrent with the reading step.* Any reading-study system can be easily adapted to become a "Doing It Right" reading-study system. This can be illustrated by comparing the popular SQ3R method with the "Doing It Right" SQ3R method:

SQ3R	"Doing It Right" SQ3R
Survey	Survey
Question	Question

Read	Read *and Monitor Comprehension: summarize, clarify, reread, question, predict*
Recite	Recite
Review	Review

The PQRST system would look like this as the "Doing It Right" adaptation:

PQRST	**"Doing It Right" PQRST**
Preview	Preview
Question	Question
Read	Read *and Monitor Comprehension: summarize, clarify, reread, question, predict*
Summarize	Summarize
Test	Test

And so it goes. Every reading-study system can become a "Doing It Right" system and as a result become a more effective system. To be the best student you can be, you will need to use the best reading-study system you can. You will want to become proficient in "Doing It Right."

THINKERS

Within 10 percent, what percentage of Monaco's residents regularly gamble in Monte Carlo?

Need a Hint?
This must be a trick question. What's the trick?

MARKING AND UNDERLINING A TEXTBOOK

Reading and studying textbook chapters is a long and time-consuming process that can be made much more effective by using a reading-study system. What you now need to learn is an *effective marking and underlining system* to use while you are reading or studying a textbook for the first time. Your markings will allow you to quickly relocate all the important information later without having to reread the whole text. The next few pages offer you a marking and underlining system that is easy to learn, highly effective, and easily incorporated into your "Doing It Right" reading-study system. You will be able to retrieve each chapter's important information within seconds, long after you first read the chapter. How is that possible? Read on.

Should You Underline and Mark Your Textbooks?

Most of us like to read with a pen in our hand so that we can mark important ideas or facts when we come to them. This combination of reading and marking helps our comprehension, because it serves to focus our attention on what we are reading.

You have probably learned that it is a good idea to pace yourself when you read. A pen (especially a felt-tip type) held in your hand makes an excellent pacer as you are reading and at the same time enables you to mark the passage as you read it. Should you mark in a book? Yes and no.

Yes, you should get in the habit when you study of always having a pen in your hand and marking important things as you read them. This not only helps comprehension if done correctly but also helps if you have to refer to the passage again later—and you will have to often, in preparation for quizzes and examinations. On the other hand, you should not underline as you are reading because it can be a hindrance to efficient studying—and there is a better way.

Don't be afraid to mark your textbooks. They are *your* tools for learning and should be used in any way that benefits you. Yes, you can sell and resell used textbooks that have been marked up. In fact, to some students, previously marked textbooks are very desirable.

The Problems with Underlining

In high school, along with a lot of other bad habits, you probably got in the habit of underlining when you studied—that is, dragging a felt-tip pen under the lines as you read. Usually you read halfway through a sentence without underlining (you always had to read halfway through to get some idea of what the sentence was about), decided that it might be an important sentence, and stopped reading in order to underline what you just read. So what is wrong with that? Several things: You interrupted your concentration on what you were reading to do something else, reducing your comprehension and retention. You may even have used a straightedge of some sort so that your underlining would look neat. You ended up doing so much at the same time that you probably paid little attention to the content. When you finished, you had a chapter full of pages with lots of ink on them, and you had little comprehension of what you had just read. Then, when you reviewed the chapter, you had to reread everything in order to find out what was important, because, without a marking system, you tended to simply mark everything. In addition, with all that activity, it took you much longer than necessary to read the material. *But there is a way to read faster and more efficiently, and mark the chapter at the same time, without losing comprehension.*

Don't Underline—Mark the Margins

Don't underline while you are reading. Instead, mark important information by putting a mark in the margin at the end of the line where the information is located. This is easily done, especially since you are now pacing yourself with a moving pen. Marking in the margin requires very little effort and no loss of reading speed or comprehension. You don't break your concentration as you do by underlining, and later you can find important information by glancing at the margins. When you look back at your marked margins and the lines of text opposite the marks, you may choose *at that point* to underline a passage. Or, you may choose to disregard a passage completely if it is not important.

Underlining can lead you astray when you are studying. Something that at first impression seems important enough to underline may later prove to be unimportant or even misleading in the context of the whole passage. Underlining it would give it equal (but false) weight and importance with the other underlined things and can cause you confusion later when you review. Marking the margins, on the other hand, allows you to quickly reread, reexamine, and evaluate information in the context of the whole page or section. This makes for effective studying.

USE A SYMBOL SYSTEM FOR MARKING MARGINS

Marking the margins of a passage as you read is a good idea. With just a little effort, you can mark the margins in such a way that you indicate specifically what is in the lines opposite the mark by using symbols.

Create for yourself a simple set of symbols that represent the things that you need to be able to identify and later find again for study and review. For example, in every textbook chapter you will need to know where the main ideas are located. So, when you are reading, why not use a straight line (—) in the margin at the end of the lines where the main ideas are found? Later, when you look over the margin marks and reread the main idea where you marked it, you may choose to under-line that main idea *at that time*. This reinforces your learning. Supporting details may be indicated by a broken line (– – – –), and other standard kinds of information that you always need to be aware of can be represented by any symbols you choose to use.

After you identify what you are looking for in a reading selection, cre-ate a specific symbol for each thing and use that symbol as a margin mark. You will then be able to "read" the margins at a glance to find important information without searching haphazardly. This quick "read" is especially important when reviewing for examinations.

Suggested Margin Marking Symbols

While you are encouraged to create your own unique set of symbols for the kinds of information you need to be aware of in reading, at this point you may not have enough experience to know what kinds of things you should margin-mark. The following list of items and their symbols will get you started locating the important information in what you read. Learn the symbols and what they represent, and use them until you create your own set of symbols.

"Doing It Right" Margin Symbols

Main ideas, thesis, topic sentences	(Solid line)	——
Secondary importance, supporting detail	(Broken line)	– – —
Things in a series, items that follow in order	(Number)	①②etc
A good quote, statement, "neat" thought	(Quotation marks)	(( ))
Something questionable, puzzling	(Question mark)	?
Summary (1st one, 2d one, etc.)	(Brackets)	[ ]
New/strange words or phrases; to look up	(Circle words)	◯
Strongly agree/disagree	(Capital A or D)	A/D
Check with the professor on this	(Check)	✓
Example, illustration	(Capital E)	E
Definition	(def)	def.

| Good exam question | (x) | *X* |
| Reread later | (RR) | *RR* |

If you get in the habit of dotting the margins as you read, reviewing to see why those dots are there, and identifying each dot with a margin symbol, your textbooks will take on the qualities of a well-organized filing system where information is quickly available. Textbooks marked this way are not a hindrance to learning, as are haphazardly underlined books. On the contrary, they are useful and valuable aids to achieving high grades and success in courses.

How to Mark a Library Book

Quite often in college you will need to read and study a book that belongs to someone else or comes from a library. Obviously, you are not able to mark the margins or underline in these books, but there is a way that you can mark and organize the information in them that is almost as effective as marking the books themselves. It involves using a sheet of paper and a four-step procedure. (See example on p. 458.)

Step 1. Divide a sheet of paper into vertical, half-inch-wide columns the same length as the pages you are about to read, one column for each page to be read. A piece of ruled notebook paper turned sideways is ideal. If you are reading many pages, you will need more than one sheet of paper.

Step 2. Number the top of each column with the number of a page that you will be reading. If you are reading pages 109–119, number your columns 109, 110, 111, and so on.

Step 3. Line the sheet up next to the book with the first numbered column next to its corresponding page and as close as possible.

Step 4. Read and mark, but instead of marking the margin of the book, mark the column next to the book. When you begin reading the next page, begin marking the next column (with the matching page number).

As you can see, you will end up with a sheet of "margins," columns that have the margin symbols representing the kind of information that is on each page. At a glance you will be able to identify on what page, and where on that page, you can find important information. When it is time to review the book, simply place the sheet next to the book, line up the columns next to their matching pages, and review the material opposite the symbols.

Neat, huh? And it works well, too.

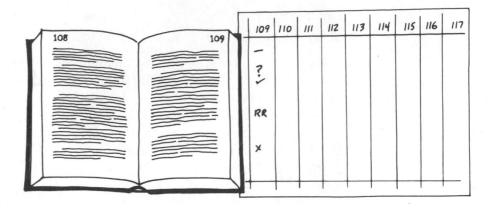

One Last Word of Advice

Students sometimes fall back into just underlining as they read, mistakenly thinking that they are saving time. As a result, they often underline too much, too little, or inappropriate information. Resist this high school habit. There is much more to reading and studying than just underlining. You now know how to do it right, and the rewards in time, knowledge, and good grades make doing it right well worth the effort.

THINKERS

Sales Per Year

In number of items sold per year, what company is the world's largest manufacturer of feminine apparel?

Need a Hint?
Think small—and think about the uses of "feminine apparel."

PREPARING FOR A TEST

As much as we don't like tests, and as justified as we are in pointing out why they do not accurately indicate how much we know, tests are here to stay. Tests of all kinds are the common form of evaluation professors use to determine if you have acquired the information that they believe you should acquire. Tests are the way you demonstrate your mastery of the course material.

In our college courses we often meet students who don't seem to work very hard but always seem to do well on tests. How do they do it?

Chances are that they are not any more intelligent than we are, but they most likely have become highly skilled at preparing for and taking exams.

In your life you will take tests that are not part of any class. For many years, tests have been required by business, industry, government, and the armed forces. Tests are used to measure fitness for entrance into college, graduate programs, and specialized training schools. These tests measure a variety of areas, including aptitude, critical thinking, and knowledge of specific topics. Obviously, doing well on tests will be important to you for the rest of your life.

So, let's figure out how to master test taking. There are various things that can be done in preparation for exams that will result in higher scores. The following tips will bring you good results—but only if you begin doing what is recommended.

Control Your Attitude

Students have different attitudes toward exams, attitudes that affect their ability to prepare for the exams. Here are three common ones:

1. *It's hopeless.* The exam is regarded as just another way to defeat students. Students with this attitude think that the purpose of exams is to weed out those who shouldn't be in college. They feel that the test is an adversary to be defeated, and many class members will be unable to do so. For them, it is pointless to prepare thoroughly because the test is going to beat them anyway. This attitude should be resisted.

2. *Tests are to be feared.* Fear of taking tests is quite common. It results in tension that can make you forget answers that you knew minutes before the test. It also results in careless errors. Fear conditions the mind for failure. You begin concentrating not on preparation and review, but on how much you fear the test, how unprepared you are, or what's wrong with the test. Preparation consists of frantic, last-ditch efforts, loss of sleep, cramming, and general complaining. All of this hinders organized review and preparation.

3. *Test results can be controlled.* This third attitude is positive. It suggests self-confidence and understanding of the nature of tests and the proper ways to prepare for them. Although they don't enjoy tests (who would?), students who have this attitude see the opportunity to demonstrate what they have learned. They prepare adequately by making use of the suggestions in this chapter. Not only is there

no room for anxiety, there is also no need for it. Test results can be controlled.

Start the First Week of Class

You should begin the following steps the first week of class and then continue them weekly.

1. Begin the first class period by making notes about information you believe the instructor will include on the exam.

2. Don't neglect to write your end-of-the-lecture questions (see page 472), and then review them weekly.

3. Keep up with your textbook reading assignments and mark your textbooks properly, as you learned on page 456. Review your margins—and the key information opposite the marks—weekly.

These steps don't take much time. Think about it. If these three things were the only things that you did, and you did no other review or exam preparation, you'd probably do well on any exam.

Think how well you'd do if you also prepared in the manner described in the rest of this chapter.

Determine What to Review and Study

Often students do poorly on tests not because they didn't study but because they studied the wrong information. Unless your instructor indicates differently, follow these guidelines to be certain of focusing on the correct materials.

1. *Review only the textbook chapters covered since the last exam.* Rarely does a professor retest old material.

2. *Review only the lecture notes taken since the last exam.* As is the case with textbook chapters, material in lecture notes is rarely retested.

3. *Review previous exams given by the instructor.* Occasionally a professor will pass out copies of exams given in past terms, or students in your dormitory, fraternity, or sorority may keep old exams on file. By reviewing these, you will get a good idea of the questions that will be asked on this term's exam. Most instructors concentrate on the same areas each term.

4. *Review any quizzes given in class.* The areas the quizzes focused on are likely to be the same areas covered on the exam.

5. *Review teacher handouts.* Any materials the instructor prepared and handed out are likely to contain important information. At the least, consider that the *subject* of the handout is likely to be included on the exam.

6. *Review out-of-class assignments.* Why were the assignments given? Were they problems to solve, a research report to give, an evaluation to write, or perhaps a concert to attend?

These six guidelines will give you some idea of what to review and study in preparation for an examination, but there is an even better way to find out what the test is going to cover: ask the professor.

Ask the Professor

Teachers are seldom asked what *specifically* is going to be on the test. When a test is announced, students usually ask just one nonspecific question. A voice from the back of the room asks, "What's the test going to cover?" The teacher responds, "Everything we've covered since the last test." And that's the end of the questions.

If *specific* questions were raised, the instructor would probably be glad to respond with specific answers.

Here are some suggested questions and possible answers. Notice how much you can learn about what to study.

1. What day will the exam be? "A week from Wednesday."

2. How much time will we have for the exam? "Fifty minutes."

3. Will the exam be objective or essay? "About fifty objective questions and two essay questions."

4. Will the objective portion be multiple choice? "Mostly. There will be a few short answers, and some matching."

5. Will the objective portion of the test cover material primarily from the textbook or from the lectures? "Primarily the textbook."

6. Will the essay portion cover the lectures primarily? "Yes."

7. Are there certain chapters in the text that you think we ought to concentrate on when we review? "Chapters 3, 4, 7, 9, and 10 are the most important."

If the opportunity to ask your instructor these questions doesn't occur in class, then ask them in the instructor's office. Often your professors will discuss coming exams in more detail in their offices than they will in class. Take advantage of this fact to help you master the course materials and pass the exams.

Allow Sufficient Time for Review

This is so obvious it almost sounds trite to say it: Be certain to allow yourself enough time to review all information, including lecture notes and the textbook chapters that are likely to be on the exam. Waiting until the last minute will result in disaster.

Know When to Study and When to Stop

You've allowed yourself sufficient time to prepare for the exam, but how do you use that time? Here are some guidelines.

1. *Study every day.* Try to review your notes and textbook a little every day. Raise questions about the material. This keeps the material fresh in your memory, and it is more effective and less stressful than cramming.

2. *Start your review a week before the exam.* A week before the exam, schedule several review sessions and plan to study certain material or specific chapters at each review session. Don't attempt to study everything in one review session. That will simply waste your time because you will not retain everything. Divide what you have to study into manageable chunks. Your retention will be considerably improved.

3. *Identify what you don't know a few days before the exam.* Many students review by going over information they already know well. They ignore the things they don't know, with the hope that the instructor won't ask questions about it. That's foolish. Don't pat yourself on the back for what you know, find out what you don't know. Scan every page in the textbook chapters, and look for names, terms, theories, and so on. As you come to each one, ask yourself if you understand it or its significance. If you do, continue until you come across an unfamiliar term. Write down the term and the page number, and then continue scanning. When you are finished scanning each chapter, turn back to the pages with unfamiliar terms and reread until you understand them and their significance. This system allows you to check yourself on every term, person, idea, or detail in each chapter.

4. *Review the night before.* Reserve ample time the night before the test for a last review. Don't study new material. Focus on the most difficult material, checking your recall of facts and material that may be the subject of an essay question.

   And don't cram—unless you're desperate. Staying up all night trying to learn material that you should have learned earlier is largely a waste of time. Your mind will only take in so much information in one sitting and then it just closes down. You may think you're absorbing information as the hours pass, but 90 percent of it will not be there in the morning. Reviewing material in smaller chunks over a period of several days results in significantly higher retention.

5. *Get a good night's sleep.* This is important, so do it. A well-rested test taker always does better on exams than a tired test taker, even though they both know the same information.

6. *Review shortly before the test.* Browse through your notes and the chapters, lightly reviewing everything you've already studied. This quick review will stimulate your recall of what you know.

Write It Out

For many college students, writing is an aid to studying and it is definitely an aid to thinking. It often provides the additional reinforcement necessary to grasp and retain difficult material. Write summaries of chapters and lectures, write out sample questions that you believe might make good exam questions. All of this reinforces your learning and retention.

Use—Don't Abuse—Group Study

Group study can be very helpful if all members of the group share equally in reviewing and answering potential questions, explaining difficult concepts, and so on. Group study is a waste of time if participants in the group have not prepared, don't share, or only participate so that they can hear from good students what is likely to be on the test. Pooling information can be helpful. Pooling ignorance is a waste of valuable review time.

Use Every Place to Study

It is best to study for exams at your regular study spot, but you can study for exams everywhere. Study at home or in your dormitory room. Study at school when you have a few minutes between classes. Study in the library, in an empty classroom, or in the learning center. Study whenever possible, while traveling, while waiting for a movie or an appointment, or even when visiting relatives or friends.

ELIMINATING TEST-TAKING ANXIETY

It is very common to be nervous or anxious because you must take a test. You may have a difficult time sleeping the night before the test. You may even experience rapid heartbeat, stomachache, headache, or shortness of breath as you enter the classroom. If this test-taking anxiety becomes acute and disabling, you should seek professional help from the college counseling center.

The majority of students, however, do not experience extreme test-taking anxiety. More likely it is nervousness and fear of being inadequately prepared that causes excitement and anxiety. This can be controlled. Check with the learning center or student services office to see if there are any courses being offered in reducing text anxiety.

If you are well prepared for a test, you will have less to fear and will thereby reduce your anxiety. By practicing the test-preparation strategies we have already discussed, and by being well rested when you arrive for the test, you will be able to do your best.

In addition, there are several things to keep in mind when you take the exam that will also reduce your anxiety and permit you to do the good job for which you prepared.

Be Prepared

Prepare thoroughly and then relax. You can do no more. If you gave yourself plenty of time and prepared well in advance, and if you were thorough in your preparation, you'll do well.

Preview the Test Before You Do Anything

On the day of the test, pay close attention to everything the instructor says as he or she gives directions and passes out the test. Resist the urge to ignore what the instructor is saying and to start reading the test. The instructor may be clarifying an important point or indicating certain questions that should be skipped.

After the instructor finishes, resist the urge to begin answering the questions, and use your previewing skills instead. Look over the test quickly to determine the nature of the questions and the number of sections. Are there questions printed on the back of each page? Now look at the test directions for each of the test sections. Do you answer all the questions, or do you select two out of four essay questions to answer? Is there extra credit for answering more questions? Are you penalized for guessing?

Schedule Your Time

After you have previewed, quickly figure out how much time to allocate for each portion of the test.

You will want to determine how many questions you have to answer, how many points each question is worth, how well you know the information, and how much time you have to answer the questions. This will allow you to determine how much time you can spend answering each question and still finish all the questions in the allotted time.

A professor may indicate verbally or on the test that twenty-five multiple-choice questions are worth two points each, four short-answer questions are worth five points each, and one long essay question is worth thirty points. This means that half your time, twenty-five minutes, should be spent on the multiple-choice questions (about one minute apiece), ten minutes should be spent on the four short-answer questions (about two and a half minutes each), and fifteen minutes should be spent on the essay question.

It is a mistake not to schedule your time. A high percentage of your fellow students will not plan their answering time, or will not stick to the time limits as planned, and as a result their test scores will suffer.

One last point: Always save a few minutes at the end of the test period to look over your exam to make certain you have completed everything, including putting your name on the test or answer sheet.

Answer the Easiest Questions First

When you read multiple-choice or true-false questions and the correct answer does not spring out at you, put a mark in the margin and move on, answering the easy or obvious questions first. You may find answers to the tough questions revealed in subsequent questions, or you may read something that triggers your memory so you remember the answer. You can then go back and answer the question. Answer quickly as many easy, familiar questions as you can, thereby giving yourself some extra time to seek answers to the tough questions. You will mess up your time schedule struggling with a question to which you don't know the answer.

Treat essay questions the same way. Do the easiest one first, saving as much time as you can for the more difficult questions. The act of writing often triggers a flow of information that is useful in your essay answers.

Usually essay questions should be answered after objective and short-answer questions because the information in the objective questions may be of use in writing the essay questions. Often you can use examples and illustrations in your essay answers that you read in the objective questions.

Answer All the Questions, Somehow

Tests that penalize you for guessing are becoming less common, so unless your professor indicates that you will be penalized for wrong answers, *always* answer every question somehow.

If you are running out of time and you don't know the answer to a question, guess. You might answer correctly. You have a fifty-fifty chance with true-false questions and a 25 percent chance with multiple-choice questions that have four possible answers.

For short-answer and essay questions that have you stumped, take your best guess and write *something*. You might get some credit.

Be the Last Person Finished

Don't be intimidated by other class members who finish early and leave the room. That's not smart. Even if you have finished and answered everything, use all the available time to check your answers carefully. Make certain that you have made no careless errors. Add more examples or illustrations to your essay question answers.

Rarely Change Answers

Often students will reread their answers to objective questions, get nervous, and change their answers. This often leads to wrong answers. First impressions are frequently correct when taking a test. Sometimes, however, other questions make us realize that we answered a question incorrectly. When that happens to you, then change your answer, but only if you are *certain* that the answer is wrong. We all occasionally mess up because we are nervous and change a correct answer to an incorrect one. Occasionally is OK, but resist getting into the answer-changing habit.

Don't Cheat or Allow Cheating

You know it is wrong to look at another student's test for correct answers. It is equally wrong to know that another student is looking at your answers, and to allow it. If you suspect another student is looking at your test, move the test or position your body so that your test is covered.

Cheating in college is a serious offense, and you want to avoid any contact—even passive contact—with students who cheat.

STIR IT UP 8.1   **Evaluate Your Anxiety**

On the following checklist, evaluate your attitudes about taking exams by indicating how strongly you agree or disagree with the following statements. Put an X in the appropriate boxes.

	Strongly agree	Somewhat agree	Somewhat disagree	Strongly disagree
I fear exams.	☐	☐	☐	☐
I dislike exams.	☐	☐	☐	☐
I don't mind exams.	☐	☐	☐	☐
I look forward to exams.	☐	☐	☐	☐
I always feel prepared for exams.	☐	☐	☐	☐
I lose sleep thinking about a coming exam.	☐	☐	☐	☐
I panic when I take an exam.	☐	☐	☐	☐
I always do worse than I know I'm capable of on exams.	☐	☐	☐	☐
I have trouble remembering during exams.	☐	☐	☐	☐

STIR IT UP 8.2   In a brief paragraph or two, describe the attitude that you would like to have toward taking exams. How could you achieve that attitude?

_____

_____

_____

_____

THINKERS

Next?

What are the next two letters in the following series, and why?

A E F H I K L M

Need a Hint?
What makes these letters look alike?

EFFECTIVE LISTENING AND NOTE TAKING

The average college student spends between fifteen and eighteen hours a week in class listening to lectures. If you have a good lecturer, you may find the lecture so interesting that you think you will easily be able to remember it. Unfortunately, our memories fade quickly because our listening skills often leave much to be desired.

You can teach yourself to become a good listener, but you must work at it. It does not happen automatically. In fact, there are factors that make efficient listening the most difficult study skill to master:

- You can't control what is said, when it is said, how rapidly it is said, and how loudly it is said.

- You can't control the speaker's logic, argument, or reasoning, and it may not make sense to you.

- Your mental processes must move through the speaker's topic at the same rate as the speaker. If not, you may lose chunks of information and become confused.

- You may have received little training in improving listening skills beyond having teachers tell you to pay attention or "sit up and listen."

But there is hope. Many students have been able to improve their listening proficiency dramatically by focusing on the specific listening skills and procedures discussed in the next several paragraphs. You too will improve.

Speaking Rates vs. Writing Rate

If you could write as quickly as your professor lectures, you wouldn't have much trouble taking notes in class. You would just have to sit close enough so that you could be certain you heard everything, copy down *everything* the professor said, and review it later to determine what was important and what wasn't. For most of us this is not possible, because we are limited in writing longhand to about 40 words per minute and the average lecturer speaks at about 150 words per minute, with rates frequently increasing to 200 words per minute. Obviously, even a skilled stenographer would have difficulty copying it all down. There are, however, some things you can do to maximize your listening and note-taking skills.

Recognize the Importance of Your Class Notes

Just listening in class without taking notes will lead to disaster. Within forty-eight hours of hearing a lecture, you will have forgotten about 75 percent of what you heard. A week later, you will have forgotten nearly everything about the lecture except perhaps that you attended it. You will certainly not be able to review and prepare for tests.

The notes you take in class are usually the best source of help for understanding the important material covered in the course. So it is necessary for you not only to attend class regularly and listen, but also to take efficient notes.

Use a Spiral Notebook and a Pen

Get started right by having the right tools. In high school you probably used a ring binder and ruled notebook paper to take notes on. And you probably used pencils rather than pens in class so you could erase. In college a ring binder is not a good idea for the following reasons:

- A ring binder is relatively bulky and awkward.

- You don't want all your class notes in one place. It's too easy to lose them all, and they are valuable.

- You have to three-hole-punch any handouts your teacher gives you before you can include them with your notes.

- It's a bit of work to keep the binder filled with paper.

Don't use a pencil for the following reasons:

- Pencil smears and fades on paper, making your notes illegible.

- Pencil points keep breaking and keep needing to be sharpened. What a pain!

Instead, use a spiral notebook and a pen for the following reasons:

- A *separate* spiral notebook for each class is portable and convenient.

- Spiral notebooks can be purchased with pockets to hold instructor handouts and blank paper for in-class writing.

- You can easily keep notes from one class separate from notes from another class.

- Class notes in spiral notebooks are convenient when you are studying for tests.

- Pens (any kind you choose) come with different color inks for making notes stand out. Moreover, they don't fade and they don't need sharpening.

Follow a Note-Taking Pattern

It is important to establish an effective pattern of copying down notes on the page in such a way as to capture the most information in the shortest possible time, and in a format that doesn't need to be reorganized later.

The sample page that follows shows an effective format for taking notes in any class. Make certain that you date each class's lecture notes, and that you leave plenty of white space between main points. If you miss a point, leave additional blank space. You can fill it in later by checking with a friend in the class.

Recommended Note-Taking Format

Your comments and questions go in this column. Remind yourself of important points or things to question or clarify.

Date: _____

Outline of Class Notes

If the professor lectures in outline form, copy it down this way:

I. _____

　A. _____

　B. _____

　C. _____

　　1. _____

　　2. _____

II. _____

　A. _____

Exam!　B. _____

If the professor doesn't lecture in outline form, don't try to outline. Copy down points as they are made.

1. _____

Know this →

2. _____

Exam (probably)　3. _____

_____

4. _____

? _____

Questions: Immediately after the lecture, write two potential exam questions over the material on each page of notes. These questions force you to summarize important points on each page and are very useful in pre-test review.

The center portion   The center portion of each page is where you write your notes. Don't try to outline a lecture if the professor doesn't lecture in outline format. Most don't. Some lectures are disorganized and seem to ramble. Just copy down what appear to be the main points. Take the most complete notes you can about each point. Numbering different points helps to keep them separate.

The left column   The left-hand column on the same page should be used for your observations and reminders about the points in the lecture.

You do not want to constantly interrupt the lecturer with questions, but you do want to identify the parts of the lecture that you have questions about and raise the questions at the first opportunity. A question mark in the left column opposite a point in the lecture, or a hastily written question, will remind you to raise the question or clarify the point later.

Often a professor will indicate that a piece of information is going to be on a test, or he or she may give an important study hint. Note that fact in the left column immediately. Use this left column for any point you want to be reminded of later.

The right column   The narrow column on the right side of each page should be used to do one or two important things. Immediately after each class and while the lecture is still fresh in your mind, write a couple of questions *on each page* that the professor could ask about the lecture content *on that page*. These questions will anticipate (probably correctly) what you will need to know for class tests. You may also want to summarize the main points of the lecture in a sentence or two on each page. This will give you summary statements for each page of notes that you take. These summaries are great for reviews in preparation for essay exams.

How This Format Aids Lecture Review and Study

Following this note-taking format aids your review of lecture notes in preparation for an exam as follows:

- The center column makes clear what was said.
- The left-hand column highlights important parts of the lecture and identifies potential exam question material.
- The right-hand column summarizes the main points of each lecture and suggests potential essay questions.

What do you do when it's time for an exam? That depends on how much time you have for review.

If you don't have much time for review, you should first read the right-hand column only. This will give you an overview. Then glance down the left column, reading the information you've identified as probable exam material.

If you have sufficient time for review, read the right-hand column first, answering the "exam questions" without reading the rest of the notes. This will highlight what you do and do not know. Next, read the center section. Take your time. Let it sink in. Then, read the left-hand column. It will highlight important sections and points the professor indicated would be on the exam. Restudy that information.

For Some Lectures, Take Notes in the Textbook

Some professors lecture by highlighting points in the textbook. When this occurs, use the textbook to take notes. Write in the margins next to the passages the professor is discussing. Don't bother taking notes on paper. Use the text as your notebook, highlighting with colored ink and commenting in the white space.

Avoid "Scribblemania"

An important thing to remember in taking lecture notes is that you must avoid what can be called *scribblemania*. Copying down important information in a rapid, messy, incoherent form does you no good at all because you won't be able to make sense out of it. Don't try to write everything down—it can't be done. Instead, write less, not more. Condense where possible. Sift. Distill. Go after the *main* points, not all the points. Remember, your primary focus should be on listening. The ears send the information to the brain, then to the hands, and not vice versa. Listen to what is said before writing it down.

Know the Professor

Adapt your note taking to the professor. Some professors will make it easy for you, others will make it difficult. If a lecture is well organized, your notes should be organized. If a lecture is choppy, disorganized, or rambling, don't expect your notes to be any different. Adapt.

Remember, because you cannot write as quickly as your professors can lecture, all good class notes are largely summaries of what was said.

For some professors, your notes must be as detailed as possible. For other professors, broad summaries are sufficient. Know the professor.

Sit Up Front

Why sit up front? You will often find yourself in very large lecture halls where it may be difficult to hear the lecturer. Up front, it is easier to see the instructor and to catch his or her nonverbal clues. If people are in front of you, you may be distracted. You hear better and you tend to stay more alert knowing that the majority of the class is behind you and aware of what you do. Face it: you'll also tend to nod off less if you are up front.

Listen for Clues

Teachers often let you know what they feel is important—and what you will be expected to know. Be aware of the following statements instructors may make to signal important information.

- This is important.
- You'll need to know this.
- You'll need to know how to do this.
- This will be covered on the exam.
- You may be tested on this.

When your instructors make statements like these, they are giving you clues about what you will need to know. Mark these clues in your notes at the appropriate spots.

There are other important clues to watch for:

1. *A change in voice.* A speaker's voice may get higher or lower, louder or softer as he or she presents important ideas.

2. *A change in rate of speaking.* Slowing down or pausing may signal that an important point is coming.

3. *Use of visuals.* Sometimes an instructor will use an overhead projector, videotapes, or other visuals to illustrate an important point.

4. *Listing, numbering, or prioritizing.* A lecturer may say, "There are three major issues involved" or "The second most important trend is . . ."

5. *Body language.* Sometimes instructors signal the importance of what they are saying by how they move. An instructor may sit casually on

the desk when discussing relatively unimportant things, but stand and pace quickly when making important points.

Watch the Chalkboard

If it is important enough to write on the chalkboard, it is important enough to copy down. Information that is written on the chalkboard is more than likely to appear on tests. Instructors often put on chalkboards such things as important names and dates, formulas, charts, diagrams, and tables.

When you record information from the chalkboard in your notes, highlight it, note its importance in the left-hand column, or indicate in some way that it is important so that you will be certain to learn it thoroughly when you review.

Challenge the Lecture

A good listener gets in the habit of challenging the lecture mentally and, when necessary, aloud. This helps keep the focus on recording only important information. Statements like the following make your note taking more efficient and help you monitor your comprehension:

• He said *four* points, that's only *three*.

• Is that a digression?

• What is that an illustration or example of?

During Dull Moments, Review and Summarize

No matter how stimulating a class is, there will be periods when nothing important is being presented or discussed. Use this time to quickly look over the notes you have taken and to summarize important points. Using these few minutes to clarify a hastily written point or to summarize several points will be of real value to you weeks later when you are reviewing for an exam.

Avoid Listening Errors

There are some listening errors that you ought to avoid. They waste time and keep you from *really* hearing what the professor has to say.

- Don't interrupt in the middle of an explanation to say that you don't understand. Wait until the explanation is complete; you may understand by then.

- Don't talk to or otherwise disturb anyone else in class during a lecture. It is impolite, wastes your and your neighbor's time, and is guaranteed to irritate the professor—and that's not a good thing to do.

- Don't contribute your knowledge to the professor's lecture unless the professor encourages such contributions. Ask questions, but permit the professor to complete the lecture without frequent comments from you.

- Don't display impatience—impatience to speak, to be dismissed, to question. It only distracts you and everyone else.

- Don't tape-record lectures instead of taking notes. Taping class lectures is often forbidden by professors because they know listening and learning aren't taking place when taping is, and often the tapes are not even played later. Only tape (with instructor permission) when taping is your backup for active note taking.

- Don't believe that it is the instructor's job to "get the lesson across" to you. It is your responsibility to "get the lesson" from the professor.

- Don't let your mind wander. Stay critically aware of everything the professor is saying and doing.

Don't Rewrite Notes

Taking notes haphazardly in class with the idea that you'll rewrite or type them in some sort of organized way later is a bad idea. It contributes to an ineffective pattern of note taking and wastes valuable study time recopying. If you take notes properly to begin with, there is no need to recopy. Use the time you have for review and study.

Review Before Class

A helpful listening and note-taking aid is to review the last class period's notes just before class. This review brings you up to the point where the next lecture will probably begin and gives you a context that will help you understand what is going to be said.

AND NOW YOU'RE READY TO BEGIN

This chapter has a lot of critical thinking tips and helpful ideas for turning your studying into a system for improving your approach to learning. In the truest sense of the words, critical thinking, not studying alone, is the foundation for improvement in learning. But, knowing how to study and think critically is not the same as doing it. Studying well and profitably can be achieved only by doing, not by thinking about doing.

 Journal Observations (see page 13)

STUDYING AND THINKING CRITICALLY

1st Writing _____

_____

_____

_____

_____

_____

_____

_____

_____

_____

_____

_____

_____

2nd Writing _____

_____

_____

_____

_____

_____

_____

_____

_____

_____

_____

_____

_____

_____

_____

3rd Writing _____

_____

_____

_____

_____

_____

_____

_____

_____

_____

_____

_____

_____

_____

_____

SOLUTIONS to Items in This Chapter

THINKERS (p. 446)

1. Hooves on ground: hero died naturally.
2. One hoof raised: hero died of wounds.
3. Two hooves raised: hero died in battle.

THINKERS (p. 448)

Only C will give you a knot.

THINKERS (p. 453)

0%. Gambling is prohibited for residents of Monaco.

THINKERS (p. 458)

Mattel, Inc., which sells over 20 million outfits for Barbie dolls annually.

THINKERS (p. 468)

N and T. The letters in the series are made with no curves. The next two letters composed entirely of straight lines are N and T.

TEXT CREDITS

INDEX